D0044523

SMUGGLER NATION

SMUGGLER NATION

HOW ILLICIT TRADE MADE AMERICA

PETER ANDREAS

OXFORD
UNIVERSITY PRESS

OXFORD
UNIVERSITY PRESS

Oxford University Press is a department of the University of Oxford.
It furthers the University's objective of excellence in research, scholarship,
and education by publishing worldwide.

Oxford New York
Auckland Cape Town Dar es Salaam Hong Kong Karachi
Kuala Lumpur Madrid Melbourne Mexico City Nairobi
New Delhi Shanghai Taipei Toronto

With offices in
Argentina Austria Brazil Chile Czech Republic France Greece
Guatemala Hungary Italy Japan Poland Portugal Singapore
South Korea Switzerland Thailand Turkey Ukraine Vietnam

Published in the United States of America by
Oxford University Press
198 Madison Avenue, New York, NY 10016

Library of Congress Cataloging-in-Publication Data
Andreas, Peter, 1965–
Smuggler nation : how illicit trade made America / Peter Andreas.
p. cm.
Includes bibliographical references and index.
ISBN 978–0–19–974688–0 (hbk. : alk. paper) 1. Smuggling—United States—History.
2. United States—Commerce—History. 3. United States—Foreign economic relations.
4. United States—Economic conditions. I. Title.
HJ6690.A74 2013
364.1′3360973—dc23
2012022990

ISBN 978–0–19–974688–0

1 3 5 7 9 8 6 4 2
Printed in the United States of America
on acid-free paper

For my teachers at Swarthmore and Cornell

CONTENTS

PART III: WESTWARD EXPANSION, SLAVERY, AND THE CIVIL WAR

PART IV: THE GILDED AGE AND THE PROGRESSIVE ERA

PART V: INTO THE MODERN AGE

PREFACE

MY INITIAL INTEREST IN illicit trade—and the early inspiration for this book—began as a smuggler's accomplice. Shortly after graduating from college, I spent four months bumming around Bolivia, Colombia, and Peru. While crossing into Bolivia from Peru by bus, a nice elderly woman sitting next to me sheepishly handed me a large plastic bag filled with rolls of toilet paper and then pleaded with me to put it under my seat. I did what she asked; it seemed harmless enough, even if a bit peculiar. The Bolivian border guards then entered the bus, checking documents and belongings, and proceeded to confiscate large amounts of toilet paper. But they overlooked my hidden stash, perhaps because I did not fit the profile of the typical toilet paper smuggler. Later I learned that the inflated demand for toilet paper in Bolivia was partly due to the cocaine industry. Toilet paper was commonly used to dry and filter coca paste, which was then transported to remote jungle laboratories to be refined into powder cocaine—most of which would eventually end up in the noses of American consumers.

During the same trip, I caught a ride on a cargo boat—which turned out to be a smuggling boat—traveling down the Amazon River from Iquitos, Peru, to Leticia, Colombia. Leticia, a bustling town where the borders between Peru, Colombia, and Brazil meet deep in the jungle, owed much of its existence to smuggling. Some of my fellow passengers were *pisadores* (coca stompers) with distinctive scars on their feet from exposure to the chemicals used to make coca paste. Late at night, before we departed Iquitos, I watched as several dozen drums of chemicals were quietly loaded onto our boat, and then off-loaded in what seemed to be the middle of nowhere before our arrival in Leticia.

I would later find out that many of the chemicals used by the Andean cocaine industry were actually imported from the United States. Leading American chemical companies were exporting vast quantities of precursor chemicals to the region far in excess of what legitimate industry could possibly absorb. Much of it was diverted to the black market and shipped to remote cocaine-processing laboratories—sometimes via Amazonian cargo boats like the one I was on. Even as America's rapidly escalating war on drugs was trying to stop the northbound flow of cocaine, largely overlooked at the time was the equally important southbound flow of U.S. chemicals needed to cook the coke. I ended up writing a short piece about it for *The New Republic*. And this, in turn, led to an invitation to testify, alongside Gene Haislip from the Drug Enforcement Administration, before a Senate hearing on chemical diversion and trafficking (with industry lobbyists sitting nervously in the audience). I was hooked on drugs, or more precisely, hooked on trying to figure out the business of drugs and the politics of drug control. And this turned into a career-long interest in illicit economic flows and government campaigns to police them.

As we'll see in the pages that follow, the drug story is just one particularly prominent and relatively late chapter in the much bigger story of America's long and intimate relationship with smuggling—a clandestine economic practice that we can simply define as bringing in or taking out from one jurisdiction to another without authorization. It is also a far more complex and double-edged relationship than I first imagined, one characterized by intense confrontation but also by accommodation, toleration, and complicity.

In this book, I tell the story of how smuggling—and attempts to police it—have made and remade America, from the illicit molasses trade in colonial times to drug trafficking today. I highlight the profound but often overlooked role of clandestine commerce in the nation's birth, economic development, geographic expansion, and foreign relations, as well as the role of anti-smuggling initiatives in vastly expanding the policing authority and reach of the federal government. Smuggling, it turns out, has been as much about building up the American state as about subverting it. Through its long interaction with the underworld of smuggling, the United States has emerged not only with a sprawling law enforcement bureaucracy—and jails overflowing with convicted drug law offenders—but also as a policing superpower, promoting its favored prohibitions and policing practices to its neighbors and the rest of the world.

Smuggler Nation covers a lot of ground, from pot to porn. It is the first book that re-narrates the story of America and its engagement with the world as a series of highly contentious and consequential battles over illicit trade. But the coverage is also inevitably selective. I make no pretense of being comprehensive. I paint in broad strokes, identifying and making sense of the most important historical episodes, trends, themes, and underlying dynamics.

These are not merely colorful smuggling stories that are otherwise marginal to the overall American historical trajectory. Far from it. For better and for worse, smuggling was an essential ingredient in the very birth and development of America and its transformation into a global power. Only by including the lens of smuggling in looking back at the American experience can we fully answer some crucial questions. For instance, what provoked such intense colonial outrage against the British imperial authorities? How did George Washington manage to defeat the world's greatest military power? How did America industrialize and catch up to England technologically? Why did the United States fail to annex Canada in the War of 1812? Why did the American Civil War last so long given the North's lopsided military advantage? Why are the tomatoes we eat so cheap, and why is American agribusiness so globally competitive? Why do we now have such a massive criminal justice system, including the world's largest prison population? In various ways and to varying degrees, smuggling—and the politics of policing it—provides an essential part of the answer to these wide-ranging questions. It is certainly not the only thing that matters. But *Smuggler Nation* shows how and why we should place it more front and center than in conventional accounts of the American epic.

I should say a word of caution about the subject of this book. As one would expect, there are built-in limits and obstacles to doing research on smugglers and smuggling. Information on illicit trade is necessarily imprecise, to say the least; there are no quarterly business reports and annual trade balance statistics. Indeed, the very success of smuggling operations typically depends on not being seen or counted. Documentation therefore tends to be fragmentary and uneven, and it represents rough estimates at best. Readers should keep these inherent limitations in mind in the chapters that follow. In the end, I hope they will agree with me that it is better to tell the story with admittedly imperfect and incomplete data than to simply throw up one's hands and pretend that the world of smuggling doesn't exist because it cannot be precisely measured. After all, that would be the equivalent of a drunkard looking for his keys under the lightpost because it is the only place he can see.

Writing this book was very much a collective endeavor, even if only one name appears on the cover. It was made possible by the generosity of Brown University, especially the Watson Institute for International Studies, the Department of Political Science, and a Richard B. Salomon Faculty Research Award. I gave presentations based on the book at Harvard University, MIT, Brown University, the Fletcher School at Tufts University, the U.S. Naval War College, Stanford University, Connecticut College, Bates College, Pomona College, the Council on Foreign Relations, and the University of London, as well as at the annual conferences of the American Political Science Association, the International Studies Association, and the Academy of Criminal Justice Sciences. Chapter 14 draws from Eva Bertram, Morris Blachman, Kenneth Sharpe, and Peter Andreas, *Drug War Politics: The Price of Denial* (University of California Press, 1996); Chapter 15 draws from Peter Andreas, *Border Games: Policing the U.S.-Mexico Divide* (Cornell University Press, 2nd ed., 2009); and Chapter 16 draws from Peter Andreas, "Illicit Globalization: Myths, Misconceptions, and Historical Lessons," *Political Science Quarterly* (fall 2011), adapted with permission.

Many thanks to my able research assistants who helped me enormously at various stages of the project: Angelica Duran Martinez, Patrick Endress, Sol Eppel, Forrest Miller, Jack Mizerak, Michael

Skocpol, Emma Tennant, and Aaron Weinstein. Mark Blyth, Bill Frucht, Roger Haydon, Jim Ron, Joyce Seltzer, and Ken Sharpe gave me valuable input when the book was little more than a rough draft of a proposal. Joel Andreas, Richard Bensel, Nitsan Chorev, Rich Friman, Cathy Lutz, Tom Naylor, Herman Schwartz, and Rich Snyder read all or parts of the book manuscript and gave me much-needed feedback. Jim Morone was a supportive voice from the start; his commitment to scholarship aimed at a broader audience beyond narrow disciplinary confines is refreshing and all too rare. I especially appreciate his encouraging my trespassing into the study of American political development.

I cannot say enough good things about Dave McBride, my editor at Oxford University Press, who embraced the idea of doing this book even before I had written a single word. And when I sent him chapter drafts he showed that some editors still actually edit. Dave also generated reviewer reports at record speed, both on the initial book proposal and the manuscript. The helpful comments from these external readers certainly improved the final version. I'm also grateful to my agent, Rafe Sagalyn, who taught me much about the world of books. My biggest thanks (as always) go to Jasmina, for tolerating my scholarly obsessions more than she should and distracting me from them as often as she could.

Peter Andreas, Providence, Rhode Island

SMUGGLER NATION

INTRODUCTION

A Nation of Smugglers

THE AGENTS MOVED IN to seize the illicit shipment, but the traffickers turned on them, shooting the senior officer and torching his vehicle. With the local courts hopelessly compromised and corrupt, the outraged authorities wanted to extradite the perpetrators of the brazen crime. But this only made them more defiant and violent, and they were never caught or prosecuted.

This may sound like Tijuana or Juarez in recent years, or Medellín not so long ago. But the year was 1772, and the place was near my adopted hometown of Providence, Rhode Island. The ringleader of the attack, John Brown—a prominent local merchant whose business interests included smuggling, privateering, and slave trading—was one of the founders of the university that bears his name (and that happens to be my employer). The famous incident came to be known as the *Gaspee* Affair, in which a British customs vessel, the HMS *Gaspee*, was stormed, looted, and torched late at night by an armed group of local citizens in retaliation for cracking down on their illicit trade. The tiny colonial outpost had long been a notorious smuggling hub, greatly advantaged by the geography of Narragansett Bay.

Today, this historical episode is so celebrated by local residents that they put on an annual festival, Gaspee Days, and proudly point to it as Rhode Island's opening salvo in sparking the American Revolution.

A plaque on South Main Street near downtown Providence, a short walk from where I live, commemorates the event. Gaspee Street is also a few blocks away. Of course, most Americans no longer have such a sanguine view of illicit trade, and U.S. officials, like the frustrated British imperial authorities before them, are increasingly preoccupied with fighting it.

In this book I reexamine the history of America as a battle over smuggling, from evading tariffs and embargoes to violating prohibitions and immigration controls. Focusing on the smuggling of goods and people, the book tells the story of how these illicit flows—and the campaigns to police them—defined and shaped the nation. As we'll see, smuggling has been a major force in the broader historical evolution of America: as a distant colonial outpost in the British empire (heavily involved in smuggling untaxed goods); as a developing nation partly based on slavery (including illicit slave trading) and clandestine importation of British machines and skilled workers; as an advanced capitalist industrial and agricultural economy built on the influx of migrant labor (legal and illegal); and as a highly urbanized economy and society increasingly geared toward personal consumption and pleasure (including smuggled porn, bootlegged booze, prohibited drugs, and pirated music). At the same time, battling these illicit trades has been a powerful motor in the development and expansion of the federal government, greatly extending its policing power at home and abroad.

An underlying dynamic I highlight throughout this book is how the state makes smuggling (through laws and their enforcement), and how smuggling in turn remakes the state.[1] But this is not to imply a simple, mechanical interaction. There is nothing natural or automatic about it. Throughout American history we see the full range of state interactions with smuggling, from collusion and toleration to discouragement and condemnation. This is why politics is such a vital part of the story. After all, deciding which activities are labeled as smuggling in the first place is inherently political, and this has varied enormously across time and place. So too has the intensity, form, and focus of anti-smuggling efforts—drugs such as cocaine and cannabis, for example, were not even law enforcement concerns until the last century.

In other words, smuggling is not just about economics—market exchange, supply and demand, and so on. It is all that, of course, but much more. Beyond the mechanics of illicit trade, it includes the morally charged politics of deviance and vice that is so often wrapped up in the issue of smuggling and the policing of smuggling. Here, politics, economics, and culture intersect and mix, often in explosive ways and with unanticipated and long-lasting repercussions for American society and America's foreign relations.

Why retell the American story as a smuggling story? The reasons are many. One is simply that the big-picture story has never really been told in a sustained and focused way; up to now, we mostly have pieces and fragments.[2] Viewing American history through the lens of smuggling sheds new light on the dynamics of borders, foreign relations, government expansion, economic development, and societal transformation. It reveals that the oft-celebrated rise of American capitalism is also about contraband capitalism, including the creation of some of the country's first family fortunes (America's first multimillionaire, John Jacob Astor, was also America's first multimillionaire smuggler).[3] It shows that the transformation of America into a consumer society is also very much about illicit mass consumption. It reminds us that the economic opening of borders has always been selective and incomplete. More broadly, it takes illicit economic activities such as smuggling out of the shadows and places them more front and center in examining U.S. and global politics.

Rereading the American experience through smuggling and anti-smuggling campaigns forces us to look more closely down the side streets, backstreets, and dark alleys of our economic history, not just at what is happening on Main Street and Wall Street (and even here there is sometimes a smuggling connection). This is of course not meant to suggest that everything can simply be reduced to smuggling. But smuggling is too often hidden and out of sight in the conventional narrative of the American epic.

Perhaps the most important reason to tell this story is to inject a strong dose of historical perspective into today's overheated policy debates about securing borders and fighting global crime. Political appeals to "regain control" of the nation's borders are afflicted by an extreme case of historical amnesia, nostalgically implying there was once a time when our borders were actually "under control." This is pure myth; there never was a golden age of secure borders. Smuggling and state making in America grew up together. To be sure, it has often been an antagonistic relationship. But far more than is typically acknowledged, it has also been an interdependent and even symbiotic relationship (sometimes unintentionally so).

Smuggler Nation tells the long and complicated story of this double-edged relationship. In doing so, the book provides a corrective of sorts to today's overly alarmist depictions of the illicit dark side of globalization as an entirely new and unprecedented threat to America and the world. These popularized accounts of a booming illicit global economy overstate its contemporary novelty and overlook its historical significance.[4] For centuries, smuggling has enriched and subverted empires, shaped patterns of global trade, and fueled wars. As the American experience shows, the same illicit commercial activities that are today viewed as besieging borders, undermining legitimate business, and spreading violence and corruption were instrumental in the country's birth, economic development, and geographic expansion. It is therefore perhaps more than a little ironic that a country made by smuggling has now become the world's leading anti-smuggling crusader. Although America's founders rebelled against the policing of illicit trade, and illicit trade helped to create and develop the nation, illicit trade today increasingly frustrates the federal government's policing ambitions.

As the chapters that follow emphasize, the American story reads rather differently when reread as a smuggling story. And this is not simply a detour to obscure places, events, and characters. It includes watershed episodes in American history. Take, for instance, the War of Independence. In many respects, the rebellion was a backlash against the militarized British crackdown on illicit trade. Colonial merchants were leading players in the Atlantic smuggling economy—most notably the smuggling of West Indies molasses to New England distilleries—and conflicts over smuggling and overzealous British customs enforcement played a critical role in the tensions leading up to the outbreak of war. Intensified British policing of clandestine commerce in the decade prior to the Revolution provoked mob riots, burning of customs vessels, and tarring and feathering of customs agents and informants. Pivotal incidents and protests, such as the Boston Tea Party, were closely connected to smuggling interests. It is perhaps appropriate that the first signer of the Declaration of Independence was Boston's most well-known merchant-smuggler, John Hancock.

Smugglers also put their illicit transportation methods, skills, and networks to profitable use by covertly supplying George Washington's troops with desperately needed arms and gunpowder. Motivated as much by profit as patriotism, they also served as privateers for Washington's makeshift naval force. And as we will see, this was just one of a number of major American military conflicts in which success on the battlefield was tied to entrepreneurial success in the underworld of smuggling. Smuggling and war fighting went hand in hand, from trading with the enemy in the War of 1812 to blockade running during the American Civil War.

A focus on smuggling also gives us a rather different perspective on the American Industrial Revolution. Conveniently forgotten in today's intellectual property protection debates is that early U.S. leaders such as Alexander Hamilton enthusiastically encouraged intellectual piracy and technology smuggling during the country's initial industrialization process, especially in the textile industry. Such smuggling also depended on the illicit importation of skilled workers (in violation of British emigration laws) to assemble, operate, and improve on the latest machinery. The most famous British artisan to illegally move to America was Samuel Slater—credited as the "father of the American industrial revolution"—who was then hired to work on and perfect smuggled cotton-spinning machinery in Pawtucket, Rhode Island. Only much later, once it was a major industrial power, did the United States become a forceful advocate for intellectual property protection. In other words, the message to China and other countries today is, "do as I say, not as I did."

Similarly, the standard story of westward expansion reads a bit differently when retold through the narrative of smuggling. As we will see, the West was won not only through military conquest but also through illicit commerce. Many nineteenth-century Americans interpreted Manifest Destiny to include a divine right to smuggle. The American frontier was a smuggling frontier. Smugglers of all sorts and smuggling of all types were at the forefront of the nation's aggressive territorial expansion (by the mid-nineteenth century, the United States purchased or conquered almost 900 million acres of new land). This ranged from large-scale smuggling of alcohol into Indian country—in violation of federal law—to trade for much-coveted furs, to illicit slave importing for the rapidly expanding cotton plantations of the Deep South. Westward expansion also included the mass movement of illegal settlers and squatters—the "illegal immigrants" of their time—who unlawfully moved to and settled on federal, Indian, and Mexican lands, often provoking violent confrontations. Weak government enforcement made such illicit frontier activities possible, and the extension and strengthening of the government's reach in turn often pushed these activities further outward to the new edges of the frontier. These borderland dynamics came at the expense of a decaying Spanish empire, a newly independent Mexico, and ever-shrinking Indian lands. In this sense, frontier smugglers were America's first pioneers, helping to lay the groundwork for territorial expansion and annexation.

The prevalence of smuggling throughout American history also complicates the image of the United States as a champion of free trade. After all, in a truly free-trade world there would be no smuggling. In one form or another, we have always imposed restrictions on cross-border economic flows, and these restrictions have created all sorts of incentives and opportunities for smuggling. In a sense, then, smugglers are the real free trader pioneers, relentlessly pushing the frontiers of commerce and challenging any and all trade obstacles in their way. No wonder, then, that Adam Smith was such an admirer of smugglers—they were at the forefront of breaking down rigid trade barriers. He viewed a smuggler as "a person who, though no doubt highly blamable for violating the laws of his country, is frequently incapable of violating those of natural justice, and would have been, in every respect, an excellent citizen, had not the laws of his country made that a crime which nature never meant to be so."[5]

But while America happily subverted British mercantilism through smuggling in the eighteenth century and denounced the Crown's anti-smuggling efforts, as a newly industrializing country, it rejected free trade and imposed high tariffs in the nineteenth century—prompting widespread evasion via smuggling. Smuggling was further fueled when the United States increasingly imposed not just tariffs but prohibitions, with eradication rather than regulation the official goal. And this created new smuggling incentives and opportunities, ranging from illicitly imported slaves and Chinese laborers to outlawed pornography and condoms, to banned booze and drugs.

Conventional notions about American government are also challenged when smuggling is introduced into the story. The standard story is of an America defined by a minimalist and unobtrusive central government for much of its early history.[6] But this image of a disengaged, hands-off state doesn't really fit with the everyday experience of those who were involved in international commerce. When it came to regulating trade—and therefore policing smuggling—the reach and presence of the state was very real in the form of the local customhouse and customs collector.[7]

The new federal government's constitutional right to regulate commerce was the cornerstone of its authority and provided a key mechanism for expanding its policing powers. Indeed, the regulation and policing of trade was a driving motivation to create a central state apparatus in the first place. Concerns about smuggling prompted government growth from the start, with the establishment of a customs service and its revenue cutters as a core component of the federal bureaucracy. Attempts to suppress maritime piracy and embargo busting also sparked the early development of the country's naval forces. Illicit trade and related activities therefore not only challenged but also empowered the new American state.[8]

So even though warfare and welfare are typically viewed as the main drivers of big government, *Smuggler Nation* highlights another motor: increased government size, presence, and coercive powers via the policing of smuggling. Consider, for example, the transformation of ports of entry. This began with an almost exclusive focus on seaports, but it later added land ports and then extended to airports and even cyberports. As the mechanisms and locations of border crossings (both licit and illicit) have diversified and expanded, so too has policing—including reaching well beyond the nation's borders through cross-border police cooperation, international agreements, deploying agents abroad, and so on.[9]

Equally important, such border policing began with revenue collection as its core mission, but over time this increasingly expanded to immigration controls and enforcing prohibitions—greatly adding to the pressures on federal law enforcement. A closer look at smuggling and anti-smuggling campaigns therefore also gives us insight into the changing role and expectations of government in American society. This shift from an almost exclusive focus on the imperative of revenue collection to a much broader mandate of keeping out "undesirable" people and things has often been entangled in the highly charged politics of moral panics and crusades.[10] Moreover, there has often been a built-in dynamic of escalation in which increased law enforcement stimulates more organized, sophisticated, and geographically dispersed smuggling, prompting calls for even more intensive and expansive enforcement. Regardless of their effectiveness and sometimes counterproductive consequences, such enforcement crackdowns have often proven politically popular for their symbolic value in projecting an image of government authority and resolve.

The end result is that alongside the welfare state and the traditional national security state we also have seen the rise and growth of a formidable policing state, with both inward- and outward-looking faces. And as some smuggling issues have come to be redefined as security issues, we also see a blurring of law enforcement and national security missions—nowhere more apparent than in the creation of the Department of Homeland Security (the largest reorganization of the federal government in half a century) and the proliferation of military hardware and technologies for anti-smuggling tasks along the nation's borders.

As we now turn to look in more detail at the role of smuggling and anti-smuggling campaigns in shaping the course of American history, it is useful to ponder some "what if" questions. For instance: What if the British had continued to tolerate rather than crack down on illicit trade in their American colonies? Would the colonies still have rebelled? And what if the rebellious colonies had failed to obtain gunpowder and other supplies through smuggling channels before France formally intervened? Would the British have won? What if the newborn country had not been able to illicitly acquire British technologies and skilled workers? Would America's early industrialization have been derailed? What if local communities on both sides of the U.S.-Canada border during the War of 1812 had been more interested in fighting instead of illicitly trading (including feeding British troops in Canada with smuggled American beef)? Would the war have lasted so long and ended in a stalemate?

Equally provocative counterfactuals can be asked about other major nineteenth-century episodes and developments. What if bootleggers and fur traders had not flooded Indian lands with illicit rum and whiskey in violation of the federal ban? Would Native American populations have been so easily and quickly pacified and displaced without "white man's wicked water" as a deadly lubricant? What if the foreign slave trade had not been able to rely on American slavers, American-built and -outfitted slave ships, and the American flag (all prohibited by U.S. law) to defy the British warships policing the trade? What if the Confederacy had been unable to illicitly export cotton to fund illicit imports of arms and other war materials? What if the Union blockade of Confederate ports had been more effective in stopping blockade runners? Would the Civil War have been so long and bloody? What if contraband contraceptives had not been so widely available in the last decades of the century? Would the country's birthrate still have fallen as much as it did?

Moving into the twentieth century: What if rumrunners and gangsters had not made such a mockery of Prohibition and kept dry America wet? Would alcohol still be illegal? And what if drugs such as cocaine, opium, and cannabis had never been criminalized? What would our criminal justice system look like without drug prohibition? What if American agribusiness and other sectors of the economy had not had such easy access to a large, cheap, and compliant pool of unauthorized migrant workers during the past century? What would the economic and demographic profile of the country look like in the absence of such large-scale evasion of immigration laws? Readers should keep these sorts of questions in mind in the chapters ahead.[11]

There is nothing uniquely American about smuggling, of course.[12] To varying degrees and in varying ways, all nations are smuggler nations. Indeed, some have even been smuggler empires; consider, for instance, the crucial role of opium smuggling in financing the British Empire in the nineteenth century. No so-called drug cartel today comes remotely close to matching the power of the British East India Company, which enjoyed a near monopoly on the China opium-smuggling trade in its heyday.

In a sense, then, this book is the story of just one case out of many—but a particularly prominent and important one. What makes the U.S. experience so striking is that not only has the country had such an intimate relationship with smuggling since before its founding, but today it has the distinction of being the world's leading importer of smuggled goods and labor (given its sheer size and wealth) and simultaneously the world's leading anti-smuggling campaigner. It is also a leading smuggling source country, if one considers all the smuggled American guns, cigarettes, pirated software and entertainment, hazardous waste, and dirty dollars circulating around the globe.

Today, America's policing spirit and illicit entrepreneurial spirit continue to thrive and coexist. We have built a vast anti-smuggling policing bureaucracy with global reach, and partly thanks to the war on drugs we also have the largest prison population on earth. At the same time, the business of smuggling never seems to lack new recruits. Barriers to entry, as economists would say, remain low. Amateur smugglers can even order "how to" books at a discount on Amazon, with titles such as *Duty Free: Smuggling Made Easy* and *Sneak It Through: Smuggling Made Easier*.[13] There are books with smuggling tips tailored especially for aspiring drug traffickers, among them *I Am the Market: How to Smuggle Cocaine by the Ton, in Five Easy Lessons*.[14] And if one wishes to also produce the drugs, there are popular books on this as well—*Marijuana Growers Handbook* and *Marijuana Horticulture* are listed as top sellers in the Amazon categories of "gardening and horticulture" and "crop science."[15] Although not nearly as profitable as smuggling itself, writing user guides for wannabe smugglers is certainly less risky. For that matter, so, too, is writing a book about the history of smuggling in America.

PART I

THE COLONIAL ERA

I

The Golden Age of Illicit Trade

AMERICA WAS BORN A smuggler nation, and indeed smuggling helped give birth to the nation. How exactly did this happen? To pinpoint the time of conception, we must go back some three hundred years, to the early colonial era. The tale of the rise of colonial smuggling unfolds within the context of highly restrictive British trade rules, in which maritime smugglers can be viewed as leading the push for more open trade. In this sense, colonial smugglers were truly pioneers of free trade, defying and circumventing restrictive trade barriers whenever and wherever they could. Britain's official trade rules were designed to keep its distant colonial outposts subordinate, weak, and dependent. The realities in the American colonies, particularly in port cities such as Boston, New York, and Philadelphia, dictated otherwise. Colonial merchants in many ways enjoyed the best of both worlds, reaping the benefits of imperial restrictions while evading imperial restrictions with relative ease. As we'll see, this peculiar arrangement persisted until the early 1760s through a mix of British neglect, tolerance, and corruption.

Formal Rules, Informal Realities

On paper, the British imperial trading system was tightly controlled. Its mercantilist policies were codified in the Acts of Navigation and Trade, a series of ambitious statutes put in place in the second half of the seventeenth century. For certain commodities, such as tobacco and sugar, the British colonies in North America were allowed to trade only directly with each other and with England, and vessels engaged in trade with any English territory had to be English and mostly manned by English crews. Trade was also subject to import and export duties, sometimes prohibitively. Competing European powers had similarly restrictive trade rules, creating a rigidly mercantilist commercial world.

Informal practice was another matter entirely. Mercantilism leaked like a sieve.[1] Indeed, trade that defied mercantilist rules was integral to the very functioning of the Atlantic trading system: "What made all this possible—what helped bind the widespread and intensely competitive Atlantic commercial world together—was the mass of illegal trade that bypassed the formal, nationalistic constraints," explains historian Bernard Bailyn.[2] Smuggling-related corruption was so institutionalized in some places that manuals were even printed up listing the standardized bribes.[3] Beyond bribing, smugglers used many tricks of the trade to disguise the origins and contents of their illicit cargoes, ranging from counterfeit clearance papers to mislabeled containers and doctored ship manifests.[4]

Merchants in British North America were at the forefront of this bustling Atlantic smuggling economy, developing an illicit trading network linking colonial ports to the West Indies and continental Europe. The type and extent of smuggling in the colonies, however, was far from uniform. For instance, smuggling was less pervasive in Virginia than in Massachusetts. There were fewer incentives to smuggle in the South, given that England provided a ready export market on favorable terms for leading Southern products, most notably tobacco (the strain used for export was introduced to Virginia by John Rolfe, who had smuggled in strictly controlled Spanish seeds from the Caribbean in the early seventeenth century). The Northern colonies, in contrast, produced little of value to English consumers and therefore sought out alternate markets through illicit channels. The Southern colonies did nevertheless engage in intracolonial smuggling—evading duties, for example, on tobacco exports to Northern colonies—as well as contraband trade with the West Indies. Northern merchants also served as smuggling intermediaries for the Southern colonies.[5]

We'll never know the exact amount of illicit trade in the American colonies—or anywhere else, for that matter, past or present. For obvious reasons, few records were kept—frustrating quantitative economic historians and making nonsense of official trade data.[6] But what is clear is that both the opportunities and the incentives to smuggle were enormous. Ambitious British trade restrictions clashed with the limits of actual enforcement, a long and minimally monitored coastline, and fierce local resistance. Not only was there little social stigma attached to smuggling in the colonies, but in port cities, where trade was the primary generator of wealth, smuggling enjoyed considerable community support. This made it extremely difficult for British authorities to rely on provincial courts to uphold seizures and convict smugglers. Indeed, the legal system could even be creatively used to retaliate against overly diligent customs agents.

Even though we lack precise measures of smuggling, we do have clues. These include uneven balance in cargo between incoming and outgoing ships, private correspondence, and travel accounts.[7] The magnitude of the illicit trade in molasses is revealed by the discrepancy between official imports and the amount of molasses actually needed to keep colonial distilleries running. For instance, a mere 384 hogsheads of molasses per year officially arrived in Boston in 1754–55, but 40,000 hogsheads per year were required to run the region's sixty-three distilleries.[8] It was largely this illicit molasses trade, Bailyn suggests, that made possible a positive balance of payments for the New England colonies.[9] Colonial merchants predictably balked when Britain suddenly stopped turning a blind eye to such smuggling in the 1760s. In a revealing line, John Adams would later write, "I know not why we should blush to confess that molasses was an essential ingredient in American independence."[10]

The Early Years

British trade laws were subverted in the American colonies from the very start. But for the most part, evasion by colonial traders in the seventeenth to mid-eighteenth centuries was met with imperial accommodation more than enforcement. The reasons were both strategic and practical. Great Britain was first and foremost preoccupied with geopolitical rivalries and therefore wished to ensure the loyalty of its colonial subjects—even if this came at the cost of overlooking a certain amount of illicit commerce. Moreover, sporadic and short-lived British attempts to improve colonial customs administration had produced dismal results, generating more resentment than revenue. Colonial merchants developed an impressive repertoire of evasive maneuvers to conceal the origins, nationality, routes, and content of their illicit cargoes. This included frequent use of fraudulent paperwork to make the cargo appear legal and authorized.[11] And much to the frustration of the British authorities, when seizures did happen local merchants were often able to use sympathetic provincial courts to reclaim their confiscated goods and have their cases dismissed.[12] For instance, Edward Randolph, the appointed head of customs in New England, brought thirty-six seizures to trial from 1680 to the end of 1682—and all but two of these were acquitted. Alternatively, merchants sometimes simply took matters into their own hands and stole the illicit goods back while impounded.[13]

It should be little surprise that Britain had such difficulties with smuggling in its remote colonies, given the magnitude of illicit trade in its own backyard: English smugglers (known locally as "free traders") engaged in large-scale tea smuggling and other contraband commerce across the English Channel, often in open defiance of the authorities and with considerable popular support in coastal communities. In the American colonies, by comparison, British trade rules were both more restrictive and more difficult to enforce.[14]

The first six decades of the eighteenth century can be described as the golden age of illicit trade in the American colonies. Britain's "salutary neglect" and pragmatic tolerance trumped enforcement and revenue collection. In 1710, there were only thirty-seven customs officers in the colonies; the number had increased to only fifty by 1760.[15] During this same time period the estimated colonial population increased from 331,700 to 1,593,600. The imperial customs administrative apparatus in the colonies was fragmented and in disarray; enforcement was typically lethargic.[16] The British authorities had neither the will nor the capacity to put a serious dent in the smuggling business. At the same time, restrictive trade rules remained on the books, new restrictions were added (most notably the Molasses Act), and a formal pretense of customs administration was maintained. All sides kept up appearances. Colonial traders continued to use circuitous routes to smuggle goods, disguise their cargo, and dole out bribes rather than publicly challenge the king's right to collect duties and enforce the trade laws. Customs officials, for their part, went through the ritualistic motions of inspecting ships and collecting modest amounts of duties (while routinely lining their pockets with payments to look the other way).

Institutionalized corruption had a pacifying effect; informal financial accommodation meant that violence between smugglers and customs inspectors was rare. For the most part, bribing trumped bullying, producing a win-win situation for the smuggler and the customs agent—even if not for imperial coffers. Corruption was in fact competitive: colonial ports competed with each other to attract shipping business, and those ports that offered the most laxity in inspections and most bribable customs houses enjoyed a competitive advantage.[17]

Customs administration was in such a sorry state of neglect that the royal collector in some places was not even present and instead rented out his post to a deputy. Such was the case in Rhode Island, where in 1742 the judge of the Vice-Admiralty court noted that the collector for the colony "for many years last past has not resided there but farms out the same." The judge also later reported that the port "at present is filled by a Deputy Collr who must be presumed to Rent ye Office from his Principle." Consequently, Rhode Island was "virtually a free port."[18]

Although historians disagree about the extent of eighteenth-century smuggling in the American colonies, it is clear that the passage of the Molasses Act in 1733 was a de facto invitation to smuggle, stimulating the development of a smuggling superhighway between the West Indies and the American colonies. The new law, aimed at protecting English planters in the British West Indies, imposed prohibitive duties on non-English sugar products. Yet it was so poorly enforced and so widely violated that it was treated as virtually a "dead letter" from the start. The restrictive law was first announced as a temporary five-year measure, but it was renewed again and again for three decades. "If any serious attempt had been made to enforce the statute," suggests historian Arthur Schlesinger, "the prosperity of the commercial provinces [New England] would have been laid prostrate. It was the West India trade, more than anything else, which had enabled them to utilize their fisheries, forests and fertile soil, to build up their towns and cities, to supply cargoes for their merchant marine, and to liquidate their indebtedness to British merchants and manufacturers."[19]

In exchange for molasses and other sugar products, colonial merchants supplied the non-British West Indies with timber, horses, grain, bread, meat, and fish—especially low-grade dried cod and mackerel, used to feed plantation slaves. They not only shipped these smuggled goods to the West Indies but also sold smuggled ships, contributing to New England's rapidly growing shipbuilding industry.[20] Smuggling in violation of the Molasses Act was not merely the domain of small-time traders. Some of the most well-known New England merchant elites, such as the Hancock family in Boston, became enmeshed in the West Indies trade.[21] Thomas Hancock (uncle of the famous John), wrote to his captain Simon Gross in December 1743 to take advantage of both licit and illicit trade opportunities in the Caribbean: "You have liberty to go to any of the English Islands, & if you think it Safe, to any of the French Islands . . . I'd have you unload at Nantasket [Boston's outer harbor] if no man of War there." The letter concludes: ". . . [A] load of Molasses will be the best Cargo you can bring here; write me all Opportunitys."[22] Smuggling was so institutionalized in the Boston merchant community that merchants were able to buy insurance policies to cover them in the event of seizure.[23]

Figure 1.1 South-East view of the town of Boston 1723 (American Antiquarian Society).

Molasses had many uses in colonial America. It was a popular ingredient for cooking; it was commonly used in a soft drink called "beverige" (molasses and ginger-flavored water); and it was used for home-brewed beer.[24] But its most important use was for rum production. Fueled by illicit imports of Caribbean sugar and molasses, business boomed for New England rum distilleries (heavily concentrated in Massachusetts and Rhode Island).[25] By 1770, there were as many as 143 distilleries in the colonies producing nearly five million gallons of rum annually.[26] British molasses suppliers could not have possibly kept up with this demand: "The entire molasses output of the British islands did not equal two-thirds of the quantity imported into Rhode Island alone, and was estimated to amount to only about one-eighth of the quantity consumed annually by all the provinces."[27]

Most New England rum was consumed in the mainland colonies.[28] The colonists were heavy drinkers by any standard, and rum was the drink of choice.[29] Some of this domestic supply was also diverted—often in violation of colonial prohibitions—to the "inward" trade with American Indians. But although exports were small compared to mainland consumption, rum was nevertheless an essential ingredient in the infamous Triangle Trade: American merchants exchanged barrels of rum for slaves on the West coast of Africa (with slave prices denominated in gallons of rum); slaves were then shipped to work on West Indies plantations; and these plantations then resupplied New England rum distilleries with sugar and molasses. And the cycle would repeat itself. Rum was thus the "currency of the slave trade, which in turn was the backbone of New England commerce."[30] The rum trade also enabled the importation of slaves to the Southern colonies: "Rum was practically the only commodity that could have been exchanged for the African slaves and it is this consideration that the Southern colonies became dependent on the trade between the Northern colonies and the West Indies."[31]

Newport, Rhode Island, was the epicenter of the rum trade in colonial America. Today we tend to associate Newport with yacht racing and gilded-age mansions, but the origins of this northern port's fortunes were less glamorous. The tiny colony of Rhode Island produced little of trading value—with the notable exception of rum. And no

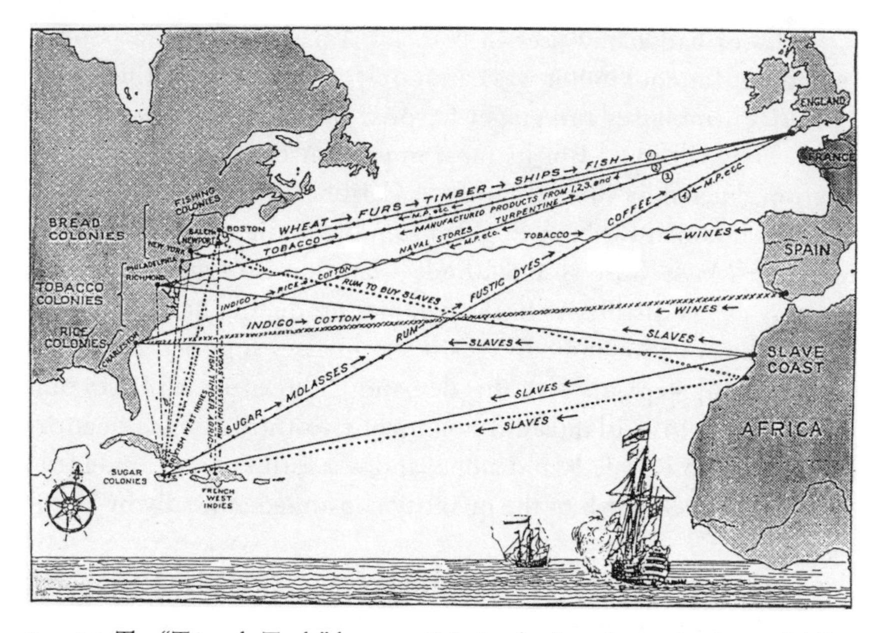

Figure 1.2 The "Triangle Trade" between Britain, the American colonies, and Africa in the seventeenth and eighteenth centuries (Granger Collection).

town exploited this commercial niche more successfully and aggressively than Newport. By the mid-1760s, twenty-two of the thirty Rhode Island distilleries were based in Newport.[32] As one historian has remarked, "If merchants from all the American seaports evaded the navigation laws to some extent, those from Newport stood alone as the greatest offenders."[33] No wonder then that the inhabitants of the town—and of the rest of the colony, for that matter—were denounced by the British Admiral John Montagu as "a set of lawless piratical people . . . whose sole business is that of smuggling and defrauding the King of his duties."[34]

Producing large volumes of rum required large-scale smuggling, carried out through all sorts of creative methods to hide illicit cargoes. As Sydney James describes it, this could include clandestinely landing an entire shipment, paying duties on part of a shipment while secretly off-loading the other part, or use of false papers (bought from customs agents in the Caribbean) for the entire shipment to disguise its non-British origins. Bribing of local customs officials also helped to ensure that they would not pry too much. It is perhaps no surprise then that during its thirty-one years in existence the Molasses Act generated "only a trickle of revenue" for the crown.[35]

But even while defying official British trade rules, this and other illicit colonial trades had an economic upside for Britain: the profits from smuggling helped the colonies pay for their growing appetite for British manufactured goods. The official balance of trade heavily disadvantaged the colonies and thus should also have greatly restricted their purchasing power. But even though the official balance of payments was lopsided, this was unofficially "balanced" through smuggling.[36] More purchasing power in the colonies, even if illicitly generated, translated into more British imports—which grew by more than 600 percent between 1700 and 1770.[37] Illicit trade did not simply undermine licit trade: rather, the two grew up and expanded together. In a sense, the breaking of British trade laws made it possible for the colonists to afford to live like the British.

Smuggling helped to create a consumer society in the colonies.[38] The historian Cathy Matson suggests that smuggling even gained a certain amount of respectability by feeding new and growing consumer tastes, ranging from tea to silks.[39] Other illicitly imported luxury goods included coffee, chocolates, wines, and French brandies. William Bollan of New England wrote in 1742 to "The Lords of Trade" in London that from Holland his area was illicitly supplied with "Reels of Yarn or spun Hemp, paper, Gunpowder, Iron, Goods of various sorts used for Men and Women's Clothing." To underscore his point, he finished by noting that "I need only to acquaint you that I write this clad in a Superfine French Cloth, which I bought on purpose that I might wear about the Evidence of these Illegal Traders having already begun to destroy the Vital parts of the British commerce; and to Use as a Memento to Myself and the Customhouse Officers to do everything in our power towards cutting off this Trade So very pernicious to the British Nation."[40]

Merchant correspondence reveals some of the tricks of the illicit trade with Holland. Thomas Hancock, for instance, wrote to one of his ship captains in Holland instructing him to divert and clandestinely unload his Boston-bound cargo at Cape Cod: "[W]hen you have finished your Business proceed for Cape C[od] New England, speak with nobody upon your passage if you c[an] possibly help it."[41]

The off-loaded cargo would then be quietly transported to Boston. This type of smuggling scheme was not limited to New England. New York Governor Charles Hardy described the situation in the colony in 1757: it was routine for ships "to come from Holland, stop at Sandy Hook, and smuggle their Cargoes to New York, and carry their Vessels up empty." He complained that smugglers who countered his efforts to curb this practice "took another Course, by sending their Vessels to . . . Connecticut"—from where the cargo was sneaked into nearby New York.[42]

Treasonous Trade

Unauthorized colonial trade with Britain's rivals violated the Acts of Navigation and Trade and undermined imperial revenue collection. But in wartime such illicit trade was also treasonous trade. Providing "aid and comfort" to the enemy was prohibited by English statutory law. This did not, however, dampen colonial enthusiasm for smuggling—and indeed, the shortages induced by war conditions simply furnished a greater incentive to smuggle. Given the frequency of war between Britain and its European rivals, "trading with the enemy" was common practice in the American colonies and elsewhere.[43] But this form of clandestine commerce reached new heights during the Seven Years War (1756–1763) between France and England; the conflict played out in their North American colonies as the French and Indian War, which started two years earlier. Even though Britain won the war, smuggling added greatly to its cost and longevity by keeping French forces supplied and neutralizing British efforts to starve them into submission. A captured letter from a Frenchman on one of the Caribbean islands explained the dire wartime situation in September 1758: "Every day we are on the verge of great want; without the help of our enemies we would be obliged to live, as you told us, on what the colony produces. Our condition is hard . . . we know very well that it is not within the power of French commerce to aid us."[44]

American merchants profitably played both sides. As British subjects, they formally contributed to the war effort by supplying troops and serving as deputized privateers (essentially legalized piracy) on the high seas to attack French supply lines. Informally, they also supplied the French and used privateering to facilitate illicit provisioning. Such disloyalty was not a self-conscious political act of rebellion; there was little sympathy for the French cause, and indeed a French victory was not in the interests of the American colonies. Rather, it was simply a pragmatic response to a business opportunity. For colonial merchants long accustomed to smuggling as a routine and "normal" form of commerce, trading with the French during wartime was merely a continuation of past practice—even if it was viewed far less benignly in London.

Wartime illicit trading with the French primarily took two forms: directly through "flags of truce," and indirectly through neutral islands in the Caribbean. The official purpose of the flags-of-truce permits, issued by colonial governors to ship captains, was to enable exchange of prisoners with the French. In practice, much more than prisoners was "exchanged." Sometimes the prisoners were entirely imaginary, with fictional names written in the paperwork for the sake of appearances. The pretense of prisoner exchanges was such a useful cover for illicit trade that some colonial governors, most notably in Rhode Island and Pennsylvania, set up a lucrative business selling flags-of-truce permits to merchants.

William Denny, Pennsylvania's lieutenant governor, was a particularly notorious seller of blank permits.[45] A November 1760 letter to William Pitt from Deputy-Governor James Hamilton (who had recently replaced Denny) described the situation in blunt terms:

> Mr. Denny, now in England . . . about the Month of May in the year 1759, began the practice of selling flags of truce; at first indeed in small numbers, and under the pretence of transporting French prisoners, of whom, tis well known we have not had more during the whole War more than might have been conveniently embarked in one, or at most, two small ships: Yet Mr. Denny or his agents received for each flag so granted, a Sum not less than from three to four hundred pistolen, and having once relished the sweets of this traffick, he became more undisguised, and as it were open'd a shop at lower prices to all Customers, . . . [including those] of the neighboring provinces, to which they came and purchased freely.

The business peaked during Denny's last months in office:

> Towards the end of his administration, the matter was carried to such a pitch, that he scrupled not to set his name to, and dispose of great numbers of blank flags of Truce, at the low price of twenty pounds sterling or under; some of which were selling from hand to hand at advanced prices, several months after my arrival. In consequence of this iniquitous conduct, by which he amassed a great sum of money, I found at my arrival . . . a very great part of the principal merchants of this city, engaged in a trade with the French islands in the West Indies.[46]

Rhode Island was the New England hub of the "flags of truce" illicit trade. Massachusetts Governor Francis Bernard complained to the Board of Trade in London: "These practices will never be put an end to, til Rhode Island is reduced to the subjection of the British Empire; of which at present it is no more a part than the Bahama Islands were when they were inhabited by the buccaneers."[47] In September 1758, Virginia Governor Francis Fauquier reported on one prisoner exchange scheme by Rhode Island merchants: "The Rhode Island Men knowing there were 60 French prisoners at Boston, sent four Ships from Providence to Boston at their own Expense, and put fifteen on board each ship by which they skreen'd four cargoes of provisions . . . to Port au Prince."[48]

The Browns of Providence profited handsomely from the flags-of-truce trade. But not all of the voyages they sponsored were successful: several of their ships were seized and condemned by the British admiralty courts at the Bahamas for engaging in "wicked, illegal unwarrantable, clandestine and prohibited trade."[49] For one ship, the *Speedwell*, it was the final of seven voyages to enemy ports; on this last trip, Rhode Island Governor Stephen Hopkins authorized that the *Speedwell* carry only one French prisoner of war to justify the journey.[50] Robert Rogers reported from his visit to Rhode Island:

> The form of government here is in all respects the same as in the colony of Connecticut. They are not, however, scrupulous in keeping up to the terms of their charter, often dispensing with it in some

> pretty essential points, and taking liberties, not only detrimental to the other provinces, but even to the nation, especially in times of war, by carrying on an illicit trade with the enemy, and supplying them with the most material articles. This they have repeatedly done with impunity, to my certain knowledge, in the course of the late war, when many scores of vessels went loaded with beef, pork, flour, &c. under the pretext of flags . . . [and] could at any time be procured from their Governor, when at the same time perhaps they carried not more than one or two French prisoners, dividing the crew of one French merchantman they had taken, among a whole fleet of flags of truce, laden with articles more welcome to the enemy than all the prisoners, with the ship and cargo, they took from them.[51]

The British Navy took over responsibility for prisoner-of-war exchanges in 1761, putting an end to the flags-of-truce trading scam.

Illicit trade with the French was also carried out less directly through neutral Spanish, Danish, and Dutch Caribbean islands serving as intermediaries. The Dutch island of St. Eustatius became a bustling free port where American colonists brought provisions in exchange for French molasses. The Spanish settlement of San Fernando de Monte Cristi on the north coast of Hispaniola was particularly convenient, since it was contiguous with French territory. In June 1757, Lieutenant Governor De Lancey of New York forwarded evidence of a "pernicious trade" at Monte Cristi, in which American merchants would use Spanish go-betweens on the island to transfer goods to nearby French ports: "By this indirect Way his Majesty's Enemies are supplied. What remedy to apply to this Evil may be difficult to say."[52] One British warship sent to investigate reported with great dismay that in early February 1759 twenty-eight of the twenty-nine vessels at the port were from the North American colonies. The British Board of Trade reported to the Privy Council later that year that all of the Northern colonies were involved in illicit trade with the French, noting that more than 150 ships from the continent had been identified "at one time in the Road of Monte Christi."[53] French ships even brazenly loaded their goods directly onto American vessels rather than first off-loading them on land.[54] A few years later, in May 1761, thirty-six of the fifty vessels in port were reportedly from North America.[55] A British army officer on the headquarters staff in New York wrote in 1760: "The greatest part of the vessels belonging to the ports of Philadelphia New York and Rhode Island, are constantly employed in carrying provisions to and bringing sugars &c. from Monte Cristi; or the enemy's islands."[56] Although increasingly alarmed by the provisioning of the French via Monte Cristi, British authorities nevertheless had to respect the island's neutrality to avoid dragging Spain into the war.

On August 23, 1760, William Pitt summed up Britain's frustrations in his instructions to provincial governors:

> The Commanders of His Majesty's Forces, and Fleets, in North America and the West Indies, having transmitted repeated and certain Intelligence of an illegal and most pernicious Trade, carried on by the King's Subjects, in North America, and the West Indies, as well to the French Islands, as to the French Settlements on the Continent of America . . . by which the Enemy is, to the greatest Reproach & Detriment of Government, supplied with Provisions, and other Necessities, whereby they are principally, if not alone, enabled to sustain, and protract, this long and expensive War; . . . In order, therefore, to put the most speedy and effectual Stop to such flagitious Practices . . . so highly repugnant to the Honor, and well-being, of this Kingdom, It is His Majesty's express will and pleasure, that you do forthwith make the strictest Enquiry into the State of this dangerous and ignominous Trade.[57]

The reply to Pitt from Governor Stephen Hopkins of Rhode Island was particularly candid, noting that the colony's ships "have indeed carried Lumber and Dry Goods of British Manufacture to sell to the French, and in Return have brought back some Sugars, but mostly Melasses." He also acknowledged that it was "highly probable" that some vessels officially headed for friendly ports instead "deviated from the Voyage pretended," stopping at French ports. But because these voyages were clandestine, the identity of the smugglers "may never come to the Knowledge of any Officers of the Colony, by whom they are sure to be prosecuted should they be discovered." Hopkins also delicately noted that the earnings made from this illicit trade helped the colony purchase British manufactures—thus ultimately benefiting Britain.

Hopkins concluded with a promise to "put a total stop" to the trade with the French.[58] Predictably, Hopkins's letter was not well received. Rhode Island's colonial agent in London reported back to the governor that "some of our leading men have taken great disgust at the trade with the French mentioned in thy letter."[59]

The port of New York was even more active than Rhode Island in trading with the enemy. Far from being a business of the socially marginal, such commerce involved not only the city's merchant elite but also the political class—including the mayor and the families of Supreme Court justices.[60] At the same time, New York served as the communications and supply hub for British forces, and it was the leading colonial privateering port—significantly outperforming all other British-American ports in terms of enemy ships captured or destroyed. As historian Thomas Truxes documents in detail, New York's wartime prosperity was based on the twin pillars of British military spending and illicit provisioning.[61] In some cases, colonial privateers who were officially commissioned to disrupt enemy supplies would instead lend protection for vessels selling goods to the enemy.[62] This would sometimes involve going through the make-believe theatrics of "capturing" an enemy vessel while in practice actually offering an escort.[63]

A code of silence in the city made informers scarce and frustrated investigations. Would-be informers had good reason to keep quiet. When one local informer, George Spencer, dared to come forward in 1759 claiming to have evidence of fraudulent paperwork masking illicit trade with the French via the island of Hispaniola, he was promptly arrested on trumped-up charges (thanks to an arrest warrant supplied by a complicit court clerk) and attacked by a mob of sailors while being escorted to the jailhouse. Bruised and battered, Spencer sat in jail for 27 months. He fled the city soon after his release.[64] "So many people I suspect have been interested in this illicit Trade from this place," New York's Lieutenant Governor Cadwallader Colden wrote in a letter to Jeffery Amherst, commander of British forces in North America, on April 23, 1762, "that it is very difficult to find Persons to execute any orders who have not connections with them, or who are not afraid of their resentment, so that however solicitous I be to bring the guilty to consign punishment, and to put an entire stop to the pernicious Trade, my endeavors may not have the desired effect."[65]

New York's merchants, Colden complained, were "accustomed to despise all laws of trade."[66] And he was determined to change their illicit ways—so much so that at one point he imposed an embargo on the New York port and brought criminal charges against eighteen merchants. On May 29, 1762, fifty-four of the city's merchants signed a petition to Colden promising to stop trading with the enemy and pleading with him to relax his crackdown.[67] Much to their dismay, however, the end of the war the following year did not stop the British squeeze on smuggling. As we'll see in the next chapter, it was, in fact, just the beginning. To make matters worse, the end of the war brought with it a sharp economic downturn, adding to colonial anxieties about diminished smuggling revenues. The boom years of illicit trading and war profiteering were now over.

2

The Smuggling Road to Revolution

THE STANDARD, FAMILIAR NARRATIVE of the roots of the American Revolution is that it was about defending freedom and protesting taxes. But a too-often-overlooked aspect of this was the freedom to evade taxes in the form of smuggling. Smuggling was certainly not the only contentious issue in the years leading up to the War of Independence, but it is striking how much of colonial outrage toward the British crown was directed at customs agents and their crackdown on illicit trade. The enforcement of trade laws was the most concrete, visible manifestation of imperial presence in the colonies. And the violation of these laws and the increasingly hostile reaction to their enforcement were the most concrete expressions of colonial opposition to imperial rule. Growing resentment toward the king's customs became a unifying cause in the otherwise fragmented and loosely connected American colonies.

This chapter recasts the founding story as a smuggling story. This does not mean reducing everything to a battle over smuggling, of course. But it does place it more front and center than in conventional accounts.[1] British reform efforts, including a crackdown on smuggling that began in the early 1760s, played no small part in fueling calls for independence in the American colonies. Not surprisingly, Boston—the port city that experienced the highest number of customs seizures in the 1760s and 1770s—was also at the forefront of the colonial challenge to British rule.[2] For many, the lofty rallying cry of "freedom" really meant freedom to smuggle—or at least freedom from harassment by overzealous customs inspectors. It was not so much Britain's burdensome trade and tax rules that provoked such outrage in the colonies. Rather it was the attempt for the first time to strictly enforce the rules—and thus threaten long-established smuggling activities—as well as the crass opportunism and abuses on the part of customs officials doing the enforcing. Britain's belated efforts to build up a credible customs capacity in the colonies provoked an intense backlash and ultimately backfired. It turned out that the reach of the British Empire was far greater than the strength of its grip. When the empire suddenly tried to tighten the grip—putting a squeeze on illicit trade and alienating colonists with heavy-handed enforcement tactics—Britain lost it entirely.

Crackdown and Backlash

Decades of British tolerance of smuggling turned to hostility as the Seven Years War came to an end. Alarm replaced apathetic neglect. Old accommodations gave way to confrontation. Now the imperial mind-set in London was to treat all American merchants as potential smugglers. Regardless of how much smuggling was actually going on, concerns about smuggling provided the pretext for tightening the screws on colonial trade. The British increasingly treated colonial merchants as smuggling suspects, harassing their business and subjecting them to more invasive scrutiny. With a mandate from London to clamp down on smuggling and increase revenue, some of the new inspectors deployed to the colonies treated this as license to loot, making busts on technicalities and enriching themselves with a portion of the proceeds from the seized goods. This upset the old unstated rules of the game in the American colonies and helped set the stage for open rebellion. British and colonial interests were now on a collision course. Until the 1760s, the collision was averted through lax enforcement. In other words, the colonists accepted British rule because it did not actually involve much enforcing of the rules. And as long as the colonies formally acquiesced to British authority, the imperial administrators showed little enthusiasm and stamina for vigorous enforcement.

What soured British attitudes toward smuggling? Debt and disgust provide much of the answer.[3] The long and costly war with the French left Britain saddled with a massive war debt—and stricter customs enforcement in the colonies, it was hoped, would help pay the mounting bills. The war, including large-scale trading with the enemy, also made London more outraged at colonial defiance and more painfully aware of the dismal state of customs administration. Getting serious about customs would therefore generate revenue and be a punitive lesson at the same time. It would also backfire.

In 1763, a few years after coming to the British throne, King George III turned to the former Whig George Grenville to replenish His Majesty's Treasury. Grenville stayed in office for only a few years, but during that time he helped launch an increasingly militarized anti-smuggling campaign in the American colonies that had profound and long-lasting repercussions. The first move was to clean up the customs service. This included ordering absentee customs officers in England back to their posts in the colonies[4] (or lose their jobs), deploying more inspectors (with higher salaries, with the expectation that this would make bribes less tempting), and pushing out customs agents viewed as too corrupt and cozy in their relations with the colonists. Importantly, the new officers would be selected from London rather than the colonies.

The second move was to give customs more power and authority. In particular, the expanded use of the controversial writs of assistance (unrestricted search warrants), first introduced in 1760, enabled more aggressive inspections and seizures. Moreover, smuggling cases could now be tried in admiralty courts without juries—designed to bypass local courts viewed as too sympathetic to colonial merchant interests.[5] Customs enforcement was also militarized through the deployment of naval cutters off the coast of the American colonies, tasked with patrolling bays and inlets used for clandestine landings. Prior to 1764, the Royal Navy had largely been on the sidelines in the battle against smuggling, but it would now be given a frontline role, with commissioned naval officers deputized as customs officials.

Trade laws were also revised. In 1764, the Sugar Act replaced the Molasses Act. In a September 1763 report, the Commissioners of Customs acknowledged that the provisions of the Molasses Act "have been for the most part, either wholly evaded, or Fraudulently compounded." They therefore recommended both lower duties to "diminish the Temptation to Smuggling," and more stringent enforcement—the combination of which, they argued, would enhance revenue collection.[6]

The colonies bitterly opposed these measures to clamp down on smuggling and improve revenue, which reversed a long history of neglect and non-enforcement. Even the Sugar Act, which lowered duties on molasses from six pence to three pence a gallon, was strenuously resisted, for it signaled an intention to actually start enforcing duties on the trade for the first time. And it imposed other duties, such as on Madeira wines, which had become a popular drink in the colonies. The act's provisions also included stricter compliance procedures, creating more cumbersome paperwork for merchants in securing manifests and listing cargo.

Of all the tools the British used to tighten the screws on illicit trade, none was more controversial and hated than the "writs of assistance." These open-ended warrants gave customs officials extraordinary leeway in conducting searches for smuggled goods. James Otis, a lawyer who seemed to specialize in representing disgruntled Boston merchants, gained instant fame with a fiery speech denouncing the writs of assistance as a violation of the rights of the colonists as British subjects. Otis lost the case but won the crowd. John Adams, who witnessed the speech, later described its impact: "Every man of an immense crowded audience appeared to go away as I did, ready to take arms against writs of assistance. Then and there was the first scene of the first act of opposition, to the arbitrary rule of Great Britain. Then and there the child Independence was born."[7] The loyalist Peter Oliver was certainly less impressed by Otis, commenting that "He [Otis] engrafted his self into the Body of Smugglers, & they embraced him so close, as a lawyer & an useful Pleader for them, that he soon became incorporated with them."[8]

One response by colonial smugglers to the British crackdown was simply adaptation, a shift in smuggling routes and methods to get around tighter enforcement. This helped keep smugglers in business. Still, stepped-up enforcement continued to put a squeeze on what was previously a minimally policed illicit trade. Smugglers were doing their best to cope, but business was not good. Smuggling had become a riskier and less predictable trade, and this translated into more costs. Some evasive moves prompted countermoves—for example, when smugglers shifted to transferring goods from large vessels to smaller boats offshore (which would then be unloaded in small coves away from major ports and harbors), the British responded with the "hovering vessel" legislation in 1764, which enabled the seizure and forfeiture of vessels loitering within two leagues of the coastline.

Part of the difficulty for colonial smugglers was that corruption—in the form of bribes, "fees," and other payoffs to customs officials—was no longer as dependable a tool to keep business running smoothly. Informal financial accommodation between merchants and customs agents had long served as pacifying glue. As Governor Francis Bernard in Massachusetts described the situation as the British were beginning to crack down on corruption in 1764, "[I]f conniving at foreign sugars and molasses and Portugal wines and fruits is to be reckoned corruption, there never was, I believe, an uncorrupt customs officer in America."[9] Old corrupt arrangements and relationships, however, were now coming unglued, making bribery less effective and reliable. Consequently, bullying increasingly replaced bribing. The old smuggling game had been win-win, based on personal profit for both law evaders and law enforcers. The new game, in contrast, was zero-sum, based on seizures rather than accommodation; it was purely predatory rather than mutually beneficial.

Colonial opposition to the crackdown on smuggling took many forms. It ranged from legal challenges, protest letters, and boycotts of British goods to mob riots, tarring and feathering of informants, and sacking of customs vessels. Forcible rescues of seized ships and goods by angry mobs became more frequent. A series of humiliating and embarrassing episodes made British authorities increasingly aware that their grip on the colonies was tenuous, at best. For instance, when the first naval cutter sent to patrol off the coast of Rhode Island attempted to stop a vessel on suspicion of smuggling, the British naval captain reported that a group of "riotous" inhabitants forced the gunners of the harbor fort to open fire on his naval vessel. A stunned Treasury ordered that the incident be thoroughly investigated, instructing that those engaged in "an Act so highly criminal as resisting all legal authority, and actually firing the Guns of his Majesty's Ports against ships of War" should be fully prosecuted. The order was simply ignored by the colonists and the investigation went nowhere.[10] This was not an isolated episode. In another Rhode Island incident in 1764, an impounded vessel was forcibly rescued by a mob of disguised colonists. And in April of the following year, a mob at Dighton in Massachusetts boarded a seized ship, the *Polly*, and ran off with all cargo and furnishings. To add insult to injury, the customs officer responsible for the *Polly* seizure was then arrested and jailed after the ship's captain filed charges against him for the loss.[11]

Seizures on land were equally contentious. In one well-known Boston incident in September 1766, Daniel Malcom, an outspoken critic of the trade laws, refused to allow customs agents to search a room in his house suspected of containing a stash of smuggled Madeira wines. When the customs officers returned with a writ of assistance, a crowd formed outside the house in support of Malcom. Intimidated and fearing escalation, the officers backed off. Locals cheered and celebrated Malcom's bold defiance.[12]

Customs officials made matters worse by taking advantage of their expanded seizure powers for personal gain. The situation was ready-made for abuse and manipulation. Little oversight and accountability and the potential for high rewards from seizures made for an explosive mix. Officers typically took a sizable cut of the prize money on every seizure made—making overzealous enforcement more tempting. Colonial merchants resented not only the squeeze on smuggling but also the exploits by unscrupulous customs agents that came with it. Such "customs racketeering" was, in the view of colonial merchants, essentially legalized piracy.[13]

The Royal Navy was especially heavy-handed in carrying out its new policing mandate. Military forces created for fighting wars can be a blunt instrument when deployed to fight smuggling. This was certainly evident in the American colonies, where in the aftermath of the Seven Years War the navy turned its attention to the war against illicit trade. Post-1763 legislation opened the door for greater naval involvement and made seizures on technical grounds easier. The militarization of customs enforcement was bitterly resented in the colonies. Benjamin Franklin described the navy's new anti-smuggling job in especially harsh terms with a heavy dose of sarcasm:

> Convert the brave, honest officers of your *navy* into pimping tide-waiters and colony officers of the *customs*. Let those who in the time of war fought gallantly in defense of their countrymen, in peace be taught to prey upon it. Let them learn to be corrupted by great and real smugglers; but (to show their diligence) scour with armed boats every bay, harbor, river, creek, cove, or nook throughout your colonies; stop and detain every coaster, every wood-boat, every fisherman; tumble their cargoes and even their ballast inside out and upside down; and, if a penn'orth of [dressmakers'] pins is found unentered [on the cargo manifest], let the whole be seized and confiscated. Thus shall the trade of your colonists suffer more from their friends in time of peace, than it did from their enemies in war. . . . O, *this will work admirably!*[14]

Deploying the Royal Navy to battle illicit trade not only antagonized merchants but also created feuds and rivalries between customs and naval officers competing over turf and claims to the proceeds of seized goods. Relations between the navy and the customs service were strained, at best. In one incident, a seizure off the coast of Massachusetts initiated by a naval captain was even re-seized and claimed by a customs officer.[15]

Seizures also depended on informers, who served as the "eyes and ears" for customs—and in turn were rewarded with a portion of the proceeds. It is little surprise, therefore, that they were greatly despised locally. A comment from the *Pennsylvania Journal* reflected the intensity of resentment: "The swarms of searchers, tide waiters, spies, and other underlings, with which every port in America now abounds, and which were unknown before the Board of Commissioners was established among us, are not it seems, quite sufficient to ruin our trade, but infamous informers, like dogs of prey thirsting after the fortunes of worthy and wealthy men, are let loose and encouraged to seize and libel."[16] In October 1773 the *Journal* even published a description of an informer who had been dispatched from Boston, and urged that "All lovers of Liberty will make diligent search and having found this bird of darkness will produce him tarred and feathered at the Coffee-House, there to expiate his sins against his country by a public recantation."[17]

Colonial leaders attempted in vain to persuade London that it was in its own self-interest to tolerate smuggling and return to the status quo ante. Such candid pleas were an open admission of colonial reliance on illicit trade. "Putting an end to the importation of foreign molasses," warned Rhode Island Governor Stephen Hopkins, "at the same time puts an end to all the costly distilleries in these colonies, and to the rum trade to the coast of Africa, and throws it into the hands of the French. With the loss of the foreign molasses trade, the cod fishery of the English in America must also be lost and thrown also into the hands of the French."[18] Without the revenue from the foreign molasses trade, Hopkins and other colonial leaders emphasized, the colonies would simply not be able to afford British goods. The Assembly of Rhode Island explained the situation in blunt terms. Rhode Island, they reported, purchased £120,000 sterling of British manufactures annually yet produced not much more than £5,000 sterling in exports. The profits from the molasses trade made up the difference, making it possible for the colony to keep importing British goods. In New York, a memorial to the British Parliament was equally blunt and offered even more startling figures: New York's imports exceeded exports by nearly £470,000 sterling—with the difference made up by the trade in French molasses.[19]

These arguments were repeated in private correspondence. For instance, William Cooper, secretary of the Boston town meeting, wrote to a fellow Bostonian in England in 1768: "You know what has been called an illicit trade has been wink'd at by all former Administrations, it being eventually more profitable to Britain than the Colonies. Our trade with the Spanish Main & Spanish & French W Indies, as also the Mediterranean, furnished us with large Remittances for the British Merchants." He went on to complain that, "[T]hese Channels are now dryed up . . . [and] for every penny drawn from us in the way of Revenue, Britain misses ten in the way of trade."[20]

London remained undeterred. To centralize and coordinate customs in the colonies, the British set up the American Board of Customs Commissioners, headquartered in Boston. This move—part of the Townsend Acts of 1767, which placed new duties and other restrictions on colonial trade—quickly backfired. With customs operations now centered around the activities of the American board, so too did colonial opposition.[21] In other words, the creation of the board and its ill-advised placement in Boston—the epicenter of hostility toward the Crown—unintentionally provided a highly visible, concentrated target for colonial outrage.[22] Long accustomed to viewing compliance with trade laws as optional, colonial merchants had an allergic reaction to the arrival of the American Board of Customs Commissioners. One particularly despised commissioner, Charles Paxton, was nearly tarred and feathered; he apparently eluded his pursuers only by disguising himself as a woman and escaping through side streets.[23] Indeed, "Within eight months' time they [the commissioners] had been forced by mob action to flee the city and take refuge in a harbor fort, protected by the guns of an English man-of-war."[24] Appalled by the level of local opposition they found upon their arrival in the colonies in November 1767, members of the board early on concluded that "[W]e . . . expect that we shall find it totally impracticable to enforce the Execution of the Revenue Laws until the Hand of Government is properly strengthened."[25]

Boston merchants became increasingly outspoken in their defiance. John Hancock, one of Boston's wealthiest shippers, even publicly declared that he would not permit customs officers to inspect his vessels. On April 7, 1768, when customs inspectors boarded one of his ships, the *Lydia*, Hancock ordered his captain not to allow them to search the cargo below deck. Shortly after this incident, another of Hancock's vessels, the *Liberty*, arrived in Boston Harbor loaded with Madeira wine. The ship's captain submitted paperwork to the customs house indicating twenty-five pipes of wine, but the commissioners suspected a much larger cargo. They were also, no doubt, fed up with Hancock's bravado and eager to find cause to single him out. The evidence against Hancock was weak, based largely on a questionable account provided by an informer, but the commissioners still pushed to seize the ship. During the seizure, customs officers discovered that the *Liberty* had taken on new cargo without first receiving clearance at the customs house. This was standard practice, but it technically violated the letter of the law. The *Liberty* was condemned on a technicality.[26]

The seizure of the *Liberty* on June 10 sparked a firestorm. An angry crowd hurled insults, stones, and threats at the customs officers charged with seizing the ship. Fearful that the colonists might attempt a forcible rescue, the officers anchored the *Liberty* next to a British naval vessel. The swelling crowd then turned its anger on the commissioners, forcing them to flee to the same naval ship guarding the *Liberty*. Wary of returning to Boston, they then took refuge in the fort in Boston Harbor.

The trial of Hancock and his alleged collaborators began in October 1768 and continued until the following March. The British authorities had hoped the high-profile trial would set an example and help restore their much-tarnished authority. But their legal case proved to be thin—so much so that in the end it was simply dropped. Hancock was hailed as a hero throughout the colonies. For the British, the affair was a total fiasco.[27]

In this tense atmosphere, the commissioners reported to London that they were fearful of leaving the safety of the harbor fort and returning to Boston without greater protection. The English ministry responded by dispatching troops—a provocative show of force meant to awe the colonists into submission, but one that would instead lead to bloodshed and further escalation. The British regiments arrived in September 1768; their intensely resented presence would culminate in the Boston Massacre a year and a half later. Thus, as one historian has described it, "Indirectly Hancock and his ship, the *Liberty*, had commenced a series of events leading to open revolution."[28]

In one respect, historian Clyde Barrow points out, the American Board of Customs Commissioners had been a modest success: the customs service in the colonies actually showed a profit for the first time between 1767 and 1774. The revenue generated was still much less than had been hoped, and operating costs had also risen due to greater enforcement, but it was a major turnaround.[29] This improved revenue collection, however, came at a high political cost. Through its stepped-up enforcement and implementation of the Townsend duties, the customs service became the main target of colonial anger toward the crown, increasingly in the form of mob violence.

In Salem, Massachusetts, for example, customs officer James Rowe persisted in making a seizure rather than accept a bribe in 1769, and in response he was tarred and feathered, wheeled around the town in a cart, and forced to wear signs labeling him an informer.[30] The situation was equally volatile elsewhere. That same year, Providence customs officer James Saiville "was seized while on duty." He was "gagged; had his clothes cut from his body; was covered in turpentine and feathers from head to foot; was beaten; had dirt thrown on him; was carried about in a wheelbarrow."[31] Further south, in November 1770, not only was a vessel seized by John Hatton, the customs collector at Salem and Cohensy in New Jersey, forcibly rescued, but Hatton was arrested and jailed for wounding one of the crewmen on the seized boat. Not giving up, Hatton then dispatched his son to try to recover the rescued vessel headed for Philadelphia. When the young Hatton discovered the vessel in the city's harbor, the crew organized an attack in which Hatton was beaten, dragged, and tarred and feathered, and had hot tar poured into his wounds. Hatton barely survived. Without any witnesses willing to testify, the investigation into the matter was quickly dropped.[32] The head of customs in Philadelphia commented on the incident: "In short, the truth of the matter is, the hands of Government are not strong enough to oppose the numerous body of people who wish well to the cause of smuggling . . . What can a Governor do, without the assistance of the Governed? What can the Magistrates do, unless they are supported by their fellow Citizens? What can the King's officers do, if they make themselves obnoxious to the people amongst whom they reside?"[33]

One of the most brazen attacks on customs occurred a few years later in Rhode Island. On June 9, 1772, the Royal cutter *Gaspee* was stormed and burned late at night in Narragansett Bay. Earlier that day, the *Gaspee* had run aground while chasing a suspected smuggling vessel. Realizing it was stranded and vulnerable, local merchants, led by John Brown, quickly formed a raiding party that snuck up on the ship under cover of darkness and overwhelmed its crew. Long known as a particularly troublesome colony and a haven for illicit trade, Rhode Island more than lived up to its reputation on this particular night. After the *Gaspee* was ransacked and set ablaze, Governor Thomas Hutchinson warned London that if England "shows no resentment against that Colony for so high an affront . . . they may venture upon any further Measures which are necessary to obtain and secure their independence." He concluded that if the perpetrators were not found and punished "the friends to Government will despond and give up all hopes of being able to withstand the Faction."[34] The ministry of Lord North appointed a

Figure 2.1 John Brown (1736–1803), prominent Rhode Island merchant, privateer, slave trader, and politician. Brown led the attack on the British customs schooner *Gaspee* in 1772 and later was the first American tried and indicted for violating the federal government's 1794 Slave Trade Act. He was also one of the founders of the university that bears his name. Painting by Edward Malbone 1794 (New York Historical Society).

commission to investigate the incident, but the inquiry generated little local cooperation and was eventually dropped. To deflect attention and criticism in the aftermath of the attack on the *Gaspee*, Providence leaders went into damage control mode: they conveniently blamed fringe elements of society and promised to look into the incident, while well aware that the ringleaders included some of the town's most prominent merchant elites.[35]

As provocative as the *Gaspee* affair was, London showed some restraint in its response. The same was not true, however, in what became known as the "Boston Tea Party," which served as not only a lightning rod for colonial opposition but also a trigger for British overreaction. On the

Figure 2.2 Burning of the British customs schooner *Gaspee* in Narragansett Bay, 1772. Painting by C. Brownell (Granger Collection).

evening of December 16, 1773, a group of irate Boston colonists, some thinly disguised as Mohawk Indians, boarded three ships of the British East India Company and for the next three hours proceeded to dump 342 chests of tea into Boston Harbor—cheered on by the crowds watching from the dock. The incident had a polarizing effect. Samuel Adams and other colonial opposition leaders celebrated and defended the "party" as a principled protest. Startled and appalled when news of the incident reached London, British politicians pushed to take a hard line. London retaliated by closing the port of Boston and introducing a series of punitive measures known as the Coercive Acts. This proved to be a tipping point: both the Boston Tea Party and the punishing British response served as a catalyst for mobilizing opposition throughout the colonies.

What provoked this incident that proved to be such an historic turning point? The Boston Tea Party is remembered in the popular imagination as a protest against taxes. But it actually had more to do with smuggling interests than tax burdens. Relatively low-priced tea supplied to the colonies by the British East India Company—which had been given a monopoly on tea imports—undercut the sale of smuggled Dutch tea, which at that point dominated the local market in violation of the Townsend duty on tea. "The Smugglers not only buy cheaper in Holland but save the 3d duty," complained Governor Thomas

Original in the John Carter Brown Library at Brown University

Figure 2.3 “The Bostonians Paying the Excise-Man or Tarring & Feathering,” London, 1774 (John Carter Brown Library, Brown University).

Hutchinson.[36] He speculated that three-quarters of the “prodigious consumption in America” was illicitly imported, and in another letter wrote, “We have been so long habituated to illicit Trade that people in general see no evil in it.”[37] In the summer of 1771 Hutchinson guessed that more than 80 percent of the tea consumed in Boston was smuggled in.[38] No doubt many colonists found the granting of monopoly trade rights to the British East India Company irksome. But most threatened were the economic interests of those colonial merchants who had invested heavily in the illicit Dutch tea trade and enjoyed wide profit margins. As one economic historian puts it, "The 'Party' was organized not by irate consumers but by Boston's wealthy smugglers, who stood to lose out."[39]

As conditions continued to deteriorate in 1774, the focus of British customs activity in the colonies shifted from collecting revenue to interdicting war supplies, particularly Dutch gunpowder. A Royal proclamation in October 1774 banned the sale of arms and ammunition. Some customs collectors reported that colonists were already stocking up on gunpowder and other war supplies, with the Dutch island of St. Eustatius suspected as the conduit.[40] In this sense, the War of Independence actually began in the form of smuggling long before the first shots were fired at Lexington and Concord in April 1775. Indeed, for months up to that point the only instructions London sent to an anxious General Thomas Gage and his troops holed up in Boston were to interdict smuggled arms from Europe.[41] Gage warned London that many colonists were "sending to Europe for all kinds of Military Stores." Moreover, some British traders were ignoring the prohibitions and clandestinely shipping munitions to the Americans.[42] In November 1775, Parliament extended the embargo to all trade with the colonies by passing the American Prohibitory Act. All American commerce would now be considered a violation of the British naval blockade and subject to seizure. As a powerful symbol of having reached a point of no return, in 1776 a mob of New Yorkers tore down the equestrian statue of King George III at Bowling Green, melting it down to make more than forty-two thousand bullets. Tory loyalists rescued fragments of the statue and somehow managed to smuggle the head back to England.[43]

THERE WERE MANY COLONIAL grievances leading to armed rebellion against British rule, but grievances related to customs enforcement and the crackdown on smuggling were certainly high on the list. The passage in the 1776 Declaration of Independence denouncing the king for having "erected a multitude of New Offices, and sent hither swarms of Officers to harass our people, and eat out their substance" clearly refers to the activities of customs officials. Another passage denounces King George III "For cutting off our Trade with all parts of the world." How appropriate, then, that John Hancock, the wealthy Boston merchant-smuggler who so brazenly challenged British customs authority, was the first to sign the declaration.[44]

"A smuggler and a Whig [an opponent of England]" are first cousins, wrote Loyalist Daniel Leonard under the pseudonym "Massachussettensis" in early January 1775, "the offspring of two sisters, avarice and ambition. . . . The smuggler received protection from the whig, and he in his turn received support from the smuggler."[45] On the eve of the Revolution, an American merchant in London commented that the British colonies in North America had finally been unified "from no object of a more respectable cast than that of a successful practice in illicit trade, I say contrived, prompted and promoted by a confederacy of smugglers in Boston, Rhode Island, and other seaport towns on that coast."[46] Britain's newfound enthusiasm for rigorously enforcing its trade laws, which had also brought with it widespread abuses, politicized colonial smuggling, so much so that it became a patriotic cause. To be sure, smuggling was about trade and economic interests, but the British crackdown transformed it into something much bigger. It came to symbolize political defiance of overbearing and abusive imperial authority, and as such it served as a unifying and mobilizing force. Economic interests and political ideology converged.

3

The Smuggling War of Independence

A RAGTAG FORCE OF colonial rebels went to war against the world's greatest military power. As the American General William Moultrie wrote in his memoirs of the Revolution, the colonists rebelled "without money; without arms; without ammunition; no generals; no armies; no admirals; and no fleets; this was our situation when the contest began."[1] No wonder, then, the British had such smug confidence that their overwhelming military superiority would quickly and easily put down the American rebellion. Indeed, at first glance the insurgency should have been short-lived.

It did not turn out that way. Why not? Smuggling is a crucial part of the answer. In other words, illicit trade not only contributed to the outbreak of the American Revolution; it also played a decisive role in the conduct and outcome. While at times subverting the Revolution by prioritizing profits over patriotism, illicit traders defying Britain's wartime embargo ultimately proved to be essential to its success. Colonial smugglers put their clandestine transportation methods, skills, and networks to good use supplying the insurgency. Part of this simply involved building on previously well-established illicit trading relationships, such as in the West Indies. But it also involved fostering new commercial connections directly with Northern Europe, such as France and Sweden—no easy task in wartime.[2]

From the very start, the Continental Army was in desperate need of clothes, arms, ammunition, food, and other supplies; with the single exception of food, all required large-scale imports from abroad in violation of the British blockade. This was especially important in the years before France formally entered the war in 1778 (followed by Spain in 1779, and Holland in 1781), tipping the military balance. Most crucial was gunpowder: "the want of powder was a very serious consideration for us," recounted General Moultrie, "we knew there was none to be had upon the continent of America."[3] Indeed, there were no powder mills operating in the colonies when the war started.[4] Virtually all of the gunpowder used by the colonists in the first two and a half years of the war had to be smuggled in, mostly via the West Indies.[5] Most of these military supplies were exchanged for colonial products, including cod, lumber, flour, tobacco, and indigo. Victory on the battlefield hinged on success in the world of smuggling. More than one hundred ships reportedly smuggled in supplies during this time period, evading the British warships attempting to blockade the Atlantic coast.[6]

Smuggled gunpowder trickled in ever so slowly. The situation was especially bleak by the end of 1775. On Christmas Day, George Washington wrote: "Our want of powder is inconceivable. A daily waste and no supply administers a gloomy prospect."[7] Some have argued that if in mid-January 1776 the British had known about the extreme scarcity of gunpowder, they "could have marched out to Cambridge and crushed the newly recruited colonial army" and "thus the revolution would have ended."[8] The British withdrew from Boston in March 1776, unaware of the anemic condition of the colonial forces. At one point, a thirteen-mile-long chain of colonial sentries around Boston did not have even an ounce of gunpowder.[9] There was also a shortage of arms, including muskets, cannon, pistols, and bayonets. But unlike gunpowder, which had to be perpetually replenished, the arms supply was cumulative, and so dependence on smuggling channels declined over time. The same was not true of other military-related supplies, however, such as tent materials, clothing, shoes, and blankets, which wore out more quickly, creating chronic shortages throughout the war.[10]

Patriots and Profiteers

Wartime smuggling blurred the line between patriot and profiteer. Smuggling was both essential to the revolutionary war effort and profitable for the well-placed and well-connected. Some illicit traders sold smuggled gunpowder and other supplies to the Continental Army at highly inflated prices. The Brown brothers in Providence, for instance, were especially well positioned to profit from the war. Their wartime business ventures included organizing "powder voyages" to France, Holland, and Spain.[11] One account of the Brown family history describes the Revolution as a "personal bonanza" for John Brown, who allegedly emerged from the war as the richest man in Rhode Island.[12] In one deal, he offered a shipment of smuggled pistol powder to colonial forces at a substantial markup. Desperate for the supplies, Stephen Moylan replied on behalf of George Washington: "The General will take it, though it is a most exorbitant price."[13]

General Washington denounced such war profiteering, at one point declaring, "There is such a thirst for gain, and such infamous advantages taken to forestall, and engross those Articles which the Army cannot do without, thereby enhancing the cost of them to the public fifty or a hundred pr. Ct., that it is enough to make one curse their own Species, for possessing so little virtue and patriotism."[14] He urged that merchants should "not take an undue advantage of the Distresses of their Country, so as to exact an unreasonable Price."[15] Nevertheless, with the colonies sometimes competing with each other for scarce provisions, smugglers could not resist inflating prices and selling to the highest bidder.[16] For instance, Elias Hasket Derby of Salem acknowledged in 1776 that 100 percent profits could be made on imported items such as gunpowder, cotton, cocoa, and sugar, and that 150 percent above normal prices was "more than common" on linens and paper.[17]

For all the patriotic fervor of the American Revolution, more base economic opportunism was also at work in keeping both civilians and rebel soldiers supplied. And even though they were supplying the Continental Army, smugglers also used this as a cover and opportunity to bring in high-value civilian goods: private trade piggybacked on supply ships restricted by contract only for military purposes.[18] This was a form of "smuggling within smuggling," often involving clandestine importation of consumer luxury goods that served no military purpose but were in high demand.

Military dependence on smuggling necessitated dispatching brokers abroad to arrange secret shipments. Maryland, Georgia, and Pennsylvania all sent commercial agents to the West Indies to arrange for the transshipment of European supplies.[19] Congress also deployed its own agents. For instance, Oliver Pollock, a New Orleans—based merchant, smuggled in Spanish supplies to western outposts and the southern backcountry via Louisiana and the Mississippi River. Congress also sent William Hodge to Europe to covertly acquire munitions from various firms.[20] By the end of 1776, Congress had created a web of American commercial agents linking Dutch and French ports to the colonies via the West Indies.

In the spring of 1775, Benjamin Franklin quietly began negotiating with merchants in England, France, and Holland to secure shipments of munitions.[21] Foreign merchants were more-than-willing business accomplices so long as the British blockade remained sufficiently porous.[22] As historian Neil York writes, "merchants in France, the Dutch Republic, Spain, Sweden, and the West Indies viewed the revolution as an opportunity for expanding their commerce and profits. Though the governments of these countries and their dependencies avoided direct complicity, they seldom interfered with entrepreneurs involved in contraband trade. Some merchants were permitted to remove 'outmoded' arms from royal arsenals for a nominal sum even though their destination was obvious. Dutch arms makers were operating their mills at full capacity by mid-1776."[23] Some especially energetic European merchants traveled to the colonies to make deals in person for smuggled military supplies. In one early case, the directors of a leading Nantes shipping company traveled to visit General Washington at his Cambridge headquarters in late 1775, and by the following November they were covertly supplying thousands of dollars' worth of war supplies.[24]

The most successful American commercial agent was Silas Deane from Connecticut, dispatched by the Continental Congress to Paris in July 1776 to covertly procure arms and other war supplies.[25] Posing as a Bermuda merchant, he collaborated with Pierre-Augustin Caron de Beaumarchais, the head of a bogus mercantile firm—Roderigue Hortalez and Company—set up to obscure French government complicity. France was willing to help the American cause, but this had to be handled clandestinely and at arm's length until the French formally entered the war. Supplying the American colonies was considered contraband and a violation of neutrality under international maritime law.[26]

Eight supply ships secured through Deane's clandestine dealings with Beaumarchais brought some two thousand tons of desperately needed supplies for the Continental Army in 1777.[27] The ships

> carried eight thousand seven hundred and fifty pairs of shoes, three thousand six hundred blankets, more than four thousand dozen pairs of stockings, one hundred and sixty-four brass cannon, one hundred and fifty-three carriages, more than forty-one thousand balls, thirty-seven thousand fusils, three hundred and seventy-three thousand flints, fifteen thousand gun worms, five hundred and fourteen thousand musket balls, nearly twenty thousand pounds of lead, nearly one hundred and sixty-one thousand pounds of powder, twenty-one mortars, more than three thousand bombs, more than eleven thousand grenades, three hundred and forty-five grapeshot, eighteen thousand spades, shovels, and axes, over four thousand tents, and fifty-one thousand pounds of sulphur.[28]

The vessels *Amphitrite* and *Mercure*, which carried "more than eighteen thousand stands of arms complete, and fifty-two pieces of brass cannon, with powder and tents and clothing, reached Portsmouth, New Hampshire, in the spring in season for the campaign of 1777."[29]

According to one Deane biographer, "It is impossible to exaggerate the importance of those supplies in the battles which culminated in the fall of British General Burgoyne, who was sweeping down powerfully from Canada to New York with the purpose of separating the northern from the southern colonies."[30] These clandestine shipments are widely credited as decisive in the defeat of the British at Saratoga in October 1777, a key turning point in the Revolution leading to France's formal entry into the war.[31] As the historian C. H. Van Tyne puts it, although the battle of Saratoga was "won by American soldiers," it was also "won with ammunition and guns of which ninety per cent were obtained through French channels."[32] Just a few months earlier, in July

1777, General Philip Schuyler wrote to Washington from Saratoga that his "prospect of preventing them [the British] from penetrating is not much. They have an army flushed with victory, plentifully provided with provisions, cannon, and every warlike store. Our army . . . is weak in numbers, dispirited, naked, in a manner, destitute of provisions, without camp equipage, with little ammunition, and not a single piece of cannon."[33] All of this would change with the influx of smuggled military supplies, much of it procured by Deane.[34]

Only one of the smuggling ships launched by Deane and Beaumarchais, the *Seine*, was captured en route after unloading part of its cargo at Martinique. The ship had false papers directing it to the French island of Miquelon, but the British seized it after finding hidden papers—which the pilot and captain failed to destroy in time—indicating the real destination. Yet even this loss had a silver lining for the revolutionary cause: implicating the French in violations of neutrality was damaging to Anglo-French relations, which American leaders hoped would accelerate France's entry into the war.[35]

Even though Deane was good at making covert deals for war supplies, he was notoriously bad at keeping track of his receipts and expenses, leading to accusations of financial fraud, abuse, and personal enrichment. Apparently, both Deane and Beaumarchais used the cover of purchasing supplies as an opportunity to also line their own pockets.[36] Recalled from Paris, Deane ended his career as an arms broker in a cloud of controversy; he was later branded a traitor for advocating reconciliation with Britain and rejoining the empire.

Wartime profiteering was even more starkly at play in the realm of privateering, which itself was intimately intertwined with smuggling. The shifting geography of war shaped the business of war. Britain's initial occupation of Boston gave a competitive advantage to Providence-based privateering and smuggling. And Providence shipping, in turn, was negatively affected by the British occupation of Newport in December 1776. Business subsequently boomed in Boston once the British withdrew and the city recovered from occupation, and it was especially advantaged by the British occupation of New York. At least 365 ships of Boston were commissioned as privateers during the Revolution.[37] The privateer investor John R. Livingston was so impressed by Boston's bustling wartime harbor that he worried that peace, "if it takes place without proper warning, may ruin us."[38] James Warren lamented the privateering-induced changes in Boston: "Fellows who would have cleaned my shoes five years ago have amassed fortunes and are riding in chariots."[39] Privateering helped to create "the Revolution's nouveau riche. . . . Their future heirs would exemplify American old money at its most genteel."[40] For instance, the sailor Joseph Peabody rose from deckhand to investor through nine successful voyages between 1777 and 1783. He became Salem's leading shipping magnate, with more than eighty vessels and eight thousand employees. Similarly, Israel Thorndike, who started out as a humble cooper's apprentice, became a skipper on a privateer ship; he would later become one of New England's wealthiest bankers and textile manufacturers.[41] Privateering also enriched the Cabots of Beverly: the firm owned by John and Andrew Cabot became one of the most lucrative in Massachusetts.[42]

As in the earlier Seven Years War, colonial merchants signed up to take advantage of privateering—except now they were commissioned to subvert rather than serve the British Empire. From the British perspective, they were therefore criminals and pirates (and defined as such in the Pirate Act of 1777); but they also became George Washington's de facto private navy. The war at sea was at least as important as the war on land, yet for the colonies it was fought almost entirely by what was essentially a profit-driven mercenary force. Though there were only a handful of Continental Navy ships, several thousand privateering ships set sail during the course of the American Revolution.[43] They rarely could take on the Royal Navy, but they wreaked havoc on supply lines by targeting British merchant vessels.

At the same time, there was a serious downside to relying on a loot-seeking private naval force. For example, the few Continental Navy vessels that existed had great difficulty attracting able seamen, given the higher rewards from signing on with privateering vessels.[44] Many navy servicemen deserted to work on privateering ships, wooed by the prospect of loot.[45] The financial allure of privateering was captured in new sea chanties: "Come all you young fellows with Courage so Bold / Come Enter on Bord and we will cloth you with gold. . . ."[46] Following orders was also a challenge for some privateers. They did not always distinguish between friendly and enemy ships in their attacks.[47] And prisoners captured were supposed to be used for prisoner exchanges, but at times they were instead ransomed at sea. Benjamin Franklin dispatched the privateering vessels *Black Prince*, *Black Princess*, and *Fear Not* from France with the explicit mission of capturing men to use for prisoner exchanges. Franklin was outraged when he discovered that the captains of these vessels, who had been recruited from the ranks of Irish smugglers, were instead trading captured prisoners for ransom money.[48]

Privateering was also a high-stakes investment opportunity for colonial elites. Among them was Nathanael Greene from Rhode Island, who discreetly invested in privateering ventures on the side while serving as quartermaster general in the Continental Army. Hinting at some ethical unease and reputational concerns about his privateering investment ventures, Greene's private correspondence expressed the desire that his efforts to cash in on the Revolution remain a secret. He wrote to an associate in 1779: "By keeping the affair secret I am confident we shall have it more in our power to serve the commercial connection than by publishing it."[49] Greene even proposed using a fictitious name, suggesting that "This will draw another shade of obscurity over the business and render it impossible to find out the connection."[50] Suspecting that Greene was also involved in diverting public funds for his own private business ventures, the Continental Congress attempted to investigate—only to be blocked by General Washington on the grounds that it would undermine military morale.[51] Meanwhile, without acknowledging the slightest hypocrisy, Greene denounced John Brown of Providence, charging him and others of enriching themselves while army officers sacrificed for the revolutionary cause.[52]

Similarly, the wealthy Philadelphia businessman Robert Morris wrote to his partner William Bingham in Martinique in December 1776: "I propose this privateer to be one third on your account, one third on account of Mr. Prejent and one third on my account. I have not imparted my concern in this plan to any person and therefore request you will never mention the matter." Just a few months earlier he had written to Silas Deane: "Those who have engaged in Privateering are making large Fortunes in a most Rapid manner. I have not meddled in this business which I confess does not Square with my Principles."[53]

By the spring of 1777, Morris had become so enthused about privateering that he not only urged Bingham "to increase the number of my engagements in that way . . ." but also wrote, "it matters not who knows my concern."[54]

More than any other individual, Morris was in charge of the business side of the war. He headed the Secret Committee of Trade, created by Congress in September 1775 to covertly procure supplies from abroad.[55] Morris used his business contacts in Europe to help supply the Continental Army and later became known as the "financier of the American Revolution."[56] Much of the activities of the Secret Committee of Trade went through his own company, Willing and Morris. His business attitude toward the Revolution is summed up in a message to Deane: "It seems to me the oppert'y of improving our Fortunes ought

Figure 3.1 Robert Morris (1734–1806), politician, signer of the Declaration of Independence, and "Financier of the American Revolution." Morris organized the clandestine effort to supply American rebels through smuggling networks to the Caribbean and Europe (Corbis).

not to be lost, especially as the very means of doing it will contribute to the Service of our Country at the same time."[57] For Morris, being a patriot and a profiteer was the same thing.

Privateering was not simply predatory; it contributed to the exchange of scarce goods in wartime, diverted British supplies to supply colonial forces, and intersected with smuggling in multiple ways. Benjamin Franklin encouraged privateers to sell their captured prizes in French ports—a form of illicit trade that violated French neutrality and outraged the British.[58] Complaints from London were met by French promises to crack down, but the captured goods continued to be smuggled in. The smuggling methods included use of false papers to disguise the origins of the goods, off-loading cargoes onto French ships at sea, and selling captured prizes just beyond the harbor, thus technically outside French waters.[59] Franklin penned formal apologies to the French for the infractions, helping them publicly save face with the British and keep up appearances even as they continued to tolerate and outright encourage the clandestine trade. Franklin wrote to Congress in September 1777: "England is extremely exasperated at the favor our armed vessels have met with here. To us, the French court wishes success to our cause, winks at the supplies we obtain here, privately affords us very essential aid, and goes on preparing for war."[60] Indeed, at one point French officials informed port authorities at Le Havre and Nantes that they should cease their embarrassing inquiries about suspicious goods headed for the West Indies.[61]

The sale of British prizes sometimes took peculiar forms. For instance, British merchants from Antigua, Bermuda, and Grenada reportedly made regular trips to Martinique to buy back goods that had been seized by American privateers. One British captain allegedly even repurchased his captured slave ship through agreement with William Bingham, who had been sent to the island to oversee the procurement of military wares.[62] Bingham mastered what he termed "the art of uniting war and commerce," and Martinique provided the perfect locale.[63] The island turned into a bustling wartime commercial center, including trade in captured goods and a transshipment point for French war supplies destined for the American colonies. Once France officially entered the war, however, the boom times were over. Martinique lost the neutrality that had provided such a convenient cover for wartime commerce.

Bingham, meanwhile, returned from Martinique a rich man: "The sum total of Bingham's public and private ventures in Martinique provided the capital for his later career."[64]

As business on Martinique went bust with the end of French neutrality, it boomed on the still officially neutral Dutch island of St. Eustatius (otherwise known as "Statia" by merchants and seamen), becoming the shopping center for the American Revolution and the wealthiest port in the Caribbean.[65] The island also served as a market outlet for smuggled American exports, such as timber, tobacco, horses, and indigo. Dubbed the "Golden Rock" for its profitable trading opportunities, St. Eustatius had all the ingredients to make it an ideal transshipment point: the cover of Dutch neutrality, the status of a free port with no customs duties, a convenient location amid many foreign territories (English, French, Spanish, and Danish), and a harbor able to accommodate some two hundred ships at a time. The island's population boomed along with its economy, increasing from just a few thousand residents before the outbreak of the American Revolution to eight thousand by 1780.[66]

British warships patrolling the international waters around the tiny island played a high-stakes cat-and-mouse game with the vessels coming and going from the American colonies. In an effort to pacify outraged British officials, in early 1775 the Netherlands imposed an embargo that formally prohibited supplying munitions and other war materials to the American colonies. The local authorities, however, ignored the order and continued to turn a blind eye.[67] The American agent on the island, Abraham Van Bibber of Maryland, reported that "the Governour is daily expressing the greatest desire and Intention to protect the trade with us here. Indeed they begin to discover their Mistake and are now very jealous of the French's running away with all their trade."[68] The motive was commercial interest more than political sympathy; the island's livelihood was dependent on the mushrooming contraband trade. As Van Bibber also reported, "The Dutch understand quite well that enforcement of the laws, that is, the embargo, would mean the ruin of their trade."[69] The English captain of the *Seaford*, anchored at the nearby British island of St. Kitts, complained that the port of St. Eustatius was "opened without reserve to all American vessels."[70] Dutch merchants could sell gunpowder to the Americans in

Figure 3.2 The Continental warship *Andrew Doria* receiving a cannon salute from the Dutch fort at St. Eustatius, West Indies, November 16, 1776. This was the first official salute to the American flag in a foreign port. Formally neutral St. Eustatius owed much of its existence to smuggling arms and other supplies for the American revolutionary war effort. Painting by Phillips Melville (U.S. Navy Art Collection).

St. Eustatius at up to six times the going rate in Holland. To disguise their destination, Dutch ships would at times set sail for Africa as the official destination but end up at St. Eustatius. Gunpowder was also disguised as nonmilitary supplies, hidden in containers such as tea chests and rice barrels.[71]

The Golden Rock also brought together the twin businesses of smuggling and privateering, affording a convenient place for American privateers to dispose of captured British goods. Perhaps appropriately, St. Eustatius was famously the first foreign port to salute the American flag, greatly offending the British and provoking loud official protests.[72] No wonder, then, that when Holland entered the war in 1781 one of the first British moves was to sack the island, where they found more than two thousand American merchants and seamen.[73] St. Eustatius had been operating as virtually a fourteenth colony, devoted largely to smuggling and other related illicit commercial activities.

Trading with the Enemy

Wartime illicit trade also included trade between the rebel colonies and British possessions that was prohibited by both sides. Rather than trade between England and the colonies simply ceasing with the outbreak of war, direct trade was replaced by more indirect forms of illicit trade. American tobacco was shipped to England via St. Eustatius and St. Thomas, and British manufactures were smuggled into the colonies via Nova Scotia.[74] Make-believe "captures" also constituted a mechanism to access markets in enemy territory. At one point, American agents in Holland allegedly even purchased British-manufactured clothing for the Continental Army.[75]

Yet economic incentives and the profit motive did not always coincide with serving the revolutionary cause. For example, private contractors in Pennsylvania opted to sell flour to the New England colonies at higher prices rather than supply Washington's troops nearby, who were desperately short on rations. Even more worrisome was that colonists were trading directly with the enemy. For instance, some farmers near Philadelphia chose to supply the British in exchange for hard cash rather than accept Washington's promises of future payment.[76] Even lumber—which is particularly bulky and thus difficult to hide and transport—was quietly sold to the British. In 1780 the Philadelphia authorities arrested a number of lumber smugglers and charged them with trading with the enemy.[77]

The British occupation of New York in 1776 stimulated an extensive illicit trade with neighboring areas. New Jersey smugglers brought foodstuffs to British headquarters in New York City and returned with luxury items such as silks and satins.[78] According to Governor Livingston, this illicit trade was so extensive in 1777 that shops were even set up to sell British goods.[79] Connecticut farmers similarly supplied British forces in the city, reducing their dependence on European provisions. Some of this illicit trade was more about basic survival than profits, carried out by desperate refugees who had escaped to Connecticut in the aftermath of the British occupation of New York. Connecticut produce was clandestinely exchanged for much-coveted British dry goods and West Indian produce. In the summer of 1782, John Chester of Wethersfield wrote of the "cursed illicit trade" that "our own people begin to get into" and "some few of us" began to justify openly.[80] The Connecticut government became increasingly alarmed about this illicit trade but was unable to do much about it, given its tenuous hold over southern Connecticut and the large British military presence in New York.[81] The frontier zone between Connecticut and New York was a fertile environment for trading with the enemy. Such illicit commerce also made this frontier zone less violent than one might otherwise have expected. The profits from continuous trading would sometimes trump raiding, and indeed some of those commissioned to carry out raiding missions instead used it as an opportunity for trading.[82] Similarly, a number of ship captains commissioned to police such illicit trading instead facilitated it.[83]

Clandestine trading was also used as a cover for intelligence gathering by both sides.[84] But Washington was skeptical of its value: "Those people who undertake to procure intelligence under cover of carrying produce into New York," he complained, ". . . attend more to their own emoluments than to the business they have charged, and we have found their information so vague and trifling, that there is no placing dependence upon it. Besides, it opens a door to a very extensive and pernicious traffic."[85]

Part of the difficulty in stopping wartime trading with the enemy was the long-established colonial preference for British goods. At first, the patriotic fervor of the Revolution helped keep this in check. But over time, old habits and commercial preferences returned. The Virginian Carter Braxton described the situation in 1779: "They [English manufactures] are so much preferred that America now winks at every importation of their goods."[86] George Washington remarked in 1781: "Men of all descriptions are now indiscriminately engaging in it, Whig, Tory, Speculator. By its being practiced by those of the latter class, in a manner with impunity, Men who, two or three years ago, would have shuddered at the idea of such connexions now pursue it with avidity and reconcile it to themselves (in which their profits plead powerfully) upon a principle of equality with the Tory."[87]

Take, for instance, the case of the Rhode Island merchant Nicholas Brown. At first he proclaimed that purchasing British goods was unpatriotic but later backtracked to such an extent that he indicated a preference for only British goods—even if this required engaging in commerce he described as "the Clandestine Way."[88] Or consider a letter with smuggling tips sent to Jonathan Amory of Boston in June 1782: British goods "are prohibited by Congress, yet I think they might be so managed that by Invoice and mixed with Holland goods, that there would be but little difficulty. And English goods sell best."[89] Aware of the strong American preference for British goods, another Boston merchant wrote abroad that same year that French textiles could be "pack'd & marked the same as tho' manufactur'd in England to as great deception as the English formerly imitated the French for the Quebec market."[90]

The one realm of trading with the enemy that was temporarily tolerated and even encouraged by revolutionary leaders was the salt trade. Demand far outstripped supply early on in the war, so much so that it sparked riots, ration cards were used in some places, and salt even served as a form of currency. Salt had vital military as well as civilian use, since it was used for preserving meat. To cope with the severe shortages, the Virginia government authorized ships to purchase salt supplies at British-controlled Bermuda (and Bermuda, in turn, was in great need of the food supplies exchanged for salt). Scarcity created conditions for exceptionally high profits. Nicholas Brown in Providence, for instance, quietly tripled his salt investment in 1777. The historian Stuart Brandes suggests that had this "become public knowledge, he certainly would have been denounced as undevoted." Charges of price gouging were widespread. In 1781 the Continental Congress outlawed the wartime Bermuda salt trade.[91]

THE BRITISH BATTLE AGAINST the rebellion in the American colonies was also a battle against smuggling: they attempted to shut off smuggling pipelines to colonial forces by occupying major ports of New York in 1776 and Philadelphia in 1777. Cornwallis also apparently concluded that the Southern colonies could only be defeated by impeding the Chesapeake Bay smuggling of tobacco, cotton, and other exports to acquire arms and ammunition.[92] Meanwhile, smugglers trading across the English Channel were doing their part to keep London preoccupied closer to home: in 1781, Lord Pembroke was so exasperated by the extent of local smuggling that he demanded, "Will Washington take America or the Smugglers England first? The bett would be a fair, even one."[93] The British lost the war in the American colonies for many reasons, including geographic disadvantage and French intervention. But losing the war on smuggling—failing to deter and interdict desperately needed clandestine shipments of arms and other war supplies to Washington's forces—played no small role.

In the national consciousness, the American War of Independence was won through self-sacrifice and patriotism. Yet often overlooked is that it was also won by merchants enriching themselves—as smugglers and privateers—regardless of patriotic sentiment or national loyalties. As we have seen, this sometimes undermined the war effort, much to the frustration of George Washington, who bitterly denounced such profiteering. But as he was well aware, smuggling was also vital to his military success. In short, smuggling helped give birth to America, even if some forms of smuggling at times also risked aborting it.

But as we'll see in the next chapter, the very smuggling interests and practices that enriched colonial merchants, that fueled calls for independence, and that kept the Continental Army supplied during the War of Independence would prove to be a daunting challenge for the new republic. Smugglers, who had subverted British rule in the American colonies, would now also subvert government authority in the very nation they helped to create. At the same time, smuggling would be at the forefront of America's growing engagement with the rest of the world and emergence as a dominant commercial power.

PART II

THE EARLY REPUBLIC

4

Contraband and Embargo Busting in the New Nation

THE NEWBORN AMERICAN STATE faced a basic challenge: How would it regulate trade in a country partly created by evading trade laws? How could it instill a respect for customs enforcement in a nation habituated to detesting it? A functioning government, even a minimalist one, required revenue. And for Alexander Hamilton, the nation's first treasury secretary, an impost on trade was the most sensible revenue source. Indeed, in a highly fragmented country deeply suspicious of centralized state authority, inhibiting illicit trade and collecting duties on imports through a federal customs service was the main rationale for a uniform system of government in the early years of the republic.[1]

Having defeated the British in 1783, American leaders now faced the laborious task of figuring out how to run an independent nation. At the top of the agenda was regulation of trade. The widely varying state customs rules in the early Confederation period proved woefully inadequate and easy to manipulate.[2] "The need for federal authority to regulate commerce," historian George Herring reminds us, "was the major reason the [constitutional] convention had been called" in 1787.[3] Customs was not only one of the first federal agencies established—briefly predating and then becoming part of the Treasury Department in 1789—but was by far the largest agency and virtually the only generator of income for the new national government (and would continue to be the primary source of federal revenue until the income tax amendment to the Constitution in 1913). It is therefore hard to overstate its importance in the context of a virtually nonexistent central state apparatus.[4] In 1790, Congress authorized the deployment of ten revenue cutters. Within a few years, customs operated in fourteen states with 146 officers and 332 subordinates.[5] Customs personnel in port cities nearly doubled in the first decade and a half of the nineteenth century, from about eleven hundred in 1801 to more than twenty-one hundred by 1816.[6] Customs agents were the most visible face of the national state in local communities otherwise far removed from the capital. How they performed their tasks would be a crucial test for the newly created central government.

Hamilton was well aware of the delicate balance between levying duties and ensuring merchants actually paid them: "Exorbitant duties on imported articles," he noted, "would beget a general spirit of smuggling."[7] Indeed, the "general spirit of smuggling" that was so prominent in the revolutionary era remained alive and well, but in a new political context. What could previously be conveniently rationalized by some as "patriotic smuggling" in a righteous anti-imperial cause now lost any heroic veneer. In other words, earlier ideological justifications for evading British trade laws were now more transparently self-serving. Patriotism, smuggling, and profiteering had all been lumped together during the revolutionary era, but economic interests and motives were now stripped bare.

For some merchants, the popular rallying cry of "no taxation without representation" really meant "no taxation even with representation." Perhaps no one epitomized this attitude more than John Brown of Providence, who showed little respect for the newly established customs service. When Providence customs collector Jeremiah Olney wrote to Hamilton about smuggling concerns, the secretary advised: "It is fit that you pay more than ordinary attention to the vessels of Messr. Brown & Francis . . . since a disposition to disregard the revenue law has manifested itself in them on this occasion."[8] Other merchants, perhaps more concerned about their reputations, publicly renounced smuggling. In Philadelphia, merchants even formed an anti-smuggling association, announcing: "We the subscribers, Merchants and Traders of the city of Philadelphia, do hereby pledge ourselves to each other, and to our fellow citizens at large, that we will not be concerned directly or indirectly in any trade contrary to the revenue laws of the United States; but will, by every effort in our power, discourage such illicit practices."[9]

Old smuggling habits and attitudes would nevertheless prove hard to change. As Massachusetts Representative Fisher Ames described the challenge in his address to the first U.S. Congress in May 1789, "The habit of smuggling pervades our country. We were taught it when it was considered rather as meritorious than criminal."[10] Perhaps partly due to this smuggling tradition, maritime historian Joshua Smith suggests, the federal government did not classify smuggling as a criminal offense until later in the nineteenth century. It remained a civil offense in the early years of the republic, with penalties primarily in the form of heavy fines, confiscation of goods, and seizure of vessels.[11]

The American tradition of smuggling continued in familiar Atlantic ports and in distant new markets. Much of the postindependence smuggling by American traders involved evading the commercial laws of other countries, and was therefore of less concern to U.S. customs collectors (though sometimes greatly complicating U.S. diplomatic relations). This predictably included continued violations of European mercantilist trade restrictions, particularly in the West Indies. In retaliation for the American Revolution, the British Order in Council blocked U.S. trade with their possessions in the West Indies from 1783 to 1796 (when the Jay Treaty reopened the trade). Yet the trade persisted through illicit channels during these years, much to the frustration of Royal Navy officer Horatio Nelson, who became obsessed with suppressing it. Even as the British government sought to curb the illicit trade, British merchants colluded with their American counterparts.[12]

American independence also had trade repercussions in the U.S.-Canada borderlands. Local cross-border community relationships—including trading relationships—predating the imposition of the borderline set by the 1783 Treaty of Paris often trumped restrictive instructions from faraway authorities.[13] U.S.-Canadian relations were thus partly founded on smuggling, especially in the early years of the nineteenth century. Though some level of smuggling was a constant, what varied was the degree of official concern, tolerance, and complicity on both sides of the poorly demarcated boundary line.

American trade also began to expand across the Pacific by the end of the eighteenth century, becoming truly global for the first time. The globalization of American trade included the globalization of its illicit trade. Smuggling was simply part of the repertoire of tools used by American merchants to penetrate new markets in distant lands. For instance, after the authorities in New South Wales (later, Australia) barred several U.S. ships from unloading spirits in 1800, their first diplomatic correspondence with the United States involved a notification that the import of spirits was prohibited and that the penalty would be confiscation of ship and cargo.[14] U.S. trade relations with Manila began with a violation of trade laws: "The first American who ever traded at Manilla [*sic*] went off without paying his duties."[15]

Smuggling was also common practice for U.S. merchant ships penetrating the China market for the first time. Carrying a shipment of furs in 1791, a Captain Ingraham was instructed by Thomas H. Perkins in Boston that on arrival in Canton he had "best sell the furs down the River, to avoid charges."[16] Similarly, in 1797, the New York firm of Gouverneur & Kremble instructed the supercargo of the ship *Sampson* that part of his cargo "sustains a pretty heavy duty, and on that account it may be necessary to part with it to some of the smugglers."[17]

In the first decade of the nineteenth century, U.S. merchants would also begin to make inroads into the illicit China opium market, much to the alarm of the British East India Company, which jealously protected its opium-smuggling monopoly. Jacque Downs, the foremost historian of the early U.S.-China opium trade, writes: "The Americans were marvelously ingenious in their exploitation of the commerce. They managed to circumvent both the East India Company's franchise and the Chinese Government's prohibition and carried on a very lucrative, if antisocial and ultimately ruinous trade."[18] Dominated by a handful of players, opium smuggling by American shippers would become increasingly vital to U.S.-China trade relations, with opium sales generating the revenue to buy Chinese goods such as silks and teas. Many of America's most elite merchant families made fortunes in the opium trade: "Girard, Astor, Joseph Peabody of Salem, John Donnell of Baltimore, and the Perkins firm (now allied with Bryant and Sturgis) were among the larger shippers of the drug."[19]

But by far the most important early boost to American trade and to the fortunes of American merchants came from the European wars that engulfed France, England, and their allies for more than two decades starting in 1792. Here the line between licit and illicit trade was fuzzy and changed with the fluctuating conditions of war. What the United States insisted were neutral goods were increasingly treated as contraband goods by Britain and France in their attempts to deprive the other of supplies. Although the expansion of American trade pulled the country out of its post-Revolution commercial slump, it was also an increasingly risky trade that threatened to drag the country into war.[20] U.S. merchant interests in profiting from war increasingly threatened U.S. geopolitical interests in remaining neutral.

As we'll see, illicit trade in the early years of the republic was double-edged. The very merchant disregard for regulation that subverted the British Empire, aided the War of Independence, and fueled postwar economic recovery and government expansion also became a serious challenge to the newborn American state—so much so that President Thomas Jefferson's ill-conceived embargo of 1807–1809 on all U.S. trade with the outside world was massively (and sometimes violently) evaded from within.

The French Revolutionary and Napoleonic Wars

France, Great Britain, and their respective allies were at war for more than two decades during the French Revolutionary and Napoleonic Wars. For the United States, such an unusually extended period of warfare presented immense risks, but also great trading opportunities. Indeed, America's foreign relations during this period were largely driven by efforts to simultaneously exploit these conflicts for commercial gain while desperately trying to avoid becoming entangled in them. It was an increasingly precarious balancing act, made doubly difficult by the national government's tenuous authority over the commercial activities of the country's merchant class. What was good for American trade created chronic headaches for American diplomacy.

For instance, playing both sides, American merchants carried out an illicit business with French and British privateers in violation of

U.S. treaty agreements. "The French Privateers bring their prizes into Charleston, S-C, and sell them openly," lamented one British official in May 1794.[21] Indeed, historian Melvin H. Jackson notes that in Charleston the privateering commerce benefited local merchants particularly through "the clandestine trade in guns, powder, shot, and above all, in ships."[22] Meanwhile, U.S. treaties with France (1778) and Great Britain (1783) forbade the selling of their prizes in American ports. In the early 1790s, Alexander Hamilton at first advised customs officials to take an accommodating and nonconfrontational stance toward French and British privateers unloading captured goods at American ports. Later he called for barring the landing of any captured prizes, in accordance with U.S. treaty obligations. The influx of prize goods at American ports nevertheless persisted, but more quietly—a form of smuggling in which goods were purchased at a substantial discount, sometimes with the collusion of local customs officials, and then resold at market prices.[23]

America's neutral status provided the main mechanism through which U.S. merchants took advantage of and profited from war. The country's declaration of neutrality in 1793 made it possible for U.S.-flagged vessels to dominate the shipping of goods between the warring European powers and their empires, particularly when carrying West Indies goods to Europe and European manufactures to the Western Hemisphere. With British and French commercial vessels preoccupied by war and harassed by enemy navies, American vessels took full advantage. "The wars of Europe," proclaimed the *Columbian Centinel* in 1795, ". . . rain riches upon us; and it is as much as we can do to find dishes to catch the golden shower."[24] Thanks largely to this "carrying trade," American shippers tripled their profits between 1792 and 1796. Douglas North calculates that between 1793 and 1801, the value of exports and net earnings generated by the carrying trade grew nearly fivefold.[25]

What eventually derailed this trade bonanza was growing conflict over the definition of neutral versus contraband commerce. The United States insisted that neutral status meant that its ships by definition carried neutral goods—"free ships, free goods"—and even argued that provisions and naval stores should be classified as noncontraband items. To circumvent British objections that the United States was directly aiding the enemy by shipping goods from French colonies to mainland Europe, American merchants would first import belligerent goods to the United States and then reexport them as "neutral" items. Britain grudgingly tolerated this legal fiction even though it was essentially a form of laundering enemy trade. Moreover, merchants could cut corners by manipulating the paperwork and not even bother to go through the trouble of first off-loading the goods in U.S. ports prior to reexport.[26] Some would maintain the appearance of a "broken voyage" while in practice shipping directly to Europe.

This peculiar trading scheme persisted for years. Great fortunes were made, enriching merchants such as Nicholas Brown and Thomas P. Ives in Providence, William Gray and Joseph Peabody in Salem, and John Jacob Astor and Archibald Gracie in New York.[27] Under the chaotic conditions of war, American ships were at times seized and their goods declared contraband. For instance, France seized a large number of neutral American ships trading with Britain during the so-called Quasi-War of 1798–1800, an undeclared conflict between France and the United States. But the rewards still far outweighed the risks.

Then Britain suddenly changed the rules of the game. In 1805, following the *Essex* decision of the British Admiralty Court, Britain began to seize large numbers of American vessels, announcing that American merchants carrying goods from enemy ports would now have to prove that the final destination of the goods was in fact the United States. In the absence of such proof, the goods would be considered contraband and subject to seizure. Trade now became a much riskier enterprise for American merchants, with their vessels increasingly falling prey to privateers empowered by "letters of marque" to seize goods Britain viewed as aiding the enemy. But as historian Gordon Wood explains, "It was not the actual number of seizures that most irritated Americans; rather it was the British presumption that His Majesty's government had the right to decide just what American trade should be permitted or not permitted. It seemed to reduce America once again to the status of a colonial dependent. This was the fundamental issue that underlay America's turbulent relationship with Britain through the entire period of the European wars."[28] At stake here, in other words, was the very power to define what constituted contraband, and for the United

States losing this definitional battle to its former rulers was yet another unhappy reminder of its subordinate position.

In further disrespect of U.S. sovereignty, British ships increasingly stopped and boarded American vessels in search of British subjects among the crew—essentially treating them as human contraband and therefore subject to seizure. Any man without documents validating his American citizenship could be forcibly removed and impressed into the British Navy. And even those with documents were treated with suspicion, given the ease with which papers could be forged or bought. "[T]he flagrant and undeniable abuses of the official documents of American citizenship," concluded the Admiralty, "have obliged their Lordships to look at all such documents with the utmost distrust."[29] Many sailors were in fact deserters from the British navy. At the time, no British subject had the legal right to expatriate to another country. From the British perspective, then, these sailors were essentially illegal migrants who had smuggled themselves to America in violation of British emigration laws; and their numbers were not insignificant. Secretary of the Treasury Albert Gallatin acknowledged that an estimated nine thousand out of twenty-four thousand sailors aboard U.S. vessels were British subjects.[30] The excuse they provided for British interference in American shipping had serious political ramifications.

Napoleon, meanwhile, escalated his war with Britain in 1806 by stepping up his attacks on Britain's trading relations, often at the expense of American shippers. In what came to be known as the Continental System, Napoleon declared a prohibition on trade with Britain, including seizing all goods and ships (regardless of nationality) departing from British ports and those of its colonies. Already alarmed by the British crackdown on the carrying trade, this was more dismaying news for American merchants, since the combination of these restrictive English and French moves essentially criminalized all neutral commerce. American trade would continue, and even flourish, but in a far more chaotic and violent Atlantic world.[31] France had essentially declared war on American trade with England, and England had similarly declared war on American trade with France. "The English take all vessels bound to Spanish or French ports and the Spanish or French take all vessels bound to or from an English port," wrote one American merchant in 1807. "As all the Ports in Europe are either English, Spanish or French, we are therefore prevented from going any where or coming from any where."[32] Thus, unavoidably, one or the other major European powers now treated previously neutral American trade as contraband commerce.

Breaking France's Haiti Blockade

While the European carrying trade involved creatively navigating the shifting line between licit and illicit commerce, American merchants also engaged in trade that was unambiguously illegal.[33] American merchants trading with Haiti's rebels, for instance, involved violating both French and U.S. laws, and this starkly revealed the tenuous nature of the federal government's authority over the country's merchants. Trade between the United States and the French colony of St.-Domingue grew rapidly in the second half of the 1780s, with American merchants exchanging dried fish, pickled fish, processed beef, livestock, and flour for coffee, rum, and sugar. By 1790, almost all U.S. molasses and sugar imports came from the island.[34] This trade not only persisted but also expanded after the outbreak of the Haitian Revolution in 1791, with American merchants in New York, Philadelphia, and Baltimore dominating the market.[35] At the end of the decade, American arms and other supplies were so crucial that the black rebels started calling Americans "the good whites."[36] French envoy to the United States Louis Pichon complained that despite his country's efforts to militarily interdict the illicit trade, "the American merchants . . . would still find some means of trading" with the island "by resorting to trickery at first and finally to force."[37]

After taking office in 1801, President Jefferson publicly expressed sympathy for the French position, yet in practice he took a hands-off approach toward the country's merchants. In response to French accusations that the United States was continuing to illegally arm the Haitian rebels, Secretary of State James Madison emphasized the distinction between the official policy stance of the American government and the behavior of the country's merchants.[38] There was mounting evidence, however, that the latter were not only arming their vessels without authorization (to fend off French privateers and break through the French naval blockade of Haiti) but doing so with the complicity of U.S. customs agents in ports from New York to Charleston.[39] Pichon charged that American merchants were engaged in "a private and piratical war against a Power with which the United States are at peace."[40]

Ever-louder French complaints compelled the Jefferson administration to finally push to put a stop to the Haiti trade. This would be just the beginning of a long and difficult campaign by Jefferson to more forcefully police American merchants, in this case not over the payment of customs duties but rather over trade that violated national policy and undermined U.S. diplomacy. Jefferson wrote in his Fourth Annual Message to Congress in 1804:

> Complaints have been received that persons residing within the United States have taken on themselves to arm merchant vessels and to force a commerce into certain parts and countries in defiance of the laws of those countries. That individuals should undertake to wage private war, independently of the authority of their country, can not be permitted in a well-ordered society. Its tendency to produce aggression on the laws and rights of other nations and to endanger the peace of our own is so obvious that I doubt not you will adopt measures for restraining it effectually in the future.[41]

Jefferson's call for action prompted not only political resistance but charges of hypocrisy and government complicity. Federalist Senator William Plumer of New Hampshire bluntly stated in November 1804, "Our merchants have traded to St. Domingo [Haiti]—Our government has never once intimated to them that that trade was unlawful—or that they ought not to arm their vessels in carrying it on." He continued: "On the contrary our Merchants have at our Custom houses cleared out their vessels for that island, when they were known to be fully armed & manned. Not a single Collector has refused, or even hesitated, to give them a Clearance. Will our government now . . . expose our innocent merchants to ruin!"[42] After extended debate, Congress passed a watered-down law in 1805. Congressman George Logan, a strong backer of the administration, acknowledged that the new law had "operated as a deception" and that, in practice, "the trade with St. Domingo has been carried on to as great if not greater extent than formerly."[43]

The French were well aware of the growing disconnect between official U.S. policy and commercial practice. Only months after the law was enacted, French General Louis Ferrand, commander of Napoleon's forces in Haiti, declared war on all American shipping in the West Indies. Ferrand listed by name a number of armed American merchant vessels that "are not only engaged in that execrable commerce, but actually transport the arms and ammunition of Dessaline's [*sic*] army from one port to another, thereby becoming auxiliaries of the black rebels against France."[44]

Scrambling to salvage relations with France, Jefferson now pushed to fully prohibit the Haiti trade. But skeptics in Congress argued that such a prohibition was unenforceable. Congressman Jacob Crowninshield of Massachusetts commented that regardless of what restrictions are passed, "you cannot stop the intercourse between citizens of the United States and the inhabitants of St. Domingo."[45] And indeed, historian Donald Hickey notes that despite the February 1806 ban on U.S. trade with Haiti, "American supplies reached Haiti anyway, carried either in foreign ships or in American ships operating clandestinely."[46] American merchants had no particular political affection for the Haiti rebellion. Far from it: many were nervous that it could inspire slave revolts at home. But this was a business opportunity too good to pass up.

These clashes between national law and local practice in American ports—including widespread complicity of customs officials—would be just the opening salvos of an all-out battle between the Jefferson administration and American merchants. Historian Gautham Rao emphasizes that, as relations with France and Britain deteriorated, the national government's approach toward regulating America's merchants shifted from an initial pattern of loose accommodation late in the eighteenth century—including tolerance of local complicity between customs houses and merchants in ignoring the law—to growing confrontation in the first years of the nineteenth century. Yet as Jefferson's ill-fated embargo would starkly reveal, more policing of merchants and merchant-friendly customs houses did not automatically translate into a successful policy. Indeed, merchants would become even craftier and more brazen in defying trade restrictions. Customs houses consequently "became the terrain of a pitched battle over the institutional and political character of the early American republic."[47]

Evading Jefferson's Embargo

In what surely qualifies as the boldest and most ambitious experiment in restricting trade in American history, in December 1807 Jefferson imposed an embargo on all U.S. commerce with the rest of the world. What provoked such a radical move, especially from an administration otherwise loath to expand centralized political power and authority? Indeed, the series of progressively more coercive and invasive embargo laws between late 1807 and early 1809 violated the core minimalist government tenets of Jeffersonian republicanism. Circumstances trumped ideology. Jefferson calculated that, denied the benefits of U.S. trade, France and especially England would come to realize the importance of American commerce and treat the country and its vessels with more respect. The embargo, it was hoped, would both punish and teach a lesson. England was viewed as especially vulnerable to an embargo, given the sheer magnitude of her trade with the United States.

Most importantly, Jefferson saw the embargo as an alternative to going to war—a war he was both ill prepared to fight and desperate to avoid. But instead he found himself at war with America's merchants, which turned into the biggest blunder of his administration. Secretary of Treasury Gallatin doubted the wisdom of the embargo from the start. He wrote to Jefferson shortly before the passage of the Embargo Act, "Governmental prohibitions do always more mischief than had been calculated" and concluded that the law was "of a doubtful policy."[48] He warned Jefferson that customs collectors must "depend on physical force to detain vessels, and there are many ports where we have neither the revenue cutters nor perhaps more than one single officer."[49]

Resistance to the embargo intensified and spread over time, starting in trade-dependent New England. Jefferson nevertheless proclaimed that the embargo necessitated sacrificing "private interests for this greater public object."[50] But merchants were in no mood for such lofty appeals.[51] Jefferson's optimism seemed naïve and disconnected from commercial realities. In May 1808, he explained to a former member of the Continental Congress, Benjamin Smith, that the embargo would continue to be enforced because America is a country where "every man feels a vital interest in maintaining the authority of the laws, and instantly engages in it as in his own personal cause."[52] Yet just a few months later, in August, Jefferson was noticeably less upbeat, writing to Gallatin: "This embargo law is certainly the most embarrassing one we have ever had to execute. I did not expect a crop of so sudden & rank growth of fraud & open opposition by force could have grown up in the U.S."[53] Jefferson nevertheless remained staunchly committed to the embargo to the very end, and he was greatly dismayed when Congress finally lifted it in 1809.

Embargo busting took three main forms. The first involved overland smuggling into Canada by inland farmers in Vermont and New York long accustomed to (and indeed dependent upon) selling their produce across the border. The second involved violations committed under the guise of the coastal trade (maritime trade between U.S. states). This could involve legally transporting goods to border towns and then smuggling them into British Canada or Spanish Florida. Alternatively, it could involve blaming an equipment malfunction or a bogus distress such as inclement weather for "forcing" the ship into a foreign port, often in the West Indies.[54] The third form of embargo evasion

Figure 4.1 Political cartoon of a smuggler during Jefferson's unpopular trade embargo. "Ograbme" is "embargo" spelled backwards (Granger Collection).

involved clandestinely sailing from an American harbor directly to foreign ports without clearance papers (most often to Canada, Florida, or the West Indies, but also to Europe).

The ease and methods of evading the embargo varied from place to place, partly depending on the degree of cooperation or conflict between merchants and local customs houses. Many customs agents, as in Delaware, New Jersey, North Carolina, and Maryland, simply threw up their hands, claiming they lacked the manpower to effectively enforce such a far-reaching prohibition. Moreover, repeating a pattern from earlier colonial times, some merchants predictably responded to stepped-up enforcement in major ports by shifting to smaller nearby inlets and bays where there was no customs presence. Alternatively, they used fraudulent paperwork to disguise their trade as domestic coastal commerce rather than foreign. Given the magnitude of the enforcement task, some customs agents found it easier to simply turn a blind eye to, or even directly collude in, embargo busting. Merchants would sometimes deliberately divert their cargoes to customs houses known for accommodation.[55]

Enforcement was most challenging—and most openly defied—along the nation's remote northern and southern frontiers. In the north, the "hot spots" were Passamaquoddy Bay (where Maine, then still part of Massachusetts, met British Canada) and the Lake Champlain region of Vermont and upstate New York.[56] As Carl Prince and Mollie Keller write in their history of the U.S. Customs Service, "The demand for flour and grain in Europe had generated a profitable illegal market in ports along the borders of Maine, Vermont, and New York. Merchants claimed that they were loading flour, corn, rice, or rye for their coastal trade. Little found its way to other American ports, however, for in Canada these goods sold for up to eight times their American value."[57] Jefferson labeled the smugglers the "most worthless part of society."[58] Yet the perpetrators clearly enjoyed considerable popular support. New York Governor Daniel Tompkins even warned Gallatin that the embargo threatened to provoke "open insurrection" along the Canadian border.[59]

In Passamaquoddy Bay, where the embargo was dubbed "the Flour War" (flour was the leading smuggled export to Canada[60]), Benjamin Smith explains, "borderland residents possessed an attitude that rejected the arbitrary authority of the state, an almost libertarian view that de-emphasized commercial restrictions and borders imposed by distant governments. Smuggling was the most obvious manifestation of this disregard for governmental interference in the economy. The more government forces attempted to halt unregulated trade, the more apparent it became to locals that the state was an unwelcome and alien force."[61]

Adding to the enforcement problem was Britain's active encouragement of such embargo busting. For instance, they designated official "places of deposit" to facilitate smuggling, and the Royal Navy sometimes even escorted smuggling vessels.[62] Open boats of various sorts—rafts, skiffs, reach boats, canoes—were the favored vehicles used by local fishermen to ferry goods across the short distance of water to the New Brunswick side.[63] "Only the timely arrival of American military and naval units," notes Smith, "prevented the complete collapse of federal authority in the area."[64]

Boston served as a key transshipment point for Maine smuggling, legally shipping flour and other supplies up the coast where they would then be ferried illegally into Canada. Faced with intense anti-embargo sentiment in his state, the Republican governor of Massachusetts facilitated this trade by providing clearance papers to ships carrying "needed" flour to Maine coastal towns.[65] Tiny Maine ports experienced a sudden economic stimulus from an influx of supplies that far outstripped legitimate local demand.[66] The town of Eastport became a particularly important entrepôt for smuggled goods, attracting merchants from far and wide hoping to cash in on the embargo-busting trade boom.

The country's southern periphery was equally porous, particularly the St. Mary's River and Amelia Island along the Georgia-Spanish Florida border, as well as the newly acquired port city of New Orleans. Gallatin reported to Jefferson in December 1808 that "the system of illegal exportations is carried on the largest scale, and embraces all the sea-coast of Georgia."[67] St. Mary's Georgia, the southernmost port of entry, and Amelia Island on the Florida side of the border a mile away at the mouth of the river was a particularly busy smuggling hub for illicit cotton exports to England.[68] The cotton was typically ferried by small boats to waiting ships offshore. An alarmed Jefferson called for the destruction of "all boats" in the area, but the order was never carried out.[69]

Customs agents on the ground were placed in an impossible situation, squeezed between growing national government pressure from above and intensifying local merchant resistance from below. With close ties to the merchants and communities within which they worked and lived, customs officials could not be expected to suddenly become stringent enforcers of a deeply unpopular embargo that strangled the local economy. Those who did so risked ostracism, intimidation, or worse. In Vermont, for instance, where resistance to the embargo approached armed insurrection, smugglers shot and killed several government officials attempting to seize their vessel.[70] Typically, however, smugglers did not need to resort to such lethal methods. They often used sympathetic local courts and juries to block many federal prosecutions of embargo violations.[71] "As to judiciary redress," observed Gallatin with dismay in July 1808, "there is very little hope."[72] In other words, embargo busters successfully used local legal instruments to subvert national laws—very much reminiscent of the colonial experience, except now U.S. laws rather than British laws were being undermined. Sometimes, seized goods would simply be stolen from warehouses. The smuggling sloop *Hope* was captured by a revenue cutter in March 1809 and placed under guard in New Haven, Connecticut. But the guards were overwhelmed on the very first night by a mob, and the sloop was plundered and then burned.[73]

The mounting backlash against the embargo was an eerie replay of the pre-Revolution years of increasingly brazen and violent resistance to British customs enforcement. Outraged mobs revived protest songs from the Revolutionary era, some commentators disparagingly compared Jefferson to King George III, and there was even talk of secession.[74] And similar to the colonial-era British rulers, Jefferson's response to resistance and protest was to stubbornly escalate rather than reevaluate—including turning to military force. Embargo enforcement became the Navy's main mission.[75] The most draconian and coercive of the embargo laws, the Enforcement Act of 1809, called for arming thirty new federal gunboats and authorized the president "to employ such part of the land or naval forces of the United States . . . for the purpose of preventing the illegal departure of any ship . . . or riotous assemblage of persons, resisting the custom-house officers."[76] Also replicating a move by his British predecessors, Jefferson replaced many customs collectors considered too accommodating and compromised, and he gave collectors sweeping new search and seizure powers without a court order.

Yet these moves did more to inflame local passions than tame smuggling. For example, Providence customs collector Jeremiah Olney wrote to Gallatin that in response to a seizure under the Enforcement Act "a large body of men had in a riotous manner assembled at and about the wharf" where the vessel was detained, with plans to "run off with said vessel . . . to a foreign port." When confronted, the mob "refused to obey the orders" to disperse. "A large body of rioters, from two to three hundred assembled . . . and forcibly took possession" of the vessel. Governor James Fenner informed Olney "he would not turn out his [militia] company in support of the embargo laws." In the aftermath of this incident, Olney received a credible warning that "the life of a Collector . . . would not be safe if he attempted to enforce the last Fatal Embargo Act." Olney resigned in frustration and wrote to Gallatin that the longer Congress "continue[d] to enforce with military aid, the fatal System" of the embargo, "in my candid opinion . . . it will shake the Empire to its centre, and deluge this once happy land in Blood."[77]

Further north, Naval Captain William Bainbridge, stationed in Portland, Maine, similarly reported that "an armed and riotous mob" threatened the lives of the customs officers. Collector Isaac Ilsey described the scene: "The wharves were taken possession of by a large number of disguised and armed men, supposed to be one or two hundred and they loaded and carried out of the harbor two vessels."[78] The situation had deteriorated so badly by early 1809 that in Alburg, Vermont (the port of entry on Lake Champlain), some of the troops originally deployed to help enforce the embargo instead became hired help in loading goods on Canada-bound smuggling rafts.[79]

Wary of further rebellion, an anxious Congress finally moved to repeal the embargo. It was officially lifted the same day Jefferson stepped down from office in March 1809. Yet the trade war was not over, and the precarious international conditions that had prompted the embargo in the first place only worsened. The new Madison administration replaced the embargo with a weaker, face-saving measure, the

Non-Intercourse Act of 1809, which restored trade with all countries except France and England. American shippers, in turn, could evade this restriction with relative ease by trading with the French and British via neutral ports, or even clandestinely ship directly to England and France.

The Non-Importation Act of 1811 followed the Non-Intercourse Act and had equally dismal results. The magnitude of the illicit trade was clearly evident by the American ships routinely returning to port loaded with British merchandise. This included a large influx of British rum from the West Indies, where accommodating Rhode Island customs inspectors happily served as taste testers to confirm its non-British origins.[80] Thus, the smuggling boom sparked by the embargo continued under conditions of Madison's high restrictions and low enforcement capacity.

THE 1807–1809 EMBARGO AND the trade prohibitions that replaced it had important implications for early American state building. Jefferson's administration was guided by principles of small government and states' rights. But ironically, Jefferson's stubborn commitment to enforcing the embargo ultimately led him to push for the very centralization of authority and power he so strenuously opposed—opening him up to charges of hypocrisy on the part of his Federalist opponents. For instance, in an effort to crack down on embargo busting, he reversed his long-standing policy of downsizing the navy and also pushed for and was given sweeping federal enforcement powers. Prior to the embargo, Jefferson had similarly pushed to scale back the number of revenue cutters, but he then reversed himself in order to enforce the embargo.[81] The series of embargo laws, each progressively more invasive and coercive, and Jefferson's willingness to resort to extreme measures to enforce them altered the legacy of what was otherwise a rather minimalist presidential administration.

The embargo also further entrenched the smuggling economy in already difficult-to-control borderlands—nowhere more evident than along the U.S.-Canada border, such as Maine's Passamaquoddy Bay, where smuggling would continue to thrive in the War of 1812 and beyond.[82] At the same time, the embargo propelled a buildup of federal policing presence in the region that persisted well beyond the embargo.[83]

Smuggling, in the context of the embargo and subsequent trade restrictions, also shaped American foreign policy by undermining economic coercion as a viable policy instrument. Illicit trade forced the Jefferson administration to go much farther than it would have wanted to enforce the embargo. The embargo had made supplies less plentiful and more expensive, yet England and other foreign powers continued to access American goods through clandestine channels and viewed large-scale smuggling as evidence that America's resolve and ability to maintain the embargo was limited. Illicit trade therefore challenged not only federal authority at home but also the government's legitimacy and credibility abroad.[84]

Perhaps the greatest irony is that whereas Jefferson's embargo and Madison's subsequent trade prohibitions were meant to punish England and France for treating neutral American trade as illicit trade, these self-imposed restrictions had a far greater criminalizing effect on American trade. And in the process, this only reinforced the already deep-seated merchant hostility toward the interventions of a distant federal government. Such hostility, as we will see in the next chapter, would turn to outright treason during the War of 1812.

5

Traitorous Traders and Patriotic Pirates

JEFFERSON AND MADISON HELD out hope that "peaceful coercion" through embargoes and other trade prohibitions would substitute for war. But as we saw earlier, these efforts were repeatedly sabotaged from within through rampant smuggling. And the main targets of economic coercion, France and especially Britain, never proved to be as economically vulnerable as expected. For Secretary of State James Monroe, America's credibility was at stake: "We have been so long dealing in the small way of embargoes, non-intercourse, and non-importation, with menaces of war, &c., that the British government has not believed us. We must actually get to war before the intention to make it will be credited either here or abroad."[1]

So in the end, Madison resorted to the very war that Jefferson had for so long been trying to avoid. In retaliation for Britain's continued predations on American trade and impressments of sailors on American ships, the United States declared war against its former colonial rulers in June 1812. It was a war the adolescent country was ill prepared to fight, yet Madison remained confident it would be relatively short and painless, and some even dreamed that it would lead to vast territorial expansion through a quick and easy conquest of Canada.[2]

It didn't work out that way. The War of 1812 instead turned into a stalemate that dragged on for two and a half years, with British forces kept well fed and supplied with the help of American smugglers pursuing illicit profits over patriotism. But even as the profit motive undermined the American war effort by reviving the old and familiar practice of trading with the enemy, the lure of quick fortunes also aided the military cause in the form of privateering. The success of American privateers at sea contrasted sharply with the less impressive U.S. military performance on land. Prominent American merchants who had earlier profited from violating U.S. trade prohibitions now invested heavily in privateers.[3] Pirates and smugglers would also go on to play a celebrated role in defeating the British in the battle of New Orleans, and they were granted presidential pardons as a reward for their contributions to the war effort. In what was otherwise a deeply divisive and unpopular war, the stunning victory at New Orleans provided a desperately needed psychological boost that helped unify the young republic and create the false impression that the United States had actually won the war.

A Traitorous Trade

The smuggling patterns that emerged during the War of 1812 were in many ways simply a continuation of the embargo-busting trade of earlier years, except this time American merchants were not just violating U.S. trade laws; they were aiding the British war effort against their own country. Similarly, U.S. wartime trade prohibitions were essentially an extension of the prewar restrictions, but the stakes were now much higher and domestic opponents of the measures were more muted in voicing their displeasure. Just as the Madison administration had earlier attempted to use economic coercion as an alternative to war, it now tried to use economic coercion as an instrument of war.[4] The Enemy Trade Act of 1812 outlawed trade with America's enemies, banned the sale of American war stores to Canada, and permitted only American vessels in U.S. ports. This was followed by the sweeping but short-lived embargo of 1813 (outlawing all exports and giving officials more invasive powers), and the Enemy Trade Act of 1815, passed shortly before the conclusion of the war. These restrictions included a further militarization of customs enforcement, as naval and other military forces were increasingly tasked with fighting not only British troops but also smugglers.

Despite these efforts, trade with the enemy flourished, and it mushroomed with the heightened demand generated by the influx of British forces in 1814.[5] "We have been feeding and supplying the enemy," bemoaned a Republican newspaper, "both on our coast and in Canada, ever since the war began."[6] Indeed, much to Madison's dismay, America's trading spirit often seemed stronger than its fighting spirit. "Self, the great ruling principle, [is] more powerful with Yankees than any people I ever saw," one British officer commented disparagingly.[7]

Nowhere was this more apparent than in the U.S.-Canada borderlands, where Americans proved more enthused about illicitly trading with their northern neighbors than conquering them. This diverted scarce supplies to the enemy, increased the costs of feeding U.S. soldiers, and undermined popular support for the war.[8] Even as some state militia units simply refused orders to march into Canada,[9] American smugglers were far less inhibited in their border crossings and engagements with the enemy. And indeed, some militia members deployed to secure the border instead colluded in border smuggling. Military intelligence also covertly flowed across the border. "The turpitude of many of our citizens in this part of the country," commented Navy Lieutenant Thomas Macdonough in dismay, "furnishes the Enemy with every information he wants."[10] Colonel Zebulon Montgomery Pike, commander of the 15th Infantry based in Burlington, described soldiers and civilians on the border as "void of all sense of honor or love of country" because of their cross-border dealings.[11]

The U.S.-Canada border became the most important back door for wartime trading, building on the illicit trade routes and networks that flourished during the embargo era. Smuggling was not only good business for border communities but good for relieving cross-border tensions in a time of war. Vermonters in the Lake Champlain Valley, for instance, remained largely unprotected from a British invasion and had good reason to maintain peaceful relations with their immediate neighbors in Lower Canada. Smuggling fostered an informal local cross-border interdependence that had a pacifying effect. Smuggling thus became a peculiar mode of peacemaking.[12] Indeed, the importance of illicit imports from northern Vermont apparently even influenced British military strategy. In preparing for the failed invasion of 1814, the Canadian governor noted that thanks to Vermont's "decided opposition to the war, and very large supplies of the Specie daily coming in from thense, as well as the whole of the cattle required for the use of the Troops, I mean for the present to confine myself in any offensive Operations which may take place to the west side of Lake Champlain."[13]

Despite some 170 seizures in northern Vermont alone, the potential for high profits outweighed the risks.[14] According to the Salem *Gazette*, smuggling had turned into "the most lucrative business which is now carried on." Smugglers could "afford to lose one half by customs house spies, and yet make money faster than those who follow the 'dull pursuits' of regular business."[15] And even when goods were seized, authorities had great difficulty making convictions. Judges in border areas were often sympathetic to the smugglers, and some even invested in the illicit trade.[16] Adding to the challenge of securing convictions, the attorney general ruled that simply visiting the enemy by itself was not a crime; the burden of proof was therefore on the prosecution to demonstrate that the accused had actually provided the enemy with "improper information" or "supplies."[17] Smugglers could even avoid any incriminating evidence of direct and improper exchange with the enemy by simply leaving goods at prearranged remote drop-off points.

Commercial interest in trading with the enemy extended well beyond the borderlands and crossed party lines. For instance, despite being a member of the prowar party, the prominent Republican New York merchant John Jacob Astor—America's first multimillionaire—was heavily invested in importing furs with his business partners in Montreal and was determined not to let an inconvenient war get in the way. In one of his smuggling schemes shortly after the war started, Astor hired the Burlington-based smuggler Gideon King, "the Admiral of Lake Champlain," to clandestinely import thousands of wolf skins.[18] No doubt Astor did not consider himself disloyal and unpatriotic. Business was business, after all.

Some illicit trade across the U.S.-Canada line was seasonal. During the winter months, one wartime smuggler from Orleans County, Vermont, later recalled, "the goods and merchandise which came from Canada were smuggled in winter when the swamps and rivers were frozen and when the deep snows could be made into a hard road over the roughest ground." He noted that the main threat in the Vermont countryside was not confiscations by the authorities but rather the armed gangs who used the cover of patriotism as an excuse to rob smugglers.[19] Meanwhile, during the summer, entire herds of cattle were smuggled through the forests of Vermont, New Hampshire, Maine, and New York into Canada to feed the Royal Army.[20] With the largest herds of cattle in the Northeast, Vermonters were especially well placed to take advantage of a tripling of the price of beef during the war.[21]

In late July 1813, an exasperated American General George Izard complained, "On the eastern side of Lake Champlain, the high roads are found insufficient for the supplies of cattle which are pouring into Canada. Like herds of buffaloes, they press through the forest, making paths for themselves. . . . Nothing but a cordon of troops, from the French Mills [in northern New York] to Lake Memphramagog [in northern Vermont] could effectively check the evil.—Were it not for these supplies, the British forces in Canada would soon be suffering from famine, or their government subjected to enormous expense for their maintenance."[22] Two years into the war, the British governor-general in Canada reported to the Foreign Office that "Two-thirds of the army in Canada are at this moment eating beef provided by American contractors, drawn principally from the States of Vermont and New York."[23] Some New England cattle smugglers never even had to step foot into Canada: after marching their livestock to the border, their Canadian counterparts would woo the animals across with a basket of corn.[24]

The border was equally porous further east, with the major smuggling hot spots changing with the shifting geography of the war.[25] When the British invaded and then occupied part of eastern Maine in the summer of 1814, British merchants flocked to the town of Castine to exploit wartime trading opportunities for the next eight months. The British authorities fully encouraged the brisk cross-border illicit trade to compensate for the severe shortage of foodstuffs and other supplies in Canada.[26] Wartime smuggling was about everyday survival, but it was also about profits. Take the case of William King, a successful Maine merchant who also headed the local militia: he supplied the British military with provisions, and the British supplied him with blankets, which he then sold at a profit to the American military.[27] King went on to be elected the first governor of Maine in 1820 and later served as the collector of customs at Bath from 1830 to 1834.[28]

Early on in the war, the British government even sold trading licenses to American merchants that exempted them from seizure by British privateers and the Royal Navy. American naval officers had an especially difficult time identifying U.S. merchant ships operating with these licenses, since the captain would keep the license hidden unless boarded by a British ship. To dupe the captain into voluntarily producing the incriminating license, American naval officers would at times masquerade as British when boarding the vessel, wearing British uniforms and showing the British flag. These ruses sometimes worked, but smugglers became less gullible and warier of such deceptions over time. The owners of a licensed American merchant ship smuggling goods into Canada warned the master that "you must be aware of the facility with which American cruisers may pass as English. . . . When in with any of the B.[ritish] B.[lockading] squadron, come forward with your Ex.[port] Li.[cense] which will safely pass you. . . . If you have any suspicions destroy all at once."[29]

The British favored New England shippers in allocating trading licenses, since the commercially oriented Northeast was most opposed to the war.[30] Britain's blockade of the eastern seaboard initially did not extend to New England, a strategy meant to secure illicit supplies but also to create division and discord between the antiwar Federalist Northeast and the Republican administration in Washington. It was certainly politically awkward that New Englanders were supplying British vessels blockading the rest of the American seaboard. Even after the Royal Navy extended its blockade to include New England in April 1814, the British continued to facilitate and encourage illicit American trade (especially to Canada) so long as it aided their subjects and military forces.[31] Rhode Islanders on Block Island, for instance, regularly brought both supplies and intelligence to British ships off the coast.[32] The British openly used the harbor at Provincetown, Massachusetts, to resupply their ships: small American vessels reportedly brought "[f]resh beef, vegitables, and in fact all Kind of supplies" to these ships on a regular basis.[33] "The fact is notorious," announced the Lexington *Reporter*, "that the very squadrons of the enemy now annoying our coast . . . derive their supplies from the very country which is the theatre of their atrocities."[34]

At the same time as American smugglers supplied enemy forces, the battle against smuggling distracted U.S. troops from their war-fighting mission. In October 1813, General Wade Hampton even ordered military raids into Canada from the Lake Champlain region of Vermont to try to disrupt the "shameful and corrupt neutrality of the lines, for the purpose of gain."[35] Similarly, the following March, Colonel Clark headed a detachment toward Missisquoi Bay, Vermont, "with a view to cut up by the roots the smuggling intercourse which had been carried on to a great extent; besides it was necessary to prevent the constant supply of provisions which were daily passing to the enemy from this state."[36]

These militarized U.S. interdiction efforts not only failed but at times backfired. In 1813 a lieutenant and his soldiers attempted to apprehend a gang of smugglers in a small northern New York border town. Yet not only were the smugglers released from jail but the lieutenant himself was arrested in retaliation (his commander ended up bailing him out).[37] In another incident, in 1814 near Burlington, Vermont, thirteen infantrymen sent to apprehend smugglers were assaulted by a group of thirty smugglers; one soldier was killed and five taken prisoner.[38]

Finally, privateering, for all its contribution to the war effort, also presented an added smuggling challenge. While American privateers traumatized British commercial shipping, at times they also used this as a cover for illicit trading. When ships were prohibited from leaving U.S. ports in late 1813, this did not include privateers—leading some vessels, particularly in New England, to declare privateering intentions but in reality load up with hidden supplies for the British. Privateers also engaged in mock captures at sea as a ploy to trade with the enemy.[39] And after disposing of the "seized" goods, the privateer could ransom the vessel back to the original owner—which itself was an opportunity to ship illicit goods in the other direction.[40] Mock captures also took place on Lake Champlain, where the entrepreneur John Banker Jr. used his vessel, *The Lark*, to make prearranged "captures" of barges loaded with U.S.-bound goods, which he would then send on for sale in New York duty-free.[41]

The Baratarian Pirate-Smugglers and the Battle of New Orleans

The southern port city of New Orleans was far removed from the main battlefields during the first years of the war, but it took center stage in dramatic fashion at the conclusion. Geography and historical timing conspired to make the city and surrounding area one of the most notorious havens in the Gulf of Mexico for pirates, privateers, and smugglers. The alliance of convenience that developed between outlaws and government authorities in repelling a British invasion of New Orleans is one of the most remarkable stories of the war.

When the United States acquired New Orleans as part of the Louisiana Purchase, the change in government authority did not change the attitudes and behavior of the city's merchants, many of whom were French and Spanish and long accustomed to openly disregarding the law. It also did not change the consumer habits of the city's twenty-five thousand residents, primarily of French origin. They had become accustomed to deeply discounted prices on goods captured by pirates and privateers in the Gulf and then smuggled into New Orleans or illicitly sold at regular auctions on islands in the swamps and bays near the city. The influx of cheap smuggled merchandise captured at sea was especially welcome by city residents during a time of shortages and inflated prices induced by the embargo and subsequent war. Smugglers also won the support of plantation owners in the lower Mississippi Valley by supplying them with clandestine shipments of slaves in defiance of the 1808 federal prohibition on the slave trade.

With no convenient French ports remaining in the Caribbean, privateers flying the French flag turned to the Louisiana coast and the port of New Orleans to illegally dispose of their captured goods.[42] One favorite privateer ploy was to feign distress and make an emergency stop in New Orleans for repairs, where they could then clandestinely unload their goods.[43] But the less risky and increasingly favored alternative was to entirely bypass the New Orleans port and its customs agents. Barataria Bay, some fifty miles south of New Orleans—with its many canals, marshes, waterways, bayous, and islands at the mouth of the Mississippi—provided a perfect base and depot for privateers and pirates to warehouse their captured merchandise. From there the goods could be moved into the city with relative ease through various smuggling routes.

The pirate-smugglers candidly acknowledged the nature of their business and even boasted they were performing a vital public service. In response to a letter to the *Louisiana Gazette* complaining about the introduction of illicit cargoes into the city, a spokesperson (who signed his name "The Agent of the Freebooters") wrote:

> Gentlemen:
> Your paper of Wednesday contained a letter written by some idiot . . . [who] makes a great outcry against a few honest fellows of us, who are using extraordinary exertions to punish the common enemy, the British and their allies, the Spaniards. . . . Does he wish to discourage our profession and put an end to trade altogether?
>
> Cannot the booby perceive that without us there would not be a bale of goods at market; and does he not see, by the open manner in which our business is done, that the government of the United States has no objection either to the fitting out of our prizes and the sale of their cargoes, without troubling ourselves about the payment of duties; which I assure you we would find extremely inconvenient when we sell so low for real cash in these hard times. . . .[44]

The spokesperson concluded with a promotional pitch, informing readers where they could purchase captured ships and their cargoes at wholesale prices; he even expressed hopes for opening convenient retail shops in Conde and Toulouse streets in New Orleans.[45]

New Orleans businessmen and brothers Jean and Pierre Laffite emerged as the ringleaders of the sprawling Barataria operation. At first they simply served as brokers, handling the purchase and transport of the illicit merchandise from Barataria into the city. "In the streets of New Orleans," observed architect and businessman Arsène Lacarrière Latour, "it was usual for traders to give and receive orders for purchasing goods at Barataria, with as little secrecy as similar orders are given for Philadelphia or New-York."[46] Eventually, Jean Laffite relocated to Barataria to directly oversee operations, becoming the de facto head of the rapidly growing community of outlaws. His brother Pierre, meanwhile, remained in town as a silent business partner, maintaining close connections to local merchants and compromised officials.

In addition to clandestinely moving merchandise into New Orleans, the Laffites also organized regular auctions at places such as "The Temple," a large shell mound halfway between the Barataria smuggling headquarters and New Orleans. Buyers from New Orleans and other nearby areas flocked to the auctions to purchase trafficked slaves and smuggled goods at bargain prices. Showing little apparent concern about hiding their business, the Laffites would even publicly advertise their auctions in advance. Outraged by such open violation of the law, the collector of customs dispatched a small force to shut down one of the auctions, but they were repelled by gunfire, leaving one customs officer dead and two others wounded. The auction went on as scheduled.[47]

The war with England made the Laffites even more ambitious, aspiring to control every stage of the business, from capturing goods on the high seas to distributing and selling smuggled merchandise. The war conditions created the opportunity. As William Davis writes, the Laffite brothers sought to take "advantage of the shortages caused by the war and the British blockade, and the distraction of the authorities thanks to the war."[48] The Laffites didn't even bother to try to obtain a legitimate letter of marque for their vessels; and even if they had secured a privateering commission, it was still easier, faster, and more profitable to dispose of their captured cargoes illegally via Barataria.[49]

But while the wartime business boomed for the Laffites, their blatant lawbreaking brought with it more government attention and concern. The more open and brazen their piracy and smuggling activities, the more embarrassing it was for the authorities. "As regards the principal offenders I am persuaded that nothing short of the most vigorous measures will put a stop to their evil practices and a resort to force is in my opinion indispensible," Louisiana Governor William C. Claiborne told General Wilkinson in 1813.[50] The customs collector for New Orleans reached the same conclusion and put in a formal request for the army and navy to assist in suppressing the Barataria smuggling operation.[51] At least for the time being, these pleas fell on deaf ears. Claiborne also appealed to the citizens of New Orleans to boycott Laffite merchandise, but the smugglers enjoyed considerable local support, especially among the French and Creole communities. As Claiborne put it, ladies would, in conversation, respond to his denouncements of the smugglers as criminals by simply saying, "*That is impossible; for my grandfather, or my father, or my husband, was, under the Spanish government, a great smuggler, and he was always esteemed an honest man.*"[52]

In March 1813 Claiborne issued a formal proclamation against the "banditti" from Barataria "who act in contravention of the laws of the United States . . . to the evident prejudice of the revenue of the federal government." He called on all officers "to seize and apprehend every individual engaged in these criminal practices."[53] The Laffites nevertheless remained openly contemptuous of the authorities. When Claiborne offered a $500 reward for the capture of Jean Laffite in 1813, the pirate-smuggler mockingly countered by posting a signed handbill offering a $1,000 reward for the capture of the governor. Laffite's proclamation was apparently in jest, but the governor was not amused.[54]

Although the governor's proclamation and award offer did not lead to the capture of Jean Laffite, in 1814 the local authorities managed to arrest and indict Pierre Laffite in New Orleans. Shortly after, Jean Laffite appealed directly to the public's consumer self-interest in a letter to a local newspaper. He charged that his opponents were simply monopolists wishing to do away with market competition by denying the citizens of New Orleans access to his discounted goods. He even suggested establishing "a press in the Empire of Barrataria" so that the public could be kept better informed of the arrival of new merchandise for sale. The not-so-subtle subtext of this message to the public, historian William Davis notes, was that "if Pierre were convicted and Barataria broken up, everyone would be the poorer for paying more for their imported goods thereafter. Favorable opinion might make it difficult to assemble a jury that would convict."[55]

Even as Louisiana officials were trying to put the Laffites out of business, the British were hoping to entice Jean Laffite and his men to join their cause. The growing animosity between the government authorities and Baratarians, the British calculated, would make them more amenable to joining the British in their planned attack on New Orleans. While Pierre Laffite sat in jail in early September 1814, the British dispatched messengers to Barataria to try to bribe his brother Jean to fight on the British side.[56] Laffite stalled, telling the British he needed fifteen days to consider the terms of the offer. He then quickly forwarded the offer letter to a trusted intermediary in New Orleans in the hopes that the authorities would view this as a sign of his true patriotism and be lenient on his brother.

Along with the British offer letter, Laffite enclosed his own note, stating, "You will see from their contents the advantages I might have derived from that kind of association." He went on to defend himself: "I may have evaded the payment of duties to the custom house; but I have never ceased to be a good citizen; and all the offence I have committed, I was forced to by certain vices in our laws." Laffite then turned to the issue of his brother's arrest, indicating that he hoped to secure his release by providing information about British intentions (this proved unnecessary, since Pierre had just broken out of jail).[57]

Jean Laffite also wrote a letter to Governor Claiborne, assuring him of his loyalties and offering his services:

> Monsieur:
> . . . I offer to return to this State many citizens who perhaps have lost to your eyes that sacred title. I offer . . . their efforts for the defense of the country.
>
> This point of Louisiana that occupies great importance in the present situation, I offer myself to defend it. . . . I am the lost sheep who desires to return to the flock . . . for you to see through my faults such as they are. . . .
>
> In case, MonSieur Le Gouverneur, your reply should not be favorable in my ardent wishes I declare to you that I leave immediately so not to be held to have cooperated with an invasion. . . . This cannot fail to take place, and puts me entirely on the judgement of my conscience.
>
> I have the honor to be, MonSieur Le Gouverneur,
> *Laffite.*[58]

Unfortunately for Laffite, his appeal was not enough to stop an already planned U.S. naval expedition to destroy the Barataria smuggling base. The September 16 flotilla assault met no resistance; the base was looted and dismantled after the Laffite brothers and most of their men scattered. Apparently, the Laffites had already made plans to abandon the base and relocate operations.[59]

But all was not lost for the fugitive Laffites and their crew. In October 1814, Governor Claiborne, worried about the lack of coastal defenses, wrote to the attorney general that "the Baratarians might be advantageously employed against the enemy."[60] General Andrew Jackson arrived on the first of December to quickly organize the defense of the city against an expected British invasion. The city was woefully unprepared, and with British troops only sixty miles away, by mid-month Jackson was eager for any help he could find. The general was at first skeptical when Claiborne informed him of the Laffite offer but warmed to the idea, given the desperate circumstances. Jackson, who at first denounced the Laffites and the Baratarians as "hellish banditti," now embraced them, even if reluctantly.[61] Jean Laffite apparently even "got along so well with Jackson that he became the general's unofficial aide-de-camp."[62] Both Laffite brothers were assigned to Jackson's

Figure 5.1 Depiction of the pirate and smuggler Jean Laffite meeting with General Andrew Jackson and Louisiana Governor William Claiborne. From Charles Ellms's *The Pirates Own Book, 1837* (Harvard College Library).

headquarters staff.[63] Ironically, the Baratarians would now be fighting side by side with the very military officers that had looted and destroyed their smuggling base just a few months earlier.

The Laffites, along with as many as four hundred of their fellow Baratarians, had much to offer in exchange for full pardons. Although numerically a tiny percentage of Jackson's defense force, they were exceptionally skilled artillerymen, knew the local terrain intimately, and provided much-needed supplies. Particularly crucial, the Laffites offered 750,000 gunflints, making up for an otherwise extreme shortage. Given the open terrain, artillery was especially decisive in the defense effort. Laffite's lieutenants, Dominique You and Renato Beluche, proved to be invaluable gunners. After the battle, a grateful Jackson reportedly exclaimed, "Were I ordered to storm the very gates of hell with Dominique You as my Lieutenant, I would have no misgivings as to the outcome."[64]

On January 8, 1815, General Andrew Jackson and his forces—an assortment of regulars, militia, and volunteers, along with the Barataria smugglers, privateers, and pirates—overwhelmingly defeated five thousand British regulars. It was easily the most lopsided and impressive American victory of the war, and it could not have come at a better time.[65] In his congratulatory address to the army, Jackson praised You, Beluche, and the Laffites: "Captains Dominique and Belluche, lately commanding privateers at Barataria, with part of their former crew and many brave citizens of New Orleans, were stationed at [batteries] Numbers 3. and 4. The general cannot avoid giving his warm approbation of the manner in which these gentlemen have uniformly conducted themselves while under his command, and of the gallantry with which they have redeemed the pledge they gave." He went on to note that "The brothers Laffite have exhibited the same courage and fidelity, and the general promises that the government shall be duly apprized of their conduct."[66]

As the battered British forces retreated, the Laffites were hailed as heroes in New Orleans, and early the next month they and their followers received the promised presidential pardons. All charges of smuggling and piracy were dropped. A few months later, before returning home, General Jackson sent Jean Laffite a thank-you note in which he praised his "activities and zeal," described him as "one of those to whom the country is most indebted," and even expressed his "sincere assurance of my private friendship and high esteem." The note concluded: "I am, Sir . . . your most Obed and humble servant."[67]

One can easily inflate the importance of the Baratarians in the Battle of New Orleans, especially given the cult-figure status the Laffites have come to enjoy in popularized accounts. At the same time, their tactical contribution—in the form of manpower, intelligence, and arms supplies—should not be discounted.[68] Perhaps most important is what Jean Laffite and his followers *didn't do*: accept the British offer and participate in the attack on New Orleans. As the historian and former Marine Corps Major General Wilburt Brown argues, "it is possible that Jackson might have defended the city successfully without the aid of the Baratarians, but it is probable that he could not have done so if Laffite and his men had accepted British offers of amnesty, alliance, and bribe money and had thrown their weight against the American defense."[69]

The battle of New Orleans actually took place after the peace treaty ending the war with Britain had already been signed, but no matter. The two events coincided so closely, and communications were so slow, that when the combined news of the treaty and the victory arrived, Americans convinced themselves that the country had actually defeated the British. A deeply unpopular and often incompetently managed war ended with a perfectly timed victory with huge political repercussions. Madison and the Republicans felt vindicated, while the antiwar Federalists were now discredited and on the defensive (and would never make a comeback). General Jackson, now catapulted to the status of a war hero, would eventually go on to become president. The victory at New Orleans had a huge psychological impact, inflating the country's self-confidence and sense of national pride. Remarkably, what had often been a frustrating and even humiliating war ended on such a celebrated high note that the war itself was reinterpreted in the popular imagination as an American success story.

THE WAR OF 1812 has now largely fallen into obscurity. But it left a number of important legacies, one of which was much greater national concern and awareness about illicit trade. The customs service, which had been challenged like never before during the war, would emerge beaten and bruised but also more expansive and empowered. The most onerous trade restrictions of the embargo and war years were now lifted, but the coercive capacity of customs would remain strengthened.[70]

Perhaps most importantly, the War of 1812 should be remembered for what it failed to do: conquer Canada. Hugely consequential, this non-event has nevertheless long been forgotten (along with the war itself) in the popular imagination in the United States, but certainly not in Canada. Massive smuggling was just one of the factors that undermined American territorial ambitions during the war, but it was certainly the most embarrassing and even scandalous. During the war, it is fair to say that Canadians and Americans proved far more interested in illicitly trading than in fighting with each other, and indeed trade would continue to be the defining feature of their relationship for the next two centuries.

As for the Laffites, it is perhaps ironic that they contributed to a victory that led to the strengthening of government authority—including a beefed-up U.S. naval presence in the Gulf—making the area less hospitable for their illicit business. The Laffites subsequently moved their base of operations further west, to the more remote Texas coast in Mexico beyond the reach of U.S. authorities. But they would never again experience the same profitable opportunities that the embargo and war years provided in New Orleans and the Mississippi River Valley.[71] Although historians continue to debate the significance of the role of the Laffites and the Baratarians in the battle of New Orleans, Louisianans have immortalized Jean Laffite's contribution to the state's history by naming a 20,020-acre park and wildlife preserve the "Jean Laffite National Historical Park and Preserve." The city of Lake Charles, Louisiana, also puts on an annual festival, appropriately named Contraband Days, in honor of Jean Laffite.

6

The Illicit Industrial Revolution

THE AMERICANS NOT ONLY fought the British on the battlefield and on the high seas but also systematically stole from them as part of the nation's early industrialization strategy. Although typically glossed over in the sanitized accounts found in U.S. high school textbooks, as a young and newly industrializing nation the United States aggressively engaged in the kind of intellectual property theft it now insists other countries prohibit and crack down on. So we now turn to examine how America became such a hotbed of intellectual piracy and technology smuggling in its adolescent years, particularly in the textile industry. Only after it had become a mature industrial power did the country vigorously campaign for intellectual property protection—conveniently overlooking its own illicit path to industrialization.[1]

In the aftermath of the American Revolution, the smuggling of industrial technologies into the new republic was the one form of smuggling still viewed as unquestionably patriotic—especially since Great Britain was the main target. Indeed, it was encouraged and celebrated as essential to building the new nation and reducing its dependence on old colonial masters. It wasn't usually called "smuggling," but this is certainly what it was. It was also not called "intellectual piracy," as it is today, but it was certainly a form of theft.

Illicit industrialization involved both smuggled machinery and smuggled migrants with the skills, knowledge, and expertise to assemble and operate the equipment. There was an overwhelming demand for both in the early years of the nation. Smuggled machinery violated British export laws. Smuggled migrants—which really meant self-smuggling even if sometimes involving aggressive recruiting by covert American agents abroad—violated British emigration laws. The two were closely intertwined. After all, the illicitly obtained machinery was of no use if no one knew how to use it. In this regard, the machinist was more valuable than the machine: ideally, he could not only re-create but also improve upon the original design. British prohibitions slowed the clandestine outflow of brainpower and technology but ultimately failed to stop it. By 1825, cotton textile production was entirely mechanized, with the United States "only slightly trailing, if at all, Britain in the adoption of power weaving."[2] By midcentury, the United States had become one of the world's leading industrial powers.

A Backward but Ambitious New Nation

The United States emerged from the Revolutionary War acutely aware of Europe's technological superiority. But it also had enormous ambitions and aspirations to rapidly catch up and close the technology gap. The acquisition of new industrial technologies from abroad, it was hoped, would help solve the country's chronic labor shortage and enhance its economic self-sufficiency and competitiveness. As the *Pennsylvania Gazette* put it in 1788, "Machines appear to be objects of immense consequence to this country." It was therefore appropriate to "borrow of Europe their inventions."[3] "Borrow," of course, really meant "steal," since there was certainly no intention of giving the inventions back.

The most candid mission statement in this regard was Alexander Hamilton's *Report on Manufactures,* submitted to the U.S. Congress in December 1791.[4] The secretary of the treasury argued that "To procure all such machines as are known in any part of Europe can only require a proper provision and due pains. The knowledge of several of the most important of them is already possessed. The preparation of them here is, in most cases, practicable on nearly equal terms."[5] Notice that Hamilton was not urging development of indigenous inventions to compete with Europe but rather direct procurement of European technologies through "proper provision and due pains"—meaning, breaking the laws of other countries.[6] As the report acknowledged, most manufacturing nations "prohibit, under severe penalties the exportation of implements and machines which they have either invented or improved."[7] At least part of the *Report on Manufactures* can therefore be read as a manifesto calling for state-sponsored theft and smuggling.

Hamilton appointed Tench Coxe as assistant secretary of the treasury and tasked him with writing the initial draft of the report. Coxe was one of the most well-known and outspoken advocates for illicitly acquiring European manufacturing technologies, and personally invested in several technology-smuggling schemes.[8] He was a spokesman for the

Figure 6.1 Tench Coxe (1755–1824), a leading proponent of industrializing through the clandestine importation of British machinery and machinists. Coxe served as assistant secretary of the treasury when Alexander Hamilton was secretary of the treasury, and he wrote the *Report of Manufacturers* with Hamilton (Granger Collection).

Pennsylvania Society for the Encouragement of Manufactures and the Useful Arts, which early on helped turn Philadelphia into the nation's leading center for acquiring foreign technologies and the artisans to operate them.[9]

Other American statesmen were equally enthused about illicitly acquiring European industrial technologies, even if they were less public than Hamilton and Coxe in advocating official government sponsorship. After all, doing so entailed violating the export laws of another country and was thus diplomatically awkward and delicate, to say the least. Benjamin Franklin, for instance, enthusiastically encouraged British artisans to violate British emigration laws and come to America, providing letters of introduction to facilitate the move—but was reluctant to provide material assistance and inducements.[10]

George Washington was also a strong supporter of acquiring European manufacturing technologies, but as president he was wary of the reputational consequences of appearing directly complicit in such illicit schemes. In January 1791 he explained why he was backing away from direct involvement in setting up a Virginia textile factory using smuggled machines. "I am told that it is a felony to export the machines, which it is probably the artist contemplates to bring with him," Washington wrote to the governor of Virginia, Beverly Randolph, "and it certainly would not carry an aspect very favorable to the dignity of the United States for the President in a clandestine manner to entice the subjects of another nation to violate its laws."[11] Nevertheless, the president had no qualms about encouraging others to do so. In his first State of the Union Address in January 1790, Washington declared, "I cannot forbear intimating to you the expediency of giving effectual encouragement as well to the introduction of new and useful inventions from abroad."[12]

The first U.S. Patent Act and its subsequent revisions reflected the government's eagerness both to adopt new technologies through any means and also to maintain the appearance of upholding the rule of law. At least on paper, the patent law of 1790 protected inventors. But as historian Doron Ben-Atar explains: "this principled commitment to absolute intellectual property had little to do with reality. Smuggling technology from Europe and claiming the privileges of invention was quite common and most of the political and intellectual elite of the revolutionary and early national generation were directly or indirectly involved in technology piracy."[13] The revised U.S. Patent Act of 1793 required patent applicants to take an oath certifying that their invention was original, but the administrator of the patents did not even insist that the oath be taken. The Patent Board lacked the will and the capacity to check the originality of patent requests.[14] Moreover, the Patent Act did not protect foreign inventors; they could not obtain a U.S. patent on an invention they had previously patented in Europe. In practice, this meant that one could steal a foreign invention, smuggle it to the United States, and develop it for domestic commercial applications.[15] The patent registration system "allowed wealthy importers of European technology, such as the Boston Associates, to claim exclusive rights to imported innovations and use the courts to validate their claims and intimidate competitors."[16] In other words, the law could be used to protect lawbreaking. Through its discriminatory patent rules, America became the world's most notorious haven for industrial piracy.[17]

Especially sought after—and especially protected—were the new textile manufacture technologies. "Strange as it may appear," observed Coxe, "they also card, spin, and even weave, it is said, by water in the European manufactories."[18] In the 1750s, historian Carroll Pursell reminds us, textile production still remained largely a medieval enterprise based on manual labor. It had not substantially changed for centuries but was suddenly revolutionized in just a few decades with the introduction of mechanical power. In Britain, James Hargreaves invented the spinning jenny in 1764 and patented it in 1770; Richard Arkwright patented his water frame in 1769 and a carding engine in 1775. Around the same time, Samuel Crompton created his mule (integrating the tasks of the water frame and the jenny). These various machines all performed the same key task of turning cotton fiber into thread. In 1790, England was the only country in the world with the technology to spin yarn by waterpower. But that was about to change.[19]

Indeed, by mid-1791, note Anthony F. C. Wallace and David J. Jeremy, there were already copies of Arkwright's water frame, Hargreaves's jenny, and perhaps even Crompton's mule in America, and the British were launching a "clandestine counterintelligence operation to recover them. Several British agents or patriotic merchants were buying the American machines wherever possible and shipping them back to England, and, in some instances, when the machines could not be procured, allegedly burning down the factories that contained them. And American agents—some of them secretly financed by the secretary of the Treasury—kept on bringing in more plans, more models, and more English mechanics."[20]

British officials viewed the clandestine transatlantic movement of men and machines with growing alarm. George Hammond, the first British minister to the United States, sent a secret dispatch to Lord Grenville, the British foreign secretary, cautioning that "No small degree of vigilance will be required in Great Britain to prevent the emigration of artists and the export of models of machines." He promised to give "unremitting attention" to the task of uncovering British-based labor recruiters.[21] Phineas Bond, the British consul in Philadelphia, similarly warned that the drain "of many useful and laborious inhabitants" out of England was so embraced in the United States and "lucrative to those who are engaged in it will be carried on extensively, and with great spirit unless speedily corrected."[22] By 1788 London ordered its consuls in the United States to keep tabs on the entry of British immigrants and collect any information on how they made the trip, how it was paid for, whether they were induced, and so on.[23]

Evading British Prohibitions

British efforts to guard its industrial secrets began in the colonial era.[24] Britain banned most manufacturing in its American colonies as part of the larger imperial strategy of privileging domestic manufactures and keeping the colonies dependent. England prohibited the export of all silk and woolen manufacturing tools in 1749, and this ban was expanded in 1774 to include cotton and linen equipment. In 1749 it also outlawed attempts to entice a skilled immigrant from the British Isles to the colonies and in 1774 imposed a ban on the emigration of mechanics to the colonies. These restrictions were further tightened after the American Revolution, with the period between the 1780s and 1824 the height of the British prohibition laws. Starting in the early 1780s, skilled artisans were prohibited from leaving British territories for work, and textile printers could not even leave the British Isles. Britain, which had jump-started its own textile industry by wooing Flemish weavers,

Huguenot silk workers, and other foreign artisans to England, was now determined not to let other countries do the same.[25] The penalties for lawbreakers were severe. Emigrants could lose both property and citizenship; recruiters could be fined £500 per worker enticed to leave and serve a twelve-month prison term. Shipmasters could be fined £100 for each passenger leaving Britain illegally. The smuggling of a machine brought a fine of £200 (£500 if involving textile machines), confiscation of equipment, and a one-year prison sentence.[26]

At least six British government departments took part in enforcing these prohibition laws.[27] Nevertheless, the controls proved difficult to implement. In the case of interdicting illicit machinery exports, port inspection facilities were typically lacking, large cargoes were difficult to sift through without causing long delays, and even when customs officials discovered machinery they did not always know how to identify what was banned. To further confuse inspectors, smugglers would mix up and combine parts of different machines, frustrating efforts to identify the equipment.[28]

Those who managed to smuggle equipment back to America were celebrated as heroes. For instance, after Joseph Hague traveled to England and illicitly brought back a cotton-carding machine to Philadelphia, the Pennsylvania Society for the Encouragement of Manufactures and the Useful Arts hailed his success in the press, announcing "that the ingenious artizan, who counterfeited the Carding and Spinning Machine, though not the original inventor (being only the introducer) is likely to receive a premium from the Manufacturing Society, besides a generous prize for his machines; and that it is highly probable our patriotic legislature will not let his merit pass unrewarded by them. Such liberality must have the happy effect of bringing into Philadelphia other useful artizans, Machines, and Manufacturing Secrets which will abundantly repay the little advance of the present moment."[29] Historian Doron Ben-Atar notes that when Philadelphia celebrated July 4, 1788, with a large parade, the Pennsylvania Society for the Promotion of Useful Knowledge sponsored a float that "featured workers operating a carding machine and a spinning machine—both of which had been smuggled by Joseph Hague."[30]

But there were built-in constraints to smuggling textile equipment. The machines were bulky, heavy, and cumbersome, making them especially hard to import illicitly. Loading heavy machinery required heavy-duty wharves—which also tended to be the most policed. Unlike other forms of smuggling, illicit traders could not circumvent inspections by using smaller and more remote docks.[31] An American industrial spy in Ireland wrote to George Washington in November 1791 about the difficulty of smuggling out the new Crompton mule machines:

> [They were] of such a size as not to be admissable in the hold of any common Ship, & are brought coverd upon the quarter deck, one on each side only; They might be got to America with a little address, & some risque both to the person shipping them & to the ship—The Vessell must be English & she cannot clear out direct for America, but may clear for Cork or the Isle of Man & so proceed on—They stop no sorts of Machinery coming from Manchester or Liverpool to this Country wch are not pattented or can be got from the Inventor. But they are so watchful in England as well as here for any going to America that upon the slightest suspicion they stop & search the Ship.[32]

But the most important limitation to smuggling machines was that they were useless without knowing how to assemble, use, and maintain them. After all, they did not come with operating instructions or user manuals.[33] In Philadelphia, a disassembled carding machine and three spinning machines illicitly imported from Britain shortly after American independence sat idle for more than three years. At first, no one could figure out how to even put the machines together; and once the machines were sold to someone who managed to assemble them, he still could not figure out how to get them to work. The machines were eventually bought by a patriotic Manchester cotton merchant, Thomas Edemsor, who then shipped them back to Britain in 1787—as he put it, "to Check the Advancement of the Cotton Manufactory in America."[34] This provoked such outrage in Philadelphia that Edemsor had to go into hiding and sought refuge in the office of Phineas Bond, the British consul.

Thus, even more important than the machines were the machinists from the British Isles who knew how to build and operate them. Thousands made the clandestine crossing to America, though we will never know exactly how many. And yet we do have one telling indicator. When war broke out between the United States and Britain in 1812, the U.S. State Department announced that all male "alien enemies" over the age of fourteen were required to register. Some ten thousand men and youths complied with the order. Of the seventy-five hundred whose occupations are identified, at least three thousand can be categorized as industrial workers. Therefore, from the British perspective they were illegally in the United States. One-seventh self-identified as engaged in manufacturing cloth, and they made up the single largest occupation group in Delaware, New Jersey, Rhode Island, and Pennsylvania.[35]

Despite strict prohibitions, British efforts to interdict the outflow of industrial workers had clearly failed; at best they slowed the flow. And the tremendous turmoil and conflicts in Europe between 1793 and 1815 only further fueled the exodus. It was simply too difficult for the authorities to weed out and differentiate skilled from unskilled emigrants on U.S.-bound ships. Checking passenger manifests was not enough, since travelers could lie about their occupational backgrounds, give false names, and avoid carrying incriminating evidence such as a bag of machine tools.[36] Other emigrants bypassed the departure checks entirely, going out in rowboats or small sailboats to board ships after they had cleared port. Complicit ship captains would hover close to shore to pick up the additional passengers. In one case, a mechanic put his wife aboard the ship in port and then "with much difficulty and hazard, and by the aid of respectable friends" met up with her shortly after the ship had set sail; but he had been "obliged to leave his tools behind him, lest his departure might have been prevented."[37] Samuel Paterson, a bookseller from Edinburgh, wrote to Hamilton in February 1791 advising that shippers be given extra compensation for smuggling artisans to counter British enforcement: "Penalties & Forfeitures, are so very heavy & so easily incurred, that No person Unacquainted with the Laws durst Venture upon Such a Measure. But the European Captain & owners know how to agree with Passengers so as to Escape the Penalties."[38]

The Englishman Henry Wansey, visiting the United States in 1794, observed the proliferation of British machines and workers to operate them. One New York factory he toured had "twelve or fourteen workmen from Manchester" who used "all the new improvements of Arkwright and others." These machines "were made on the spot from models brought from England and Scotland."[39]

To encourage the British brain drain, a handful of labor recruiters covertly operated in England in the late 1780s and early 1790s. Abel Buell—a Connecticut inventor, silversmith, and convicted counterfeiter—traveled to England on a recruiting mission. One of his recruits, William MacIntosh, an Essex Worsted manufacturer, set up shop in New Haven in 1791.[40] The American Thomas Digges was probably the most successful industrial spy and recruiter of skilled labor, and certainly the most controversial. Based in England during the Revolutionary War, he had organized the smuggling of munitions to the Continental Army. But he had also developed a shady reputation as a kleptomaniac and embezzler and was despised by Benjamin Franklin and distrusted by many others.[41] Fortunately for Digges, his old Virginia neighbor George Washington came to his defense and vouched for his character. "I have no hesitation in declaring," wrote the president in April 1794, "that the conduct of Mr. Thomas Digges . . . has not been only friendly, but I might add zealous." He added: "Since the War, abundant evidence might be adduced of his activity and zeal (with considerable risque) in sending artizans and machines of public utility to this Country."[42]

Even as America's first president praised Digges, the British denounced him as a spy and criminal and threw him in jail multiple times.[43] A British pamphlet aimed at discouraging emigration, published in the mid-1790s, railed against Digges and other recruiters as "agents hovering like birds of prey"; it singled out Digges as a "designing villain" and a "very dangerous character" who preyed upon the "credulity of his audience."[44]

The covert nature of the recruiting effort meant that one could not openly advertise in British newspapers and other outlets. As a substitute, in 1792 Digges printed up a thousand copies of Hamilton's *Report on Manufactures* in Dublin and distributed it as a recruitment tool in targeted manufacturing communities in England and Ireland. In April 1792 Digges wrote to Hamilton that he was confident the report would "induce artists to move toward a Country so likely to very soon give them ample employ & domestic ease."[45] Digges devoted much of his recruiting efforts to the manufacturing towns of Lancashire and Yorkshire. Here, he believed, "many are ready to move for America, but the difficultys of so doing are very great. By the laws of England they can stop an Artist from migration, & the smallest particle of machinery, tools &ca. will stop the Ship if informed against—the person attempting to inveigle away an artist is subject not only to a very rough treatment, but a fine of 500 £ & 12 months imprisonment."[46] Writing from Dublin, Digges reported to Thomas Jefferson that his recruiting of "useful mechanics" had caused him troubles, and that several of his new recruits were "under rigorous trial in the Courts here for attempting to ship themselves with their Tools implements &ca &ca."[47] Digges informed Jefferson that England was "making Laws and trying all possible means to stop the Emigration of Artists and their tools. I need to tell you," he said, "that it is not only difficult to get such away, but highly dangerous to those concerned; Therefore, the more secret it is kept the better."[48]

Digges claimed to have recruited, "by some art, and very little expense," between eighteen and twenty "valuable artists and machine makers" over a twelve-month period in 1791–92.[49] His most prized recruit was William Pearce, a mechanic from Yorkshire who claimed to have worked for Arkwright and Cartwright. Digges reported to Jefferson that "a box containing materials and specifications for a new Invented double Loom" was about to leave for America and that Pearce and two assistants would soon follow to reassemble the machines for production in the United States.[50] Pearce, whom Digges called "a second Archimedes," barely managed to evade the British authorities. According to Digges, "A Cuter pursued and search[ed] the Vessel twice for His double Loom and they would have brought him back had He not entered and given a different name—this was done in my sight and within a half hour after I had parted with him sailing out to Sea."[51] Pearce arrived in America with letters of introduction from Digges to key figures, including Washington, Jefferson, and Hamilton. Pearce was subsequently hired by the Hamilton-led company, the Society for the Establishment of Useful Manufactures. President Washington and his entourage visited Pearce's cotton manufactory in 1792. According to the local newspaper, the President "attentively viewed the Machinery, etc. and saw the business performed in its different branches—which received his warmest approbation."[52]

Not all recruits turned out so well, and indeed some proved to be better con artists than artisans. One immigrant pocketed a $10,000 advance and fled to Ireland.[53] One of Hamilton's correspondents sent a warning: "I repeat it, Sir, unless God should send us saints for Workmen and angels to conduct them, there is the greatest reason to fear for the success of the plan."[54] Part of the problem was the lack of documentation certifying the individual's skills and work experience. This reflected the clandestine nature of the transatlantic crossing: machine workers attempting to move to America purposefully destroyed such documentation prior to boarding U.S.-bound vessels to avoid being detained by British port inspectors. Consequently, as Jeremy notes, hiring was based on assurances rather than records.[55]

Meanwhile, many other skilled workers made the clandestine trip across the Atlantic without the prompting and assistance of a recruiter. The most celebrated self-smuggled British artisan was Samuel Slater, who started out as a teenage apprentice and then worked his way up to middle management at the Jedediah Strutt mills in Milford, England, which used Arkwright's new water frame. Enticed by stories of opportunity and success in America, the ambitious and risk-taking Slater pretended to be a farmhand or some other nonskilled laborer and boarded a U.S.-bound ship in 1789. Leaving tools, machines, models, and drawings behind, all he brought with him was his memory. Meanwhile, Moses Brown in Rhode Island was looking for someone to figure out how to use the spinning machines he had illicitly imported. Slater took on the job and moved to Pawtucket. Brown's smuggled machines proved inoperable, but Slater was able to cannibalize them for parts and built his own.[56] He had production up and running in Pawtucket by the winter of 1790–91.

Slater was certainly not the first to introduce the Arkwright-style water frame to America, but he was the first to turn it into a real commercial success, helping to spread the technology throughout the northeast.[57] Slater's brother, John, also later made the clandestine move across the Atlantic and brought with him the latest cotton technology.[58] Slater-style mills proliferated throughout Rhode Island and New England, becoming the most successful early model of family-owned

Figure 6.2 Samuel Slater (1768–1835), the "father of the American industrial revolution." Slater sneaked out of England in violation of strict emigration laws and was then hired by Moses Brown to work on and improve illicitly imported textile machinery in Pawtucket, Rhode Island (Granger Collection).

textile manufactures in America.[59] By 1813, the *Niles' Weekly Register* reported that Providence was at the center of a sprawling cotton mill production zone, with seventy-six cotton mills operating within a thirty-mile radius of the city.[60] New England cloth manufacturing boomed, increasing fiftyfold between 1805 and 1815.[61] This initial phase of illicit industrialization was a stunning success story for Rhode Island and the region.

Historians credit Slater as being the "father of the American industrial revolution." But Boston businessman Francis Cabot Lowell is credited with truly transforming New England textile manufacturing into a mass-production and internationally competitive factory system. Doing so involved pulling off the most remarkable case of industrial espionage in American history. Lowell traveled to Britain in 1810 for an extended stay, allegedly for "health reasons." The wealthy Boston merchant was not considered a rival manufacturer and therefore not treated with suspicion in local business circles. Lowell toured the Glasgow factories in the spring of 1811. Soon after, he visited other factories to obtain "all possible information" on cotton manufacturing "with a view to the introduction of the improved manufacture in the United States," as his business partner later recounted.[62]

Lowell's bags were searched before he returned to the United States, but the British customs agents came up empty-handed.[63] What they could not search was his memory. Lowell, who had majored in mathematics at Harvard and possessed an exceptional memory, used his mind to smuggle out British industrial secrets. In addition to memorization, Lowell also apparently obtained a sketch of Radcliffe and Johnson's patented dressing frame.[64]

With the assistance of mechanical expert Paul Moody, Lowell was able to not only reproduce the machines back home but even improve on the original models. Backed by his newly formed Boston Manufacturing Company (the first company in America to sell shares as a method of raising funds), Lowell opened his first cotton mill in Waltham, Massachusetts, in 1813. Lowell's was the first mill in the country to combine all aspects of the textile production process—from carding and spinning to weaving and dressing—in one building. This integrated cotton mill was a transformative development in the history of textile manufacturing, replacing the smaller Slater-style family-run mill operations and making the American textile industry truly competitive with Britain for the first time (though Lowell lobbied for and received a heavy protective tariff on cotton products in the Tariff of 1816). This early version of the American factory system of the nineteenth century also required much larger scale investment, epitomized by the development of an entire mill town, appropriately named Lowell in 1822.[65]

Britain loosened its restrictions in phases between 1824 and 1843. The emigration bans, which cut against growing public support for freedom of movement, were lifted in 1824. Though strict controls remained on the export of spinning and weaving machinery, a licensing system replaced the prohibition system for other industrial equipment. Licensing, in turn, created opportunities for new forms of smuggling: an exporter could receive a license to ship one machine and use it as a cover to ship a different one—gambling that port inspectors would either not check beyond the paperwork or not be able to tell the difference. Apparently, this practice was sufficiently institutionalized that illicit exporters could even take out insurance to protect them against the occasional seizure.[66] British export controls were finally repealed in 1843 with the spread of free-trade ideology. But by that time, the United States had already emerged as one of the leading industrial economies in the world—thanks, in no small part, to the successful evasion of British emigration and export prohibitions.

AMERICA'S EARLY ECONOMIC DEVELOPMENT strategy relied heavily on theft-aided industrialization. The nation's early industrial revolution was made possible by the illicit acquisition of machines and machinists. But as we'll see in the next chapter, the country's economic development also greatly depended on smuggling-enabled territorial expansion. Smuggling played a crucial—if often overlooked—role in the push across the continent, though the form, function, and content of the smuggling was entirely different from that in the industrialization story. We therefore now turn our attention westward and examine how the West was really won.

PART III

WESTWARD EXPANSION, SLAVERY, AND THE CIVIL WAR

7

Bootleggers and Fur Traders in Indian Country

CONTRARY TO THE IMPRESSION given in Hollywood movies, white populations pushed west into Indian country not simply through brute force. They also did it through trade, with smuggled alcohol exchanged for much-coveted Indian furs leading the way. In this sense, frontier smugglers were early pioneers, helping to lay the groundwork for westward expansion. Moreover, even as government authorities passed laws banning the sale of alcohol to Indians (an often forgotten early chapter in the history of American alcohol prohibition), they used copious amounts of rum and whiskey to lubricate Indian treaty negotiations. And the treaty terms, often involving generous land concessions and removal of tribes to more distant western territories, included dispensing millions of dollars in federal annuity payments—no small portion of which ended up in the pockets of whiskey peddlers. In other words, as part of the process of being displaced or wiped out, Indian populations were softened up by, and became dependent on, illicit supplies of "White Man's Wicked Water"—with devastating consequences.[1] We focused earlier on the illicit side of Atlantic trade during the colonial era and the first decades of the new republic; we now turn our attention to the illicit side of trade on the frontiers of continental expansion. But even here there is a transatlantic dimension, with most of the

Figure 7.1 "Manner of Instructing the Indians," frontispiece of William Appess, *Indian Nullification of the Unconstitutional Laws of Massachusetts Relative to the Marshpee Tribe; or, The Pretending Riot Explained*, Boston, 1835 (American Antiquarian Society).

Indian furs bought with smuggled alcohol exported to meet booming demand in European markets.

Rum and Fur in the Colonial Era

The first pioneers were fur traders, not settler farmers. Their wide-reaching economic exploits in North America stimulated imperial rivalry and territorial ambition.[2] The trade began early on in the colonial era and rapidly expanded in the first decades of the nineteenth century. The scramble for profitable pelts was inherently expansionist. Sea otters, beavers, raccoons, and buffalo were an exhaustible natural resource. Their depletion through intensive hunting pushed ambitious traders to venture into new lands, often trading alcohol for Indian pelts.[3] Indeed, rum was so dominant in the colonial fur trade that Iroquois called fur traders "rum carriers."[4]

But even though alcohol provided fuel for the fur trade, its negative repercussions inspired prohibitions dating back to the early colonial period.[5] We therefore need to briefly return to this earlier era as the starting point of our story. The settlers in the British colonies were exceptionally heavy drinkers by today's standards, with rum and its various concoctions the drink of choice. According to one estimate, by 1770 each colonist imbibed an average of three pints of alcohol per week—the equivalent of about seven shots per day.[6] Extending such heavy drinking to Native American communities with no previous exposure to alcohol had devastating consequences. It also greatly alarmed white colonists. "It was not the amount Indians drank that concerned colonists, it was the way they behaved when they drank," explains historian Peter Mancall.[7] "The most noteworthy aspect of Indian drinking styles, and the feature that most often caught the attention of colonial observers, was Indians' insistence on drinking to the point of intoxication."[8] Other alcohol researchers have pointed to the widespread Indian drinking pattern of "maximal dosing" that exhausts available alcohol supplies in the absence of social controls.[9]

Such bouts of binge drinking reinforced white stereotypes of Indians as out-of-control "savages," morally deficient, and racially inferior. It also ignited intense fear and anxiety. Terror-stricken by the specter of bands of inebriated natives running wild through white settlements, legislatures in almost all the American colonies at various points banned the selling of alcohol to Indians.[10]

British General Jeffrey Amherst also attempted to prohibit alcohol sales to Indians in the west during the Seven Years War and its aftermath. When Pontiac launched an unsuccessful attack on the British fort at Detroit in 1763, the commander of the British troops, Major Henry Gladwin, advised Amherst that the most effective reprisal would be to lift the alcohol ban: "[I]f yr. Excellency still intends to punish them further for their barbarities, it might easily be done without any expense to the Crown, by permitting a free sale of rum, which will destroy them more effectually than fire and sword."[11] Later, an English trader paid an Indian from the Peoria tribe a barrel of rum to kill Pontiac.[12]

Colonial efforts to restrict the Indian alcohol trade met stiff merchant resistance. In March 1764, seventy-two Albany fur traders sent a petition to the Lords of Trade in London requesting that they allow them to trade freely and to reject the prohibitionist pleas of Iroquois tribal leaders. They argued that "other Tribes with whom your Petitioners carry on a far more considerable Trade, look upon such a Prohibition as the greatest Indignity, and as an encroachment on their liberty to trade." They also warned that cutting off the alcohol supply would devastate the fur trade: "[W]hen the Indians have nothing farther to provide for than bare necessities, a very small quantity of Furs in Trade will abundantly supply that defect, Whereas when the Vent of Liquors is allow'd amongst them, it spurs them on to an unwaried application in hunting in order to supply the Trading Places with Furs and Skins in Exchange for Liquors."[13]

Some British officials were persuaded by such blunt economic arguments, well aware of the growing importance of the fur trade for imperial commercial interests in North America. Sir William Johnson, superintendent of Indian affairs, commented, "With regard to the sale of Rum . . . the [fur] Trade will never be so Extensive without it." Without the liquor trade, "the Indians can purchase their cloathing with half the quantity of Skins, which will make them Indolent, and lessen the furr Trade."[14] In 1770, Johnson reported that fur traders brought with them little else to trade other than alcohol "because the profits upon it are so considerable."[15]

Indian leaders, unable to curtail rampant alcohol abuse in their tribes, often made appeals to the colonists to cut the supply. As a Shawnee spokesman declared in July 1771, "It is You that make the Liquor, and to you we must look to Stop it."[16] Colonial authorities often replied that they could impose laws but do little to actually enforce them. As the governor of Pennsylvania told a group of Indians in 1722, "The sale of Rum shall be prohibited . . . , but the Woods are so thick & dark we cannot see what is done in them."[17] Presiding over negotiations between provincial officials and Iroquois leaders in Philadelphia in 1736, James Logan commented: "The Traders of all Nations find the Indians are so universally fond of Rum, that they will not deal without it." He added, "We have made many Laws against carrying it . . . but the Woods have no Streets like Philadelphia, the Paths in them are endless, & they cannot be stopt."[18]

Beyond sustaining the lucrative fur trade, rum also helped induce Indians to negotiate and sign treaties. In his *Autobiography*, Benjamin Franklin recounted how he and his fellow negotiators used rum as a diplomatic tool in Carlisle, Pennsylvania, in 1753, enticing Indians to sign a treaty by promising to reward them with plenty of rum at the conclusion of the talks.[19] Similarly, George Cadagan informed South

Carolina Governor James Glen in March 1751 that supplying rum was essential to getting Indians to the negotiating table, noting that it was "impossible for me or any other without Rum to be very useful on such Occasions."[20] So even as colonial authorities passed laws against the selling of alcohol to Indians, alcohol was also strategically used in negotiations with them.

"Rum was a potent ethnic cleanser," Ian Williams notes in tracing the history of rum in early America. "It was not just the effect of alcohol and binge drinking on the individuals, their families, and their societies that prepared for the spread of European settlement; by tying the Indians into the transatlantic trading system, rum helped transform and destroy their subsistence economies. It lubricated the move of the colonists westward and across the Appalachians."[21] Colonial leaders were well aware of the lethal effects of the illicit rum trade in Indian country, as evident in this startling passage from Benjamin Franklin's *Autobiography*: ". . . if it be the Design of Providence to extirpate these Savages in order to make room for Cultivators of the Earth, it seems not improbable that Rum may be the appointed means. It has already annihilated all the Tribes who formally inhabited the Sea-Coast."[22]

Whiskey and Westward Expansion in the Nineteenth Century

Rum was displaced by whiskey as the drink of choice in the aftermath of the American Revolution, a shift in drinking habits reinforced and accelerated by the logistical challenges of westward expansion. As historians Mark Edward Lender and James Kirby Martin point out, "Both molasses and finished rum were too bulky and expensive to ship far inland, and as the eighteenth-century settlement line advanced, frontiersmen shifted their loyalties to grain whiskeys. Indeed, whiskey was particularly suited to the frontier. Grain was plentiful . . . and a single bushel of surplus corn, for example, yielded three gallons of whiskey. This assured a plentiful liquor supply for Westerners and gave them a marketable commodity, which both kept longer and was easier to transport to market than grain."[23] As a commodity and form of currency, whiskey had ideal properties: it was high value relative to weight, non-perishable, and could be watered down for even greater profits. And last but not least, quick and addictive consumption created its own demand for more supply.

Just as authorities in the colonial era attempted to impose controls on the sale of alcohol to Indians, so too did the nascent federal government—with equally poor results. Beginning with the Trade and Intercourse Act of 1802, Congress authorized the president to restrict the "vending or distribution of spirituous liquors to Indians," and this was amended in 1822 to allow for greater search and confiscation of alcohol in Indian country.[24] The federal ban was further tightened in 1832 and 1834 and again in 1847.[25] Territorial laws restricting alcohol sales to Indians also proliferated in the first two decades of the nineteenth century, from Illinois and Michigan down to Louisiana and Mississippi.[26]

Alcohol policy was increasingly restrictive on paper, but enforcement was anemic and had little effect in curtailing supplies. Indeed, as historian William Unrau documents, "the more restrictive Indian prohibition became . . . the greater the amount of alcohol consumed by Indians."[27] Federal Indian agents were almost routinely reporting that "illicit alcohol was destroying the tribes more rapidly than gunpowder or the advance of white yeomen with the plow."[28] Not only was there limited capacity to police the alcohol trade in the country's vast and remote frontier regions, but there was also little political will to prioritize the problem, reflected in the minimalist fines and penalties imposed in cases where there were actual convictions. There was no broad societal outcry about the devastating impact of alcohol on Indian tribes; the nation's burgeoning temperance movement was primarily based in the East and urban in focus. Lethargic enforcement on the remote western frontier went largely unnoticed despite the occasional complaints by high-minded officials and calls on the part of missionaries for abstinence.

Illicit alcohol continued to be the most important lubricant for the Indian trade, and supplies grew rapidly in the first half of the nineteenth century as white traders and settlers extended their westward march. "The farther west the white man proceeded," notes Unrau, "the more alcohol figured as a necessary staple in both private and government relations with the Indians."[29] Even as alcohol smuggling violated federal law and frustrated what little enforcement existed, it ultimately contributed to the larger government objective of pacifying native populations and enlarging the area of white settlement. The alcohol trade prohibitions nevertheless allowed the government to formally express disapproval of the commerce while largely turning a blind eye to those who engaged in it—often including its own frontier agents. Indeed, there were reports of Indians purchasing alcohol at military outposts throughout the West.[30]

The intensely competitive nature of the fur trade created a powerful added incentive to sell alcohol in defiance of government laws. Traders used alcohol to gain the upper hand or at least keep up with competitors. Fur traders were especially reluctant to give up selling alcohol, given that there were no assurances competitors would do the same. This meant that regardless of its legal status alcohol was an "indispensable" trade item.[31] As Colonel J. Snelling, the commander at the Detroit garrison, wrote to the secretary of war in August 1825, "He who has the most whisky, generally carries off the most furs."[32] Similarly, a contemporary fur trader and liquor smuggler on the Upper Missouri wrote in his memoir, "It must be remembered that liquor, at that early day, was the principal and most profitable article of trade, although it was strictly prohibited by law."[33]

Fur traders relied on all sorts of creative evasive maneuvers to get around the alcohol ban. Superintendent of Indian Affairs Thomas L. McKenney reported in February 1826 that "the forbidden and destructive article is considered so essential to a lucrative commerce, as not only to still those feelings [of revulsion] but to lead the traders to brave the most imminent hazards, and evade, by various methods, the threatened penalties of the law."[34] Some smugglers transported flat kegs overland by pack mule rather than by boat to avoid river inspection stations. Others camouflaged their illicit liquid cargo within containers for licit goods, such as flour barrels, that would likely be overlooked by a superficial inspection. A favorite ploy was to obtain a license from the Indian Office for fur company boatmen to carry a daily supply of alcohol officially for their own personal use. This boatman allowance was easily abused and impossible to supervise. In a particularly blatant case in 1832, the fur trader William Sublette was granted a permit for 450 gallons of whiskey when in fact he traveled overland and his "boatmen" were entirely fictional. St. Louis Superintendent Lewis Clark reported to officials in Washington that the profits from illicit sales are so great that "very little of the liquor taken to the Indian country is actually used by the boatmen."[35]

The most glaring and exploited loophole in the federal prohibition was that the law did not technically cover selling alcohol to Indians in non–Indian designated country. Consequently, whiskey vendors would set up shop just outside of Indian lands. In an 1847 letter to the governors of Missouri, Arkansas, and Iowa, Secretary of War William L. Marcy asked for their help in dismantling the whiskey traffic: "The most stringent laws have been passed by Congress for this purpose, but as these are operative only in Indian country, they fail to reach the most prolific source of this great evil, which is within the limits of the States adjoining our Indian territory."[36] Indian Agent John Beach reported to his superiors in 1832 that along the Wisconsin-Iowa frontier "two-thirds of the frontier population was engaged in trading with the Indians with whiskey as the bait."[37] Another loophole was that the law technically covered only non-Indians selling alcohol to Indians, creating an opening and incentive for Indians to enter the illicit trade as middlemen. According to Unrau, "Indians selling to Indians was the most convenient and profitable way for non-Indian suppliers outside of Indian country to evade the law."[38]

The fur-for-alcohol trade created great fortunes, most famously that of John Jacob Astor, America's richest man at the time and now remembered as the country's first multimillionaire. Illicit alcohol, more than fur, was arguably the secret of Astor's extraordinary financial success. "It is fair to state," writes W.J. Rorabaugh, "that Astor's wealth came from selling liquor rather than from buying furs, a fact that may explain why later, with a touch of conscience perhaps, he gave money to the temperance movement."[39] Alcohol was fantastically profitable for Astor's American Fur Company, which he ran until 1834. For instance, in 1817 and 1818 the company "sold the Indians at Mackinaw 'whiskey' made of 2 gallons of spirits, 30 gallons of water, some red pepper, and tobacco." This concoction sold for fifty cents a bottle but cost only five cents a gallon to produce.[40]

The American Fur Company, established with the approval of Thomas Jefferson in 1808, soon had a near monopoly over the fur trade through its subsidiaries across the country, starting in the Great Lakes

Figure 7.2 John Jacob Astor (1763–1848), America's most famous fur trader and first multimillionaire. Nineteenth-century wood engraving depicts Astor's first fur-buying expedition up the Hudson Valley, ca. 1787 (Granger Collection).

region and the Midwest and then expanding to the Great Plains and the Rocky Mountains. In the process, the company played a lead role in developing and settling the vast western frontier, including the outposts of St. Paul, Detroit,[41] Milwaukee, and Chicago,[42] and building up key transportation routes such as the Missouri River and the Santa Fe Trail. At its height, the company controlled three-quarters of the U.S. fur trade.

Astor and his company strenuously opposed a total alcohol ban, arguing that this put the company at a competitive disadvantage relative to the Hudson Bay Company and other British traders across the northern border who were not similarly constrained.[43] Moreover, Astor complained that the British traders had the additional advantage of cheaper access to legal goods, such as blankets, used in the Indian trade. He wrote to Senator Thomas Hart Benton in January 1829 that "It is known that none of the woolen goods fit for the Indian trade . . . are as yet manufactured in this country. We are therefore obliged to import them from England, and it so happens that those are just the articles paying the heaviest duty. The English [fur] traders have theirs free of duty, which enables them to bring their goods 60 percent and over cheaper than what we pay and they are thereby enabled to undersell us."[44] What Astor didn't mention is that this disadvantage made his company especially dependent on illicit alcohol as a trade item to stay competitive in the international fur business.

The American Fur Company was both creative and brazen in subverting the federal alcohol prohibition.[45] In October 1831 Andrew Hughes wrote from St. Louis to Lewis Cass, the secretary of war: "The traders that occupy the largest and most important space in the Indian country are the agents and engages of the American Fur Trade Company. They entertain, as I know to be the fact, no sort of respect for our citizens, agents, officers or the Government, or its laws or general policy."[46] For example, Kenneth McKenzie, nicknamed the "King of the Missouri" for his exploits as the company's agent in the Upper Missouri River frontier, set up a crude whiskey distillery at Fort Union in 1833, a major trading post in present-day North Dakota. McKenzie's rationalization was that the law applied only to *introducing* whiskey, not to *making* it. In a boastful letter to a company associate, McKenzie wrote: "For this post I have established a manufactory of strong water, it succeeds admirably. . . . I believe no law of the U.S. is hereby broken though perhaps one may be made to break up my distillery but liquor I must have or quit any pretension to trade at this post, especially while our opponents can get any quantity passed up the Mo or introduce it as they have done by another route."[47] In time, the government found out about the distillery—probably through informants from rival companies—and shut it down.[48]

The company's bootlegging business nevertheless continued to thrive: "Although the still house had been destroyed," wrote a contemporary fur trader, "the Company found means to smuggle plenty of liquor."[49] In 1842 the company even used its political connections to have a former employee, Andrew Drips, appointed to the post of special agent in the Indian service in 1842. Historian Jeanne Leader writes that "as a special agent in the Indian service he notified company men of impending inspections and advised them as to the best techniques for destroying or concealing whiskey. . . . When the office of Indian affairs dismissed Drips in 1846, the American Fur Company immediately welcomed him back into their ranks."[50]

After years of mounting evidence of the company's alcohol smuggling activities, the government finally brought it to trial in 1846. The suit called for a $25,000 fine as well as the recovery of a minimum of forty-three hundred gallons of alcohol illegally brought into Indian country. But the company's obstructionist tactics, including bribing and disappearance of key witnesses, repeatedly bogged down proceedings. After several years of delays and a greatly weakened case, the government settled the suit for $5,000. After the company's license for the upper Missouri Indian trade was renewed, one of its first cargoes into Indian country in the spring of 1849 included a shipment of sixty gallons of pure alcohol—officially approved for the purposes of combating cholera.[51]

Even as the fur trade began to decline in the 1840s, whiskey smuggling continued to grow as westward expansion accelerated. This was made possible by the provision of millions of dollars in federal funds to Indian tribes in exchange for land concessions.[52] Federally allocated annuity funds increasingly replaced furs as the means for Indians to purchase illicit alcohol. The federal government's annuity payment system, in other words, ended up as a subsidy to an alcohol trade based on violating federal law. And this, in turn, further weakened Indian communities while stimulating non-Indian population growth and economic development of the western frontier. The annuity payments were meant to pacify. As Senator John C. Calhoun noted in 1836, as long as Indians were paid annuities, it "made it their interest to keep at peace."[53] But the side effect was to also fuel the illicit alcohol trade.

This dynamic did not go unnoticed, and indeed it was applauded in some quarters. When the Iowas and Kickapoos obtained a substantial supply of whiskey at St. Joseph, Missouri, after receiving their annuity payments in 1854, a St. Louis newspaper praised the exchange as "the cheapest way of exterminating them."[54] "A few years ago," reported a local newspaper in 1858, "the Iowas numbered 15,000 souls; now they scarcely exceed 400—and not the least among the causes is the facility with which they get whiskey."[55]

Meanwhile, even as the government formally banned alcohol sales to Indians, government agents continued the old practice of dispensing alcohol as a diplomatic tool in Indian treaty negotiations. For example,

Michigan territory Governor Lewis Cass (who went on to become secretary of war) was one of the government commissioners at the 1825 treaty at Prairie du Chien, where whiskey was given to the Chippewas. In 1827 he exclaimed: "Every practicable method has been adopted by the government of the United States, effectually to prevent this [liquor] traffic."[56] Yet Cass had previously provided more than six hundred gallons of whiskey for the Saginaw Chippewa treaty of 1819 and in excess of nine hundred gallons of whiskey for the Ottawa, Chippewa, and Potawatomi treaty of 1821.[57]

Echoing their colonial-era predecessors, some Indian leaders made impassioned pleas to the federal government to stem the tide of alcohol. A leader of the Miamis, Little Turtle, said to President Jefferson in 1802, "When our white brothers came to this land, our forefathers were numerous and happy; but since their intercourse with the white people, and owing to the introduction of this fatal poison [alcohol], we have become less numerous and happy."[58] "We are afraid of the wicked water brought to us by our white friends," a Kickapoo tribal spokesman told U.S. Commissioner E. A. Ellsworth in 1832. "We wish to get out of its reach by land or water." Ellsworth responded with promises to put a stop to it.[59]

Government authorities also used such concerns about alcohol as a convenient rationale to push for Indian removal to more distant lands. In its efforts to negotiate a removal treaty, an executive commission warned the Miamis: "If you continue here where you now are . . . and let the white people feed you whiskey and bring among you bad habits, in a little while where will be the Miami Nation? They will all be swept off." But the commission also suggested an alternative: "Situated as you are, your Great Father cannot prevent his white people from coming among you. He wants to place you in a land where he can take care of you [and] protect you against all your enemies, whether red men or white."[60] Conveniently left unstated was that alcohol smugglers moved west along with the Indians being pushed west, and that the government had little will or capacity to stop them. From 1825 to 1847, the federal government relocated some seventy thousand Indians to Indian country west of Missouri and Arkansas. Soon, the new "boundary of Indian country became literally inundated with whiskey dispensed by prominent merchants and small-time hucksters whose principal customers were Indians."[61] And flush with annuity payments from the federal government, Indians could now pay with cash, not just furs. In 1842, Superintendent Mitchell wrote to his superiors in Washington that "whenever money is around it soon finds its way into the hands of the whiskey dealers who swarm like birds of evil omen around the place where annuities are paid."[62] He also reported that hundreds of Indians had died of alcohol in the previous two years alone.

Missouri grain and distilleries kept the lower Kansas and Platte valleys and the Sioux country to the northwest well supplied with alcohol. There were a dozen distilleries based in the St. Louis area by 1810, with production rising sharply by the 1830s. One need only look at prices to understand the incentive to smuggle into nearby Indian country: in the early 1830s, a twenty-five-cent gallon of whiskey in St. Louis was worth thirty-four dollars at Fort Leavenworth, and as much as sixty-four dollars at the intersection of the Missouri and Yellowstone rivers. Bellevue, on the west bank of the Missouri River in present-day Iowa, served as both a bustling fur trade center and a distribution hub for alcohol brought in by steamers from St. Louis distilleries, earning it the title of the "whiskey capital" of Indian country.[63]

The illicit alcohol trade, coupled with the lethargic enforcement of the federal ban, left a powerful impression on foreign travelers. Charles Dickens noted in 1842 that the alcohol ban was "quite inefficacious, for the Indians never fail to procure liquor of a worse kind, at a dearer price, from traveling peddlers."[64] Another Englishman, George Frederick Ruxton, observed, "The misery entailed upon these unhappy people by the illicit traffic must be seen to be fully appreciated. . . .With such palpable effects, it appears only likely that the illegal trade is connived at by those whose policy it has ever been, gradually, but surely, to exterminate the Indians, and by any means to extinguish their title to the few lands they now own."[65] One British visitor to Kansas in 1855, traveling with a wagon train that was also transporting several dozen barrels of alcohol for the Indian trade, was especially struck by the openness of the illicit business:

> It seems almost impossible that a blind man, retaining the senses of smell, taste and hearing, could remain ignorant of a thing so

> palpably plain. The alcohol is put into wagons, at Westport or Independence, in *open day-light*, and taken into the territory, *in open daylight*, where it remains a week or more awaiting the arrival of its owners. Two Government agents reside at Westport, while six or eight companies of Dragoons are stationed at Fort Leavenworth, ostensibly for the purpose of protecting Indians and suppressing this infamous traffic,—and yet it suffers no diminution from *their vigilance!* What *faithful* public officers! How prompt in the discharge of their *whole duty*! . . . These gentlemen cannot plead ignorance as an excuse. They well know that alcohol is one of the principal articles in Indian trade—this fact is notorious—no one pretends to deny it; not even the *traders themselves*.[66]

Given the context of a federal prohibition on alcohol sales to Indians, European visitors were also taken aback by the common practice of government officials providing alcohol to Indian leaders while negotiating treaties. The English traveler Charles Latrobe was startled to find that whisky was available at official negotiations, and he lamented that this tarnished the government's image and the legitimacy of the treaties:

> However anxious I and others might be to exculpate the United States Government from the charge of cold and selfish policy toward the remnants of the Indian tribes, and from that of resorting to unworthy and diabolical means in attaining possession of their lands,—as long as it can be said with truth, that the drunkenness was not guarded against, and that the means were furnished at the very time of the Treaty, and under the very nose of the Commissioners—how can it be expected but a stigma will attend every transaction of this kind. . . . Who will believe that any act, however formally executed by the chiefs, is valid, as long as it is known that whiskey was one of the parties to the Treaty.[67]

ILLICIT ALCOHOL WAS ONLY one ingredient that fueled the motor of westward expansion. It played multiple roles in Indian relations: as a form of currency, high-value commodity, diplomatic tool in securing land concessions, and health hazard and community destabilizer.

Its potent effects should not be overstated or oversimplified, but they are an important and often untold part the story of America's territorial enlargement. Commerce soaked in illicit alcohol went hand in hand with blood-soaked conquest, weakening native populations while enriching bootleggers and fur traders. But booze was not the only illicit trade that facilitated territorial expansion; as we will see next, the illicit trade in human cargo also played a crucial role.

8

Illicit Slavers and the Perpetuation of the Slave Trade

ADAM SMITH LONG AGO noted that of all things that cross borders, people are the most cumbersome and difficult to transport. This is especially true of smuggled people, and even more so if done forcibly. Nevertheless, this did not impede the mass trafficking of African slaves to the Americas in the nineteenth century in defiance of prohibitions and policing campaigns. Our smuggling story therefore continues, but in this case what is being illicitly procured, transported, and sold is a shackled human being. In the face of a British-led international suppression effort, the African slave trade morphed into a vast transatlantic criminal enterprise. It was enabled by American merchant complicity—in violation of U.S. antislave-trade laws—and fueled by growing demand for slave labor in new world plantations economies, especially Cuba and Brazil. Only the abolition of slavery itself finally closed the darkest chapter of illicit trade in American history.

The United States was both an illicit import market for African slaves and a leading player in the trafficking of slaves to foreign ports. The smuggling of slaves into the United States was especially prevalent up to the 1820s. Illicit slavers brought their human cargoes through the porous southern borderlands to feed the rising demand for plantation workers in Louisiana and other frontier regions. These importations supplemented natural reproduction within the domestic slave population.[1]

More economically and demographically consequential was America's role in the carrying trade to foreign ports such as Havana and Rio, which was especially significant after the 1830s. So even as imports into the United States declined sharply after an initial flurry of smuggling, American involvement in clandestinely transporting slaves to foreign ports greatly expanded. Indeed, in this particular illicit trade America shaped the trade as much as the trade shaped America. American complicity in illicit slave trafficking helped to perpetuate the institution of slavery, enriched slave traders, caused enormous human suffering, and revealed the hypocrisy of American rhetoric about freedom.

In this chapter we examine the dynamics of slave trafficking, its links to territorial expansion, and the nature and extent of American collusion. We also briefly look at reverse slave smuggling—the self-smuggling of fugitive slaves to northern states and to Canada and Mexico—and how the increasingly politicized fugitive slave issue not only strained relations with immediate neighbors but greatly amplified sectional divisions, fueling calls for abolition and stoking the flames of the secessionist movement.

Criminalizing and Policing the Foreign Slave Trade

The year 1808 is typically marked as the starting date of the federal prohibition on American involvement in the international slave trade. But this historic date was actually the culmination of a series of state and federal efforts to restrict U.S. participation in slave trafficking that began years earlier.[2] Indeed, all states had imposed prohibitions on slave imports by 1798, and only South Carolina defected by reopening the trade from 1803 to 1808. In 1794 the first federal antislave-trade law made it illegal for Americans to participate in the trafficking of slaves to non-American ports, and in 1800 Congress expanded the ban to include the actions of investing in foreign slaving voyages and serving as a crewmember on a foreign slave ship. Penalties included steep fines, forfeiture of vessels, and imprisonment. Moreover, in 1803 Congress took its first action to restrict the importation of slaves, outlawing bringing "any negro, mulatto, or other person of colour" into a state that had banned such entry.[3] The 1808 federal law imposed a total ban on American participation in the foreign slave trade. And in

1820 Congress passed the toughest antislave-trade law of any nation by classifying slave trading as the equivalent of piracy and punishable by death.

Although actual enforcement of these laws was another matter entirely, the act of a major slave-holding country criminalizing the slave trade begs for some explanation. The ban did not simply reflect humanitarian concern and abolitionist sentiment. Far from it. Fear and economic self-interest explains why southern slaveholding states were often the most vigorous promoters of antislave-trade legislation. The Haitian Revolution sent shock waves through American slaveholding communities, intensifying southern fears and anxieties that a further influx of African slaves and shift in the balance between white and black populations could provoke violent revolts. Established slaveholders also supported a ban on slave imports to prop up the market value of the slaves they already owned. In other words, the ban functioned as a de facto price support and form of protectionism for a thriving domestic slave market, much of it based on moving slaves from eastern seaboard states such as Virginia and North Carolina to the expanding plantations of the Deep South. Meanwhile, northern abolitionists enthusiastically lobbied for the end of the foreign slave trade even while realizing they were still too weak to make much headway in eliminating the institution of slavery. From their perspective, ending the slave trade was an important first step toward their ultimate goal of ending slavery itself. Support for criminalizing the foreign slave trade thus made for some strange bedfellows, to say the least.

However tortured the logic, American politicians were careful to distinguish between the evils of the foreign slave trade and the legitimacy of domestic slavery, arguing for suppression of the former while reaffirming support for the later. Despite all the lofty talk of liberty and freedom during America's founding, in this case property rights—specifically the right to own slaves—clearly trumped.

Moreover, even though some of the country's founders expected and hoped that slavery would simply wither away and die out on its own, the use of slave labor not only endured but became more economically entrenched. To a far greater extent than anyone could have imagined just a few decades earlier, the slave-based plantation economy was booming in the early nineteenth century, thanks to the invention of the cotton gin in 1793 and the rapid spread of cotton cultivation in the South.[4] North and South became more economically interdependent even while more politically divided: as northern entrepreneurs smuggled in British technologies and illicitly imported skilled British workers to set up the New England cotton mills that sparked the American industrial revolution, slave-based southern cotton plantations expanded to supply them. Northern shipbuilders and shipping companies similarly profited by keeping English textile factories supplied with southern cotton. In just a few decades, cotton became the country's leading export by a considerable margin. Cotton production skyrocketed from 3,000 bales in 1790 to 178,000 in 1810, and it reached 732,000 bales in 1830.[5] By 1850 cotton comprised two-thirds of American exports. New York's rapid rise as a leading commercial center owed much of its success to the cotton trade—so much so that the city's mayor, Fernando Wood, even proposed seceding from the Union.[6]

America's antislave-trade laws coincided with Britain's turn away from the slave trade early in the nineteenth century. But here the similarities ended. The United States lacked both the will and capacity to vigorously enforce its prohibitions, but Britain unleashed the Royal Navy to police slave ships on the high seas between West Africa and the slave markets in the Americas. The contrast between Washington's lethargic approach to enforcement and London's aggressive stance became a chronic diplomatic irritant, with frustrated British officials bitterly complaining that the United States was doing more to help than hinder slave trafficking. At the same time, American politicians and merchants alike greatly resented Britain's self-appointment as policeman of the high seas.

Anglophobia long outlasted the War of 1812 and crippled cooperation in suppressing the slave trade. For instance, the U.S. Navy's "Africa squadron" was deployed to patrol Africa's west coast in 1843, but its priority mission was protecting U.S. commercial vessels from the British rather than policing slavers.[7] The squadron, initially consisting of four vessels totaling eighty-four guns, failed to intercept a single slaver in its first two years of operation, and its crews seemed to spend as much time vacationing on Madeira Island as patrolling the far less hospitable African coast. Yet by deploying the squadron and going through the motions of carrying out patrols, Washington met the bare minimum obligations stipulated in the 1842 Webster-Ashburn treaty with Britain.[8]

In 1850 the navy reported that seven slave ships had been captured by the squadron in its first seven years. The British Navy, in contrast, made more than five hundred captures during the same period.[9]

Most importantly, it was not until June 1862—after the American Civil War had already begun—that the United States finally agreed to a right of mutual search with Britain.[10] American sensitivities about boarding parties (especially British) dated back to the battles over neutral shipping in the late eighteenth century. When the British foreign secretary asked U.S. Secretary of State John Quincy Adams if there was a greater evil than the slave trade, Adams responded, "Yes, admitting the right of search by foreign officers of our vessels upon the sea in time of peace, for that would be making slaves of ourselves."[11]

Decades of Washington's resistance to British wishes to search U.S.-flagged ships made the stars and stripes the favored flag of illicit slavers. The American flag became an especially favored shield for slave ships once other maritime powers, such as Spain and Portugal, caved in to British pressure to allow searches of their vessels. Consequently, as other nations became increasingly cooperative—even if not always willingly—in fighting the slave trade under British leadership, the United States continued to insist on going it alone. Traditional American anglophobia played right into the hands of slave traffickers. The Royal Navy's inability to search American flagged vessels, regardless of whether they were actually American, until near the end of the transatlantic slave trade was the Achilles' heel of its antislaving campaign.

On the rare occasion when an American-flagged slave ship was seized by a U.S. patrol, U.S. courts typically either failed to convict or handed out light sentences.[12] The burden of proof was so stringent and the loopholes so great that slavers had little to fear from the legal system.[13] For instance, even though certain types of supplies were a sure sign of intent to traffic in slaves, American courts were far less willing than the courts of other nations to consider this as evidence of a slaving voyage.[14] Quite a few convicted slave traffickers received a presidential pardon after serving only a portion of their sentence, and President James Buchanan even publicly vowed that he would refuse to ever allow a slaver to be hanged.[15] To make matters worse, slavers could sue naval officers for damages, which predictably had a chilling effect on enforcement.[16]

On February 21, 1862, Nathaniel "Nat" Gordon was the first and only American ever hanged for illicit slave trading—more than four decades after the passage of the federal law making slave trafficking the equivalent of piracy and punishable by death. Gordon's sentence generated much interest not only because of its severity but also because it was so unprecedented. It was a powerful political statement as well for the new administration of Abraham Lincoln.[17] Just a few years earlier, another slave trafficker, Captain James Smith, had been found guilty, only to be pardoned by President James Buchanan.[18] But with the outbreak of the Civil War the political climate radically changed. Lincoln rejected multiple pleas for leniency in the case, including a petition for mercy signed by eleven thousand New Yorkers.[19]

So even though on paper America's antislave-trade prohibitions certainly had plenty of teeth, there was no real bite until near the end of the transatlantic slave trade. In practice, Washington's approach to suppressing slave trafficking was defined more by negligence and

Figure 8.1 "Hanging Captain Gordon." *Harper's Weekly*, March 8, 1862. Nathaniel Gordon was the first and only American slave trader executed for violating the federal crime of slave trafficking (John Hay Library, Brown University).

apathy than by committed and sustained policing. Enforcement was woefully inadequate, but criminalizing the slave trade nevertheless mattered. It pushed the trade more out of sight, and therefore more out of the public mind. It signaled the government's disapproval of the trade without requiring a substantial commitment of federal resources or undermining of its support for domestic slavery. It added to the growing social stigma associated with international slave trafficking. And it created an enormously lucrative opportunity for illicit slavers and their accomplices.

American Collusion in the Carrying Trade

The American government's policing of the foreign slave trade was anemic, erratic, and ambivalent; the country's illicit commercial involvement in the trade was anything but. This was especially true of northern seaports. Indeed, the United States went from being a secondary player in the international slave trade when it was legal to the leading player in the trade after it was prohibited. Criminalization ended up giving America a competitive advantage in the foreign slave trade, capturing market share as other nations grew susceptible to ever more intensive British pressure to curb their involvement.

American slave traders openly flouted the first state and federal prohibitions, considering them little more than a nuisance. Nowhere was this more apparent than in tiny Rhode Island, the first state to ban the slave trade but also the most commercially involved. In October 1787, Rhode Island abolitionists, led by Moses Brown in Providence, successfully pushed through a bill making it illegal for any citizen of the state to "directly or indirectly import or transport, buy or sell, or receive on board their vessel . . . any of the natives or inhabitants of any state or kingdom in that part of the world called Africa, as slaves or without their voluntary consent."[20] The abolitionist minister Samuel Hopkins wrote with pride the next month: "Is it not extraordinary, that this State, which has exceeded the rest of the States in carrying on this trade, should be the first Legislature on this globe which has prohibited that trade? Let them have the praise of this."[21] Moses Brown and his fellow abolitionists were also instrumental in pushing through the first federal antislave-trade law in 1794, prohibiting "the carrying on the slave trade from the United States to any foreign place or country."[22] The law established penalties for violators, including forfeiture of ships and steep fines.

Rhode Island slave traffickers, meanwhile, went about their business as usual. In fact, the number of ships setting sail from Rhode Island to the African coast substantially increased in the mid-1790s.[23] In Providence, John Brown not only invested in illicit slaving voyages but was the most outspoken critic of the state and federal antislave-trade laws that his abolitionist brother, Moses, passionately lobbied for. He defiantly exclaimed, "in my opinion there is no more crime in bringing off a cargo of slaves than in bringing off a cargo of jackasses."[24] He also told Congress that restricting American participation in the international slave trade unfairly placed the country's merchants at a competitive disadvantage. U.S. citizens, he argued, had as much a right as anyone to the "benefits of the trade," and banning U.S. ships would do nothing to impede the trade: "We might as well therefore enjoy that trade as leave it wholly to others."[25]

In August 1797, John Brown was the first person convicted for violating the new federal antislave-trade law, receiving the relatively mild punishment of forfeiting his ship, the *Hope* (a separate trial in 1798 failed to convict him on offenses that would have also imposed substantial financial penalties). Forfeiture was a small price to pay and well worth the risk relative to expected profit, given that the value of the ship paled in comparison to the profits from the shipload of slaves John Brown had already successfully delivered abroad.[26] Moreover, even though federal forfeitures were standard practice in Rhode Island convictions, it was also standard practice for owners to simply purchase back their vessels at a deeply discounted price through rigged public auctions. Competing bids were locally frowned on, ensuring a low price—sometimes as little as ten dollars—for the original owner. Court costs for the government, meanwhile, were nearly one hundred dollars.[27]

To counter this common ploy, William Ellery, the Newport customs collector, sent Samuel Bosworth, the Bristol surveyor, to participate in bidding for a seized ship, the *Lucy*, at a Bristol auction in July 1799. Well aware of the local hostility this would generate, Bosworth accepted the task "with considerable fear and trembling."[28] The night before the scheduled auction, John Brown and the local owner of the

Lucy paid Bosworth a visit at his home. They cautioned that it would be unwise and inappropriate for him to carry out his assigned task. He received another visit and warning the next morning. Undeterred, Bosworth headed out to the auction but was kidnapped en route and dumped two miles out of town. The *Lucy* was auctioned off as scheduled, sold to a Cuban captain who worked for the ship's original owner.[29] The federal ban was clearly proving to be ineffective. In fact, the number of Africa-bound ships from Rhode Island reportedly tripled between 1798 and 1799, increasing from twelve to thirty-eight clearances.[30]

Though slave trading was never more than a side business for John Brown, it was the core business for the DeWolf family in Bristol. The DeWolfs were allegedly the country's leading participants in the foreign slave trade from the late colonial years to around 1820. Their ability to continue in the international flesh trade long after it had been outlawed was made possible by the complicity of the local customs inspector, Charles Collins, appointed in 1804 by Thomas Jefferson despite having served as a captain on DeWolf slaving ships. The DeWolfs and their political allies had successfully petitioned Jefferson to fire the previous inspector, Jonathan Russell. Russell bitterly complained to Treasury Secretary Albert Gallatin that whereas he did not object to his own removal, he considered Collins to be a criminally inappropriate replacement given his involvement in "numerous and notorious" evasions of the law. Indeed, at the same time as Collins was being appointed customs collector he was also informed that his slave ship had successfully delivered its human cargo in the West Indies.[31]

The very creation of a separate Bristol customs district came about through John Brown's political maneuverings during his stint in Congress, allowing the DeWolfs to circumvent stricter enforcement of the Newport customs collector, Ellery.[32] Collins, who was also the brother-in-law of the slave trafficker James DeWolf, stayed on as the Bristol collector for nearly two decades. During this time, Bristol slave traders enjoyed de facto legal immunity. Africa-bound departures soared.[33] Critics were intimidated and informants silenced. When a local abolitionist dared to push for the prosecution of a slave ship, he was attacked in his sleep and had an ear sliced off.[34] Although Jefferson may very well have simply been duped into firing Russell and appointing

Figure 8.2 James DeWolf (1764–1837) of Bristol, Rhode Island. DeWolf may have been America's richest slave trader, flagrantly violating state and federal antislave-trade laws (New York Public Library, Astor, Lenox and Tilden Foundations).

Collins as the Bristol collector, he took no action when later informed of the criminal consequences.[35] Collins remained collector until 1820, when President James Monroe declined to reappoint him—bringing to an end the heyday of Bristol slave trading.

Officially retired from slave trading, James DeWolf went on to be elected to Congress, providing political ammunition for South Carolina Senator William Smith in his 1820 speech denouncing Northern hypocrisy. "The people of Rhode Island have lately shown bitterness against slaveholders, and especially against the admission of Missouri," Smith stated. "This, however, cannot, I believe, be the temper or opinion of the majority, from the late election of James DeWolf as a member of this house, as he has accumulated an immense fortune in the slave trade."[36] Smith also submitted documents from the Charleston customs house showing that of the twelve thousand slaves imported on American vessels between 1804 and 1808, almost two-thirds were brought in on Rhode Island ships.[37]

Other eastern seaports also became enmeshed in the foreign slave trade, especially in later years. New York City came to be known as the world's leading center for financing, organizing, and outfitting slaving voyages in the 1850s and early 1860s. The combination of having one of the busiest seaports in the world and a tolerant legal climate made New York an excellent cover and hub for illicit slavers. When New York Senator William Seward met opposition from New York businessmen after he proposed new legislation in 1858 to curb the slave trade, he bluntly responded: "The root of the evil is in the great commercial cities and I frankly admit, in the City of New York. I say also that the objection I found to the bill, came not so much from the slave States as from the commercial interests in New York."[38]

That same year, the *Times* of London described New York as "the greatest slave-trading mart in the world."[39] In 1857 the *New York Journal of Commerce* editorialized, "Few of our readers are aware . . . of the extent to which this infernal traffic is carried on, by vessels clearing from New York, and in close allegiance with our legitimate trade; and that down-town merchants of wealth and respectability are extensively engaged in buying and selling African negroes, and have been, with comparative little interruption, for an indefinite number of years."[40] The *New York Evening Post* even published a list of eighty-five vessels outfitted in New York Harbor from early 1859 to mid-1860 engaged in the international slave trade.[41] Cuba provided the main market. Perhaps up to 170 Cuba-bound slave voyages were organized in New York in 1859–1861; British authorities estimated that almost eighty thousand slaves were brought in during this period, with each slave selling for $1,000.[42] In 1863, the U.S. consul in Havana, Robert Shufeldt, reported: "However humiliating may be the confession . . . nine tenths of the vessels engaged in the slave trade are American."[43]

Sympathetic judges made it next to impossible to vigorously prosecute illicit slavers in the courts of the Southern New York district.[44] And those charged with violating the U.S. antislave-trade laws had access to the best legal counsel available in the city, including Beebe, Dean & Donahue, top admiralty lawyers located at 76 Wall Street.[45] Of the cases that went to court, few ended with convictions, let alone serious penalties.[46] One federal judge in New York, Samuel Betts, once even released a slave ship captain on bail so he could travel to Brazil to obtain evidence for his defense. The captain never returned and allegedly bragged, "You don't have to worry about facing trial in New York City. . . . I can get any man off in New York for $1,000."[47]

New York specialized in outfitting slave ships. Other eastern ports built them, including Baltimore, Boston, Beverly, Portland, Providence, and Salem. Baltimore shipbuilding firms such as those owned by Samuel and John Smith, William van Wyck, John Hollins, and Stewart and Plunkett had long supplied vessels for the slave trade, and they continued to do so after the federal prohibitions.[48] Baltimore shipbuilders, famous for their fast clippers, became especially favored suppliers for slave traders as British naval patrols stepped up their enforcement in the 1830s.[49] As historian Warren Howard explains: "The trim Baltimore clippers, which had become a specialty of the city's shipbuilders, made very handy slavers. They were fast enough to outrun ordinary British cruisers. . . . Spanish and Brazilian slave traders paid good prices for Baltimore clippers, and some of the city's businessmen took advantage of this market."[50] Howard notes that the "get-rich-quick schemes" of the Baltimore ship sellers produced a "mild boom in Baltimore shipyards" in 1838.[51]

The American flag became even more important to the slave trade than American-built and American-outfitted ships. By the 1830s the United States was one of the last remaining maritime powers unwilling to grant Britain the right to search suspected slave ships sailing under its flag. Consequently, the Stars and Stripes became the flag of choice not only for American slave traffickers but for traffickers of all nationalities trying to keep British patrols at bay. In 1844, George Proffitt, the U.S. minister in Rio, conceded that the slave trade was "almost entirely carried out under our flag, in American-built vessels."[52] But American-flagged did not necessarily mean American-owned, even if the ship was American-built and Americans were among the officers and crew.[53] A U.S. citizen was often designated to play the role of "flag captain" on a slave ship as added insurance against capture.[54] But only American-built ships could receive U.S. registers, which added further incentive for traffickers to favor U.S.-made vessels.[55]

Unable to legally board and search even the most blatant slave traders flying the American flag, in June 1839 a British naval patrol created quite a stir by escorting American-flagged slaving ships from the African coast to New York Harbor and handing them over to local authorities to prosecute.[56] The Royal Navy also sometimes boarded and searched American-flagged ships without permission, much to the irritation of Washington. In 1850, in response to a request from Congress to produce a report on illegal searches, the Millard Fillmore administration reported that of the ten American vessels recently inspected unlawfully by Britain, nine turned out to be slave ships.[57]

American officials stationed in foreign ports often had a lax attitude toward U.S. complicity in the slave trade, motivated as much by disdain for British meddling as sympathy for slave trafficking. They viewed their main job and priority to be protecting American commerce from British interference, even if this meant a high tolerance for slave-trade-related abuses. The most egregious case was the American consul in Havana, Nicholas Trist, appointed in 1833. Havana-based British authorities singled him out in their reports, claiming that Trist routinely signed off on papers allowing suspected slave traffickers to fly the American flag. John Quincy Adams concluded that the British documents persuasively showed "either the vilest treachery or the most culpable indifference to his duties."[58] The *New York Herald* reported that there seemed to be cause for Trist's "instant removal."[59] The politically well-connected Trist nevertheless managed to hold on to his post and was not replaced until a change in administration in 1841.

When less Anglophobic U.S. officials in foreign ports expressed alarm about American complicity in the slave trade, their reports simply gathered dust in Washington. Such was the case in Brazil during the 1840s. David Tod, the American consul in Rio de Janeiro, often reported on American complicity in the slave trade and recommended various actions, including banning all commerce carried on American ships between Africa and Brazil. Yet Tod did not even receive a reply about the matter from his superiors for three years. The pleas by his predecessor, Henry Wise, were similarly ignored.[60] Meanwhile, as historian Don Fehrenbacher writes, "Slave traders landed more than 350,000 Africans in Brazil during the 1840s, and according to most contemporary estimates, at least half of those importations were achieved with American help of some kind."[61]

Illicit Importation and the Southern Borderlands

The illicit importation of slaves into the United States was only a small part of the foreign slave trade. Nevertheless, it was not inconsequential, especially early on in the southern borderlands, where it was closely connected to territorial expansion. Estimates of the number of slaves smuggled into the United States vary dramatically, from tens of thousands to hundreds of thousands. In his classic work on the slave trade, W.E.B. Dubois estimated that a quarter million slaves were illicitly imported into the United States between 1807 and 1862. More recent scholarship considers this number greatly inflated.[62] At the same time, it should be noted that Dubois's estimate does not include the substantial smuggling of slaves into the country in violation of state laws prior to the federal ban. Historian Warren Howard describes the quantification conundrum:

> Anyone who believed all the rumors of slaving voyagers would paint a lurid picture of lawbreaking on an incredible scale: of small slavers successfully landing twice as many Africans as they could possibly have carried; of slaving expeditions so numerous that the Africans could hardly have found enough slaves to sell to them, and the plantation owners found work for so many slaves. Unfortunately, this sort of distortion has been committed. On the other hand, satisfactory proof of illegal voyages is so rare that anyone demanding it will close his eyes to most of the lawbreaking that went on.[63]

Although the numbers debate will never be settled, there is general agreement that there was a major influx of smuggled slaves between the 1790s and 1820s when state and federal antislave-trade laws were in their infancy and demand for slaves was rapidly growing in southern frontier regions with severe labor shortages. And this early influx of smuggled slaves contributed to the growth of the domestic slave population through natural reproduction. It should also be noted that even when illicit shipments of foreign slaves were seized during this period, the slaves were typically simply sold at public auctions rather than freed, further adding to the domestic slave population.[64]

The porous southern borderlands, which had a tiny federal policing presence and a long tradition of smuggling, served as the gateway for illicit slave imports to the plantations of the Deep South (the area that became the states of Louisiana, Mississippi, and Alabama). The Louisiana Purchase, which more than doubled U.S. territory, both facilitated the smuggling of slaves through the Gulf and opened up new lands for the expansion of the slave-based plantation economy. As we saw earlier, Louisiana and its port city of New Orleans proved to be especially attractive for all sorts of smuggling, not just slave trafficking. Louisiana's best-known illicit traders, the Laffites, were also leading slave traffickers. They effectively integrated the business of piracy and slave trading, specializing in capturing foreign slaving ships in the Gulf and then clandestinely diverting their human cargo to Louisiana's expanding sugar plantations.

The congressional ban on the importation of foreign slaves into the newly acquired territory clashed with growing demand for slave labor, making locals resentful of federal authorities and supportive of slave smugglers such as the Laffites. Consequently, slave smuggling was a widespread practice for several decades after the Louisiana Purchase.[65] As the mayor of New Orleans declared, "I defy all the vigilance of man to prevent the introduction of slaves by some means or other."[66] Rising prices also increased the rewards from smuggling. A German merchant doing business in New Orleans reported that in 1813 slaves purchased from the Laffites for under $200 each were selling for at least $600 in the city.[67] Five years later, one slave buyer reported that "fresh imported Guinea negroes were lately sold in NOrleans at $1,500."[68]

To distance themselves from the reach of U.S. authorities, in 1817 the Laffites and their accomplices moved their base to Galveston Island in Spanish Mexico, some seventy miles from the Louisiana border, turning it into a bustling contraband depot and slave-trading center. The island, about twenty-seven miles long and three miles wide, provided an ideal smuggling hub: good natural harbors and a location remote from central authorities, yet still in close proximity to the U.S. border and slave plantations. The U.S. Navy took notice of Galveston's slave-smuggling business in 1817 when the captain of the USS *Congress* reported to his superiors that several hundred slaves in Galveston were destined for New Orleans planters. "Every exertion will be made to intercept them," he said, "but I have little hope of success."[69] That same summer, the New Orleans customs collector reported that a New York ship had reached Galveston carrying nearly three hundred slaves, sold "to the Laffites . . . and other speculators in this place, who have or will resell to the planters."[70]

James Bowie (the American folk hero who is mostly remembered for the Bowie knife, as well as for his role in the battle of the Alamo) joined the Laffites at Galveston, where he and his brothers specialized in trafficking slaves across the border into nearby Louisiana. According to historian William Davis, "James himself did the most dangerous work of conveying the contrabands through the swamps and bayous, bringing them in lots of forty at a time."[71] Between 1819 and 1820, he reportedly smuggled at least 180 slaves.

The Bowie brothers also devised an ingenious import scheme that exploited the fact that smuggled slaves captured by the authorities were typically sold off at public auctions. The Bowies would take on the role of informants, turning in their human cargo to the local customs officials without revealing that they were actually the smugglers. They would then purchase the slaves back at auction, with half the purchase price refunded to them by the government as a reward for having originally turned the slaves in. As one of the Bowie brothers wrote, we "fitted out some small boats at the mouth of the Calcasieu [River] and went in to trade on shares. Our plan of operation was as follows: We first purchased forty Negroes from Lafitte at a rate of one dollar per pound, or an average of $140 for each negro: we brought them into the limits of the United States and delivered them to a customs-house officer."[72] Through this creative manipulation and abuse of the legal system, illegally imported slaves became legal domestic slaves with a bill of sale, at great profit to the smugglers-turned-informants.

Spanish Florida, bordering Georgia, was also a key entry point for smuggling slaves into the United States in the first two decades of the nineteenth century. Illicitly importing slaves via Florida began with Georgia's ban on the foreign slave trade in 1798, and it continued to grow after the federal ban took effect in 1808. According to Richard

Drake's "Revelations of a Slave Smuggler," after the U.S. prohibition Florida became a "nursery for slave-breeders, and many American citizens grew rich by trafficking in Guinea negroes, and smuggling them continually, in small parties, through the Southern United States."[73] One investor in the illicit importation of newly arrived slaves in Florida was the former governor of Georgia, David B. Mitchell. He resigned as governor to take the position as federal Indian agent to the Creek nation, which he then used as a convenient cover to traffic slaves from Florida into the Creek lands.

Just as Galveston Island supplied Louisiana with smuggled slaves, Florida's Amelia Island and its port town of Fernandina supplied Georgia. Its economic advantage came from proximity to the United States, conveniently located at the mouth of the St. Mary's River, which marked the border between Spanish Florida and Georgia. Jefferson's embargo in 1808 and the War of 1812 provided a tremendous boost to the island's smuggling-based economy; the U.S. ban on importing slaves simply added another profitable trade item.[74] But at the same time as the smuggling boomtown of Fernandina was building more warehouses to store U.S.-bound slaves, the town also had a tolerant attitude toward free blacks and escaped slaves—much to the frustration of Georgia slaveholders across the border.[75]

Spain's control of Amelia Island was already tenuous, but it lost total control in 1817 when the Scottish adventurer and South American revolutionary Gregor MacGregor invaded the island.[76] Many in MacGregor's invasion force were American sailors and officers recruited in Philadelphia, Baltimore, Charleston, and Savannah. MacGregor boldly announced the independence of the Republic of the Floridas and for a brief time turned the island into his own privateering, smuggling, and slave-trading fiefdom. Another European adventurer, Louis Aury, supplanted MacGregor in September 1817, relocating his slave-trading base from Galveston to Amelia Island. Although Aury's rule was similarly short-lived, it was more significant. In less than two months Aury reportedly sold more than a thousand Africans. Many runaway slaves were also captured and sold off.[77] At the same time, there were widespread reports that Aury employed black mercenaries and sailors, making Georgians especially anxious about the presence of armed blacks so close to their plantations.[78]

Spain was already under growing pressure from the United States to cede Eastern Florida, so losing control of Amelia Island only made matters worse for the decaying empire. Indeed, to the dismay of Spanish officials, Washington quickly pounced on the opportunity to use concerns about slave smuggling and a lawless border as a pretext to invade and occupy the island in late December 1817. Rampant smuggling, U.S. officials declared, demonstrated that Spain was simply incapable of controlling its side of the border. In his first annual message to Congress, on December 2, 1817, President Monroe announced his decision to take Amelia Island, claiming that it had become "a channel for the illicit introduction of slaves from Africa into the United States, an asylum for fugitive slaves from the neighboring states, and a port for smuggling of every kind."[79] A congressional investigating committee was appointed in early December to report on the situation. South Carolina Representative Henry Middleton, the chairman of the committee, announced the findings on January 10, 1818: "Your committee are of opinion that it is but too notorious that numerous infractions of the law prohibiting the importations of slaves into the United States have been perpetuated with impunity upon our southern frontier. . . ."[80]

American concerns about smuggling along its southeastern border thus offered a convenient rationale for a U.S. invasion and occupation that happened to coincide with diplomatic efforts to convince Spain to relinquish Florida. Regardless of the sincerity of these concerns, alarm over border smuggling and illicit slave trading ultimately advanced Washington's annexationist ambitions.[81] American forces never left Amelia Island, and in 1819 the Florida Purchase added forty-three million acres to the United States. The U.S. seizure of Amelia Island, which had been officially justified as an anti-smuggling intervention, helped to set Florida on the road to statehood.

The illicit slave trade also played an important role in America's territorial ambitions in the southwest. The smuggling of slaves contributed to the early development of a plantation economy in Texas, where Anglo settler thirst for slave labor was increasingly at odds with national laws after Mexico's independence from Spain in 1821. Mexico banned the slave trade in 1824 and outlawed slavery in 1829. A variety of exemptions and creative settler schemes to import and hold slaves, including the legal fiction that slaves were long-term contract laborers, helped to circumvent these laws. And local Mexican officials showed little enthusiasm for enforcing rules handed down by a distant central government in disarray.[82] The introduction of slaves into Texas by American settlers also violated U.S. antislave-trade laws, since it was illegal for a U.S. citizen to traffic slaves into a foreign land. Slavery and the slave trade became growing irritants in settler relations with the increasingly antislavery Mexican government and played no small part in calls for revolution in 1835 and the war of independence in 1836.[83] Mexico's decree of April 6, 1830, outlawed further immigration into Texas, yet the influx of slaveholding Americans continued unabated, and by 1836 they greatly outnumbered native Tejanos.

In defiance of the Mexican authorities, maritime slave smuggling into Texas grew in the years leading up to the Texas Revolution: "Beginning in the early spring of 1833 . . . one boatload after another of Africans (totaling four documented cases in the next eighteen months) arrived by way of Cuba at Galveston Bay for distribution to labor-hungry farmers. At least two ventures lured free blacks from the Caribbean into Texas and then treated them as slaves on their arrival."[84] Buying their slaves in Cuba, Texan blackbirders (slave traders) "included such future luminaries as Benjamin Fort Smith and James W. Fannin, and prominent planters like Monroe Edwards and Sterling McNeel purchased human cargoes."[85] Slave smugglers also helped finance and supply the Texas Revolution,[86] and some, such as James Bowie, directly participated in fighting Mexican General Antonio López de Santa Anna's forces.

The illicit importation of slaves into Texas continued after independence. Of course, when Texas entered the Union on December 29, 1845,what had previously been illegal slave smuggling between the United States and Texas became part of the legal interstate slave trade. With legal access to the domestic U.S. slave market, Texas slaveholders were now no longer dependent upon illicitly importing labor; and slaves previously smuggled into Texas became part of the legal U.S. slave population.

The Divisive Politics of Policing Fugitive Slaves

Just as it was illegal to import foreign slaves into the American South, so too was it illegal for southern slaves to leave without their masters' consent. But just as profit-seeking smugglers defied the law by bringing in new slaves, freedom-seeking slaves stole and smuggled themselves to northern states and neighboring countries. This reverse form of slave smuggling—the illegal cross-border movement of slaves to freedom—typically involved self-smuggling (and self-stealing, since slaves were defined as property) more than the highly organized "underground railroad" wildly imagined by both slaveholders and abolitionists alike. As historian Larry Gara notes, both slaveholders and abolitionists found much propaganda value in constructing an image of runaway slaves being aided by a sophisticated clandestine network. For southern slaveholders, this represented a vast abolitionist smuggling conspiracy to woo otherwise content slaves away from their protective masters. For abolitionists, in contrast, this was boastfully celebrated as evidence of their humanitarian reach, influence, and risk taking. In both constructions, the slave is passive, with abolitionist outsiders depicted as either predators or rescuers. In reality, slave escapes tended to be more self-planned and reliant on self-sufficiency than either of these narratives suggested. Yet these dominant accounts were politically useful for all sides and long outlived slavery (and indeed the abolitionist version continues to shape the popular imagination).[87]

The problem of runaway slaves had long frustrated slave owners. Indeed, George Washington and Thomas Jefferson were among the many slaveholders who took out advertisements for the return of their runaway slaves.[88] Though the number of escaped slaves was always small relative to the overall size of the slave population, it became a hugely consequential political issue, especially in the divisive years leading up to the Civil War. The possibility of escape was of greatest concern to slaveholders who lived in close proximity to free states or to countries where slavery was banned. U.S. officials turned this concern into a high-priority foreign policy issue.[89]

Thousands of slaves (including several owned by Sam Houston) found refuge by crossing the Rio Grande into Mexico despite U.S. diplomatic protests and incursions to recover fugitives.[90] Most slaves had to find their way to the border on their own, but in one clever scheme the abolitionist smuggler John Short colluded with sympathetic slave "buyers" in repeatedly selling and reselling the escaping slaves all along the route to the border. In other words, transportation to the border was carried out through a series of legal ownership-transfer schemes as a cover for escape. The humanitarian side of Short's criminal career came to an end, however, when his cattle theft and counterfeiting operations were busted and he and his son were put to death at a public hanging.[91] In any event, the fugitive slave issue remained a great source of tension in U.S.-Mexico relations all the way up to the Civil War, with Mexico persistently refusing to sign an extradition treaty with the United States that included rendition of escaped slaves.

Canada was the favored foreign destination for escaped slaves, with an estimated twelve thousand former slaves crossing the northern border by 1842.[92] In the 1850s, the number of blacks in Ontario alone reportedly doubled to eleven thousand.[93] Even if opposed to slavery, most northerners did not welcome fugitive slaves (or free blacks, for that matter[94]). Northern states remained deeply racist; only a few considered free blacks to be citizens. Part of northern opposition to the slave regime, in fact, was that it was viewed as an incentive for slaves to smuggle themselves north. The anxiety-producing specter of a mass influx of fleeing slaves was one strand of abolitionist sentiment. Ending slavery, many hoped, would end the motivation for blacks to leave the South.

Canada was also a more attractive destination for escaped slaves because U.S. fugitive slave laws made it possible, with enough funds and persistence, for owners to hire a slave catcher to reclaim their "stolen property." The jurisdiction of such laws did not extend across the border, of course, and Canada typically refused U.S. requests for cooperation in rendition of fugitive slaves.

The fugitive clause in the Constitution denied escaped slaves legal protection in nonslave states. George Washington signed the first fugitive slave law in 1793, and enforcement obligations were federalized with the passage of the Fugitive Slave Act as part of the Compromise of 1850. These fugitive slave laws contributed to a climate of fear not only for escaped slaves but also for free blacks, since they facilitated kidnapping free blacks and selling them into slavery in the South.[95] The kidnappers ranged from part-time opportunists wishing to make a quick buck to veteran slave catchers fraudulently claiming free blacks as fugitive slaves. Some were members of gangs that also engaged in other forms of theft, such as horse thieving.[96] Many states passed antikidnapping laws, but the abuses continued. Southern politicians blocked efforts to pass similar legislation at the federal level.[97]

The most important impact of the fugitive slave issue was ultimately political rather than demographic. As a political lightning rod, it greatly contributed to the deepening and widening sectional cleavages and gave entrepreneurial abolitionists their most potent issue. For most northerners, even if they found slavery distasteful and abhorrent it was still distant and abstract, far removed from their daily lives. The fugitive slave issue, in contrast, made slavery much more visible and immediate. It personalized slavery, brought it home, and gave it a human face. Equating slave catching with the evils of the slave trade, in 1843 the Illinois abolition society resolved that "to aid the slave catcher in the free States, is no better than to aid the kidnapper on the coast of Africa."[98]

With the antislavery movement gaining steam and making the fugitive slave issue a focal point, southern slaveholders and their hired slave catchers found northern states increasingly uncooperative in their efforts to recapture runaway slaves. In 1850, southerners countered by pushing through the Fugitive Slave Act, which for the first time gave the federal government jurisdiction over the detention and return of runaway slaves.[99] Southerners viewed the enforcement of the new law as a litmus test of the government's commitment to upholding its constitutional obligations to defend slavery. "The continued existence of the United States, as one nation," warned the *Southern Literary Messenger*, "depends upon the full and faithful execution of the Fugitive Slave Bill."[100] Beyond its questionable utility in dealing with runaway slaves, the real value of the law for southerners was to make a loud statement reaffirming and strengthening national commitment to slavery.

But the unintended consequence of the law was to provide new ammunition for the abolitionist movement and greatly magnify public awareness and antislavery sympathy.[101] Most famously, the law inspired the publication of *Uncle Tom's Cabin* in 1852, with twenty thousand copies printed in the first three weeks, three hundred thousand in the first year, and more than two million within a decade. It was also a huge hit in England and was translated into multiple foreign languages. Frederick Douglass commented that "The fugitive slave bill has especially been of positive service to the anti-slavery movement." It showed the "horrible character of slavery toward the slave, . . . revealed the arrogant and overbearing spirit of the slave states towards the free states."[102]

The new law, which gave the federal government sweeping new powers and responsibilities in defending slavery and policing slaves, provoked highly publicized episodes of resistance and confrontation. Forcible rescue incidents were rare but dramatic, and thus useful as antislavery spectacles. The first forcible slave rescue took place in Boston in February 1851. A waiter named Shadrach was arrested on a federal fugitive slave warrant, but then set free by a crowd of black Bostonians who broke into the courtroom and spirited him away to Canada. Outraged southerners demanded forceful action from Washington. President Fillmore responded by calling for the prosecution of those who had aided the escape, and Secretary of State Daniel Webster denounced such illegal actions as the equivalent of treason.[103]

Even as enforcement of the Fugitive Slave Act in its first three years led to the return of about seventy escaped slaves, antislavery militancy continued to grow and exploded again in 1854. In March, a fugitive slave named Joshua Glover was forcibly freed from a Milwaukee jail by an angry mob, and local authorities refused to cooperate with federal officials in punishing the perpetrators. In a direct challenge to federal power, the Wisconsin Supreme Court declared the Fugitive Slave Act to be unconstitutional. In Boston a few months later, a guard was fatally shot in a botched effort to liberate a captured slave, Anthony Burns. Marines and army troops were deployed to escort Burns to the Boston wharf, keeping thousands of antislavery protesters at bay. Although such a heavy-handed display of force was effective, it generated intense political aftershocks and would be the occasion for the last fugitive slave recovered from New England.[104]

Meanwhile, in the wake of the Burns case, state governments in Michigan, Wisconsin, and throughout New England unleashed a flurry of new personal liberty legislation from 1854 to 1858 aimed at hobbling the enforcement of the Fugitive Slave Act. A hostile local environment had already made it virtually impossible for slave owners to recover fugitive slaves in these states, but such legislation represented blatant defiance of federal authority, further alienating and angering southerners. From the southern perspective, the issue was less about the failure to apprehend a relatively small number of escaped slaves than about the failure to protect constitutionally guaranteed rights.[105] Flagrant disrespect of the fugitive slave law was thus viewed as a broader threat to the very institution of slavery and was commonly cited as justification for breaking from the Union.[106]

Even with the outbreak of the Civil War, the fugitive slave issue remained far from resolved. And it was further complicated and magnified by the sheer number of slaves fleeing to the protection of Union forces. Some Union officers returned escaped slaves—labeled "contrabands"[107]—to their owners, until Congress prohibited the practice in 1862. And even then, there were documented cases of Union soldiers being paid to smuggle escaped slaves back across the line to the original owners.[108] The fugitive slave laws remained on the books until 1864, long after contrabands had been fighting in the Union army.

THE ILLICIT SLAVE TRADE was not the only (or the numerically most significant) episode of smuggled human cargo in American history, but it was the first and certainly the most inhumane. As we will see later in our story, millions of foreign workers clandestinely came to America through the back door, but in violation of U.S. immigration laws rather than antislave-trade laws. As cheap immigrant workers came to replace slaves as America's most exploitable labor force in the late nineteenth century, the federal government became far more involved in immigration control than it had ever been in policing the slave trade. But before we get to that story, we must first turn to the illicit-trade side of the war that finally brought slavery to an end.

9

Blood Cotton and Blockade Runners

MORE AMERICANS PERISHED IN the nation's Civil War than in any other conflict; well over six hundred thousand soldiers lost their lives, and hundreds of thousands more were injured. Smugglers contributed to this heavy human toll by arming Confederate forces and thus enabling the war to drag on much longer than would otherwise have been possible. The illicit flow of arms and other materials could not in the end shift the military balance on the ground and change the ultimate outcome of the war, but it did profoundly shape its character and longevity. Although attracting far less attention than the Civil War's famous battles, southern success on the battlefield depended on commercial success in the underworld of smuggling. The North attempted to impede such clandestine commerce by imposing an ambitious naval blockade on southern ports. Yet at the same time, the Union undermined its own blockade through extensive trading with the enemy across the front lines. Profits and politics often trumped military logic.

King Cotton

The South entered the war hugely disadvantaged. It had no navy and no real capacity to build one. The nation's industry was overwhelmingly concentrated in the North—including virtually all of the capacity to manufacture arms, rails and locomotives, cloth, pig iron, and boots and shoes.[1] The South suffered from supply problems from the very start, including an arms and gunpowder shortage. The Confederate rebels, much like the revolutionary rebels of 1776, attempted to compensate for these severe deficiencies by developing clandestine commercial links to the outside world, especially Britain. This time, the British would be supplying, rather than fighting, the American rebels. The Confederacy sent James D. Buloch to the Liverpool shipyards in early 1861 with the task of covertly acquiring warships. Caleb Huse was similarly dispatched to England to acquire arms and ammunition. These Confederate representatives, posing as private citizens, hired commercial agents to buy up large quantities of war materials.[2]

More than anything else, the Confederacy counted on cotton as a political and economic weapon. The South placed all bets on its near monopoly of the world's supply of cotton to outweigh the many disadvantages it faced at the start of the war. British mills, in particular, depended upon the South for some 75 to 80 percent of their cotton imports. British textile manufacturing, the country's most important industry, imported almost two million bales of southern cotton per year.[3] Deprived of cotton, Britain would have little choice but to intervene on the side of the South. Or so the Confederate government hoped. It was assumed to be just a matter of time before the pain of cotton shortages took an unbearable toll. And to try to hurry things along, southerners imposed an informal embargo on cotton exports in 1861 and even burned some 2.5 million bales at the beginning of the war to show they were serious.[4]

The intensity of southern faith in "King Cotton" was captured by a Charleston merchant who told a reporter for the London *Times* in early 1861 that "if those miserable Yankees try to blockade us, and keep you from our cotton, you'll just send their ships to the bottom and acknowledge us. That will be before autumn, I think."[5] In Montgomery that spring, W. H. Russell reported to *The Times* that Southerners "believe in the irresistible power of cotton to force England to intervene. . . . The doctrine of 'cotton is king' to them is a lively, all powerful faith."[6] And that summer, Confederate Vice President Alexander Stephens asserted that "in some way or other [the blockade will] be raised, or there will be revolution in Europe. . . . Our cotton is . . . the tremendous lever by which we can work our destiny."[7]

But King Cotton was a mirage. The Confederacy badly miscalculated. There was no British intervention; Britain never even formally recognized the Confederacy or openly challenged the Union blockade.[8] King Cotton was partly a victim of its own success. Bumper cotton crops in 1859 and 1860 had saturated the British market. Large stockpiles of cotton and a surplus of cotton manufactured goods in British warehouses dampened and delayed the impact of sharply reduced cotton imports in 1861. British textile manufacturing was hit hard by the cotton shortages starting in the summer of 1862, and nearly two million people in Britain were left destitute by the end of the year.[9] But this was not enough to provoke intervention. And other British industries, such as armaments and shipbuilding, were stimulated by the war and profited by its perpetuation.

Moreover, by this time the Confederacy had abandoned trying to use cotton as a political tool to provoke British intervention and was instead eagerly encouraging the clandestine shipment of cotton through the Union blockade to obtain desperately needed arms and other supplies. The Confederacy was aggressively selling "cotton bonds" in Europe at attractive prices as a creative mechanism to finance imports of war materials. The catch was that the bondholder could redeem bonds for cotton only at certain southern ports—which meant smuggling, in the form of breaking through the Union blockade. Whereas King Cotton had failed politically, the South now held out hope that it would succeed economically, enticing foreign merchants to aid the South in the pursuit of profits.

Britain's proclamation of neutrality in May 1861 proved to be not only politically pragmatic but also financially rewarding. Just as American merchants had commercially exploited their country's neutral status during the Napoleonic Wars, British merchants were now doing the same. And just as American merchants had earlier risked having their cargoes seized by the British as contraband, so too were British merchants now taking similar risks as they attempted to sneak contraband cargoes through the northern blockade. When London complained about Union warships harassing, searching, and seizing British-flagged commercial vessels, Washington could point to British precedent from more than a half-century earlier.[10] And when Washington complained about British commercial complicity in the war, London could similarly point to American precedent. The solicitor general reminded Parliament in 1863 of the words of U.S. Secretary of State Daniel Webster from two decades before. "It is not the practice of nations," Webster stated in 1842, "to undertake to prohibit their own subjects from trafficking in articles contraband of war. Such trade is carried on at the risk of those engaged in it under the liabilities and penalties prescribed by the law of nations."[11]

Diplomatic relations between London and Washington were often tense, but both sides exercised restraint by limiting conflicts to disputes over contraband of war rather than actually going to war. The Union resented British neutrality and commercial complicity in supplying the South; this was, however, far preferable to London formally recognizing the Confederacy, openly challenging the legitimacy of the Union blockade, and intervening militarily. Even as the British government was unwilling to forcibly break the blockade, British merchants were more than willing to profit by evading it. In this case, commercial interest in supporting the slaveholding South trumped British antislavery sentiment.

Blockaders and Blockade Runners

On April 19, 1861, President Lincoln announced a naval blockade on the South—soon dubbed the "Anaconda Plan"—with the aim of squeezing the Confederacy into submission by blocking contraband of war. Although it was an impossible task to police the 3,549-mile Confederate coastline, blockaders could focus primarily on the handful of major southern ports with the requisite infrastructure and transportation links to handle large volumes of external supplies. During the course of the war, the Union's four blockading squadrons captured 136 blockade runners, and eighty-five more were destroyed.[12]

But the runners usually outmaneuvered the blockaders. Historian Stephen Wise calculates that almost three hundred steamships were involved in blockade running between the fall of 1861 and spring 1865, and out of an estimated thirteen hundred runs, more than a thousand succeeded.[13] Blockade runners managed to smuggle out roughly half a

Figure 9.1 "Scott's Great Snake." Cartoon map in 1861 illustrates General Winfield Scott's strategy to blockade the South, which was dubbed the "Anaconda Plan" (Library of Congress).

million bales of cotton, and smuggle in a thousand tons of gunpowder, half a million rifles, and several hundred cannon.[14] Wise estimates that blockade runners provided the South with 60 percent of its weapons, one-third of the lead for its bullets and the ingredients for three-fourths of its powder, and most of the cloth for its uniforms.[15] Clearly, the Confederacy could not have survived without this clandestine lifeline to the outside world.

Successful blockade running sometimes meant that Confederate soldiers were better supplied than their Union counterparts. At one point, General Ulysses S. Grant replaced his own rifles with captured southern weapons: "At Vicksburg 31,600 prisoners were surrendered, together with 172 cannon, about 60,000 muskets with a large amount of ammunition. The small-arms of the enemy were far superior to ours. . . . The enemy had generally new arms which had run the blockade and were of uniform caliber. After the surrender I authorized all colonels whose regiments were armed with inferior muskets, to place them in the stack of captured arms and replace them with the latter."[16]

In the first year of the war, the blockade was so thin that it scarcely deserved to be labeled as such. The Confederate government dismissively called it a "paper blockade." But over time, it tightened and thickened considerably, targeting the relatively small number of key southern ports, especially Charleston and Wilmington, that remained in Confederate hands (New Orleans, the largest southern port, was captured and occupied by the Union early on in the war, and by 1863 blockade runners were largely restricted to the ports of Wilmington, Charleston, Mobile, and Galveston). The blockade typically had multiple layers, with smaller ships patrolling closer to shore and able to signal to warships several miles out when a blockade runner was leaving port.

Blockade runners adapted to these Union tactics by deploying faster, more agile, and lower-profile British-made steamer vessels, painted gray or bluish green and burning smokeless anthracite coal for added stealth. Under the cover of fog and darkness, these blockade runners could sneak by a Union warship in close proximity without being detected. And when detected, many blockade runners could simply outmaneuver and outrun their would-be captors. Despite the wartime context, the blockade enforcement-evasion game was mostly nonviolent: blockade-running ships were typically not armed (to save weight but also to avoid being classified as an armed pirate ship, which brought much harsher penalties), and Union warships preferred to capture rather than destroy them in order to seize the cargo and receive the prize money.

Britain supplied not only hundreds of blockade-running ships but also most of the owners, captains, and crews. Investors in blockade running ranged from major stockholding firms to individual ship ventures.[17] The British had a distinct advantage in the blockade-running game: when captured by Union ships, southerners aboard blockade runners were treated as prisoners of war, whereas British subjects were simply released (after the vessel and contraband cargo were confiscated) in order to avoid any diplomatic fallout with London. Upon release, they often joined another blockade-running vessel. Not surprisingly, captured southerners sometimes pretended to be British. Secretary of State Seward complained that such deception was standard practice: "Blockade runners . . . generally resort to every possible artifice and

Figure 9.2 Confederate blockade runner *A. D. Vance*, 1863–64. Drawing by R. G. Skerrett, 1899 (Naval Historical Foundation).

fraud which promises to conceal their true nationality, the unlawful character of their voyage, and the nationality of their vessels. They simulate flags, they erase names, they throw papers overboard or burn them, they state falsehoods, and they equivocate under oath. Whether neutrals or insurgents, when captured, they lay claim to the character of innocent traders and of neutrals and . . . generally lay claim to the rights of British subjects."[18]

A British publication in 1862 summed up the country's involvement in blockade running: "Score after score of the finest, swiftest British steamers and ships, loaded with British material of war of every description, cannon, rifles by the hundreds of thousand, powder by the thousand of tons, shot, shell, cartridges, swords, etc, with cargo after cargo of clothes, boots, shoes, blankets, medicines and supplies of every kind, all paid for by British money, at the sole risk of British adventurers, well insured by Lloyds and under the protection of the British flag, have been sent across the ocean to the insurgents by British agency."[19]

Two British island ports, Bermuda and Nassau, served as the main hubs for blockade runners, not unlike the transshipment role that the Dutch island of St. Eustatius played during the American Revolution. Bermuda and Nassau became bustling island warehouses for Europe-bound cotton and Confederacy-bound contraband. Cotton—"white gold"—served as the de facto currency for purchasing European war materials and other supplies. One blockade runner described the wartime scene at Nassau's port: "Cotton, cotton, everywhere! Blockade-runners discharging it into lighters, tier upon tier of it, piled high upon the wharves, and merchant vessels, chiefly under the British flag, loading with it."[20]

Nassau, with a sympathetic governor and local population, was the favored transshipment point, given its proximity to southern ports. In 1863, some 164 steamers departed Nassau for southern ports, while only 53 cleared for Bermuda.[21] From Nassau, blockade runners could reach Wilmington (570 miles) or Charleston (515 miles) in just three days. This saved not just time but also coal, and less space devoted to

Figure 9.3 Unloading smuggled cotton from Confederate blockade runners at Nassau, the Bahamas. Wood engraving from an English newspaper of 1864 (Granger Collection).

coal meant more space devoted to profitable cargo. Secretary of the Navy Gideon Welles complained about Nassau's complicity: "Almost all of the aid which the Rebels have received in arms, munitions, and articles contraband have gone to them through the professedly neutral British port of Nassau. From them the Rebels have derived constant encouragement and support. . . . It is there that vessels are prepared to run the blockade and violate our laws, by the connivance and with the knowledge of the colonial, and, I apprehend, the parent, government."[22]

Mexico also served as a back door for smuggling cotton out, bringing in war supplies, and getting around the blockade.[23] As the only neutral country sharing a land border with Confederate territory, Mexico enjoyed a special niche in wartime trading. The Mexican border town of Matamoros became a smuggling depot, where war supplies could be ferried across the Rio Grande to Brownsville, Texas, and exchanged for southern cotton. A Union general lamented that "Matamoros is to the rebellion west of the Mississippi what the port of New York is to the United States. It is a great commercial center, feeding and clothing the rebellion, arming and equipping, furnishing the materials of war."[24] One historian describes the area as resembling the California gold rush of 1849, with entrepreneurs, speculators, agents, and brokers drawn to it like a magnet.[25] According to one estimate, more than twenty thousand speculators from the Union, Confederacy, England, France, and Germany arrived in four years.[26]

The tiny Mexican coastal hamlet of Bagdad, at the mouth of the Rio Grande some thirty miles from Matamoros, experienced an equally dramatic growth spurt, mushrooming in size from a handful of huts to a town of some fifteen thousand residents virtually overnight. In April 1863, the commander of the Eastern Gulf Blockading Squadron was informed that there were as many as two hundred ships waiting to unload their cargoes and load cotton at Bagdad. During this same period, the commander of the Confederate raider *Alabama* reported that business was booming in Bagdad: "The beach was piled with cotton bales going out, and goods coming in. The stores were numerous and crowded with wares."[27]

There was little that Union naval authorities could do about the use of Mexico to circumvent the blockade. As stipulated in the 1848 Treaty of Guadalupe Hidalgo, the Rio Grande was neutral and therefore could not be blockaded by Mexico or the United States within a mile north or south of its entrance. Union warships slowed the trade down through harassment (by constantly boarding and inspecting vessels) but could not stymie it completely.[28] This supply line was crucial in sustaining the Confederate war effort west of the Mississippi. But thanks to geographic distance and a poor transportation system, the Mexico connection was far less consequential than blockade running for supplying Confederate forces elsewhere.

Blockade-running officers and crews were well rewarded for their risk taking. This is illustrated by the pay scale of the commercial blockade runner the *Venus*. The captain received $5,000, the first officer $1,250, the second and third officers $750 each, the chief engineer $2,500, the pilot $3,500, and each crewmember $250. These wages were paid in gold, half up front and the other half after the successful round-trip run.[29] Crews and officers also greatly supplemented their income on the inbound trip by carrying scarce necessities and luxury items in their personal belongings, ranging from toothbrushes to corsets, which they could sell for many times their original value. And on the outbound trip they were allowed to carry personal supplies of cheap cotton, which they similarly sold at greatly inflated prices.

Confederate cotton exports were much reduced from prewar levels, but reduced supply also meant highly inflated prices—ensuring substantial profits for those who managed to evade the blockade. Cotton prices in Europe soared to as much as ten times their prewar levels. At such prices, the incentives to run the blockade remained high even as the risks increased over time—with the chances of being caught one in three by 1864 and one in two by 1865.[30] Blockade-running cotton traders were challenged by the blockade but also enriched by it. A popular toast captured this dynamic: "Here's to the Southern planters who grow the cotton; to the Limeys who buy the cotton; to the Yankees that maintain the blockade and keep up the price of cotton. So, three cheers for a long continuance of the war, and success to the blockade-runners."[31]

Yet, relying on private commercial shippers for desperately needed war materials had a serious downside for the Confederate government. Transportation costs were extremely high, accounting for much of the increase in cotton prices. These high transportation costs also decreased the incentives to ship bulky items, notably much-needed machinery and railroad iron.[32] Moreover, commercial blockade runners motivated more by profits than patriotism—or, in the case of Rhett Butler, "for profit only," as he told Scarlett O'Hara in *Gone With the Wind*—devoted scarce cargo space to high-value luxury goods and civilian items, ranging from books to booze, rather than strictly military necessities.[33] For instance, when the *Minho*, a blockade-running steamer, ran aground off the South Carolina coast in October 1862, her cargo was auctioned off in Charleston. The cargo included hundreds of barrels and cases of champagne and wines, more than a thousand wineglasses, seventeen hundred tumblers, cigars, coffee, teapots, and cookware.[34] By early 1864, frustrated Confederate officials finally resorted to banning the importation of luxury goods, but the practice continued.[35] Some southern states also began to purchase their own blockade runners to reduce costs and prioritize military-related imports.

Confederate officials had little choice but to outsource most blockade running to private shippers. The Confederacy simply lacked the administrative capacity and apparatus to impose centralized control over the business of blockade running even if it had wanted to. Moreover, doing so would reduce the profit incentives that sustained the blockade-running system, as was evident when the Confederacy banned the importation of luxury goods. So even as it attempted to impose greater regulation, the Confederate government remained dependent on the profit motives of foreign merchants.[36]

Blockade runners fed, armed, and clothed the Confederacy until Union forces sacked the ports of Charleston and Wilmington. In late 1864, General Robert E. Lee's army in Virginia depended almost entirely on smuggled food from Europe. The supply lines to Europe were severed when the last Confederate port on the Atlantic was shut down in the first months of 1865. With the Wilmington supply line cut, Lee's army was starving when he surrendered at Appomattox in April.[37] Some blockade running continued in the Gulf through Galveston, but this was inconsequential to the war east of the Mississippi.[38]

In the end, the northern blockade can be seen as both a failure and a success. Its porosity suggests failure, as is evident from the repeated success of blockade runners throughout the war years. Historians tend to agree that the war would have ended much sooner if the North had been able to seal off southern ports. But as historian James McPherson points out, in evaluating the effectiveness of the blockade we must also ask: what would the supplying of the South have looked like in the absence of the blockade? He notes that the South's prewar seaborne trade level was significantly higher than the wartime level despite much higher supply needs during the war years. Wartime seaborne trade was less than one-third of its prewar level. Importantly, the blockade forced the Confederacy to rely on ships built to maximize speed and stealth at the expense of cargo capacity. He concludes that the blockade succeeded in significantly reducing southern supplies, even if it did not cut them off entirely.[39] The blockade also forced the Confederacy to rely on less-convenient ports, including Matamoros, which was far from the main battlefields.[40]

The Union blockade also appears relatively more successful compared to blockades during earlier American wars. The British Royal Navy attempted to blockade American ports during the Revolutionary War and the War of 1812. As we saw early on in our story, the British lost the American War of Independence partly because they failed to adequately interdict smuggled European gunpowder and other war supplies to the colonial rebels. The Royal Navy's blockade of the eastern seaboard had more success in the War of 1812, contributing to a stalemated outcome. Fast-forward to the American Civil War, where for the first time the side imposing the blockade was the victor. On balance, it seems that the Union naval blockade was porous enough to help prolong the war and provide an enormously lucrative opportunity for contraband traders, yet was also sufficiently effective to ultimately constrain Confederate fighting capacity.

The North-South Trade

Blockade running was not the Confederacy's only supply line to the outside world. To a remarkable extent, the North supplied the South even while fighting and blockading it. Prewar economic interdependence between North and South did not simply end with the dissolution of the Union. Instead, it transformed into more informal interdependence via trading across the front lines. Trading with the enemy was an old story in America. As we saw in earlier chapters, it thrived during the Seven Years War, the Revolutionary War, and the War of 1812. But during the Civil War it reached an unprecedented level, amid equally unprecedented bloodshed. As Colonel Lafayette C. Baker put it, "It seems incredible that in the midst of the most tragical scenes that war has ever created, the very arena of conflict should be the busy field of mercenary and lawless trade."[41] Federal policy on trade with the South was often confused, conflicted, contradictory, and inconsistent. It was also easily abused, manipulated, and ultimately corrupted in the interests of profiteering.

Cotton was the fiber that tied the Union and Confederacy together even in wartime. It was as sought after by the North as by Britain. Cotton kept the blockade-running system going, and it also generated extensive North-South trading. One estimate suggests that some nine hundred thousand bales of southern cotton reached the North, almost twice the amount exported to Europe through the blockade.[42] Of course, this is a rough estimate at best, but even half this amount would still be significant.

High demand and extreme price differentials explain the powerful allure of the wartime cotton trade: cotton could be sold in the North for three to ten times the purchase price in the South. Southern cotton was paid for with gold, supplies, or Union greenbacks. Gold was especially favored by the Confederacy, since it could be used to buy arms in international markets. Salt was also a highly valued currency of exchange, given its great scarcity in the South. A pack of salt selling for $1.25 in Union-occupied New Orleans was worth $100 in nearby Confederate territory.[43] When cotton was purchased with greenbacks (the least-preferred payment method for the Confederacy), the greenbacks could be converted to northern supplies.[44]

Border states and occupied southern territory turned into conduits for trade between the belligerents. In order to maintain their loyalties, Treasury Secretary Salmon T. Chase devised a policy that allowed trade with the border states of Kentucky, Delaware, Maryland, and Missouri—under the condition that the goods would not be shipped on to the Confederacy.[45] But it was difficult to enforce this prohibition, and there was considerable leakage. This was soon evident in the cross-border trade between Maryland and Virginia. "Almost daily," Baltimore customs collector Henry Hoffman acknowledged, "we have information of goods being shipped from this port to Virginia in our Maryland craft. In some instances we have arrested the parties," but, he noted, "too many get off."[46] The Confederate sympathies of many Maryland residents added to the border control challenge.

The western borders were equally porous. The treasury secretary was upset by reports in 1861 that the Confederacy routinely received northern goods smuggled down the Ohio River, with Cincinnati customs inspectors apparently showing little concern. "It is reported," a frustrated Chase wrote to the customs surveyor, "that the agents appointed by you for the purpose of preventing this traffic are in the habit of passing their time playing cards and in other amusements to the entire neglect of their duties."[47] Chase did approve a shipment of Bibles to the Confederacy, but he also instructed Ohio customs agents to carefully inspect the boxes for tampering, noting that "disloyal or unscrupulous persons" would show no reluctance to hide "percussion caps and other contraband articles to the enemies" in the shipment of holy books.[48]

Illicit trading significantly increased in 1862 as the Union captured and occupied New Orleans, Memphis, and Norfolk. Union policy was to let "commerce follow the flag." The political rationale was that restoring economic activity would generate loyalty and support in occupied territory. But in practice, illicit commerce also followed the flag, facilitating the supplying of Confederate forces in neighboring areas. As the Union army extended its reach to the cotton belt, so too did smuggling opportunities, despite a ban on trading beyond military lines. For instance, Union occupiers allocated permits to local merchants to open up trade stores and import "family supplies" from the North, so long as they took a loyalty oath. These supplies were supposed to be restricted to "loyal" families and plantations in pacified areas, but much was funneled to nearby Confederate-held territory.[49] Union soldiers were often bribed to look the other way at checkpoints, or they became active participants in the trade.[50]

Women were especially effective smugglers thanks to the reluctance of soldiers to search them.[51] This apparently included petty smuggling by the wives of high-ranking Confederate officers, who declared their loyalty to the Union as a cover to sell cotton and buy supplies for the Confederacy.[52] One woman trying to cross through the lines had such difficulty stepping down from her carriage that it provoked suspicion.

It turned out that underneath her girdle she had strapped twelve pairs of boots containing whiskey, military lace, and other supplies.[53]

Memphis, which was captured in June 1862, became a particularly active hub for smuggling supplies into Confederate areas south of the city and bringing cotton out. Charles A. Dana, an observer for the War Department, reported (perhaps with some exaggeration) from Memphis in early 1863 that "The mania for sudden fortunes made in cotton . . . has to an alarming extent corrupted and demoralized the army. Every colonel, captain, or quartermaster is in secret partnership with some operator in cotton; every soldier dreams of adding a bale of cotton to his monthly pay."[54] Dana himself, meanwhile, was speculating in cotton.[55] The financial allure was obvious: cotton purchased for twenty-five cents per pound on the Confederate side of the line could then be sold for sixty cents on the Union side.[56] With such profits, there was plenty of money to allocate to paying off those guarding the lines. As Brigadier General Charles S. Hamilton described the situation in January 1863, "pickets are bribed, captains of outposts are bribed, colonels and generals are bribed, and the trade goes on."[57]

Senator Zachariah Chandler charged that by the middle of 1864, some $20–30 million worth of supplies had reached the Confederacy via Memphis. This apparently included arms: Grant claimed that Confederate cavalry he captured between Holly Springs and Memphis carried new carbines bought in Memphis.[58] Major General Cadwallader C. Washburn complained in May 1864 that "Memphis has been of more value to the Southern Confederacy since it fell into Federal hands, than Nassau [the most important blockade-running port in the Caribbean]."[59] Sherman had made similar complaints to Secretary of Treasury Chase in 1862, arguing that Memphis was actually more useful to the enemy after it fell to the Union.[60]

The North's occupation of Norfolk in early 1862 similarly facilitated trading with the enemy. "Loyal" local residents were given permits to sell cotton to federal officials in order to feed themselves, but the amount of cotton sold far surpassed the local production level—meaning much of it had to have been clandestinely imported from Confederate-held areas. General George Gordon testified before Congress: "There is now, and has been for many years past, little or no cotton produced in the six counties east of Chowan river for export, and the quantity produced there the last three years has been extremely small, nor was there any surplus there at the beginning of that period." He reached the conclusion that "all the cotton that passes across the Blackwater and Chowan rivers is the property of the rebel government, and passes only by their permission."[61]

The Confederacy officially denounced and prohibited trading with the enemy but at the same time recognized it as a necessary evil. The Confederate War Department stated that "all trade with the enemy" was "demoralizing and illegal and should, of course, be discountenanced, but situated as the people to a serious extent are . . . some barter or trading for the supply of their necessities is almost inevitable."[62] In some cases, such trading became a matter of survival. "The alternative," explained the secretary of war bluntly, "is thus presented of violating our established policy of withholding cotton from the enemy or of risking the starvation of our armies."[63]

Generals Sherman and Grant repeatedly complained that the cotton trade was undermining the war effort, and they attempted to impose new controls to curb it. Sherman even had several of his men shot for trading across the lines.[64] "War and commerce are inconsistent," Sherman insisted. "We cannot have commerce until there is peace and security."[65] Sherman summed up his position: "We cannot carry on war and trade with a people at the same time."[66] But that is exactly what was happening. In 1863 Grant complained that the trade "is weakening us of at least thirty-three percent of our force. . . . I will venture that no honest man has made money in West Tennessee in the last year, whilst many fortunes have been made there during that time."[67] Grant also argued that the cotton trade was eroding troop morale: "Men who had enlisted to fight the battles of their country did not like to be engaged in protecting a traffic which went to the support of the enemy they had to fight, and the profits of which went to men who shared none of their dangers."[68]

Grant especially singled out Jews to blame for black marketeering, and he even went so far as to attempt to expel all Jews from territory under his authority, until President Lincoln quickly blocked the order. Meanwhile, as historian Jonathan Sarna points out, "Grant's own father, Jesse Grant, was engaged in a clandestine scheme to move Southern cotton northward. His partners were Jewish clothing manufacturers named Harman, Henry, and Simon Mack."[69]

At the same time as Sherman and Grant were denouncing the cotton trade, other Union military leaders eagerly profited from it. Some military expeditions were actually covers for cotton expeditions. This included the early-1864 Grand Gulf expedition commanded by Brigadier General A. W. Elleter. The report of the officer in charge described the trip in blunt terms: "To sum up, we marched 250 miles, injured our transportation, exposed our lives, got but few recruits, and as far as ending the war is concerned, we did just nothing at all; but if anything, served to prolong it by assisting a lot of rebels and thieves to sell and get to market about 1,515 bales of private, C.S.A. [Confederate], and abandoned cotton, and a lot of speculators, whose loyalty I very much suspect, in making fortunes."[70] Cotton speculators sometimes joined army expeditions by purchasing journalistic passes, sold for $2,500 apiece.[71]

Some Union military leaders, such as Major General Benjamin F. Butler, commander of the Department of Virginia and North Carolina, were notorious for using their position for commercial gain. Butler somehow managed to increase his net worth from about $150,000 in 1862 to about $3 million six years later.[72] As historian Ludwell Johnson documents, Butler was so entrenched in cotton dealing that his name was "almost a synonym for contraband trade, with all its undertones of corruption and treason. Wherever Butler was, whether New Orleans or Norfolk, business boomed, and much of it was in the hands of his friends and relatives." Butler also happened to be a stockholder of the Middlesex mills and a resident of Lowell, Massachusetts, the center of the country's textile industry.[73]

Butler and his cotton-trading brother William had close ties to President Lincoln, who maintained a strikingly lax attitude toward the cotton trade. Lincoln argued that every bale of cotton that came to the North was one less bale of cotton exported by the Confederacy to Europe at greater profit through the blockade. It kept northern mills running and maintained the loyalties of border states and occupied southern territory. Or at least that was how Lincoln rationalized it. He was well aware of the problems associated with "cotton fever." "Few things are so troublesome to the Government as the fierceness with which the profits of trading in cotton are sought," Lincoln wrote to a friend who had asked for help in securing a cotton deal in June 1863.

"The temptation is so great that nearly everybody wishes to be in it; and when in, the question of profit controls all, regardless of whether the cotton-seller is loyal or rebel, or whether he is paid in corn-meal or gunpowder."[74]

Left unstated by Lincoln, but clear to anyone taking notice, was that cotton was also useful for patronage politics. Lincoln liberally handed out much-coveted permits to purchase cotton, many of them to close associates, friends, and family members.[75] These permits could then be sold and resold to other merchants. As Senator Justin Morrill complained, through these executive permits "a very large trade has sprung up . . . so that . . . the exception came very near being the rule itself."[76] In July 1864 Congress revoked Lincoln's power to personally allocate these special trade permits, hoping to rein in private traders. In September, however, Lincoln signed an executive order that significantly loosened restrictions on the cotton trade, with those most able to take commercial advantage typically also the most politically connected in Washington.[77] As historian David Surdam points out, despite Lincoln being remembered as "Honest Abe," the president had few qualms about facilitating the abuses, corruption, and profiteering associated with the wartime cotton trade.[78] In one case, he even personally intervened to release a merchant imprisoned for cotton smuggling.[79]

Some members of Congress were appalled by the extent of the trade with the South. Senator Grimes charged that the Union either "carry on this war as a war, or let us else disband the army and let the treasury undertake to trade us through the war." Senator Collamer facetiously advised that the government "withdraw all your Army, and enlist a large force of Yankee peddlers . . . to go down there and trade them all out; clean them out in trade."[80] A congressional investigative committee report, titled *Trade with Rebellious States*, concluded:

> It is the judgment of your committee that the trade . . . has been of no real benefit to our government; but, on the other hand, has inflicted very great injury upon the public service. It has induced a spirit of speculation and plunder among the people, who have entered into a disgraceful scramble for wealth during a time of war, waged to save the life of the nation, and has fed the greed of gain which must wound the public morals. It has tended to the demoralization and

> corruption of the army and navy by exhibition of the vast rewards which have accrued from this trade and from the temptation and bribery with which they have been constantly assailed. It is believed to have led to the prolongation of the war, and to have cost the country thousands of lives and millions upon millions of treasure.[81]

Some contraband supplies from the North also reached the South through the Union blockade rather than overland. For instance, meat from Boston or New York would be exported to Canada; then transported to Bermuda or Nassau, where it would be sold for several times the original price; and from there shipped on to southern ports through the Union blockade. Northern meat would also be shipped all the way to Liverpool, where it was reexported to southern ports via Bermuda or Nassau.[82] Through these circuitous routes, the North was feeding the very Confederate army it was fighting.

New York and Boston smugglers also took advantage of the Mexico transit trade discussed earlier. "Trade now carried on with the insurgents," General E. R. Canby noted, persisted "from New York and other Northern ports through the Mexican port of Matamoras [*sic*]." This included "[c]asks and crates of crockery freighted with rifle and musket barrels, bales of codfish with the small parts of the arms, kegs of codfish with the small parts of arms, kegs of powder in barrels of provisions." These supplies were "constantly transferred to insurgents in Texas."[83] Before 1861, requests for customs clearances from New York to Matamoros averaged only around one per year, but from August 1861 to March 1864 there were 152 cargo ships cleared.[84] Shippers used Mexican merchants as fronts, pretending to be doing business with Mexicans but actually doing business in Texas. As added insurance, customs agents were offered bribes to not ask too many questions.[85]

Cuba was also a favored neutral transit point for shipping northern gunpowder to the Confederacy early on, with Boston and Salem smugglers the leading offenders. The treasury secretary resorted to banning all gunpowder shipments from Massachusetts ports to Cuba, arguing that "the powder finds its way . . . into the hands of insurgents."[86] Boston smugglers also reportedly routed their cargoes through Canada to help disguise the final destination. "Large cargoes of Block-tin, drugs and powder are exported from Boston, for St. John's, New Brunswick, with the intent, it is believed, to forward them to the insurgent states by way of Havana," a Treasury Department official informed Boston collector John Goodrich.[87]

To deter the shipment of northern supplies to the Confederacy through Havana and other neutral ports, port collectors in New York were instructed to impose a bond equivalent to the value of the cargo if there was suspicion that the cargo would be diverted to the Confederacy. The flaw in this seemingly sensible policy, however, was that it simply meant another opportunity for customs authorities to collect fees rather than inhibit clandestine trade. New York port officials charged shippers $25 to cancel a bond, which was sometimes paid even before the bond was issued. American consuls in neutral ports were supposed to provide another check on the transit trade, since it was their job to verify that the arriving goods were in fact intended for local use. But owing to either corruption or incompetence (or both), lax oversight was the norm. Trade from the port of New York to Cuba and the British West Indies doubled during the war years, a peculiarity that can be explained only by the transit trade to the Confederacy.[88]

New York customs agents were cashing in on the wartime trading in other ways as well. Take the case of Hiram Barney, appointed by Chase as customs collector for the Port of New York in 1861. Chase was in debt to Barney, owing him at least $45,000. It is unclear whether the loan was ever repaid, but Barney enriched himself through his position. His duties included serving as the Union's "cotton agent," receiving and selling cotton from occupied territory in the South—for which he received a 5 percent cut.[89] These activities were legal, but congressional investigators unearthed many illegal commercial dealings in which Barney was complicit. Historians Carl Prince and Mollie Keller note that the position of customs collector for the port of New York was "long believed to be the most lucrative post in American government."[90]

ALL SIDES EXPECTED THE American Civil War to be short-lived. But it dragged on for four years, turning into a war of attrition. How and why did this happen? Wartime commerce, in the form of blockade running and trading with the enemy, is a crucial part of the answer. Much attention has been given in recent years to the importance of "conflict commodities" in fueling contemporary civil wars, such as so-called blood diamonds in West Africa. Such profit-driven trade is characterized as a defining feature of these "new wars."[91] But as our own historical experience dramatically demonstrates, this is far from a new phenomenon. Cotton played an equivalent if not greater role in the American Civil War; indeed, we could label it "blood cotton." And as we have seen, many commercial and political actors far removed from the battlefield had blood on their hands. Cotton is what gave the South the confidence to secede in the first place, and illicitly trading cotton for arms and other supplies is what helped the Confederacy sustain its war effort for such an extended period of time.

The Union victory brought peace, but it certainly did not bring an end to smuggling. Rather, as we'll see in the next chapter, smugglers were very much a part of America's extraordinary economic development and growth spurt in the late nineteenth century. War was good for illicit trade, but so was peace.

PART IV

THE GILDED AGE AND THE PROGRESSIVE ERA

10

Tariff Evaders and Enforcers

AMERICA AND ITS POSITION in the world were radically transformed in the decades after the Civil War. No nation benefited more from the revolutions in transportation and communication, and no nation experienced such rapid economic growth and industrialization. These late-nineteenth-century changes also transformed the world of smuggling and America's role in it. Booming trade and travel increased the opportunities to smuggle, high U.S. tariffs provided the incentive, and a burgeoning consumer culture yielded much of the demand. New York City, with some two-thirds of all imports entering through its port and being the place where three-quarters of all customs revenue was collected (the government's main source of income before the national income tax), was the epicenter of tariff evasion and enforcement—and is thus the main focus of this chapter.[1]

The Protectors of Protectionism

The years between the Civil War and the Great Depression have been called the "golden era of American protectionism."[2] Between 1871 and 1913, the average tariff on dutiable imports was never less than 38 percent.[3] Although America was born espousing free trade and condemning British mercantilist restrictions, the country now embraced protectionism. And Britain, ironically, had become the world's leading proponent of free trade. Indeed, in the heated debates over protectionism, free-trade advocates were disparagingly labeled "English free traders."[4] Epitomizing this remarkable metamorphosis was Rhode Island, which went from being one of the most trade-dependent and pro-free-trade colonies to an industrial manufacturing center nurtured by protectionist policies. Its jewelry makers, for instance, were protected by an 87 percent tariff. By 1907, Rhode Island was described in the *American Magazine* as a "tariff made" state—"high protection's most perfect work"—with three-fourths of its population tied to factory jobs.[5]

Thousands of customhouse workers—appraisers, collectors, inspectors, surveyors, gaugers, and weighers—served as the protectors of protectionism. They also enforced import bans on an increasingly long list of items, but their main job was revenue collection.[6] They sifted through luggage, inspected and weighed cargo, checked papers and documents, collected duties and imposed fines, and made seizures and arrests. Customs was the second largest federal employer after the postal service, with a workforce of more than thirteen hundred in New York alone by 1877.[7] Between July 1869 and July 1874, customs agents at the New York port seized more than thirty-six hundred shipments, secured sixty-eight smuggling-connected indictments, and collected more than $4 million in fines. Penalties were stiff. A complicit sea captain could face fifteen years in prison, a $5,000 fine, and loss of vessel; penalties for others could include up to a two-year prison term, a $10,000 fine, court costs, and payment of duties double the value of the smuggled item.[8]

Like their British colonial predecessors, customs officials were often viewed as abusive, heavy-handed, and corrupt. Far from deferring to the "invisible hand" of the market, the customhouse was the most "visible hand" of the state.[9] Indeed, customs was the most striking exception to an otherwise anemic central state. Customs was the main generator of revenue for government coffers but was also used to line pockets and bankroll patronage politics. Unlike a century earlier, though, the abuses, graft, and corruption within customs generated pressures for reform rather than revolution.[10]

In the years before Congress finally pushed to reform customs in the 1870s, revenue enforcement was remarkably profitable: under the "moiety system," which dated back to the eighteenth century, agents and their informants could be awarded a substantial cut of all fines and forfeitures. This could amount to many times the annual salary of a customs official.[11] Entire shipments could even be impounded if any part of the cargo was improperly disclosed. As noted by historian Andrew Wender Cohen, this was most dramatically illustrated in the winter of 1872–73, when customs agents discovered that the New York firm Phelps, Dodge and Company had undervalued its imports by $6,658.78 and failed to pay $1,664 in duty. Customs consequently seized the entire shipment, valued at $1.75 million. The company ended up paying $271,000 in fines and duties in order to get its shipment back.[12]

These financial incentives encouraged the same sort of overzealous enforcement that had so enraged colonial merchants in their dealings with British customs offices. In one bust alone, the collector of customs at the New York port reportedly pocketed $56,120—more than the annual salary of the U.S. president. The collector was Chester Arthur, who was so notorious for abusing the system that the president asked him to resign—and when he refused, it took years to force him out.[13] Arthur went on to become the twenty-first president of the United States and surprised his critics by turning into an advocate for civil service reform, including within customs.

In the face of mounting evidence of abuses and public outrage over unscrupulous profit-driven enforcement, the Grant administration finally abolished much of the moiety system in June 1874.[14] With the personal financial incentives and rewards for customs agents greatly reduced, enforcement noticeably loosened. Even as imports increased sharply, the amount collected from fines and forfeitures plummeted.[15]

The New York customhouse, by far the nation's largest, epitomized the excesses of patronage politics and the political spoils system. As one account of the history of the U.S. Customs Service describes it, "The office of the Collector of Customs at the Port of New York had become a prize second only in political prestige and influence to a Cabinet appointment."[16] Customs often served as a jobs program to reward loyal political supporters, regardless of qualifications. And those hired through political favoritism, in turn, were expected to make regular financial contributions to the political party. As a congressional commission appointed to investigate the New York customhouse reported in 1877, the amount of political contributions was set on the basis of salary level, and that "some of them repair their diminished salaries by exacting or accepting from the merchants unlawful gratuities."[17]

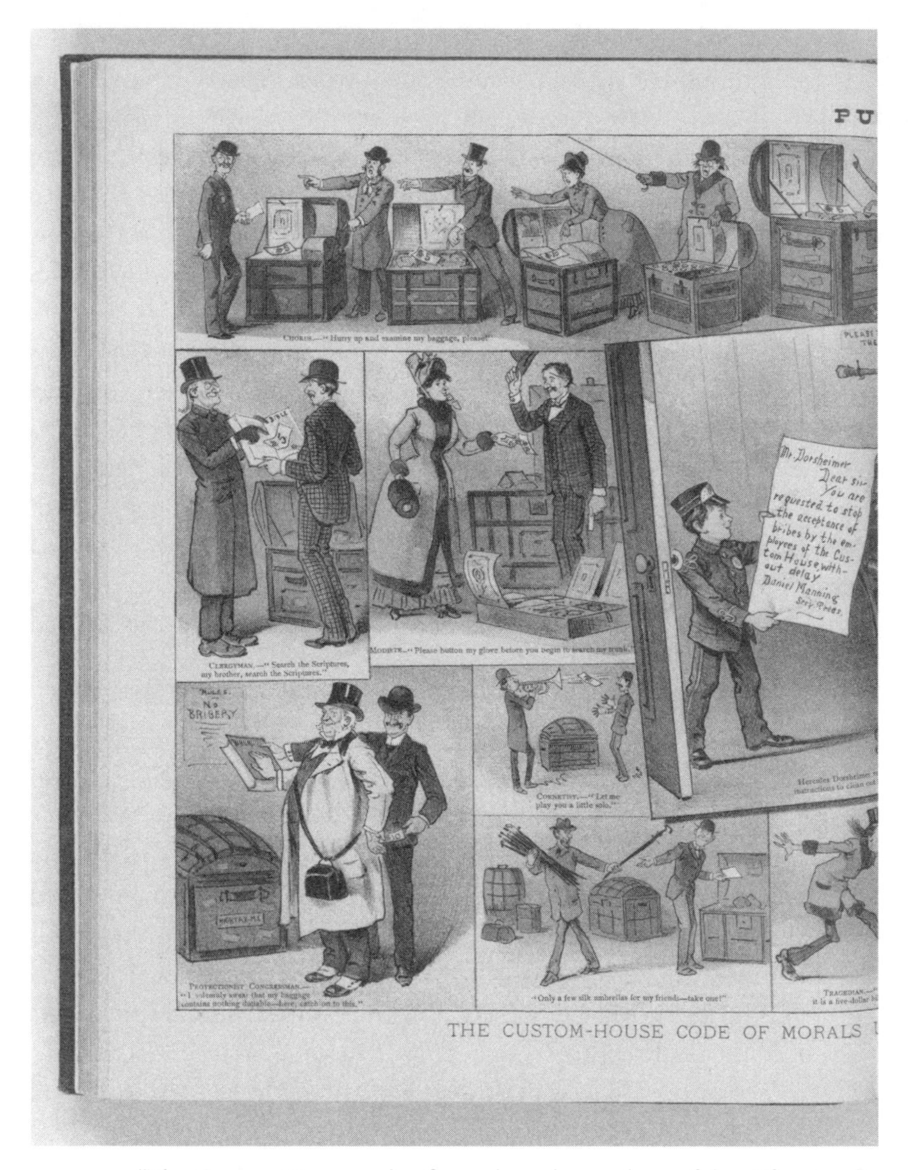

Figure 10.1 "The Custom-House code of morals under our beautiful tariff system." *Puck*, October 14, 1885. Political cartoon showing the many types of bribes offered to customs agents. (Library of Congress).

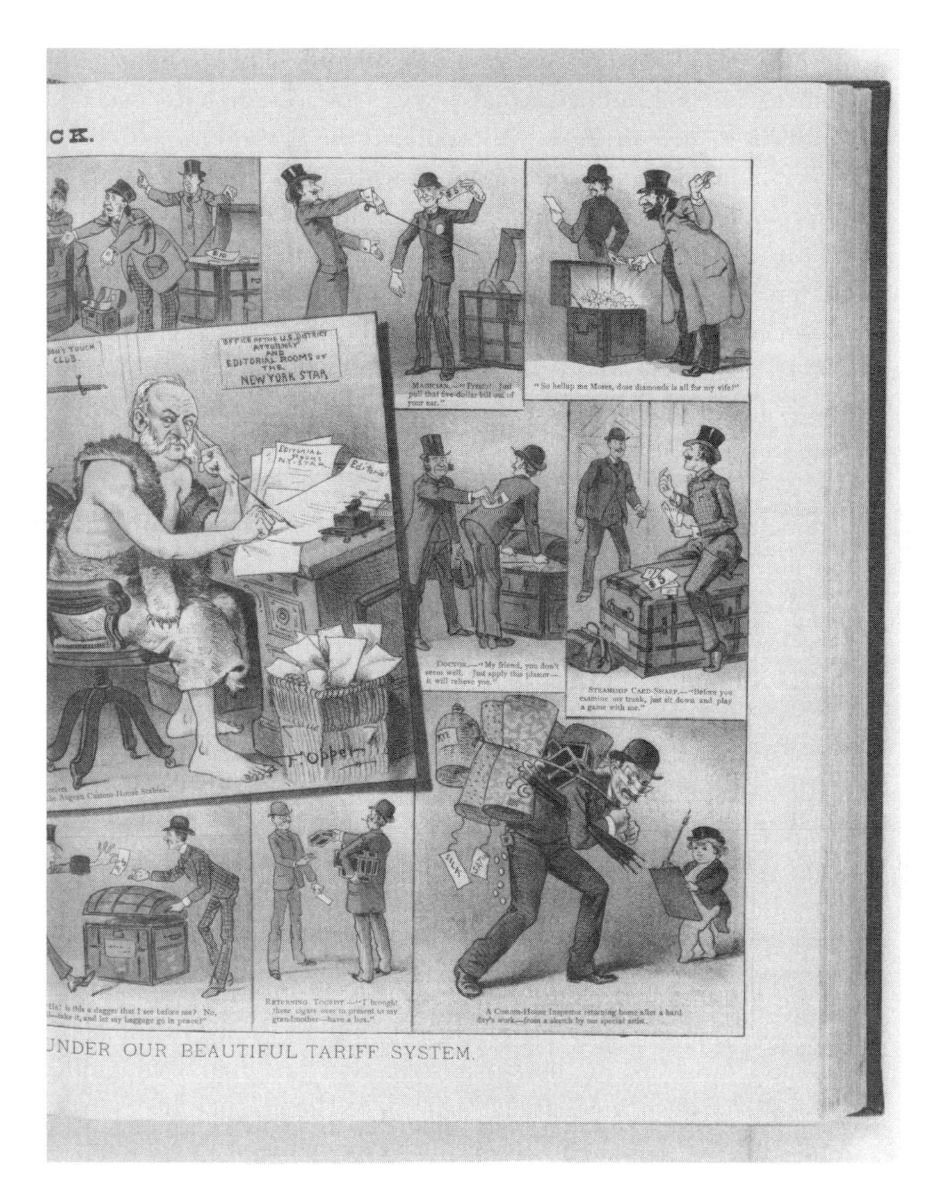
CK.
OFFICE OF THE U.S. DISTRICT ATTORNEY AND EDITORIAL ROOMS OF THE NEW YORK STAR
CLUB.
EDITORIAL ROOMS N.Y. STAR
Editorial
F. Opper
MAGICIAN.—"Presto! Just pull that five-dollar bill out of your ear."
"So hellup me Moses, dose diamonds is all for my vife!"
DOCTOR.—"My friend, you don't seem well. Just apply this plaster—it will relieve you."
STEAMSHIP CARD-SHARP.—"Before you examine my trunk, just sit down and play a game with me."
RETURNING TOURIST.—"I brought these cigars over to present to my grandmother—have a box."
A Custom-House Inspector returning home after a hard day's work.—from a sketch by our special artist.
SILK
UNDER OUR BEAUTIFUL TARIFF SYSTEM.

The New York customhouse came to symbolize corruption in a famously corrupt era. A standard scheme was for customs appraisers to take bribes from importers in return for undervaluing incoming goods.[18] "It is a fact more or less notorious among merchants," reported the *New York Herald*, that the appraiser's office within the customhouse "is rotten throughout. . . . The Place has become a disgrace even to the present administration."[19] Foreshadowing the Progressive movement's calls for reform decades later, in April 1877 the New York *Tribune* suggested that the city's customhouse was so corrupt that it should be placed at the top of the list of government operations across the country most in need of reform.[20]

Although the New York customhouse gained the greatest notoriety (partly due to its sheer size and importance), corruption also plagued the customhouse at other major ports. At the New Orleans customhouse, government investigators in 1877 found that the declared value of goods by importers was usually not questioned, and that there was "great elasticity of conscience" in such declarations—evident, for example, in keeping multiple sets of invoices (one reflecting the actual value of the goods, one below value used for entry, and one above value for selling the goods).[21] Special Treasury Department agents in San Francisco reported that in far too many instances "the luggage of passengers arriving from foreign ports were delivered to the owners without any examination, and that this was done by special order from the collector." Consequently, "hundreds of thousands of dollars worth of merchandise is brought into San Francisco and passed without payment of duty."[22] It was apparently common for passengers to bribe inspectors; as John Dean Goss wrote in his late-nineteenth-century survey of tariff administration, "the practice of bribe-taking, or the 'acceptance of gifts' by the inspectors from arriving passengers is very general, and produces a very demoralizing effect."[23]

Even as the New York customhouse faced mounting public complaints and charges of corruption, supporters rushed to its defense. In June 1871, *Harper's New Monthly Magazine* published a glowing profile of the New York customhouse, portraying it as a victim of corrupt merchants: "It is the fashion of the day to speak derisively of Custom-house officials. They are supposed to be idlers, and, if opportunity offers, dishonest." Nevertheless, "it should be remembered that no dishonest customs official can exist unless he is seduced into his fraudulent course by some unprincipled merchant trader. And yet the press and the public opinion launch their condemnation of the poor clerk, but never breathe a word of censure upon the plotter of the mischief, and receiver of the lion's share of the dishonestly obtained plunder."[24]

In June 1884, *Harper's* followed up with another glowing profile, calling the New York customhouse "the greatest institution in the city," noting that trade had almost doubled since 1866 and that most of this trade flowed through New York.[25] The city was indeed the leading beneficiary of the trade boom, becoming the world's most important trading center by the turn of the century. Astonishingly, American imports and exports doubled between 1897 and 1907, with much of it flowing through the port of New York. "Commerce," proclaimed an upbeat Charles King, the president of Columbia College, "is the interpreter of the wants of all other pursuits, the exchange of all values, the conveyor of all products."[26] He could have added, "through both legal and illegal means."

Smuggling in the American Dream

Whether by buying off, deceiving, or evading customs agents, smugglers managed to sneak in large quantities of untaxed goods. As one historian describes it, "Illegally imported goods from Europe, the Caribbean, and Asia filled store shelves, graced the dinner tables of fashionable houses, and swathed the bodies of chic women."[27] Smuggling greatly contributed to America's increasingly consumer-oriented and fashion-conscious society in the Gilded Age, an era defined by conspicuous consumption of foreign styles and tastes, imported both licitly and illicitly.[28]

In New York social circles an appearance of cosmopolitanism was attained through imitation, and imitation was attained through importation. In this "golden age of New York society," some high-society women ordered forty gowns from Paris every season, with each dress costing $2,500.[29] It should therefore be little surprise that in a period of both high tariffs and high consumption, some were tempted to keep up with changing fashion styles through tax-evading smuggling. As the *New York Times* reported, "In the Spring and in the Fall, when the styles change, there is always an epidemic of smuggling. The dressmakers, buyers, and milliners who bring back the latest Paris styles are now the subjects of constant watch."[30] One woman was even caught trying to use a fellow passenger to help her smuggle in her bridal outfit.[31] The customs commissioner estimated that in fiscal year 1872–73 36,830 travelers smuggled in goods worth $128,905,000 (the equivalent of $2.4 billion in 2010), though one must wonder how he could possibly have come up with such a precise number.[32] America in the Gilded Age, it seems, was not just a nation of shoppers but also a nation of illicit shoppers.

Illicit importers ranged from petty smugglers to major firms engaged in bulk smuggling. The former typically involved smuggling high-value and low-bulk items subject to heavy duties—such as jewelry, cigars, and watches—carried on the person or in personal luggage when returning from abroad.[33] The latter most often involved systematic undervaluing or false invoicing of commercial cargo, such as underestimating the weight of a shipment of sugar or bay oil, or listing highly dutiable silks and linens as cheaper cloth material.[34] For instance, in 1870 the *New York Times* reported that almost thirty "prominent firms" were accused of trading in smuggled bay oil, and in 1889 the paper reported on the near monopoly of the sugar trade by some twenty firms able to defraud the government and drive out competitors.[35] In 1877, the customhouse statistician Joseph Solomon Moore estimated that nearly $12 million in silk imports—some 25 percent of the total—was smuggled in.[36] In 1881, a leading New York silk manufacturer claimed that a majority of the duties on silk—which carried a 60 percent tariff—were routinely evaded through false invoicing.[37]

Books were also smuggled in to meet the demands of a rapidly growing reading public. In one smuggling operation, the book shipment was first sent from London to a broker in Montreal and then smuggled across the border into the United States.[38] But more often books were simply copied and reprinted in complete disregard of foreign copyright claims. After all, why bother smuggling in multiple copies of bulky books to get around high tariffs—typically 25 percent on books—when an American publisher could simply copy and reprint them cheaply without permission from the original publisher or author? The tariff created yet another incentive to engage in copyright piracy. In the nineteenth century the United States was notorious as "the foremost haven for international copyright piracy" in the world.[39] American copyright law did not protect most of the works of foreign authors until 1891, and even then piracy remained common.[40] Intellectual piracy in the publishing business was greatly aided by significant improvements in printing technology that made books and other publications much easier and cheaper to reproduce. The brazenness and magnitude of American reprinting outraged not only foreign publishers but also authors such as Charles Dickens, who pleaded for decades for U.S. copyright protection.[41] British author Wilkie Collins bitterly accused the Americans of making "robbery" into "the basis of national aggrandizement."[42]

Smuggling schemes carried out by steamship passengers were as varied as they were ingenious. Virtually anything could be used as a smuggling device: trunks with false bottoms and other hidden compartments, hollow canes and heels, and even infants and children. In one case, a boy was walking so stiffly and awkwardly that he caught the attention of an inspector at the New York port of entry. It turned out that the child had silver spoons sewn into his clothes, making it impossible for him to bend.[43]

Travelers returning from shopping sprees in Europe would often hide items inside their clothing, from hat to heel and everywhere in between. One Chicago smuggler somehow managed to stuff 42 chains, 112 diamonds, and 43 pearls in his boots—which were many sizes larger than his exceptionally small feet.[44] On-the-body smuggling even included dead bodies: one smuggler shipping a casket from abroad confessed to having placed forty-three rings on a dead man's fingers (the dead man was his brother). When informed by the authorities that what he was doing was smuggling, he simply replied, "Why, everybody that I know does it."[45]

Women smugglers were especially advantaged since they could conveniently stuff items inside overflowing dresses and elaborate hats and hairdos. As *Harper's New Monthly Magazine* described it, "As smugglers, women are more successful than men. The complications of their dress favor the business."[46] Usually this involved small items such as diamonds, pearls, jewelry, or watch chains, but in one case a woman was even caught trying to smuggle thirteen boxes of cigars under her dress.[47] Another woman wrapped her body in several thousand yards of expensive laces. When discovered, she insisted she was not smuggling but just trying to stay warm.[48] In another case, a woman was caught wearing a double-quilted petticoat filled with Shetland shawls, caps, and stockings.[49] The female clothing advantage diminished over time as women's fashion styles changed to tighter-fitting dresses, making it more difficult to hide smuggled items.

To handle the growing number of female smugglers, Customs hired women to search for contraband carried on the body. In March 1908, women inspectors estimated that more than half of the female passengers arriving from foreign ports were hiding dutiable goods somewhere on their persons.[50] Women who engaged in smuggling ranged from part-time amateurs to hired couriers to sophisticated professionals devising their own elaborate schemes. One of the most successful was Sophie Lyons, nicknamed "Queen of the Crooks" for her various criminal exploits; later in her career she made a small fortune in diamond smuggling. A 1902 headline in the *Los Angeles Times* called her the "Country's Greatest Woman Crook."[51]

The emergence and growth of the international tourism industry, enabled by much faster and more accessible travel via steamship, created far greater opportunities for petty smuggling and a growing headache for customs inspectors. At the turn of the century, almost 125,000 American tourists traveled overseas (nearly all to Europe), four times the number of travelers three decades earlier.[52] The number of American tourists traveling to Europe was double that number on the eve of World War I. Many viewed European destinations as not only a holiday adventure but also a shopping expedition, with the length of the transatlantic crossing—dubbed the "six-day pond"—drastically shortened by the steamship.[53]

American travelers were increasingly mobile, but so too were law enforcers. By the turn of the century, special Treasury Department agents were deployed to five European cities, headquartered in Paris, with tasks that included tracking big-spending Americans and informing inspectors back home what to look out for in the luggage on the return trip. The agents also kept busy trying to determine the true value of items (ranging from gloves to jewelry) to verify that American shoppers were making truthful value declarations when arriving back home.[54] As the New Orleans *Times-Democrat* reported, "The Treasury finds it profitable to maintain in the leading European cities agents to watch out for purchases of small articles of great value by Americans visiting abroad, and

Figure 10.2 "Home from the Old World—Examination of Baggage by Custom-House officers on a New York steamship wharf," *Harper's Weekly*, March 29, 1879 (John Hay Library, Brown University).

if the traveling American buys a tiara of diamonds or an expensive set of furs the chances are that the Treasury agents will know the purchase in a few hours."[55]

Customs agents enjoyed enormous discretion, leeway, and authority in carrying out their daily tasks. Indeed, the invasive power of the federal government in peacetime was nowhere greater or more concentrated than in customs inspections. Searches required no probable cause or warrant; mere suspicion was sufficient—and everyone was plausibly a suspect. As one headline in the *New York Times* read, "Law Stands Behind the Customs Officer," followed by the subhead "His Authority to Examine and Search a Suspected Smuggler is Almost Limitless."[56] In this regard, the policing power of the American state over citizens and noncitizens alike was most evident and concentrated at border points of entry.[57]

Highly intrusive and time-consuming customs inspections were the source of considerable anxiety, anger, and frustration among tourists and merchants alike. As the *Boston Herald* noted, "Nothing tends to make a man a free-trader as a few little bouts with the Custom

House, and even the sounder protectionists are now and then caught smuggling."[58] One prominent New York merchant went so far as to denounce the inspection process as "a system of terrorism"—though he had particular reason to complain given that his company was implicated in undervaluing imports.[59] Frequent grumbling about invasive and unreasonable customs procedures resonated widely. In one case, an overeager customs inspector provoked not only complaints but

Figure 10.3 "Another Hold-Up. This is the way Uncle Sam treats his own." Cover of *Life magazine*, May 4, 1899, depicting the treatment of returning American passengers by customs inspectors (John Hay Library, Brown University).

ridicule when he went so far as to snatch a four-ounce chocolate bar out of the hands of a fourteen-year-old girl at the New York port for failure to pay duty (the chocolate bar was returned).[60]

Americans from all walks of life enjoyed finding a good bargain, and evading the tariff could mean a steep discount. Even the superrich, who could most afford to pay duty, often took their chances at playing the smuggling game. A pearl necklace purchased at Tiffany & Company in Paris for tens of thousands of dollars was certainly expensive. But for some, the possibility of evading the 60 percent U.S. tariff made it an all-too-tempting bargain.[61] Less-high-end smugglers even found fake pearls—with a 20 percent import duty—attractive. This included, for example, the professional smuggler Ferdinand Block, who allegedly used Providence, Rhode Island, as a distribution hub for thousands of illicitly imported fake pearls.[62]

When the rich and famous were caught smuggling, it often caused them great embarrassment. In one case prominently reported in the *New York Times*, the former governor of New Hampshire along with his wife and son were arrested for smuggling.[63] In another case reported in the *Chicago Daily Tribune*, a Chicago millionaire caught smuggling insisted that the seized items—including pearl and diamond brooches, jewel boxes, and gold watches—were intended as Sunday school presents.[64]

Highly publicized cases of inspectors busting wealthy travelers for smuggling projected an image of government fairness and impartiality. At the same time, ethnic and racial profiling was both routine and accepted—with Jews and Chinese especially targeted, harassed, and crudely stereotyped as predisposed to engage in smuggling. They typically received extra scrutiny and more intensive inspections, including full-body searches.[65]

Bitter battles over the tariff question included denouncing smugglers, but also sometimes defending them. One prominent New York reformer, David A. Wells, even outdid Adam Smith in portraying the smuggler as "the knight-errant of civilization," who, acting "in disregard of the law, and sustained in a high degree of popular opinion . . . compels the letting down of barriers by which a false political economy seeks to isolate nation from nation."[66] In this view, the smuggler was at the forefront of bringing America and the world closer together.

At the same time, those who defended the tariff and denounced the smuggler reflected not just industrial interests but nationalist anxieties about bringing America and the world too closely together. These intense political debates over the tariff and its evasion, Cohen suggests, reflected America's deep ambivalence about globalization.[67]

THE COMBINATION OF HIGH tariff walls, rapidly expanding trade and transportation links to the outside world, and a flourishing consumer culture translated into extraordinary incentives and opportunities for tax-evading smuggling in America's Gilded Age. In 1869, *Harper's New Monthly Magazine* warned, "it is the opinion of men experienced in trade and political economy that we will soon become a nation of smugglers."[68] Overlooked in this pronouncement, of course, was that America had been a nation of smugglers from the very start. But by the first decades of the twentieth century it was a much more mature—and vastly richer and more powerful—smuggler nation. Sixty years after the prediction published in *Harper's*, a May 1929 article in the *Chicago Daily Tribune* asked: "Are we a nation of smugglers? The answer is that we are, if the 800,000 Americans who annually journey abroad may be regarded a fair cross section of our population." Indeed, petty smugglers came from all ethnicities and classes. The article went on to note that U.S. customs officials estimated some three-quarters of travelers returning from foreign trips were engaged in some form of smuggling, and that a mere 5 percent were probably caught.[69] Regardless of the accuracy of these numbers, U.S. customs agents clearly thought that smuggling had become as American as apple pie.

Most of this smuggling was about evading tariffs, whether on the part of tourists or professional illicit traders. But as we'll see in the next chapter, smuggling during this time period also increasingly involved evading prohibitions. And unlike tariffs, the goal of prohibitions was to eradicate rather than tax and regulate. Prohibitions were not about commercial protectionism but moral protection and condemnation. Smuggling therefore became deeply entangled in the politics of sin, deviance, and vice in a rapidly changing American society.

11

Sex, Smugglers, and Purity Crusaders

THE POLICING OF SMUGGLING in the post–Civil War era was first and foremost about revenue collecting, but it was also about purity crusading. Congress increasingly used its powers of regulating commerce to also suppress vice—providing another mechanism for enhanced policing powers. This began in midcentury with a federal prohibition on importing obscene material and then sharply escalated in the 1870s by extending the definition of obscenity to include contraceptives. Among other things, the import ban ironically helped protect and stimulate America's nascent underground pornography business, while the expanded antiobscenity laws created a lucrative trade in contraband condoms.

The flourishing illicit trade in obscene pictures, publications, and devices fueled a decades-long moral crusade, with much of the enforcement outsourced to newly deputized antivice groups. But it was the alarm over sex trafficking—the so-called white slave trade—that sparked a full-blown moral panic. The nature and magnitude of this illicit sex trade in the first years of the new century turned out to be wildly exaggerated, in no small part due to hyped-up media accounts and national anxieties about rapid urbanization and an unprecedented influx of immigrants; yet it left a lasting legacy of more expansive federal anticrime laws and policing bureaucracies.

Smut Smuggling

Beginning with the Tariff of 1842, federal law banned the importation of "indecent and obscene" pictures; in 1857 obscene books were added to the list of prohibited items. Customs was empowered to seize these materials, adding more work for inspectors otherwise preoccupied with dutiable commerce. And as was the case with tariff enforcement, New York was also center stage in the effort to ban obscene materials. The first known case of enforcing the ban at the New York port involved the seizure of nine German snuffboxes containing indecent pictures.[1]

But an ironic unintended consequence of attempting to eradicate smuggled smut was pornography protectionism—which jump-started a domestic porn industry.[2] Advances in printing technology enabled import substitution by making it possible to more rapidly and cheaply copy illicitly imported printed material. It was no longer necessary to smuggle in bulk quantities of foreign prints; a single smuggled copy would suffice. In the case of smuggled erotic literature, English publications were preferred since no translation was necessary.[3] It was standard practice for New York publishers to steal and copy English texts of all kinds, including illicit texts.

The trade in erotic photographs and other images, in contrast, faced no language barriers. Nude photographs were illicitly imported from the Netherlands and especially France. "Once smuggled into the United States," historian Wayne Fuller notes, "they were reproduced again and again in small photography shops across the country."[4] The invention and spread of photography made it possible to produce stunningly lifelike sexual images as never before, and their portability and low expense made them widely accessible. France had an especially notorious reputation as the world's leading source of erotic photographs and began to inundate the U.S. market starting in the 1860s.[5] Further technological advances in cameras and photography equipment in the late nineteenth century made such photographs even cheaper and more available.

Meanwhile, an increasingly fast, affordable, and efficient U.S. mail service—made possible by the nation's expanding railroad network—provided the ideal advertising and distribution mechanism for pornography peddlers.[6] And nowhere was this more evident than in mail deliveries to army camps during the Civil War, where Union soldiers routinely received enticing flyers and catalogs from New York–based sellers detailing their sexually arousing offerings.[7] Erotic photographs were particularly easy to distribute via the mail. Using its powers to regulate trade, Congress responded by outlawing the mailing of any "publication of a vulgar and indecent character . . ." Violators could be fined up to $500 or imprisoned for up to one year.[8] Since mail was both foreign and domestic—and could include both obscene material and dutiable items—the missions of Customs and the Post Office increasingly overlapped. This created jurisdictional tension and competition but gave way to growing cooperation by the end of the nineteenth century.[9]

The campaign against the trade in obscene materials really took off in March 1873 when Congress passed the Act for the Suppression of Trade in, and Circulation of, Obscene Literature and Articles of Immoral Use. The new law (which extended, expanded, and strengthened earlier bans) came to be known as the Comstock Act, named after the zealous antivice crusader Anthony Comstock. He made vice hunting his lifelong obsession, not only aggressively lobbying for a more expansive antiobscenity law but taking on the job of enforcing it as well. For the next four decades, no other person in America became more closely associated with stamping out the illicit trade in obscene materials, so much so that a new word, "Comstockery," was coined.[10] Although he was ridiculed in cartoons as fanatically prudish, his crusade was also cheered on in Victorian America and bankrolled by prominent wealthy New Yorkers.

Nassau Street in lower Manhattan was not only the hub of the pornography publishing business but also the headquarters for Comstock's campaign to eradicate it. Comstock was the secretary of the New York Society for the Suppression of Vice, backed by the Young Men's Christian Association (YMCA) and influential donors. Empowered by federal law and appointed as a special agent of the U.S. Mail, Comstock and his collaborators kept long, detailed lists of arrests, convictions, and seizures as a running tally of their successes.[11] Many arrests were made through elaborate "buy and bust" sting operations, with Comstock often posing as a would-be customer. Penalties for violators included one to ten years in prison and fines up to $5,000. By the time he died in 1915, he had made 3,873 arrests (with more than 2,900 convictions) for Comstock law violations.[12] Painting the obscenity threat as largely of

Figure 11.1 "Your Honor, this woman gave birth to a naked child!" One of many political cartoons that ridiculed Anthony Comstock and his antivice crusade. *The Masses*, 1915 (Granger Collection).

foreign origin, he disproportionately targeted immigrants. Highlighting statistics on the high number of nonnative citizens arrested, Comstock reported, "It will be seen at a glance that we owe much of this demoralization to the importation of criminals from other lands."[13]

In addition to arrest numbers, the New York Society for the Suppression of Vice also meticulously compiled seizure statistics. The society's 1900 annual report summed up its work to date: "Books and Sheet Stock seized and destroyed—78,608 lbs; Obscene Pictures and Photos [seized and destroyed]—877,412; Negative Plates for making Obscene Photos [seized and destroyed]—8,495; Engraved Steel and Copper Plates [seized and destroyed]—425; Stereotype Plates for Printing Books, etc. [seized and destroyed]—28,050 lbs; Indecent Playing Cards destroyed—6,436; Circulars, Catalogues, Songs, Poems, etc. [destroyed]—1,672,050."[14] By the end of Comstock's four-decade

Figure 11.2 Seal of the New York Society for the Suppression of Vice, founded in 1873. On the left, an illicit purveyor of obscene materials is taken into a cell; on the right, seized obscene materials are burned (Granger Collection).

mission to suppress smut, he had confiscated fifty tons of books and four million pictures and made some four thousand arrests. Comstock even pointed to more than fifteen suicides as an indicator of his success.[15]

One prominent suicide case was the Irish immigrant William Haines, who made a fortune selling hundreds of thousands of copies of obscene books from the 1840s to the early 1870s. He played a pioneering role in the emergence of the U.S. pornography trade, entering it the same year as the first federal ban on imports and becoming "the nation's largest and most notorious publisher of erotic print."[16] The night before he committed suicide he received a message: "Get out of the way. Comstock is after you. Damn fool won't look at money."[17]

But far from eradicating the illicit trade, Comstock's crusade instead transformed it, pushing it more into the shadows and out of sight. The

GENUINE FANCY BOOKS.

Beautifully illustrated with Colored Plates.

Every work on this circular is exactly as represented, printed from new type, on fine paper, handsomly illustrated with expensive COLORED PLATES, and richly bound in cloth.

To ensure safety and defy detection, all those books are sent privately by mail, done up in strong wrappers, closely sealed up with wax, and full letter postage paid on every book.

When those books are ordered to be sent by express, there is 25 per cent. discount allowed on the annexed prices.

In ordering any of those books, it is always necessary to order by the number instead of the title of the book. The prefixed number to each book is the regular trade-mark. In ordering in this way, there can be no possible mistake made in sending the right book.

Prices reduced

No.	Title	Plates	Price
No. 1.	FANNY HILL, large size	24 Colored Plates	$4.00
" 2.	FESTIVAL OF LOVE, or REVELS AT THE FOUNT OF VENUS (New book.)	11 " "	2.00
" 3.	FANNY HILL, HER LIFE AND AMOURS.	10 " "	2.00
" 4.	ROSE DE AMOR, THE FRENCH COURTESAN	10 " "	2.00
" 5.	LUSTFUL TURK, OR LOVE IN THE HAREM.	10 " "	2.00
" 6.	TWO COUSINS. THEIR CONFESSIONS	10 " "	2.00
" 7.	SILAS SHOVEWEL, HER AMOURS WITH THE MONKS	10 " "	2.00
" 8.	CURTAIN DRAWN UP, OR THE EDUCATION OF LAURA.	10 " "	2.00
" 9.	VOLUPTUOUS CONFESSIONS IN BED.	5 " "	1.00
" 10.	MADAME CELESTE, HER INTRIGUES.	5 " "	1.00
" 11.	CECILIE MARTIN, THE WOMAN OF PLEASURE.	5 " "	1.00
" 12.	CABINET OF VENUS UNLOCKED.	5 " "	1.00
" 13.	FLASH AND FRISKY SONGSTR	5 " "	1.00

☞ Recollect none of the above articles can be had at my office in New York, or through any agency or bookseller whatever. All orders must come by mail to be promptly and faithfully attended to.

Figure 11.3. "Genuine Fancy Books." Private circular advertising erotica, promising to make discreet deliveries through the mail in a manner that will "defy detection" (American Antiquarian Society)

trade was also increasingly pushed out of New York, unintentionally spreading it to other towns and cities across the country.[18] Pornographers creatively adjusted to the new prohibitionist climate, using aliases and false addresses and increasing their bribes and payoffs to the authorities;

some even posed as religious publishers.[19] Pornography traders also shifted to more portable and lightweight products—away from bulky books and toward more concealable items such as photographs and playing cards.[20] Similarly, as it became riskier to use the U.S. mail system, illicit traders increasingly turned to private express companies to reach their customers.[21] Comstock's targeting of the most established publishers also created openings for new market entrants attracted by the unusually high profits of the trade (with expected profit margins as high as 500 percent).[22] The illicit import side of the trade also survived Comstock's crackdown. As domestic publishing became a much riskier business, a high-end niche import trade also flourished in the late nineteenth century aimed at wealthy clientele willing to pay a premium for "luxury erotica" smuggled in from Europe.[23]

Contraband Contraceptives

Obscene texts and pictures were not the only items banned. The Comstock Act extended the definition of obscenity to include all devices and information related to contraception or abortion as well.[24] Imports were prohibited. When asked why birth control was added to the ban on obscenity, Comstock replied, "If you open the door to anything, the filth will all pour in and the degradation of youth will follow."[25] But as was the case with obscene material, the import ban on contraceptives did more to stimulate domestic production than curb supply. This was strikingly evident in the story of the condom.

Until the 1850s, virtually all condoms were imported from Europe and made from animal intestines. They were also expensive, as much as a dollar per condom in the 1830s, making them unaffordable to most.[26] Condoms were often imported via smuggling, but to evade U.S. tariffs rather than prohibitions. *India Rubber World*, an American trade journal, reported that condoms were regularly "brought in from Europe, not as a regular import, but in small carefully-guarded packets that got by the customs officials without paying duty."[27]

Condom production was revolutionized in midcentury through a technical breakthrough—the vulcanization of rubber (which made rubber resistant to both melting and cracking)—patented in 1844 by the American Charles Goodyear. Skin condoms remained popular, but the rubber revolution increased supplies, heightened competition, and drove down prices. By the early 1860s, a condom cost as little as a dime.[28] George Bernard Shaw even called the rubber condom "the greatest invention of the nineteenth century."[29] Condoms were not only more affordable than ever by the time of the 1873 ban; they remained relatively cheap afterward, with the price of a rubber condom in 1887 still ten times less than that of the animal skin equivalent of a few decades earlier.[30]

Curiously, the same year that condoms were criminalized and imports banned, the duty on legal imports of the animal intestines most commonly used to make skin condoms was lifted and never drew Comstock's attention. As historian Jane Farrell Brodie writes, the prohibition on "the importation of contraceptives was never enforced against goldbeater's skins [the outer membrane of calf intestines] or their molds, so that throughout the decades when the laws against reproductive control were most stringently enforced a constant supply of materials ready to be made into condoms was available."[31] In other words, even as the importation of condoms was banned, the legal importation of skins for clandestine domestic condom manufacturing remained legal and was even facilitated by the lifting of the tariff. Predictably, this encouraged and enabled import substitution in the condom trade.

As was the case with pornography, the main effect of prohibition was to drive the birth control business underground, making it much less public and visible even as it continued to thrive. Compare, for example, advertising before and after the Comstock law. As Robert Jutte notes, "At the beginning of the 1870s . . . a third of all advertisements in the popular New York paper the *Sporting Times and Theatrical News* consisted of publicity for methods of abortion and contraception."[32] One Manhattan-based firm advertised its wares as follows: "Best protectors against disease and accident. French rubber goods $6.00/dozen; rubber $4.00/dozen. Sample 30 cents. Trade supplied. Ladies protectors $3.00."[33] The first advertisement for condoms appeared in the *New York Times* in 1861, but the Comstock law made such advertisements increasingly scarce. After 1873, information and knowledge about birth control continued to circulate, though much less freely. Advertising continued, using less candid and blunt language. Distributors protected themselves from the law by advertising products for their hygienic value (such as "sanitary sponges for ladies") rather than for their antipregnancy uses.[34]

Some inventors even continued to apply for patents for birth control devices, but without directly labeling them contraceptives. Texas inventor Uberto Ezell applied for a patent in 1904 for a rubber "male pouch," which was a condom in all but name, described as a device to "catch and retain all discharges coming" from the "male member."[35] The patent was approved in 1906.

Comstock's crusade was noticeably selective, typically targeting lower-class immigrants while turning a blind eye to the rich and respectable.[36] This latter group included Samuel Colgate, the president of the New York Society for the Suppression of Vice; his New Jersey soap company was the exclusive manufacturer of Vaseline, a petroleum jelly advertised as a safe contraceptive aid to help kill sperm.[37] Other major companies—notably Goodyear; Goodrich; and Sears, Roebuck and Co.—advertised contraceptives without attracting the ire of Comstock and his antivice agents. They escaped scrutiny partly because contraceptives were never more than a marginal part of their commercial profile. This created space for smaller players to participate in the riskier and more criminalized business of mass distribution. The prohibitionist climate inhibited larger firms from making contraceptives a core part of their business and thus taking over the market.[38]

At the high end of the contraband condom business, the best and most reliable products continued to be shipped in from Europe.[39] But the mass-produced stuff was increasingly domestic. Clandestine condom production (both rubber and skin) required minimal start-up costs, and the product itself was highly portable, profitable, concealable, and in great demand—an ideal commodity in a dispersed and decentralized black market. As was the case with pornography, illicit distribution was facilitated by the increasingly efficient and inexpensive U.S. mail system. In the end, it was not Comstock but rather the invention of latex in the 1920s, as well as new FDA regulations, mass production, and product standardization in the 1930s, that pushed small-time entrepreneurs out of the business.[40] Until then, criminalization had a democratizing effect on the market, creating a profitable niche for small-time entrepreneurs—many of them immigrants—who were otherwise relegated to the margins of society. For those willing to take the risks, the commerce in contraband contraceptives offered few barriers to entry and provided an alternative avenue of upward mobility.[41]

Take the remarkable career of Julius Schmidt, a young Jewish immigrant from Germany who started out making animal-intestine condoms on the side while working at a meat-processing plant in New York. Harassed, arrested, and fined by Comstock, Schmidt nevertheless managed to build up an underground condom business that would not only survive but thrive. Despite raids on his home, Schmidt continued to expand his business, and he listed "cap manufacturer" as his occupation on the 1890 census.[42] Decades later, *Fortune* magazine would dub him the king of the American condom empire—without mentioning his criminal past. Changing his last name to Schmid, he also became the top condom supplier to the U.S. armed forces during World War II.[43]

Many women also turned to birth control bootlegging at a time when their economic opportunities were few and far between.[44] This included, for instance, Antoinette Hon, a Polish immigrant who specialized in mail order distribution of "womb suppositories" and "douching powders" from her base in South Bend, Indiana.[45] In the case of Margaret Sanger, birth control (a term she coined) was a cause rather than a business. Credited as the founder of the American birth control movement, she repeatedly defied and evaded Comstock in the waning years of his campaign. She was arrested multiple times, in 1916 for opening the country's first birth control clinic, which landed her in jail for thirty days. On several other occasions, she fled to Europe to avoid arrest. It was during these overseas trips, including to the Netherlands, where she expanded her knowledge about birth control practices, that she developed many of her core views.[46]

Sanger also colluded with her husband, James Noah Slee, to smuggle Mensinga diaphragms into the country. Slee, the president of the Three-in-One Oil Company, used the cover of his business to ship the diaphragms from Europe to Montreal, and from there the shipments were smuggled across the U.S.-Canada border hidden in the company's oil drums. Sanger resorted to this smuggling scheme not only to evade the prohibition on contraceptives but also to avoid dealing with domestic black marketeers such as Schmid, whom she viewed as too commercially oriented.[47]

As was the case with catching pornography traders, Comstock and his agents relied heavily on undercover purchases and buy-and-bust sting operations. But their effectiveness was limited by privacy protections and court rulings against entrapment. Much to Comstock's frustration and dismay, judges and juries tended to have a more lenient and less punitive attitude toward bootleg birth control than toward smut smuggling.[48] There were far fewer arrests and convictions for the former than the latter. Comstock's agents made fewer than five arrests related to birth control per year between March 1873 and March 1898.[49]

So despite Comstock's crusading efforts, black market contraceptives remained widely available at relatively affordable prices.[50] It is striking that the national fertility rate was declining at the same time as Comstock was busily trying to suppress contraception and abortion. Although extremely difficult to measure, it is not unreasonable to speculate that black market supplies played a role in the country's declining birthrate. Abortion was obviously not a form of smuggling, but importing and distributing information and devices related to abortion certainly was.[51]

World War I proved to be a decisive turning point in the battle over contraband contraceptives. In the context of war, concern about the spread of sexually transmitted diseases was elevated to the status of a security threat, for which the condom was increasingly viewed as an urgently needed shield. The logistical challenge, however, was that Germany was Europe's largest producer of rubber condoms. Cut off from German supplies, Allied troops looked to alternative sources—including from outlawed U.S. producers such as Schmidt—who now also became illicit exporters for the war effort in Europe. The American company Youngs Rubber began to produce the now-famous Trojan brand of condoms in 1916. As Merle Youngs, the company's founder, later acknowledged, the war generated "a tremendous demand . . . for these little articles."[52] According to Youngs, condoms were "unofficially" sold in many government-run canteens despite the military's official stance of prohibition. More than four million American men took part in World War I, and they brought back both greater familiarity with and acceptance of condom use.[53]

Growing anxiety and concern about venereal disease ultimately trumped Victorian taboos and legal prohibitions. Legal rulings began to roll back the Comstock law. In 1918, Judge Frederick Crane overturned a conviction against Sanger, ruling that condom use was legal and not "indecent or immoral" if prescribed by a doctor to prevent disease. But since there was no real enforcement of the prescription requirement—condoms marked "for the prevention of disease only" could even be bought at pool parlors and gas stations—the need for a medical justification was moot.[54] In a July 1930 New York court of appeals ruling, producers of contraceptives who promised to sell only to licensed doctors and druggists were exempted from federal prosecution.[55]

Decriminalization was therefore achieved through medicalization; the rationale of disease prevention provided the cover for pregnancy prevention. Contraceptives were not removed from U.S. obscenity statutes until 1970, a century after the Comstock Act. And until 1971 it was still illegal (and thus considered smuggling) for a layperson to import contraceptives.[56] Only after the sexual revolution of the 1960s did access to birth control come to be viewed as not just a medical necessity but also as a reproductive right.

The "White Slave Trade" Moral Panic

The only thing that enraged morality groups more than selling smut was selling sex. And not only was there plenty being sold, it was both highly visible and foreign-looking. From New York to San Francisco, the brothel business in urban America was flourishing, and many of the prostitutes were newly arrived immigrants. This coincided with the rapid growth of cities, filled by record waves of new immigrants, an increasingly restless and mobile population, shifting sexual mores, and rising public anxiety over the disorienting speed of change. This combustible mix was the backdrop for a full-blown nationwide panic over the "white slave trade" in the first decade of the twentieth century.

In following a familiar pattern, accusing fingers once again pointed at the new arrivals. And it wasn't just their sheer number that was so unsettling (some thirteen million new immigrants between 1900 and 1914); it was also where they were coming from: increasingly from eastern and southern Europe, which meant more "undesirable" Catholics and Jews. A congressional commission set up in 1907 warned of the growing connection among immigrants, vice, and crime: "The vilest practices are brought here from continental Europe" and "imported women and their men" were corrupting America with "the most bestial refinements of depravity."[57] Jewish and French pimp organizations were singled out for the most blame.[58]

Sensationalistic accounts in the popular press further fueled fears of an invasion of vice. Writing for *McClure's Magazine*, the muckraker George Kibbe Turner gained instant national attention in April 1907 when he reported that a "company of men, largely composed of Russian Jews," supplied most of the women for Chicago's brothels, and that "These men have a sort of loosely organized association extending through the large cities of the country, the chief centers being New York, Boston, Chicago, and New Orleans."[59]

Turner gained even more attention in November 1909 with another article in *McClure's*, this time claiming that New York City had become "the chief center of the white slave trade in the world." This massive illicit trade, he claimed, came from Europe and was now so deeply entrenched in New York's immigrant neighborhoods that the city's sex traders were exporting enslaved women to all corners of the globe.[60] And the victims were not only poor immigrant girls but also naïve and innocent "country girls"—wooed to the darkness of the city by slick and shady foreign men. Turner offered startling details even if very little actual evidence; but no matter. The story stuck in the national imagination because it reaffirmed and played to deep-seated anxieties and fears. Variations of the same storyline proliferated in articles and books across the country, generating a cottage industry of white slave trade horror stories.[61]

Edwin W. Sims, the U.S. attorney in Chicago, added an authoritative voice to the chorus of alarm bells. In 1909 he confidently wrote, "The legal evidence thus far collected establishes with complete moral certainty the awful facts: That the white slave traffic is a system operated by a syndicate which has its ramifications from the Atlantic seaboard to the Pacific ocean, with 'clearing houses' or 'distribution centers' in nearly all of the larger cities . . . that this syndicate . . . is a definite organization sending its hunters regularly to scour France, Germany, Hungary, Italy and Canada for victims; that the man at the head of this unthinkable enterprise it [*sic*] known among his hunters as 'The Big Chief.' "[62]

Figure 11.4 *Fighting the Traffic in Young Girls, or War on the White Slave Trade*. The provocative cover of a popular 1910 book by Ernest A. Bell depicts a young girl enslaved in a brothel and watched over by a shadowy figure (Yale University Library).

In late November of that year, President Howard Taft was briefed by Sims, along with Representative James R. Mann of Illinois, the chairman of the House Committee on Foreign and Interstate Commerce. At the end of the meeting, Mann announced to the press that investigations "have disclosed a situation startling in its nature as to the extent of the traffic in young girls, both within the United States and from France and other foreign countries. Most of these American girls are enticed away from their homes in the country to large cities. The police power exercised by the state and municipal governments is inadequate to prevent this—particularly when the girls are enticed from one State to another or from a foreign country to the United States."[63] In his first State of the Union Address the next month, Taft pointed to the "urgent necessity for additional legislation and greater executive activity to suppress the recruiting of the ranks of prostitutes from the streams of immigration into this country," concluding that "I believe it to be constitutional to forbid, under penalty, the transportation of persons for purposes of prostitution across national and state lines."[64] The *New York Times* chimed in with its support, editorializing that the "belief that the white slave trade is a great as well as a monstrous evil . . . has the support of all the commissioners and individuals who have given the matter examination at once honest and careful."[65]

The anti–white slavery crusade peaked with the passage of the White Slave Traffic Act of 1910, otherwise known as the Mann Act—named after Representative James Robert Mann, the sponsor of the bill that Congress quickly passed with little debate. The president signed it on June 25, 1910. The Mann Act went well beyond an earlier federal law, mostly aimed at Chinese immigrants, restricting the entry of prostitutes. Yet again, Congress used its authority to regulate commerce as the basis for expanding federal police powers.

Although the frenzy that created the Mann Act was specifically about stopping white slavery, the language of the law was far more sweeping, vague, and open-ended. The law penalized "any person who . . . knowingly transport[s] . . . in interstate or foreign commerce . . . any woman or girl for the purpose of prostitution or debauchery, or for any other immoral purpose, or with the intent and purpose to induce, entice, or compel such woman or girl to become a prostitute or to give herself up to debauchery, or to engage in any other immoral practice. . . ." Those last six words opened the door for federal authorities to police all sorts of other perceived vices. In the next years and decades the Mann Act would be so broadly interpreted that most arrests had little or nothing to do with anything resembling white slavery.[66]

The task of enforcing the Mann Act was handed to the Bureau of Investigation, a small upstart government agency with limited jurisdiction. The bureau seized the opportunity to expand its mandate and increase its visibility. Previously confined mostly to Washington, it opened a field office in Baltimore, significantly increased manpower, and deployed agents to cities across the country. It received a major boost when the attorney general established a specialized division, the Office of the Special Commissioner for the Suppression of the White Slave Traffic. The Mann Act gave the bureau the kind of feel-good, high-profile, righteous mission through which it could generate public and political support and make a name for itself; later, this included changing its name to the Federal Bureau of Investigation. Historians credit the Mann Act for giving the FBI its early boost.[67]

The notion that there was a vast, sophisticated, foreign-inspired white slave trade turned out to be overblown, to say the least. Many prostitutes, often immigrants, were certainly exploited and abused. Some were no doubt coerced. But the complex social realities involved many more shades of gray than the black-and-white picture of victims and victimizers painted by politicians, popular publications, and antivice groups. And historians have certainly found no evidence of a global criminal syndicate supplying the country's brothels. Even the *New York Times*, which had backed the anti-white slavery crusade at its peak in 1909 and 1910, editorialized in July 1914 that "sensational magazine articles had created a belief in the existence of a great interstate 'white slave' trust. No such trust exists, nor is there any organized white slave industry anywhere." In 1916 it described the "myth of an international and interstate 'syndicate' trafficking in women" as little more than "a figment of imaginative fly-gobblers."[68]

But even an illicit flesh trade that turned out to be more myth than reality had profound and long-lasting effects. The moral panic surrounding it was relatively short-lived, but it left an enduring legacy of greatly expanded federal policing powers. As James Morone puts it, "In the uproar" over the white slave trade, "policy makers laid down the institutional foundations for federal crime-fighting."[69]

MUCH OF THE MORAL crusading of the late nineteenth century and early twentieth century—whether against smuggled smut, contraband condoms, or sex trafficking—targeted immigrants as much as these particular illicit trades. So, as we'll see in the next chapter, it should be no surprise that the federal government also got into the business of immigration control for the first time during this period, stimulating both the business of migrant smuggling and the rise of a national immigration law enforcement apparatus.

12

Coming to America Through the Back Door

AMERICA IS OFTEN CALLED a "nation of immigrants," highlighting a long tradition of an open and welcoming front door. But this tells only part of the story. The front door has never been fully open, and became increasingly regulated at the national level in the last decades of the nineteenth century.[1] Consequently, less welcome immigrants developed alternate routes and methods of entry through the back door. They either deceived authorities at official ports of entry or evaded authorities by clandestinely crossing the country's vast land borders—smuggling themselves in or hiring the services of professional smugglers.

This chapter tells the story of this back door and how it was created, used, policed, and transformed over time. Considering the current policy preoccupation with illegal Mexican immigrants, it is especially striking that the early part of our story has so little to do with Mexicans. Indeed, Americans illegally migrated *to* Mexico long before Mexicans illegally migrated to the United States, moreover, the first illegal immigrants crossing the border from Mexico viewed by U.S. authorities as a problem were actually Chinese.

The influx of foreigners, both legal and illegal, changed the face of America. At the same time, enforcing increasingly restrictive entry laws and cracking down on human smuggling gave birth to a national immigration-control apparatus. Federal responsibility for regulating the nation's borders, traditionally focused almost entirely on the flow of goods, was now extended to also include the flow of people. Illegal entrants were numerically far less significant than their legal counterparts, but the political and bureaucratic scramble to keep them out transformed the policing profile of the federal government.

An Old American Tradition

Our story begins with a brief historical detour back to the colonial era. Illegally moving and settling, it turns out, is an old American tradition, even if it was not called "illegal immigration." Consider, for instance, colonial defiance of the British Proclamation of 1763, which imposed a frontier line between the colonies and Indian territories west of the Appalachian Mountains. King George III prohibited colonists from moving across the line and settling, and he deployed thousands of troops to the western colonial frontier to enforce the law. The British feared loss of control over their subjects, and they also wished to avoid conflicts between colonists and Indians. But the colonists simply ignored the proclamation and illegally moved into what became Kentucky and Tennessee. Tensions between the colonists and British authorities over freedom of movement intensified until the outbreak of the American Revolution. And after Independence, these Anglo-American tensions persisted, but now over the illegal emigration of skilled British artisans. As we saw in Chapter 6, thousands of ambitious artisans managed to smuggle themselves out of the country in violation of strict British emigration laws, helping to jump-start the American industrial revolution.

Meanwhile, independence from Britain opened up enormous opportunities for illegal westward movement by settlers in defiance of central government authorities.[2] With the adoption by Congress of the Land Ordinances of 1784 and 1785, the national government planned to survey and then sell off territory west of the original states. The Northwest Ordinance, passed in August 1789, created the Northwest Territory, a geographic area east of the Mississippi River and below the Great Lakes. These land ordinances, designed by Congress to raise revenue, deter squatters, and promote orderly westward migration and settlement, were quickly undermined by a flood of unlawful settlers unwilling or unable to pay for the public land. Squatters also moved onto Indian lands in violation of federal treaty obligations, often leading to bloodshed. The debates over the Northwest Ordinance included public denouncements of illegal squatters. William Butler of New York, for instance, complained, "I Presume Council has been made acquainted with the villainy of People of this Country, that are flocking from all Quarters, settling & taking up not only the United States lands but also this State's, many Hundreds have crossed the Rivers, & are dayly going many with their family's, the Wisdom of the Council I hope will Provide against so gross and growing an evil."[3]

In 1785 Congress empowered the secretary of war to crack down on illegal settlers, and the laws grew harsher as the problem persisted. The Intrusion Act of 1807 criminalized illegal settlement and authorized fines and imprisonment for lawbreakers. These measures were largely ineffective from the start. Testimony delivered to Congress in 1789 noted that the army "burnt the cabins, broke down the fences, and tore up the potatoe patches [of the squatters]; but three hours after the troops were gone, these people returned again, repaired the damage, and are now settled upon the land in open defiance of the union."[4] Some states, such as Vermont and Maine, actually won statehood after being settled by illegal squatters who refused to buy the land from the legally recognized owners and violently resisted government eviction efforts. Even President Washington found it maddeningly difficult to remove illegal settlers from his western lands and bitterly complained about it.[5]

The pattern of illegal settlement and intense (sometimes even violent) resistance to central government authority repeated itself for decades as migration accelerated and the frontier pushed westward.[6] According to one estimate, by 1828 two-thirds of Illinois residents were illegal squatters on federal land.[7] The westward demographic movement included European immigrants who entered the country legally but then settled illegally. Failing to deter and remove illegal settlers, Congress passed "preemption" acts, first in 1830 and again in 1841. These were essentially pardons for illegal settlement, providing legitimate land deeds at heavily discounted prices. The law, in other words, eventually adjusted and conformed to the realities of the situation, legalizing previously criminalized behavior.[8]

Of course, even though illegal settlers defied the authorities and undermined the rule of law, in the end they were an essential part of westward expansion, very much serving the federal government's objective of populating the West and extending the nation's geographic reach. This included the illegal influx of American settlers into what is now the state of Texas despite Mexico's decree of April 1830 prohibiting further immigration from the United States. Texas border officials paid little attention to such orders from a faraway central government. By 1836, the immigrant population greatly outnumbered Tejanos.[9] The Mexican government even deployed garrisons to try to control the influx, but the Americans continued to illegally move across the border. In this regard, the famous battle at the Alamo can be viewed as a militarized attempt to stop illegal American immigration—though that is not what "remember the Alamo" is meant to remind us of.

Last but not least, the smuggling of hundreds of thousands of African slaves into the country after the importation of slave labor was banned—first by states and then by the federal government—certainly qualifies as the most brutal form of forced illegal migration in the nation's history. The federal government's erratic and often halfhearted measures to restrict the illegal importation of slaves can be viewed as a form of immigration control. Moreover, as formally codified in the nation's fugitive slave laws, escaped slaves residing in the North were essentially illegal immigrants. They were asylum seekers denied the legal protection of asylum, and therefore lived in constant fear of being deported back to the South. And even in the midst of the Civil War, fleeing slaves crossing Union lines were labeled "contrabands"; they remained in a legal limbo until the repeal of the fugitive slave laws and abolition of slavery.

Closing the Front Door

The federal government did not get into the business of controlling immigration in a serious and sustained way until the efforts to prohibit Chinese immigration in the 1870s and 1880s, marking the beginning of Washington's long and tumultuous history of trying to keep out "undesirables." Before then, regulating immigration was mostly left to the states to sort out.

Figure 12.1 "And Still They Come." Political cartoon depicts Uncle Sam trying to manage the influx of Chinese migrants through the front door while many sneak in via the back doors of Mexico and Canada. *The Wasp*, August–December 1880 (Bancroft Library, University of California).

Starting in the 1850s, tens of thousands of Chinese laborers (many of whom left China in violation of their country's emigration laws[10]) were welcomed in the American west as a source of cheap labor, especially to build the transcontinental railroad. But they were never welcomed as people. From the start, Chinese could not become citizens. So it is little surprise that once the demand for Chinese labor dried up, an anti-Chinese backlash quickly followed. And it is also no surprise that the backlash was most intense in California, home to most of the country's Chinese population.[11] By 1870, Chinese composed some 10 percent of the state's population and about one-fourth of its workforce.

As political pressure to "do something" about the "yellow peril" intensified, Congress first passed the Page Act of 1875 (with enforcement mostly aimed at keeping out Chinese prostitutes), followed by the far more sweeping Chinese Exclusion Act of 1882.[12] These exclusions were renewed, revised, strengthened, and extended to other Asian groups in

Figure 12.2 "Throwing down the ladder by which they rose." Political cartoon of "The 'Chinese Wall' Around the United States of America." *Harper's Weekly*, July 23, 1870 (John Hay Library, Brown University).

subsequent years (and were not repealed until 1943). The front door was being closed and the welcome mat pulled up.

But the door was not entirely shut. The law barred the entry of Chinese laborers but not Chinese in other categories: merchants, teachers, students, diplomats, and travelers. Also, Chinese who were legal U.S. residents before the exclusion law took effect could leave the country and return (though this right was later revoked). These exceptions to the exclusion laws created all sorts of opportunities for illegal entry through deception, as is evident in the many creative and sophisticated schemes used to impersonate being in a legally admissible category. Identification documents were sold and resold, borrowed and bartered, forged and doctored.[13]

Laborers would pretend to be merchants, Chinese lawfully in the United States would return from trips to China with make-believe children ("paper sons"[14]), and newly arriving Chinese would claim to have been born in San Francisco; all this was made much easier after birth records were destroyed by the earthquake-generated fire of 1906. One Seattle immigration agent explained the difficulty of sorting out legitimate from illegitimate arrivals: "There is not much way of checking on the Chinese when they get here. A number will have papers, a number will not have papers, and when asked why, they say they were born in San Francisco. Cannot show birth, for fire destroyed all."[15] Former immigration inspector Clifford Perkins recollects, "At one time it was estimated that if all of those who claimed to have been born in San Francisco had actually been born there, each Chinese woman then in the United States would have had to produce something like 150 children."[16]

Steamship companies connecting China to San Francisco (notably the Pacific Mail Steamship Company, which dominated much of the shipping between Hong Kong and the United States) were well aware that many of their passengers were seeking unlawful entry.[17] Grueling interrogations of Chinese arriving by steamship at the San Francisco port could last days, weeks, or even months. An arrival and detention facility was opened on Angel Island in San Francisco Bay in 1910, where friends and relatives would smuggle in instructions—even inside peanut shells, banana peels, and care packages—to detainees on how to answer questions and fool the interrogators. Immigration guards could also sometimes be bought off to facilitate the smuggling of coaching notes to detainees.[18]

The exclusion law included heavy penalties for violators. Fraudulent use of identification documents brought a fine of $1,000 and a maximum five-year prison term; aiding the entry of "any Chinese person not lawfully entitled to enter the United States" was subject to a fine and a maximum twelve-month prison term.[19]

Over time, efforts to distinguish between lawful and unlawful entrants stimulated the development of a racially based national immigration control system increasingly reliant on standardized personal identification documents, photographs, visas, and so on.[20] These document requirements, pioneered by the Chinese exclusion laws, required creating entirely new federal administrative capacities, including document checks by U.S. consular officials in China.[21] Immigration law evasion and law enforcement thus grew up together in the last decades of the nineteenth century and early decades of the twentieth century, in a political climate otherwise hostile to central government expansion.[22] And the elaborate immigration control system of documentation and registration first developed to keep out unauthorized Chinese could then be applied more widely.[23]

The federal government had no stand-alone immigration control apparatus when the Chinese Exclusion Act was passed, so the job of implementing it was handed to customs agents within the Treasury Department. It was an awkward fit, especially at first. Customs was created to oversee the entry of goods, but it was now suddenly expected to also monitor and police the entry of people. Customs, in turn, sometimes treated people as if they were actually goods, often calling Chinese "contraband"; on one inspection list, "Chinese laborers" was even entered as a line item between "castor oil" and "cauliflower in salt."[24] A Bureau of Immigration was created in 1891 (later moved into the newly established Department of Commerce and Labor in 1903), but Customs remained in charge of enforcing the exclusion law until the turn of the century. A "Chinese Bureau" within Customs was set up in San Francisco in the mid-1890s, headed by the collector of customs and staffed by "Chinese inspectors."

Opening the Northern Back Door

As front-door entry through San Francisco and other seaports became more regulated in the late nineteenth century, more and more Chinese immigrants turned to entry though the back door: America's vast and minimally policed northern and southern land borders.[25] Canada became the favored transit country for smuggling Chinese immigrants into the United States in the late 1880s and 1890s.[26] Chinese arrivals in Canada increased sharply during this period. Regular steamship service connected China and Canada, and Chinese immigrants had no problem entering Canada so long as they paid a head tax. The Canadian Pacific Steamship Company and Canadian officials generally had a lax attitude, knowing full well that most of the Chinese were just passing through. As one Canadian official bluntly told an American journalist in 1891, "They come here to enter your country, you can't stop it, and we don't care."[27] With Canada collecting a head tax on every Chinese entry, the Canadian government was even making money from it. One Canadian official joked, "We get the cash and you get the Chinamen."[28] From 1887 to 1891 alone, Canada collected $95,500 in head taxes.[29] In 1885 the head tax was $50 on Chinese laborers, and this was raised to $100 in 1900 and to $500 in 1903.[30]

U.S. officials bitterly complained that Canada's virtually open door policy "practically nullified . . . the effective work done by the border officers."[31] In 1902, U.S. immigrant inspector Robert Watchorn reported, "Much that appears menacing to us is regarded with comparative indifference by the Canadian government." As he described it, "those which Canada receives but fails to hold . . . come unhindered into the United States."[32]

The westernmost stretch of the Canadian border was initially the favored illicit entry point. An unintended consequence of the Exclusion Act was to create a law enforcement problem far from San Francisco and the nation's capital. As Special Agent Herbert Beecher wrote in 1887, the U.S. exclusion law was "created without practical knowledge of what was required of it. A law created apparently more for California, with no thought or knowledge of its workings in Washington Territory, situated as we are, so closely to British Columbia, commanding as it does such natural advantages of evasion of the Restriction Act."[33] Customs agents long preoccupied with the smuggling of goods through the ports of entry now had to also deal with the smuggling of people through the vast areas between the ports of entry. In the 1890s, the cost of hiring a smuggler to cross the Northwest border was anywhere between twenty-three and sixty dollars.[34] The waterways of the Puget Sound were especially difficult to police and therefore conducive to smuggling Chinese migrants in by boat at night. Local Chinese served as agents and intermediaries for those being smuggled, but white men reportedly handled the actual transportation given that they enjoyed greater freedom of movement across the border.[35] Smuggling operations involved not only close business collaborations between Chinese and white merchants but sometimes also paying off U.S. border agents.[36]

Smuggling gradually shifted eastward along the northern border (greatly facilitated by the establishment of the Canadian Pacific Railway in 1885) in response to intensified U.S. enforcement in the west. Eastern states such as New York and Vermont consequently also turned into entry points for smuggled Chinese.[37] These geographical shifts in smuggling in turn stimulated a geographic expansion of immigration law enforcement.[38] The growth of human smuggling in defiance of the exclusion laws also fueled alarmist political rhetoric in Washington. In the words of one journalist covering the issue, this included "amazing utterances in Congress, in which, among others, one speaker had likened the influx of contraband Chinese to nothing less than the swarming of the Huns in early European history."[39]

The influx of smuggled Chinese across the northern border was ultimately curbed not by tighter U.S. border controls but by changes in Canadian policy that were partly induced by U.S. pressure. This included imposing a prohibitively expensive head tax,[40] turning away Chinese who had previously been denied entry to the United States, allowing U.S. inspectors to enforce U.S. immigration laws on Canadian-bound steamships and at Canadian ports of entry, and agreements with Canadian steamship and railroad companies to pre-screen passengers and curtail the transport of U.S.-bound migrants.[41] And in 1923 Canada imposed its own Exclusion Act (admitting only merchants and students), dramatically reducing the use of Canada as a conduit for smuggling Chinese into the United States.[42]

Opening the Southern Back Door

As the back door through Canada began to close, the back door through Mexico started to swing wide open in the first decade of the twentieth century. Rather than ending Chinese smuggling, U.S. pressure on Canada simply redirected it to Mexico—and Mexico was far less inclined to cooperate with the United States, given the still-festering wounds from having lost so much of its territory after the Mexican-American War. U.S. State Department efforts to negotiate agreements with the Porfirio Díaz regime to curb Chinese entries went nowhere.[43]

The U.S.-Mexico border, long a gateway for smuggling goods, was now also becoming a gateway for smuggling people. As was the case in Canada, new steamship, railway, and road networks greatly aided migrant smuggling through Mexico. But unlike in Canada, Mexican transport companies showed little willingness to cooperate with the

United States. An agent for one steamship company reportedly told U.S. authorities that his next scheduled ship was expected to carry some three hundred Chinese passengers to the northern Mexican port of Guaymas. "For all I know they may smuggle themselves into the United States and if they do I do not give a d-n, for I am doing a legitimate business."[44] Guaymas was connected by railway to the border town of Nogales.

The development of new transportation networks linking the United States and Mexico was hailed as a boon for cross-border commerce. As President Benjamin Harrison commented in his annual message to Congress at the end of 1890: "The intercourse of the two countries, by rail, already great, is making constant growth. The established lines and those recently projected add to the intimacy of traffic and open new channels of access to fresh areas of supply and demand."[45] Left unstated was that these very same channels also facilitated illicit traffic.[46]

The Treaty of Amity and Commerce signed by China and Mexico in 1899, and the establishment of direct steamship travel between Hong Kong and Mexico in 1902, opened the door for a surge in Chinese migration to Mexico. And this, in turn, provided a convenient stepping-stone for clandestine migration to the United States.[47] In 1900 there were just a few thousand Chinese in Mexico, but less than a decade later nearly 60,000 Chinese migrants had departed to Mexico. Some stayed, but the United States was a far more attractive destination.[48] A banker in Guaymas, the Mexican port in the border state of Sonora, told U.S. Immigration Inspector Marcus Braun in 1906 that about twenty thousand Chinese had come to the state in recent years, but fewer than four thousand remained.[49] In his investigations, Braun witnessed Chinese arriving in Mexico and reported that "On their arrival in Mexico, I found them to be provided with United States money, not Mexican coins; they had in their possession Chinese-English dictionaries; I found them in possession of Chinese-American newspapers and of American railroad maps."[50]

In 1907, a U.S. government investigator observed that between twenty and fifty Chinese arrived daily in the Mexican border town of Juarez by train, but that the Chinese community in the town never grew. As he put it, "Chinamen coming to Ciudad Juarez either vanish into thin air or cross the border line."[51] Foreshadowing future developments, a January 1904 editorial in the El Paso *Herald-Post* warned that "If this Chinese immigration to Mexico continues it will be necessary to run a barb wire fence along our side of the Rio Grande."[52] The El Paso immigration inspector stated in his 1905 annual report that nearly two-thirds of the Chinese arriving in Juarez are smuggled into the country in the vicinity of El Paso, and that migrant smuggling is the sole business of "perhaps one-third of the Chinese population of El Paso."[53]

With Mexico becoming the most popular back door to the United States, some smugglers relocated their operations from the U.S.-Canada border to the U.S.-Mexico border. One smuggler who made this move, Curley Roberts, reported to a potential partner: "I have just brought seven yellow boys over and got $225 for that so you can see I am doing very well here."[54] Some historians note that border smuggling operations involved cross-racial business collaborations, with white male smugglers often working with Chinese organizers and Mexicans serving as local border guides.[55] A 1906 law enforcement report on Chinese smuggling noted, "All through northern Mexico, along the lines of the railroad, are located so-called boarding houses and restaurants, which

Figure 12.3 "Dying of Thirst in the Desert." Drawing depicts the serious risks and dangers for those attempting to cross the border in remote areas. *Harper's New Monthly Magazine*, March 1891 (John Hay Library, Brown University).

are the rendezvous of the Chinese and their smugglers, and the small towns and villages throughout this section are filled with Chinese coolies, whose only occupation seems to be lying in wait until arrangement can be perfected for carrying them across the border."[56]

As U.S. authorities tightened enforcement at urban entry points along the Mexico-California border, smugglers shifted to more remote parts of the border further east in Arizona, New Mexico, and Texas.[57] And following the earlier pattern on the U.S.-Canada border, this provided a rationale for the deployment of more agents to these border areas. In addition to hiring more port inspectors, a force of mounted inspectors was set up to patrol the borderline by horseback. As smugglers in later years turned to new technologies such as automobiles, officials also pushed for the use of the same technologies for border control.[58]

With the tightening of border controls, smugglers sometimes opted to simply buy off rather than try to bypass U.S. authorities in their efforts to move their human cargo across the line. This was the case in Nogales, Arizona, where border inspectors, including the collector of customs, reportedly charged smugglers between $50 and $200 per head until their arrest by special agents of the Treasury Department and Secret Service operatives in August 1901. Covering the case, the *Washington Post* reported that "with two or three exceptions, the whole customs and immigration administration at Nogales are involved" in the smuggling scheme.[59]

Chinese were not the only ones coming in through the back door. They were simply at the top of a growing list of "undesirables." By the last decades of the nineteenth century, federal law also prohibited the admission of paupers, criminals, prostitutes, "lunatics," "idiots," and contract workers in general (not just Chinese). And the list of inadmissible aliens kept growing: "those convicted of a crime of moral turpitude," polygamists, and persons with loathsome or dangerous contagious diseases were added in 1891. By 1903 there was a lengthy list of excludable illnesses, with trachoma the most common health reason given for exclusion.[60] Anarchists were added to the exclusion list in 1903, and "imbeciles" and Japanese laborers were added in 1907. Illiterates were banned from entry in 1917. The head tax also increased sharply, from fifty cents in 1891 to four dollars in 1907 and eight dollars in 1917.[61] Not surprisingly, as seaports became more tightly regulated and policed, immigrants who feared being placed in one of these excludable categories increasingly turned to the back door. Those groups that were disproportionally being turned away at the front-door ports of entry—among them Lebanese, Greeks, Italians, Slavs from the Balkans, and Jews—found Mexico to be a convenient back-door alternative.[62]

A 1908 letter from the secretary of commerce and labor to Secretary of State Elihu Root described the situation at the Mexican border:

> On the Mexican side of the border, at towns nearest the several ports of entry, aliens, both European and Asiatic, congregate in larger numbers prior to seeking entry into the United States. By reason of the influx of foreigners into these towns, a profitable industry has grown up in the promotion of immigration, by methods seldom more than colorably legal and often simply illegal. There are "boarding houses" offering, not only food and lodging, but effective assistance in crossing the border. There are "immigrant bureaus" whose advertised promises plainly indicate the use of unlawful methods. There are physicians professing ability to remove signs of disease, and there are smugglers and guides in abundance.[63]

Chinese reportedly ran much of the smuggling business in border towns west of El Paso, but they relied on Mexicans to guide immigrants across the line.[64] Also, given the importance of railways as the primary means of long-distance transport, it is little surprise that railroad workers, ranging from brakemen to dining car cooks to conductors, were found complicit in schemes to deliver smuggled migrants from the El Paso railroad terminal to interior destinations as far away as Chicago.[65]

Since Mexicans were still of little concern to border inspectors, one deceptive ploy immigrants used to avoid being noticed was to try to appear Mexican. Almost all of the traffic back and forth through the port of entry in El Paso and in other urban areas along the border involved local residents who were typically not inspected. It was therefore not uncommon for unauthorized U.S.-bound immigrants, ranging from Greeks to Lebanese to Chinese, to attempt the border crossing simply by blending in.[66]

The relationship between smugglers and law enforcers along the border was not entirely adversarial. Not only was corruption sometimes part of their relationship but they also occasionally rubbed shoulders socially. In his memoir, former immigration inspector Clifford Perkins notes that El Paso Deputy Sheriff Mannie Clements "had been mixed up with the smuggling of narcotics and Chinese,"[67] and he also recalls drinking rice whiskey with Charlie Sam, a prominent figure in the El Paso Chinese community who was reputed to be "the brains behind the smuggling of Chinese."[68] On another occasion, Tom Kate, dubbed the "king of smugglers" in the El Paso area, apparently threw a party for the city's attorneys and judiciary members. The list of prominent attendees included federal judicial commissioners whose workload included cases involving Chinese migrant smuggling, and the assistant U.S. attorney prosecuting such smuggling cases.[69]

The Mexican Revolution between 1910 and 1920 and World War I disrupted the use of Mexico as a stepping-stone for illegal entry by non-Mexicans into the United States. But migrant smuggling through Mexico strongly rebounded when international steamship service was resumed. However, this mostly now involved smuggling Europeans rather than Chinese. Mexico had become a far less hospitable environment for Chinese during the course of the Mexican Revolution, with many Chinese residents in Mexico robbed and abused as a particularly vulnerable minority population (and many fled the chaos and violence of the revolution years by moving to the United States illegally).[70]

The popularity of the Mexican back door received a major boost by new U.S. restrictions on European immigration through the national origins quotas in 1921 and 1924 at the peak of the nationwide nativist backlash against foreigners.[71] Passport rules left over from World War I, formalized in the Passport Act of 1918, also now required immigrants to secure visas at U.S. consulates abroad.[72] The Mexico route offered a way to sidestep these new numerical restrictions and documentation requirements. This did not go unnoticed in Washington, and it provided political ammunition for calls for more border enforcement. As the commissioner general's 1922 report put it, "The experience of the past two years in dealing with Europeans unable to secure entry at our seaports who look to the back door of this country as a favorable means of ingress has demonstrated as nothing else could the ever-existing and increasing need of a strong border patrol."[73]

U.S. officials acknowledged that more restrictive laws were creating more business for smugglers and more work for law enforcement. The commissioner-general of immigration reported in 1923 that each new restriction "promoted the alien smuggling industry and furnished new and multiplied incentives to illegal entry."[74] The commissioner-general's 1923 report noted that Europeans were resorting to using the Mexican back door "because of passport difficulties, illiteracy, or the quota law."[75] The report claimed that migrant smuggling had become a sophisticated operation: "Reliable information has been received to the effect that there is now in existence a far-reaching organization that takes the alien from his home in Europe, secures a passport for him (a fraudulent one, if necessary), purchases his steamship passage to Mexico, places him on the ship, arranges for his entry into Mexico at Vera Cruz or Tampico, conducts him north to the Rio Grande, and delivers him into the United States—all for a fixed price."[76] The commissioner's report the following year predicted that the Immigration Law of 1924 "Will result in a further influx of undesirable European aliens to Mexico with the sole object in view of affecting illegal entry into the United States over the Rio Grande."[77]

The El Paso inspector expressed similar concerns, noting that "if the Mexican government continued to permit aliens to enter Mexico practically without restriction, the more stringent provisions of the restrictive immigration act of 1924 undoubtedly will result in a still higher ratio of increase in the number of European aliens proceeding to Mexico with the United States as their objective."[78] Local media reports reinforced these concerns. A December 22, 1924, article in El Paso's Spanish-language newspaper *La Patria* pointed to the booming cross-border business for "contrabandistas de carne humana" ("smugglers of human meat") in the wake of the new U.S. immigration restrictions.[79] The article (with the headline "Foreigners who want to cross over to the United States have invaded the city of Ciudad Juarez") described Juarez as a depot for foreigners—including Russians, Germans, Czechs, Turks, Syrians, Greeks, Bulgarians, Italians, French—waiting to enter the United States. The article suggested renaming one of the streets in Juarez "Foreigners Street."[80]

Just as the Chinese Exclusion Act had made front-door entry at the nation's seaports more difficult and created a smuggling problem along the nation's land borders, the same pattern was now repeating itself with the new immigration restrictions in 1924. "It must be conceded that the present law was enacted primarily for the purpose of providing for the closer inspection of aliens coming to the seaports of the United States," U.S. Immigration Commissioner John Clark stated at the time. "When we come to consider the dangers of unlawful invasion along the land boundaries, however, we find our law conspicuously weak, and almost totally inadequate to protect the interests of our Government."[81] Echoing this concern, Congress greatly expanded immigration bureau personnel's powers to search and arrest along and near the nation's borders.[82] In a country otherwise wary of increasing the power and reach of government, border control was clearly one realm where there was a push to bolster federal authority.

Political pressure had been building up for a number of years to create a uniformed border patrol force. "How many men would be required to patrol that border of 2,000 miles," Ohio Representative Benjamin Welty inquired at a February 1920 hearing, "for the purpose of protecting ourselves against all undesirables?"[83] Frank Berkshire, supervising inspector of the Mexican Border District, projected that four hundred more officers might be sufficient to "enforce it to a reasonable certainty." But, he also warned, "To absolutely sew up the border so that nobody will get across would take more than the standing army because they would have to be in sight of each other."[84]

The U.S. Border Patrol was formed in 1924 with a $1 million budget and a total force of some 450 officers, with the vast majority of them reportedly World War I veterans.[85] The primary mission was to keep out illegal immigrants, though it spent much of the time in those Prohibition years chasing bootleggers. And given the Prohibition mind-set at the time, media reports began to conflate migrant smuggling and alcohol smuggling. The *New York Times* even referred to migrant smuggling as "bootlegged immigrants."[86] The *Washington Post* similarly called it "bootlegging aliens," warning that "A cargo of rum in the wrong hands can do a lot of damage. But a cargo of undesirable aliens can easily become a national calamity."[87]

The Border Patrol's priority target was the smuggling of Europeans excluded by the restrictive immigration reforms of the 1920s. Wesley E. Stiles, one of the first border patrol agents hired in the summer of 1924, later recalled, "the thing that established the Border Patrol was the influx of European aliens." He noted that he and other agents deployed to the immigration subdistrict at Del Rio, Texas, especially "looked for European aliens." Border patrolmen "didn't pay much attention to the Mexicans" because they were considered merely cheap seasonal farm labor that returned to Mexico when no longer needed.[88] Retired immigration service officer Perkins similarly recalled that border communities were equally unconcerned: "Residents near the border paid little attention to the comings and goings of Mexicans."[89] The growing influx of unauthorized Mexican workers was largely tolerated and overlooked—at least for the time being.

Despite an 1885 law restricting the importation of contract workers, U.S. employers informally recruited large numbers of Mexicans to work in southwest agriculture in the early twentieth century. Whereas formal, legal entry was a complicated process, crossing the border illegally was relatively simple and largely ignored. Up to half a million Mexicans may have come to the United States in the first decade of the century. The Mexican Revolution, U.S. labor shortages during World War I, and the continued expansion of agriculture in the southwest fueled a further influx.

The agriculture lobby pushed hard to exempt Mexicans from the eight-dollar head tax imposed by the Immigration Act of 1917. The president of the South Texas Cotton Growers Association complained to a Senate committee in 1920 that Mexicans would stop coming because they could not afford the head tax. He bluntly suggested that Congress should therefore either exempt Mexicans or turn a blind eye to their illicit entry: "If you gentlemen have any objections to admitting Mexicans by law, cut them out and take the river guard away and let us alone, and we will get them all right."[90]

Strict controls against Mexicans crossing the border were widely perceived as neither viable nor desirable. As one observer put it, "from a practical administrative standpoint a quota system would be impossible to enforce" because the long border with Mexico "could not be adequately policed. The pressure to bring Mexicans across the border would be so great and smuggling them would become so profitable that a quota law for Mexicans would become a joke."[91] The numerical limits and nationality quotas imposed on European immigration were therefore not applied to Mexicans. And those restrictions that did apply—the head tax, visa fee, literacy requirement, and exclusions on contract laborers and "lunatics, paupers, and convicts"—were anemically enforced. Consequently, as immigration scholar Aristide Zolberg puts it, "undocumented entry became the norm."[92] There was a growing disconnect between the formal entry rules handed down from a distant capital and the realities, needs, and practices on the ground along the border.[93]

As a substitute for European and Asian workers, employers considered Mexicans an ideal labor force: flexible, compliant, and temporary—or so it seemed at the time. As we will see later, millions of unauthorized Mexican migrants would eventually settle in the United States, becoming a vital source of labor for agriculture and other sectors of the economy but also the main rationale for more intensive border enforcement. Yet in the meantime, as we'll examine in the next chapter, U.S. border agents had a new preoccupation: the flood of smuggled alcohol coming across the nation's borders.

13

Rumrunners and Prohibitionists

ALCOHOL AND SMUGGLING HAVE long been closely connected in American history. As we saw at the beginning of our story, smuggling West Indies molasses to supply New England rum distilleries was critical for colonial trade, and British efforts to clamp down on it helped provoke the backlash against imperial rule leading up to the War of Independence. Illegally trading alcohol for Indian furs was also a defining feature of frontier relations and westward expansion in the nineteenth century. But with the notable exception of efforts to ban the liquor trade in Indian Country, smuggling booze usually had more to do with evading taxes than prohibitions. Starting with Maine in 1851, there were various attempts to outlaw the sale of alcohol at the state level (prompting some smuggling between wet and dry states), but for the most part the feds stayed out of it. It remained largely a local rather than national and international matter.

That all changed with the passage of the Eighteenth Amendment to the Constitution and the implementation of the Volstead Act to enforce it. Once again, the federal government's right to regulate interstate commerce opened the door for boosting its policing powers. The national ban on the alcohol trade between 1920 and 1933 was an extraordinary and unprecedented experiment in top-down social control. In the process, it transformed both the business of smuggling and the policing of smuggling. Smuggling became more sophisticated, organized, and violent, and the federal government became more involved in crime fighting than ever before.

Banning Booze

America was born a nation of drinkers. As the historian W. J. Rorabaugh describes it, with only slight exaggeration, "Americans drank from the crack of dawn to the crack of dawn."[1] The *Mayflower* carried more beer than water; the Continental Army received regular rum rations; George Washington built his own distillery at Mt. Vernon, and William Penn owned a Philadelphia brewery; John Adams drank hard cider every morning; James Madison drank a pint of whiskey every day; and Thomas Jefferson was famously fond of fine wine and champagne at White House dinners. Benjamin Franklin was also a hearty drinker, favoring punch, Madeira, and rum, and he even penned drinking songs.[2] As he put it, "if God had intended man to drink water, He would not have made him with an elbow capable of raising a wine glass."[3] Drinking water was in fact considered unhealthy, unsanitary, and even dangerous—and often it was.

Thanks to the proliferation of distilleries, by the 1820s a mixed drink with whiskey was cheaper than a cup of tea. Astonishingly (at least by today's standards), between 1800 and 1830 annual per capita pure alcohol use in America increased to more than five gallons—nearly three times contemporary consumption levels.[4] In 1839 the English traveler Frederick Marryat was amazed by how important liquor was in everyday American life. As he wrote in *A Diary in America*:

> I am sure the Americans can fix nothing without a drink. If you meet, you drink; if you part, you drink; if you make acquaintance, you drink; if you close a bargain, you drink; they quarrel in their drink, and they make it up with a drink. They drink because it is hot; they drink because it is cold. If successful in elections, they drink and rejoice; if not, they drink and swear; they begin to drink early in the morning, they leave off late at night; they commence it early in life, and they continue it, until they soon drop into the grave.[5]

With the influx of Irish and German immigrants in the decades that followed, beer increasingly supplanted spirits as America's favorite drink. Beer consumption tripled between 1870 and 1915, and it came to be closely associated with the rapid spread of urban saloons catering to working-class immigrants.[6] The new immigrants were not just beer guzzlers but beer brewers; the leading beer companies, among them Pabst, Schlitz, and Miller, were all German.

Prohibition was the culmination of a century-long backlash against America's seemingly insatiable drinking habit. What began as a grassroots religious appeal for temperance morphed into a stunningly ambitious campaign to legislate morality by trying to put one of the country's largest industries out of business. Similar to the earlier purity crusades against commercial sex and obscenity, the push for prohibition was caught up in broader societal anxieties about rapid urbanization and mass migration. It also provided a powerful catalyst for organizing women—most notably through the Women's Christian Temperance Union—who not only resented that wages were being spent on booze rather than bread but were on the receiving end of much of the drinking-induced male violence.[7] But only by adding patriotism and the intensely anti-German climate of World War I to the mix were prohibitionists actually able to do what no other lobby group has ever done: change the Constitution of the United States.

World War I was a godsend for the Anti-Saloon League, the most powerful single-issue lobby organization the country had ever seen. German drinkers and brewers could now be cast as not just sinners but traitors. As Wayne Wheeler, the head of the league, who devoted his life to the cause of Prohibition, told the *New York Times* in 1917, "The liquor traffic aids those forces in this country whose loyalty is called into question at this hour."[8] Speaking German in public or on the phone was outlawed in Iowa, playing Beethoven in public was prohibited in Boston, and German books were burned in Wisconsin.[9] German toast became French toast, Frankfurters became hot dogs, Sauerkraut became freedom cabbage, and Kaiser rolls became liberty buns. Little wonder, then, that it was so easy to cast the country's German brewers as unpatriotic, even downright traitorous. The new fervor of wartime patriotism and long-festering moral indignation proved a potent political mix. The Eighteenth Amendment to the Constitution was passed with remarkable ease, with Congress pushing through the needed votes to overturn President Wilson's veto.

As Prohibition took effect in January 1920, the Anti-Saloon League triumphantly declared that "at one minute past midnight . . . a new nation will be born. . . . Now for an era of clear thinking and clean living! The Anti-Saloon League wishes every man, woman and child a happy New Dry Year."[10] But dry America remained thirsty. And bootleggers, moonshiners, and rumrunners were more than happy to help quench the thirst.

Enforcing Prohibition

Prohibitionists had a remarkably naïve faith in the law. Their assumption, it seemed, was that the law would largely enforce itself: Americans would simply stop buying booze because, well, the law told them to. An upbeat Wayne Wheeler assured Congress that implementing Prohibition could be done cheaply. Just a few months into Prohibition, he confidently asserted that a $5 million budget would suffice—and that the cost of enforcement would actually go down over time. By January 1921 he had already revised this number upward, calling for an $8 million appropriation from Congress.[11] Two years later, the treasury secretary told Congress that $28 million was needed.[12]

John F. Kramer, handpicked by Wheeler as the first Prohibition Commissioner, boldly proclaimed that once Prohibition took effect, no alcohol would be commercially produced in the United States, "nor sold, nor given away, nor hauled in anything on the surface of the earth or under the earth or in the air."[13] His successor, Roy Haynes, asserted two years later that Prohibition enforcement was "rapidly approaching the highest point of efficiency." At the end of the following year he announced that the Prohibition agency had made such progress that it was "nothing short of marvelous."[14] In 1923 he claimed that "The illegal liquor traffic is under control. . . . The control becomes more complete and thorough with each passing day."[15] He even went so far as to state that 85 percent of all drinkers had gone dry.[16] Such lofty official claims of success had little to do with reality. In fact, rarely in American history has there been such an extreme gap between a law and its enforcement.

Figure 13.1 New York City Deputy Police Commissioner John A. Leach, right, watching agents pour alcohol into a sewer following a raid (Library of Congress).

Enforcement was anemic. The federal government was woefully unprepared to implement such a sweeping law. A Prohibition Unit (later renamed the Prohibition Bureau) with some fifteen hundred agents and an initial budget of $6.35 million was set up within the Treasury to police the drinking habits of the entire nation. The Coast Guard, Customs, and immigration agents along the border were also drafted to enforce Prohibition. The expectation in Washington was that the states would also play a big policing role, but they never really embraced the job and devoted to it only token resources. After all of the clamor to pass Prohibition, it turned out there was little enthusiasm to actually pay for it.

To make matters worse, the appointment of the Prohibition agents was highly politicized and consequently marred by incompetence. Wheeler and the Anti-Saloon League made sure that Prohibition agents were exempt from standard civil service requirements. This ensured that appointments would be driven by patronage politics, in which connections rather than competence determined hiring. Prohibition jobs were doled out as rewards for political loyalty and support. When agents were finally subjected to civil service requirements in 1927, fewer than half of them passed the basic entrance exam.

Enforcement was chronically corrupt. Between 1920 and 1926, one out of twelve Prohibition agents was fired on corruption-related charges.[17] In New York City, the wettest of wet cities, corruption was so entrenched that the Prohibition agency resorted to cutting off outgoing telephone calls from its office on nights when raids were planned to prevent corrupt agents from tipping off bootleggers. Some agents showed up to work in fancy cars and wearing jewelry they clearly could not afford. Not only did agents take bribes to look the other way but they also sold seized alcohol—sometimes even selling it right back to

Figure 13.2 "National Gesture." Political cartoon depicts the many hands that take bribes during Prohibition (American Social History Project, City University of New York).

the original owners. By the end of the first year of Prohibition, nearly a quarter of the two hundred Prohibition agents in the city had been fired. The next year, the *New York Times* reported that more than a hundred agents had been dismissed.[18]

Mayor Fiorello La Guardia was apparently not corruptible, but it didn't matter. "I just don't understand that guy [La Guardia]," the bootlegger Charles "Lucky" Luciano told his ghost writers. "When we offered to make him rich he wouldn't even listen. . . . So I figured: what the hell, let him keep City Hall, we got all the rest, the D.A., the cops, everything."[19] La Guardia had little faith in Prohibition, claiming that it would take 250,000 cops to enforce it in New York—and that an additional 250,000 would be needed to police the police.[20]

Public support for enforcement was undermined by political hypocrisy, nowhere more evident than in the nation's capital, which was supposed to be the model of dry urban America. Not only was the capital city dripping wet but so too was the Capitol Building. In October 1930, the *Washington Post* ran a series of front-page stories written by George Cassiday, who claimed to have worked as a bootlegger for Congress for a decade, at one point taking orders and distributing booze right out of a storeroom in the House Office Building. He said he filled between twenty and twenty-five orders per day and calculated that four out of five senators and congressmen drank.[21]

When the police raided one local bootleg operation they discovered account books with the names of many congressmen and senators as regular customers. The White House also turned out to be squishy wet: the duties of the treasurer of the Republican National Committee apparently included making sure President Warren G. Harding's regular poker games had plenty of whiskey on hand.[22]

Mabel Walker Willebrandt, who stepped down as deputy attorney general in 1928, wrote a year later: "I think that probably nothing has done more to disgust and alienate honest men and women who originally strongly favored the prohibition amendment and its strict enforcement than the hypocrisy of the wet-drinking, dry-voting congressmen."[23] Journalist H. L. Mencken called these congressmen "wet dry"—"a politician who prepared for a speech in favor of Prohibition by taking three or four stiff drinks."[24] Willebrandt complained that many "have been antagonized by the discovery that the very men who made the Prohibition law are violating it and that many officers of the law sworn to enforce Prohibition statutes are constantly conspiring to defeat them. How can you justify prison and fines when you know for a fact that the men who make the laws and appropriate the money for Prohibition are themselves patronizing bootleggers?" It was well known, she said, that "Senators and Congressmen appeared on the floor in a drunken condition," and that "bootleggers infested the halls and corridors of Congress and ply their trade there."[25]

Some congressmen who had voted to toughen penalties for violating the Volstead Act even turned out to be petty smugglers; several were caught trying to sneak alcohol into the country in their luggage on return trips from abroad.[26] Particularly embarrassing was the arrest of Ohio Congressman Everett Denison, one of the most outspoken supporters of Prohibition, for attempting to smuggle in a barrel of rum while returning from a Caribbean cruise.[27]

Meanwhile, enforcement became increasingly overwhelmed and overloaded. The swamped federal courts resorted to large-scale plea bargaining to clear liquor cases on what came to be called "bargain days." In exchange for pleading guilty and waiving the right to a trial by jury, defendants avoided jail time and received a minimal fine. But even with massive plea bargaining, prisons were overflowing with Prohibition law offenders, prompting President Herbert Hoover to build six new federal penitentiaries. During Hoover's term, the number of Prohibition offenders in prison almost doubled.[28] Toughening penalties in response to the failures of enforcement, as Congress did in passing the punitive Jones Act of 1929, only made matters worse by further clogging the criminal justice system.[29] It also backfired, angering the public and turning key early supporters of Prohibition, prominent among them William Randolph Hearst and John D. Rockefeller Jr., against it.

There were some much-touted law enforcement success stories, most notably the conviction of America's most famous gangster, Al Capone. For years openly flouting the law and bragging about his bootlegging exploits in the press, he had simply become too famous for his own good. His highly publicized conviction on tax-evasion charges was a defining moment in the history of the U.S.

federal taxing agency. Indeed, historian Michael Woodiwiss suggests that no one benefited more from the rise and fall of Al Capone than the Internal Revenue Service. An ex–IRS agent later wrote than in the aftermath of Capone's conviction "tax violators began to kick in, right and left . . . floods of amended and delinquent returns, with checks attached, showing up not only in Chicago but at other Internal Revenue offices all across the country from scared tax cheaters."[30]

Enforcement also succeeded in shutting down the saloon—which had come to symbolize urban America's drinking problem and was the main target of the Anti-Saloon League—only to see it quickly replaced by the less visible, and therefore less publicly offensive, speakeasy. Alcohol use did decline by roughly a third; America sobered up, at least a bit, and especially at the beginning (it would take decades for consumption to return to the pre-Prohibition level). The price of a drink skyrocketed. In some northern urban markets, a fifteen-cent cocktail in 1918 became a seventy-five-cent cocktail in the early 1920s. Many working-class drinkers simply could not afford this.[31] But many others could, and demand remained strong enough to sustain a vast market.

It was precisely the Prohibition-induced high prices—and thus the potential for extraordinarily high profits—that made violating the law so attractive to moonshiners, bootleggers, and rumrunners. In other words, the very success of Prohibition in raising prices was also the source of its own undoing. The high financial stakes are also what made the illicit trade so violent—with such trouble mostly concentrated in a handful of major urban markets such as Chicago and New York—and so attractive to a particularly aggressive class of criminal entrepreneurs.

There were many sources of domestic supply, ranging from homemade moonshine to diverted industrial alcohol to pre-Prohibition stockpiles and even doctor prescriptions. But the largest source—and by far the highest-quality—were illicit imports shipped in by boat, car, truck, train, and airplane, and then watered down for even higher profits. The Atlantic seaboard and northern border were the two most important entry points for the illicit alcohol that helped keep dry America wet.

Rum Row

Nassau was in the right place at the right time. Just as it was a conveniently located base and warehouse for British-supplied blockade runners during the American Civil War, it served a similar function during the Prohibition era. Prohibition turned Nassau into a smuggling boomtown and depot for U.S.-bound liquor. Much of the supply came from British distillers, who used the island to illicitly access an otherwise closed U.S. market. Complaints from Washington to London fell on deaf ears. Winston Churchill in the Colonial Office took the stance that "a State is only responsible for the enforcement of its own laws" and thus refused to impede the Bahamas trade in order to help the United States enforce Prohibition—a law he described as "an affront to the whole history of mankind."[32]

The Bahamas imported only about five thousand quarts of liquor in 1917, but this increased to about 10 million quarts a year by the end of 1922.[33] And what was good for the liquor trade was also good for government coffers. The government collected six dollars in export duty on every case of liquor passing through its port. Liquor revenue skyrocketed from $44,462 in 1918 to $984,732 in 1921.[34] A Bahamian economic development brochure noted that the government's financial good fortune was due to "the conditions supervening in the United States early in 1920."[35] The British governor of the colony, Sir Bede Clifford, even went so far as to suggest that it would be fitting to build a monument honoring Andrew J. Volstead near the statues of Queen Victoria and Columbus.[36]

The real moneymakers in Nassau, Daniel Okrent points out, were not the smugglers themselves but the assortment of brokers and their financial backers who made the trade possible. The profiteers of Prohibition included, for example, Roland Symonette, who by 1923 had become a millionaire from investing in the liquor trade and who would later go on to serve as premier when the Bahamas became self-governing. Knighted by Queen Elizabeth II, his portrait now appears on the Bahamian fifty-dollar bill.[37]

Nassau not only warehoused liquor but also provided legal cover for American rumrunners by registering their ships as British. From 1921 to 1922 there was a tenfold increase in the net tonnage of vessels with

THE VOLSTEAD MARKET DAY

Figure 13.3 "The Volstead Market Day." Rollin Kirby's political cartoon of "Rum Row," the floating marketplace set up by bootleggers just beyond the three-mile limit of U.S. territorial waters. *New York World*, 1923 (Granger Collection).

Bahamian registry.[38] Flying the British flag made American smuggling ships immune from U.S. seizure in international waters. As long as the vessels stayed beyond the three-mile limit of U.S. territorial waters, the Coast Guard could not touch them.

What consequently developed came to be known as Rum Row: fleets of liquor-laden ships (very little of it rum, actually) idling just outside the three-mile limit, not far from U.S. urban markets. There were in fact many rum rows, located off of Boston and New York in the North and off of Galveston, New Orleans, Mobile, Tampa, Savannah, and Norfolk in the South. As the largest market, New York attracted the highest concentration of rumrunners.[39] These smuggling flotillas—essentially floating liquor stores—would transfer their supplies to smaller boats darting out and back from the mainland.[40] A bottle of Scotch purchased at Rum Row could be sold for twice as much once landed—and that was before cutting with water and grain alcohol to boost profits even further. U.S. authorities claimed that during a twelve-month period in the mid-1920s more than three hundred foreign-flagged ships were involved in "wholesale and organized efforts to smuggle liquor into the United States," with almost all of them flying the British flag.[41]

The tiny French possession of St. Pierre-Miquelon, some fifteen miles south of Newfoundland, became Nassau's chief competitor as a smuggling depot and Rum Row supplier. The island, the last remnant of the French empire in North America, offered many of the same advantages as Nassau but at a much cheaper price, imposing a levy of only about forty cents per case.[42] The island also became a warehouse for Canadian distillers, who could officially claim they were exporting to France. In 1923, St. Pierre handled more than half a million cases of liquor, with about one thousand vessels passing through its small port. So much booze flowed through St. Pierre that locals developed a creative form of recycling: most of the homes constructed on the island during the Prohibition years were built using empty whiskey cases.[43]

The former Florida boat maker Bill McCoy is credited as the pioneering founder of the first rum row, off Long Island, making him America's most well-known and even celebrated rumrunner. McCoy used Nassau as his supply base during his early runs, and later he was allegedly the first to use St. Pierre. The term the "Real McCoy" came to signify a high-quality, genuine product "right off the boat" (though the actual origins of the term remain disputed). McCoy prided himself on being an "honest lawbreaker" and independent operator, and he got out of the business as it became much more organized and violent after the mid-1920s. The story of his rise and exit illustrates the transformation of the rumrunning business itself. It also illustrates the perils of becoming a celebrity rumrunner. Prohibition enforcers could not put smuggling out of business, but with enough effort they could put high-profile smugglers such as McCoy out of business if their reputation and visibility made them too much of a public nuisance and embarrassment. McCoy spent eight months in a New Jersey jail—though the warden had such a lax attitude that he let McCoy stay at a nearby hotel and even "escape" for evening outings, allegedly including to attend a boxing match at Madison Square Garden.[44] McCoy retired from smuggling after his release from prison.

McCoy saw himself as simply continuing an old American tradition. Frederick F. Van de Water's biography of McCoy is written in the rum-runner's first-person voice:

> If I wished to defend myself, I have precedent right out of American history for my rum running enterprises. Americans, since the beginning of this nation, have always kicked holes in the laws they resented. The Stamp Act was law, wasn't it? Men who broke it are called "patriots" today. Sometimes I wonder what the rum runners will be called a century from now. The Boston Tea Party wasn't exactly a legal expedition, either. The Fugitive Slave Act was once as much law of the land as Volstead's legislation. I went to jail for the crime of conspiracy. Well, lots of our best ancestors conspired to break the Fugitive Slave Law, too, and established the underground railway to get runaway Negroes safely into Canada.

He continued:

> There was a man in Massachusetts who might stand as the patron saint of rum-runners. He owned or chartered fast ships, ran liquor up from the West Indies and slipped it ashore when the customs men weren't looking. . . . In the eye of the law as it stood at the time he was a bigger crook than I, for he resisted the government on other counts as well. He helped overthrow the constituted authority of those days, this original rum-runner. His name was John Hancock, and you can see it still, first of the signatures of patriots to the Declaration of Independence.[45]

The U.S. Coast Guard Service was given the daunting task of disrupting the ferrying of illicit cargoes from Rum Row to shore. Although the Coast Guard never managed to entirely shut Rum Row down, it did disperse and transform it. And this also transformed the Coast Guard. As one former officer describes it, during Prohibition the service changed from "a small organization, known chiefly to the mariner, to a well-known service of mature size."[46] Prohibition ultimately failed, he acknowledges:

> But many good things for the Coast Guard came out of these 14 years of rum warfare. The Service was greatly expanded, and while it became

> reduced at the end of the period, it remained larger and more important than it had been previously. . . . Much of the experience gained by its personnel was immensely valuable. Its *esprit de corps* was immeasurably enhanced and that enhancement has persisted down through the years. Intelligence became highly developed and has remained so. Standardization of communications procedures in line with those of the Navy was a strong plus factor in World War II.[47]

Rumrunners were also the first smugglers to take full advantage of the radio age, developing increasingly complex radio codes to coordinate their operations. This presented a new challenge to the Coast Guard, but it also helped to further stimulate the development of code-breaking expertise—which would later be put to good use in deciphering enemy communications during World War II. Some of the early pioneers of U.S. cryptography, most notably Elizabeth Smith Friedman, got their start helping the Coast Guard intercept and unravel encrypted rumrunner codes during the Prohibition years.[48]

Rumrunners and Coast Guardsmen were intimately familiar with each other, often coming from the same background. As one former Coast Guardsman, Harold Waters, recounts in his memoir about the Prohibition years: "Rummies were pretty much like us, ex-fishermen, ex–merchant seamen. Many had served in the armed forces of their respective countries. Nor was it unusual for a rummy to change sides, to decide on running with the hounds rather than the hares, especially after too many close calls from Coast Guard bullets. Ex-rummies invariably turned out to be good Coast Guardsmen."[49] Waters also notes that Coast Guardsmen were not averse to heavy drinking: "None of us regarded ourselves as crusaders dedicated to the total destruction of the Demon Rum. Most of us were, on the other hand, on remarkably good terms with the Demon, having frolicked with him the Seven Seas over. Rather, we were to regard rum-chasing in the light of a sport, as a glorified sort of cops and robbers game."[50] Waters even recounts an episode in which Coast Guardsmen stole and smuggled aboard a large amount of alcohol during a reconnaissance stop at St. Pierre and then went to extreme lengths to try to hide the supply from their outraged commanding officer.

At first, smugglers ferrying in their supplies from Rum Row operated relatively unimpeded, with little to fear from the Coast Guard.

The early 1920s was the heyday of Rum Row—an open, freewheeling market with little risk, low violence, and high rewards. An infusion of almost $14 million in new funding in 1924, however, allowed the Coast Guard to significantly beef up its fleet and hire nearly five thousand additional officers and men. By mid-decade, the Coast Guard operated a fleet of 20 converted Navy destroyers, 16 cutters, 204 patrol boats, and 103 picket boats.[51] Hundreds of seized smuggler vessels were also turned into Coast Guard boats (many others were sold at public auction, often bought back by the original owners[52]).

Moreover, the three-mile limit was pushed out to about twelve miles by treaty agreement with Britain, forcing smugglers to travel a greater distance to deliver their cargoes to shore and giving the Coast Guard more time and space to chase down suspected vessels. The government proclaimed that "a state of war—a war of patient attrition—virtually exists on the seas off New York, New Jersey, Rhode Island, and portions of Massachusetts."[53] The Coast Guard's new destroyer force was based at New London, described by one former Coast Guardsman as "the biggest concentration of anti-smuggling ships in the history of the United States, and for very understandable reasons. It was the greatest smuggling area in the United States, handy to New York, Boston, Providence, Rhode Island, and smaller ports in between."[54]

As the enforcement-evasion battles along the eastern seaboard escalated, the smaller independent operators who once defined Rum Row were increasingly pushed out. As one former Coast Guard officer recalls, "New measures brought about new counter-measures. . . . In the earlier days, most contact boats had been fairly small craft, many operated by amateurs. Now the professionals, largely controlled by the syndicates, had taken over. The boats were larger, faster, and of greatly increased capacity. Sometimes they had to run as much as fifty miles to sea to get their loads."[55]

In other words, intensified enforcement perversely and unintentionally helped to push the illicit trade into the hands of those criminal syndicates that had the greatest capacity to adapt and survive (including through greater use of violence). Sometimes they would even have new and faster smuggling boats built in the very same yards where the Coast Guard boats were built. For instance, Long Island's Freeport Point Boatyard built fifteen vessels for the Coast Guard, but also thirty vessels for smugglers. Several of these were forty-two-foot-long speedboats capable of carrying six hundred cases of alcohol each—equipped with 500-horsepower Packard Liberator engines and bulletproof gas tanks—made especially for the Bronx bootlegger and racketeer Dutch Schultz.[56]

Similarly, the Manhattan bootlegger William Vincent "Big Bill" Dwyer equipped his eighteen speedboats with surplus Army Liberty airplane engines. He became such a dominant force in rumrunning that he allegedly charged independent operators $2 per case—and those who failed to pay risked being hijacked by Dwyer's men. Dwyer sometimes simply bribed rather than evaded the Coast Guard; one Coast Guard vessel reportedly assisted Dwyer in moving some seven hundred cases of Scotch and champagne.[57]

American mobsters came to dominate the ferrying of booze from Rum Row to shore and became increasingly involved in transatlantic shipping as well. "To cut our costs and increase efficiency, we chartered our own ships to bring the Scotch across the Atlantic," Meyer Lansky noted decades later; ". . . By the middle twenties we were running the most efficient international shipping business in the world." Lansky claimed this was a cost-cutting measure, complaining that "those fine upright men in Britain [Scotch whiskey distillers] kept squeezing us for higher prices."[58]

Chases between the Coast Guard and rumrunners sometimes turned violent. In one particularly bloody confrontation off the New England coast, the fatalities on a smuggling vessel attempting to evade capture prompted outrage and protests on the streets of Boston. As an ex-Guardsman recounts, "Coast Guard recruiting posters on display in The Commons were ripped, slashed and burned by enraged mobs. Protest meetings were held around town, and we of the Coast Guard were vehemently denounced as legalized buccaneers and pirates of the worst possible sort. . . . Recruiting in the Boston area had to be suspended for a bit."[59]

The Coast Guard was under pressure from Washington to show results—meaning more seizures, confiscations, arrests, and so on. This was especially important in the congressional budget approval process. As one commandant told a Coastguardsman on his ship, "The Drys have really been clamoring for more action lately. You know the sort of pressure they can apply. They've really got us over the barrel on that big appropriations bill for new construction now pending. We've just got to have their help on this one."[60]

The Coast Guard nevertheless readily acknowledged that they were interdicting only a very small percentage of the imported alcohol. And to the extent that focused crackdowns disrupted suppliers, even if only temporarily, the leading beneficiaries included domestic moonshiners. As Harold Waters recollects from his experience on a Coast Guard offensive off the Florida coast: "Oddly enough, one segment of the population was actually glad to see us. This was the moonshining fraternity from out of the Florida backwoods and everglades whose lethal varieties of fusel-oil-laden corn whisky could not normally compete with the choice liquors coming in by sea."[61] Waters points to the "unholy alliance of the Dry lobbies in Washington and Floridian moonshiners, who naturally wanted no letup in our anti-smuggling drive, especially now that they had gained a big slice of the local bootleg market for themselves."[62]

The Canadian Leak

Even more important than Rum Row in the illicit alcohol import business, especially after the Coast Guard's tighter policing of coastal smuggling, was the virtually wide-open Canadian border. And the single most important entry point was the mile-wide and eighteen-mile-long Detroit River between Ontario and Michigan, appropriately dubbed the "Detroit-Windsor Funnel."[63] Canadian distilleries shipped some nine hundred thousand cases of liquor to Windsor in the first seven months of Prohibition alone.[64] Powerboats could ferry loads of whiskey and beer across the river in under five minutes. By 1920 applications for motorboat licenses in the Windsor area had skyrocketed. As historian Philip Mason documents, the trade developed an efficient division of labor: purchasers working the docks, river transporters, transporters to local warehouses, and distributors to markets across the Midwest.[65]

Detroit turned into a regional warehousing and distribution hub, with the liquor trade considered the city's second largest employer after the auto industry. The *New York Times* named it America's "Rum Capital."[66]

Figure 13.4 "Only 2,500 Cases a Day." Political cartoon shows the flood of alcohol between Windsor and Detroit (Walkerville Publishing).

According to a 1928 survey by the Detroit Board of Commerce, the illicit trade in alcohol employed some fifty thousand people and generated $215 million in sales per year.[67] Key players included the notorious Purple Gang, which for a number of years was allegedly the lead supplier for Al Capone in Chicago.[68] Detroit's Henry Ford, one of the staunchest defenders of Prohibition (at one point even advocating deploying the army and navy to enforce it), apparently had no qualms about hiring the well-known local gangster-bootlegger Chester LaMare as his right-hand man to help suppress labor unionization. Ford, who was clearly bluffing when he declared that he would stop making cars if Prohibition was ever lifted, also raised eyebrows by serving bootleg beer at an event celebrating the release of his new V-8 model.[69]

Bootlegging across the Detroit River initially faced little law enforcement resistance and could operate in broad daylight. But increased U.S. river patrols after 1923 forced smugglers to rely on speedier boats and the cover of darkness. Thousands of boats were seized, but smugglers often simply bought them back at public auctions; some boats were even seized multiple times in the same year. Hundreds of other boats simply vanished from U.S. custody and reappeared on the river as smuggling boats.[70]

Bootleggers also enjoyed considerable local community support on the U.S. side of the river, so much so that several towns near Detroit situated across from Canadian export docks were openly hostile toward law enforcement. In Hamtramck, the situation got so out of hand that Michigan Governor Alex Groesbeck deployed state police to take over the city in 1923. Another waterfront town, Ecorse, was described by the *Literary Digest* as "that amazing nest of smugglers, in which even large armed squads of American enforcement officers feel uncomfortable."[71]

Prohibition enforcement on the Detroit River was a frustrating and thankless job, though it could also be financially rewarding. The pay was low, but bribes were high. A 1929 grand jury disclosed that smugglers spent an average of $2 million annually on corruption to operate along the river, paying off about a hundred border agents who each collected an average of $1,700. Smugglers reportedly could even buy "free nights" on the border.[72]

It wasn't just the smugglers and corrupt law enforcers who were cashing in on the Detroit-Windsor illicit trade boom. The Canadian government took its own official cut and actively encouraged it. Twenty-nine Ontario breweries and sixteen distilleries were granted production licenses in 1920, with some of the largest conveniently located either on or near the border.[73] They were even allowed to store their alcohol at export docks along the river near Windsor.

Canada's export tax on alcohol made up about 20 percent of total government revenue. In 1929 revenue from the alcohol export tax was double the amount collected in income tax.[74] According to Canadian customs records, whiskey exports to the United States in 1928 alone amounted to 1,169,002 gallons (and this does not count, of course, unrecorded exports).[75] On top of that, Canada collected duty on British liquor imports, which increased by almost six times between 1918 and 1922. This was just the beginning; imports of British booze increased from 124,546 gallons in the first quarter of 1926 to 560,444 gallons for the same period in 1928.[76] And it wasn't just the British who were reaching the U.S. market via Canada. For example, between 1922 and 1929, the French champagne producer Moet et Chandon increased its exports to Canada more than tenfold—and they plummeted once Prohibition was lifted.[77]

Despite repeated appeals from Washington, Canadian officials insisted that enforcing Prohibition was entirely a U.S. problem. After all, no laws were being violated until the alcohol entered the United States.[78] Frustrated U.S. officials were not the only ones to view Canada as engaging in state-sponsored smuggling. A July 28, 1929, editorial in the Toronto *Globe* stated: "The situation boils down to this: The Canadian Government is operating in collusion with outlaw American citizens to break United States laws. It is a blunt way of putting it; but is it not the fact?"[79]

Ottawa became truly concerned about smuggling across the border only when it discovered that rumrunners were also smuggling high-value goods into Canada on their return trips.[80] This included evading the more than 40 percent Canadian duty on silk imports. Bowing to U.S. pressure, in 1929 Canada finally shut down the Windsor-area export docks and outlawed alcohol shipments to countries that banned imports. Rumrunners quickly adapted. With river transport less convenient, they turned more to trains, trucks, automobiles, and even airplanes.[81] Smuggling by car and truck was greatly facilitated by the remarkably well-timed opening of the Ambassador Bridge between Detroit and Windsor in 1929 and the Detroit-Windsor Tunnel in 1930; overstretched U.S. agents simply could not inspect more than a small percentage of the inbound traffic.[82] "In less than three years," commented Malcolm Bingay of the *Detroit News*, "around $50,000,000 was spent so that people could get back and forth—quickly—between Detroit and our ever-kind liquor-supplied neighbors of Windsor."[83]

Booze also poured across the border via the dozens of roads linking Quebec to Vermont and New York. Most roads had no customs stations, and the stations that did exist were closed at night and minimally patrolled. Route 9, dubbed "Rum Trail," connected Plattsburgh, New York, to the border. A case of beer bought in Canada for as much as five dollars could be sold in Plattsburgh for ten, and it fetched up to twenty-five dollars in New York City.[84]

Such high profits in a business with low barriers to entry predictably attracted many fortune seekers.[85] Consider the rags-to-riches story of Larry Fay, the New York City cabdriver who quickly realized that it was far more profitable to transport booze than people. Fay bought whiskey for ten dollars a case in Montreal and sold it for eighty dollars a case on his return trip to New York. Reinvesting these profits in his upstart illicit transport business, Fay soon owned several cabs and trucks making runs between Montreal and New York. Bootlegging provided the start-up capital for Fay's real business interest: New York nightclubs. At "El Fey," the first nightclub he opened, heavily watered-down whiskey sold for $1.50 per drink, and "champagne" (actually carbonated cider mixed with alcohol) sold for twenty-five dollars per bottle. After the feds shut it down, Fay opened an even bigger nightclub, the "Club Del Fey" at 247 West 54th Street. Fay's clientele ranged from wealthy New Yorkers to famous foreign visitors—including members of the British Royal Family.[86]

Bootleggers also took advantage of the Canadian leak along the northwestern edge of the border. The most famous of all was Roy Olmstead, a cop-turned-smuggler who oversaw a large-scale alcohol shipping and distribution business between Vancouver and Seattle in the early 1920s. He became Seattle's millionaire "rum king" in just a few years. Olmstead's fleet of fast boats, powered by Boeing engines, delivered Canadian whiskey throughout the Puget Sound area. Olmstead became a fixture in Seattle social circles, throwing grandiose parties at his Mount Baker mansion. He also established Seattle's first radio station, which was suspected of using coded messages to facilitate smuggling operations.

Although many locals—including the mayor and many of his former associates in law enforcement—hobnobbed with Olmstead, the feds targeted him, resorting to previously illegal wiretapping (including taped conversations between Olmstead and corrupt cops discussing illicit business transactions) to build their case. In 1926 Olmstead was tried for "conspiracy to possess, transport and import intoxicating liquors" and given a four-year jail term. The case made history: it was the first time a judge allowed phone wiretapping as evidence in a trial. The hugely controversial verdict was appealed all the way to the Supreme Court, which ruled in favor of the prosecution by a five-four vote—a decision that was not overturned until 1967.[87]

Ultimately, those who made the biggest profits from the Prohibition-induced smuggling boom were not the bootleggers but the big distillers. The stock value of Canada's four largest liquor producers more than tripled.[88] As the bootlegger and racketeer Moe Dalitz noted later, "I did nothing more than the head of Seagram's, than the head of G&W [Gooderham and Worts], the head of Canadian Club. They assembled all this merchandise for runners to bring it across."[89]

Leading the list of Canadian liquor magnates who made enormous profits from Prohibition was Samuel Bronfman. At the start of Prohibition his company allegedly imported some 300,000 gallons of American whiskey, significantly watered it down, and then shipped it back to the United States through smuggling channels. He also reportedly imported thousands of barrels of alcohol from Scotland, added coloring and water, and illicitly exported it to America. By the end of the first year of Prohibition, his company was moving nearly sixty-four thousand gallons of spirits across the border every month. Bronfman also dominated much of the St. Pierre transit trade. In 1928, already one of the wealthiest men in Canada, he bought Seagram and turned it into a global player in liquor distribution.[90]

The Prohibition Hangover

If World War I was the crucial context that gave birth to Prohibition, the Great Depression was the crucial context that killed it off. The great need for tax revenue in desperately hard times ultimately trumped America's waning enthusiasm for Prohibition. The Anti-Saloon League had promised that Prohibition would cleanse and purify the nation. Instead, an increasingly weary public and skeptical media came to blame Prohibition for poisoning the nation by fueling corruption, violence, and lawlessness. Although no one saw it coming—a constitutional amendment, after all, had never been repealed before—in the end Prohibition was discarded as easily as it had been imposed. Even Mormon Utah signed on for repeal.

Though America's failed Prohibition experiment was relatively short-lived, it left a long-lasting legacy. As James Morone puts it, in just thirteen years Prohibition rewrote "American federalism, criminal justice, the courts, civil liberties, crime-fighting, crime families, and national attitudes."[91] Thanks to Prohibition, the idea that crime was a federal matter requiring federal policing became more deeply embedded and institutionalized, and it helped to lay the groundwork for the subsequent expansion of the Federal Bureau of Investigation.[92] Prohibition even changed the way we speak. New slang terms were invented and popularized, many of which have lived on: "big shot," "big time," "bump off," "taken for a ride," "frame," "muscle in," "run around," "grand" (thousand dollars), "powder room" (bathroom for women at speakeasies).[93]

Law enforcement was bruised and battered during the Prohibition years but came away from the experience greatly empowered. Consider, for example, the radical rewriting of search-and-seizure rules. The proliferation of the automobile in America—from only three million in 1916 to more than twenty-six million in 1930—provided new opportunities for smuggling, but it also prompted law enforcement to test the limits of Fourth Amendment protections. In *Carroll v. United States* (1925) the Supreme Court ruled that a warrant was no longer required to search a vehicle so long as there is a "reasonable and probable cause for believing that the automobile has contraband liquor therein which is being illegally transported."[94]

The same thing happened with the spread of the telephone. It facilitated coordination of smuggling but also gave law enforcement new surveillance opportunities. The Supreme Court decision in the Olmstead smuggling case, noted earlier, granted the police sweeping wiretapping powers for the first time, powers that would not be curtailed for four decades. It is striking that the 1910 version of the *Cyclopedia of Law and Practice* devotes only fifteen pages to the issue of search and seizure, but in the 1932 version it runs 114 pages.[95]

The law enforcement infrastructure and legal precedents created by Prohibition would stay in place long after repeal—retooled and refocused on other policing concerns, including other mind-altering substances. Indeed, Harry Anslinger, the assistant prohibition commissioner, became the first commissioner of the Federal Bureau of Narcotics. And as we'll see in the next chapter, even though alcohol prohibition lasted little more than a decade, drug prohibition would not only persist but also escalate for more than a century. It offers a glimpse of what the short-lived experiment in alcohol prohibition could have looked like if it had been globalized rather than repealed. But compared to alcohol, drugs such as heroin and cocaine were much more compact, portable, durable, and concealable—making them even more difficult to suppress and prompting even more expansive and invasive policing.

PART V

INTO THE MODERN AGE

14

America's Century-Long Drug War

THE USE OF MIND-ALTERING drugs—whether for ceremonial, medicinal, or recreational purposes—has existed throughout human history.[1] What have varied over time are the particular substances, the location and methods of production and distribution, consumer tastes, societal tolerance, and laws and their enforcement.[2] The previous chapter focused on America's short-lived, failed experiment in prohibiting an especially popular drug—alcohol—and the smuggling boom it unleashed. We now turn our attention to the other drugs that were prohibited in the early decades of the twentieth century—opium and its derivatives (morphine and heroin), cocaine and other coca products, and cannabis (marijuana)—but that remain criminalized a century later and are the main targets of a U.S.-led global "war on drugs."[3]

Drug prohibition sharply accelerated and expanded the broader trend of using federal powers to police vice trades. New and more punitive laws were passed, new and more expansive bureaucracies were created to enforce them, new and bigger prisons were built to house violators, and arm-twisting drug diplomacy became a new and increasingly prominent component of U.S. foreign relations. Yet despite this sustained drug war buildup, the illicit drug business not only survived but turned into one of the most profitable sectors of global trade, with the United States as the world's leading consumer. Through the century-long enforcement-evasion game between "narcs" and "narcos," illicit drugs became the smuggled commodity most closely associated with crime, corruption, violence, and the underside of America's transformation into a consumer society.

Prohibiting Drugs

To many Americans, certain ideas about drugs such as cocaine and heroin seem commonsensical: use of these drugs is simply wrong and dangerous, distributing and ingesting them is criminal, seeking to eliminate their supply is sensible, and relying primarily on suppression is the most effective way to stop trafficking and dealing. But this set of ideas has not always held sway. Indeed, many nineteenth-century American merchants viewed opium no differently from any other commodity. For instance, Warren Delano II, the grandfather of Franklin Delano Roosevelt and the creator of the family fortune, profited from shipping opium to China, calling it a "fair, honorable and legitimate trade; and to say the worst of it, liable to no further or weightier objections than is the importation of wines, Brandies & spirits into the U. States, England, &c."[4] But he failed to also mention that the Chinese authorities considered him an outlaw and a smuggler; the opium trade had been banned by imperial edict since 1729.

In 1900 opium, morphine, heroin, cocaine, and marijuana were all legal and readily available in the United States. They were prescribed by doctors to relieve pain and sleeplessness, and they could even be purchased in grocery and general stores as well as by mail order. They were found in numerous unregulated patent medicines, claiming to cure everything from stomachaches to toothaches. Cocaine, synthesized from the coca plant, was a favorite ingredient in Coca-Cola, medicine, and wines. Historian David Musto reminds us that the Parke Davis Company "sold coca-leaf cigarettes and coca cheroots [cigars] to accompany their other products, which provided cocaine in a variety of media such as a liqueur-like alcohol mixture called Coca Cordial, tablets, hypodermic injections, ointments, and sprays."[5] The 1897 Sears, Roebuck catalog offered hypodermic kits—a syringe, two needles, two vials of morphine, and a carrying case—for $1.50.[6] In 1898 Bayer and Company promoted its own synthesized version of morphine as a

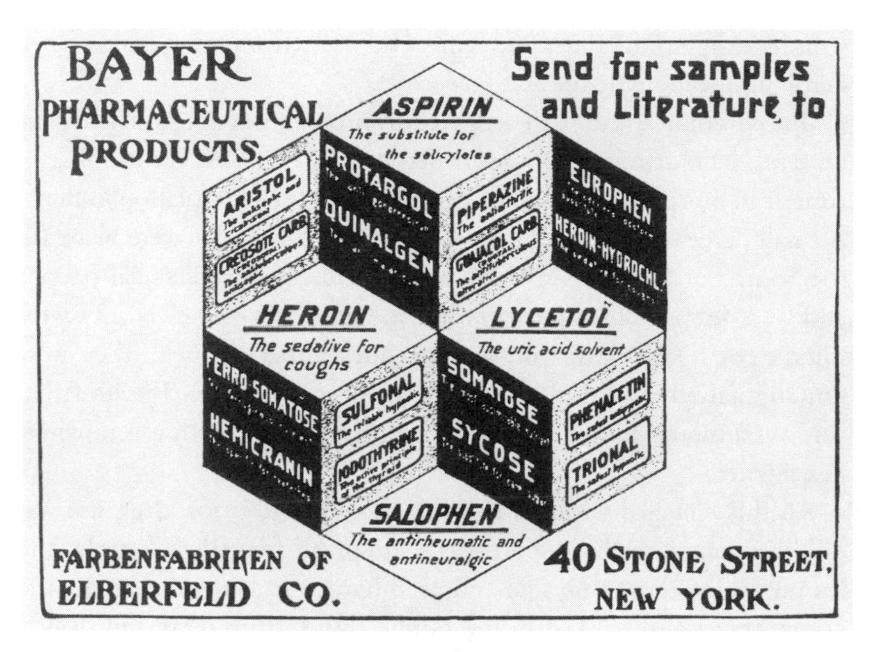

Figure 14.1 At the turn of the century, Bayer Pharmaceuticals promoted heroin as a cough suppressant (Granger Collection).

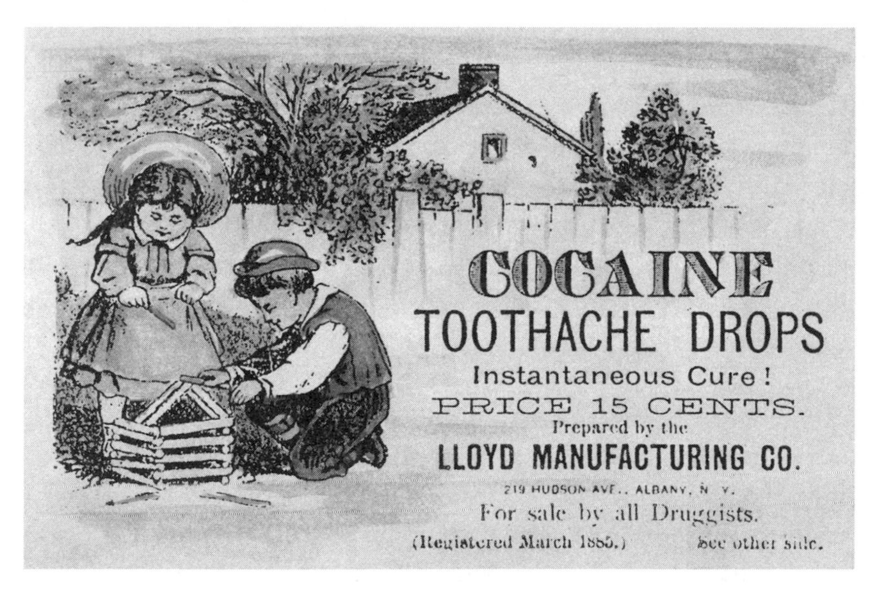

Figure 14.2 An 1885 medicine ad for "cocaine toothache drops" was clearly meant for children as well as adults (Granger Collection).

wonder drug, under the brand name "heroin" (from the German word heroisch, meaning heroic and powerful).[7]

The common use of such drugs led to problems of abuse. There were no hard data, of course, but informed estimates placed the number of American morphine addicts at 2 to 4 percent of the population in 1895.[8] A small percentage of drug users—especially those who were black (in the South) or Chinese (in the West)—were considered social pariahs and were feared. But most users in the latter half of the century were middle- or upper-class, with women outnumbering men. They were not stigmatized and certainly not treated as criminals. The idea that this was a matter for the federal government to deal with was nowhere in evidence.

All this changed within a few decades. By the 1930s, drug use was publicly condemned. Support was widespread for strict controls, and for punishing those who sold and used heroin and cocaine. Drugs and crime were tightly linked in the public mind; drug users and dealers were seen as threats to society. Stopping drug use and stemming the supply of drugs were unquestioned goals of government policy.

What happened? By the early 1900s concern about drug use was rising, though it did not generate the same sort of organized fervor as alcohol consumption.[9] There was nothing like the Anti-Saloon League leading the antidrug charge. However, groups in the medical community, reformers in the Progressive movement, moralistic anti-vice crusaders, muckraking journalists, and racist and nativist groups who feared that America would be mongrelized and contaminated by drug-consuming "inferior peoples" were all intent on establishing some kind of regimen for drug control. Their various struggles merged in the early decades of the twentieth century to forge a new public consensus on drug use.

Physicians began to pay attention to problems of addiction in the aftermath of the Civil War, when wounded soldiers who were given morphine for pain became addicted in large numbers. Of particular concern were the problems that resulted from the casual prescription of drugs to relieve aches and pains and from consumers' unwary exposure to these substances in popular patent medicines with unlabeled contents. The emerging medical professions, anxious to protect their members' interests, argued that medical officials should regulate the supply of drugs and decide what treatments were appropriate. In 1903 the American Pharmaceutical Association said that cocaine and opium derivatives should be given only under prescription and that laws should regulate—but not prohibit—drug use. Pragmatic reformers in the Progressive movement joined the doctors and pharmacists. Seeking to protect the public interest against greedy corporations and corrupt politicians, they echoed the medical community's call for close regulation of patent medicines. Their efforts paid off in the enactment of the Pure Food and Drug Act of 1906, which required that all narcotic ingredients, as well as cannabis, be listed on the labels of any patent medicines shipped in interstate commerce. The legislation dramatically reduced the patent-medicine market.

Health and professional interests were not the only concerns that motivated drug reform. An explicitly antidrug crusade also emerged as part of a broader movement against vice, including drinking and prostitution, at the turn of the century. It was rooted in a puritanical strain in American culture that demanded that public control be exercised to foster moral and upright behavior. The antivice crusade was intensified by concerns that rapid urbanization in the early twentieth century was corrupting the family and undermining traditional values.

The antidrug crusade was also linked to deep-seated racist and nativist fears. The campaign against vice and urban immorality at the turn of the century was fueled in part by widespread anxieties that the wave of immigration from eastern and southern Europe threatened America's moral (and economic) well-being. In its less genteel form, anxiety about drug use by immigrants combined with violent prejudice against blacks, Chinese, and Mexicans to spur the enactment of local antidrug laws aimed specifically at these minorities.[10]

In the South, for example, cocaine was linked to deep-rooted prejudice against blacks. Its euphoric and stimulating qualities were feared for their presumed ability to make Negro cocaine users "oblivious of their prescribed bounds" and to lead them to "attack white society."[11] There were even accusations that cocaine use "gave blacks superhuman strength, improved their marksmanship, and made them difficult to kill."[12]

There was a parallel campaign against Chinese immigrants in the West. In 1875 San Francisco forbade opium smoking, a practice closely identified with Chinese Americans. Between 1877 and 1900 anti-opium legislation was enacted in eleven western states. A 1902 American Federation of Labor (AFL) pamphlet foreshadowed what decades later would become a widely accepted "contagion" theory. Chinese smokers had spread the "deathly habit" to "hundreds, aye thousands, of our American boys and girls," the AFL declared.[13]

Despite the widespread antidrug rhetoric and local bans, opium smoking and the use of other drugs did not disappear. Users either went underground or were tolerated in limited locations. Antinarcotics groups reacted by pressing Congress to restrict supply at the national level. In 1883 the tariff on opium was raised; four years later restrictions were imposed on the importation of some forms of opium, and Chinese immigrants were prohibited from any importation of the drug. In 1890 the manufacture of smoking opium was limited to American citizens. Not surprisingly, these efforts also failed to stop the trade; instead they stimulated smuggling.[14]

The push for drug control was propelled by other developments abroad. American missionaries in China were appalled at what they saw as the moral and social degeneration resulting from the British opium trade. They circulated horror stories of opium's impact back home and began to urge the government to take a leadership role in an international effort to curb the drug trade.[15] The full impact of missionary diplomacy became evident after 1898, when the United States gained control of the Philippines. The United States was suddenly faced with the question of what to do about narcotics addiction in the territory: under Spanish rule, addicts had been licensed and opium was legal. The War Department turned to the Right Reverend Charles H. Brent, the Episcopal bishop in the Philippines. Bishop Brent convinced President Theodore Roosevelt to call an international conference on regulating the opium trade in 1906.[16] The State Department backed the request, recognizing that it served other foreign policy interests as well. In particular, it allowed the United States to increase its influence in the Pacific, notably against its major competitor, Britain, and to strengthen its relations with the Chinese government, which was strongly opposed to the British trade.[17] Perhaps more important than their impact abroad, the resulting meetings (in Shanghai and The Hague) became vehicles for organizing a campaign for stricter drug control in the United States.

In 1909 Secretary of State Elihu Root convinced Congress to ban the importation of all forms of smoking opium in order to secure "legislation on this subject in time to save our face in the conference at Shanghai."[18] Other prohibitionists wanted much more. Spearheading the campaign was Dr. Hamilton Wright, who had joined Brent in representing the United States at the international conferences. Wright and others argued that Washington should not only support an international agreement to ban the production, export, and use of cocaine and opium abroad but also pass federal legislation to ban all imports of these drugs. They were quick to join their campaign to the rising domestic tide of racist fears about narcotics and their effects. Dr. Wright pushed tirelessly for restrictive legislation and skillfully recruited the secretary of state and the secretary of the treasury in the effort.[19] Avid in his support of prohibitionist and missionary pursuits, Secretary of State William Jennings Bryan pressed for the passage of legislation to meet the requirements of the international agreements the State Department supported.[20]

New York Representative Francis Burton Harrison eventually agreed to sponsor legislation. In the wake of reports that opium use had nearly tripled between 1870 and 1909,[21] he expressed a now-familiar logic for control of the drug supply: "This enormous increase in the importation of and consumption of opium in the United States is startling and is directly due to the facility with which opium may be imported, manufactured into its various derivatives and preparations, and placed within the reach of the individual. There has been in this country an almost shameless traffic in these drugs. Criminal classes have been created, and the use of the drugs with much accompanying moral and economic degradation is widespread among the upper classes of society. We are an opium-consuming nation today."[22]

There was no mass movement, as in alcohol prohibition, to support Harrison's bill; but neither was there broad opposition. Public opinion had gradually swung to accept the view that drug use was a problem and that it was legitimate to control drugs. And, unlike alcohol users before and during Prohibition, cocaine and heroin users mounted no organized opposition to control.

The Harrison Narcotics Act, passed in December 1914, grounded federal drug control in the constitutional power to tax—which meant that enforcement powers fell to the Treasury Department. This first federal drug-control law would prove momentous. But what exactly did the new law mean? Legally, it set three major requirements for those who produced or distributed drugs: they had to register with the federal government, keep a record of all their transactions, and pay a purchase or sales tax. The Harrison Act also required that unregistered persons—drug users—could purchase drugs only with a prescription from a physician who "prescribed [it] in good faith" and did so "in pursuit of his professional practice only."

On its face, the Harrison Act seemed to be based more on a medical rather than law-enforcement model of drug control. The major regulatory mechanisms were designed to keep drugs under the control of the medical community. The law did not criminalize drug users or brand them as morally wrong. Using drugs was not made a crime: users were simply required to turn to doctors for prescriptions to buy drugs. The antivice crusaders, despite their rhetoric and pressure campaigns, appeared to have lost the fight: the law did not reflect their prohibitionist desires, nor did legislators believe they were passing a prohibition law.[23]

But the battle to define the terms of national drug policy had only begun. In the end, the prohibitionists would transform a largely medical model for controlling drug use into a law enforcement model for outlawing drug use. Powerful government agents joined them in their quest. They were aided by an increasingly fearful and vengeful social context shaped by such events as the struggle over alcohol prohibition, World War I, and widespread fear of immigrants and foreign influences.

The Treasury Department was charged with administering the Harrison Act, and its agents took the lead role in transforming it into a prohibitionist law. The department (first its Bureau of Revenue and then, after 1920, the Narcotics Division of its Prohibition Unit) began to issue regulations interpreting the law as forbidding the maintenance of addicts on drugs. The department also began to arrest physicians and druggists, in order to stop them from providing prescriptions to help maintain addicts, and to arrest addicts for illegal possession.[24] The courts rejected this prohibitionist maneuver. But Treasury persisted and was eventually able to take advantage of a changing social context increasingly shaped by the antivice movement.

In the years immediately following the Harrison Act, antivice crusaders, often supported by urban dailies and popular national magazines, sought more stringent prohibition and punishment of physicians and addicts and continued to warn of "the drug evil." Mass organizations pushing for alcohol prohibition had created a moral atmosphere that condemned such vices. The Treasury Department also helped turn public opinion against doctors and their addicted patients. Antivice crusaders and many journalists projected an image of "dope doctors" responsible for the nation's drug problems.

The growing antidrug sentiment rode the tide of other national fears. World War I and the 1919–20 Red Scare fanned the fears of foreign threats. Press stories circulated about drugs being smuggled into U.S. Army training centers by Germans and about Germans "exporting drugs in toothpaste and patent medicines in order to hook innocent citizens of other countries on drugs."[25] Alcohol Prohibition further boosted the antivice crusade, and in the early 1920s a number of antinarcotics groups formed. Richmond P. Hobson, a star orator of the Prohibition movement, was responsible for the creation of some of the more vocal organizations. Hobson not only grossly exaggerated the numbers ("one million heroin addicts") but also argued that heroin caused crime and that addicts were "beasts" and "monsters" who spread their disease like medieval vampires.[26] "Drug addiction is more communicable and less curable than leprosy," he warned, asserting that, "drug addicts are the principal carriers of vice diseases." Hobson exclaimed that "upon this issue hangs the perpetuation of civilization, the destiny of the world, and the future of the human race."[27] Meanwhile, very few voices rose in opposition to the prohibitionist tide, and those that did were weak and marginalized.

The courts also caved in. From 1915 to 1919 narcotics agents faced limits in their campaigns to intimidate doctors because the courts refused to accept the Treasury Department's prohibitionist interpretation of the Harrison Act, and Congress was unwilling to amend the law.[28] But in 1919, in *Webb v. United States*, the Supreme Court concluded that it was illegitimate for a doctor to maintain addicts on morphine with no intention of curing them. Treasury pounced on the decision, quickly putting its personnel on notice that the Supreme Court now supported the prosecution of physicians who were distributing drugs "to a person popularly known as a 'dope fiend,' for the purpose of gratifying his appetite for the drug." Such acts, the Treasury memorandum said, put physicians in violation of the Harrison Act.[29] In 1922 the Court again delivered a verdict supporting Treasury's position. In *United States v. Behrman*, the Court established that a narcotics prescription for an addict was illegal unless the addict had some other ailment requiring treatment with narcotics.

These court rulings transformed the Harrison Act into a prohibition law that conformed to the Treasury Department's interpretation. The social and political tide toward the prohibition of drugs had turned so decisively by the mid-1920s that even a reversal of position on the *Behrman* case by the Supreme Court in 1925 had little effect on policy or practice. As legal sources of drugs dried up, dope peddlers and smugglers were defined as the key problem and became the targets of government policy. The dominant interpretation of addiction, meanwhile, pointed toward harsh, punitive measures. Furthermore, a consensus arose that any nonmedical narcotics use—even nonaddictive use—was a vice and that users should be punished. Laws began to sanction not just suppliers but also users themselves. By the late 1920s, one-third of inmates in federal prisons were serving sentences for violating the Harrison Act.[30]

Driving the Drug Trade Underground

As physicians and pharmacists backed away from prescribing cocaine and opiates and as clinics closed their doors by the 1920s, those drug users who were unable to break their habits had little choice but to enter the underworld—supporting the black-market smugglers and dope peddlers who had replaced doctors and pharmacists, and sometimes stealing to meet the high prices created by prohibition.

In this growing illicit drug market, New York City emerged as the central import, distribution, and user hub. The city not only possessed the country's largest port and was well connected by transportation links to major markets across the continent but also had the largest concentration of heroin users.[31] In the second decade of the twentieth century New York was also the center of a loosely organized and decentralized underground cocaine trade. Through New York, criminologists

Alan Block and William Chambliss tell us, "Cocaine was imported, wholesaled, franchised, and retailed. . . . It was traded in movies, theaters, restaurants, cafes, cabarets, pool parlors, saloons, parks, and on innumerable street corners. It was an important part of the coin of an underground that was deeply embedded in the urban culture of New York."[32]

Initially, supplies of cocaine, morphine, and heroin could still be found through diversion and theft from American pharmaceutical companies, many of them located in the New York–Philadelphia corridor.[33] Like their foreign counterparts, these companies produced far more than the legitimate medical market could possibly absorb. A favorite diversion and smuggling scheme early on was to set up front companies in Mexico and Canada to import heroin and other drugs from the United States and then smuggle them back into the country.[34] As Treasury told a congressional committee in 1920, "drugs are exported from this country for the purposes of reentry through illicit channels."[35]

Congress targeted these trade tricks by passing the Narcotics Drugs Import and Export Act of 1922, otherwise known as the Jones-Miller Act. The new law empowered the federal government to closely track legal narcotics shipments and crack down on diversion. Treasury Secretary Andrew Mellon warned that the law would be difficult to enforce, require many more customs agents, and further fuel smuggling. Customs, he stressed, was already overwhelmed, its reports documenting "conclusively that smuggling of narcotics into the United States is on the increase to such an extent that customs officers seem unable to suppress traffic to any appreciable extent."[36] To eliminate the possibility of diversion from legal channels, in 1924 Congress banned all domestic production and medical use of heroin.

With domestically produced drug supplies drying up by the mid-1920s, dealers increasingly turned to foreign sources. Bulk quantities of heroin, morphine, and cocaine could still be secured through German, Dutch, and French firms. Taking advantage of this new international business opportunity, Arnold Rothstein became America's most famous drug trade entrepreneur of the 1920s. Already a well-established and successful New York bootlegger, racketeer, financier, and gambler who gained fame and notoriety for allegedly fixing the 1919 World

Series, Rothstein used his underworld business connections to branch out into the profitable new world of international drug trafficking. Rothstein set up and oversaw a transatlantic operation illicitly importing drugs—mostly heroin but also morphine and cocaine—legally manufactured in Europe. France was an especially important source, with French pharmaceutical firms processing far more opium than any other country in the world and far beyond legitimate medicinal needs. Excess production slipped into the black market.[37]

As European countries began to impose stricter controls on their pharmaceutical companies (as agreed to in international treaties signed in 1925 and 1931 to more closely monitor and restrict legal production), underground factories sprung up in France, the Balkans, and Turkey. Drugs were also increasingly imported from East Asia, especially Shanghai, where a freewheeling regulatory environment and chaotic political situation provided favorable conditions for heroin processing and export in the 1930s.[38]

These prohibition-induced shifts in the illicit drug trade favored heroin over morphine and opium smoking. Heroin was much more potent than morphine, and its higher value per weight made it ideal for smuggling. Moreover, heroin could more easily be diluted for higher profits at the retail distribution level. And unlike morphine, heroin users could snort the stuff (as long as it was not overly diluted) if they had an aversion to the needle.

Meanwhile, opium smoking, which was less dangerous than heroin, virtually disappeared: opium was a bulky product with a pungent smell, making it less profitable to smuggle per weight and more detectable by law enforcement.[39] A similar shift happened with coca products, with high-potency cocaine pushing out the much more benign coca tonics.[40] This essentially repeated the market dynamic we saw with alcohol prohibition, with hard liquor replacing beer as the favored drink in the 1920s.

Another parallel to alcohol prohibition was the spread of drug-related corruption. The high profits of the trade not only enriched smugglers but also made bribes and payoffs to law enforcement an affordable business expense. Investigations following the fatal shooting of Arnold Rothstein in 1928 revealed not only the magnitude of his illicit drug import business but also the extent of drug corruption. A New York grand jury found that federal drug enforcement in the city—home to the largest number of agents in the country—was plagued by gross incompetence, negligence, and corruption. Most embarrassing was the revelation that both the son and son-in-law of the deputy commissioner of prohibition, Levi Nutt, were actually employed by Rothstein.[41]

America's First Drug Czar

The New York corruption investigation following Rothstein's death contributed to the shakeup of the federal narcotics bureaucracy and its separation from the much-maligned Prohibition Bureau. Efforts in Congress to establish an independent drug-control agency paid off in July 1930, with the creation of the Federal Bureau of Narcotics (FBN) in the Treasury Department. With Nutt's career derailed by scandal, President Hoover turned to Harry Anslinger, a high official in the Prohibition Bureau with considerable international experience targeting alcohol smuggling, and appointed him as the FBN's first commissioner.[42]

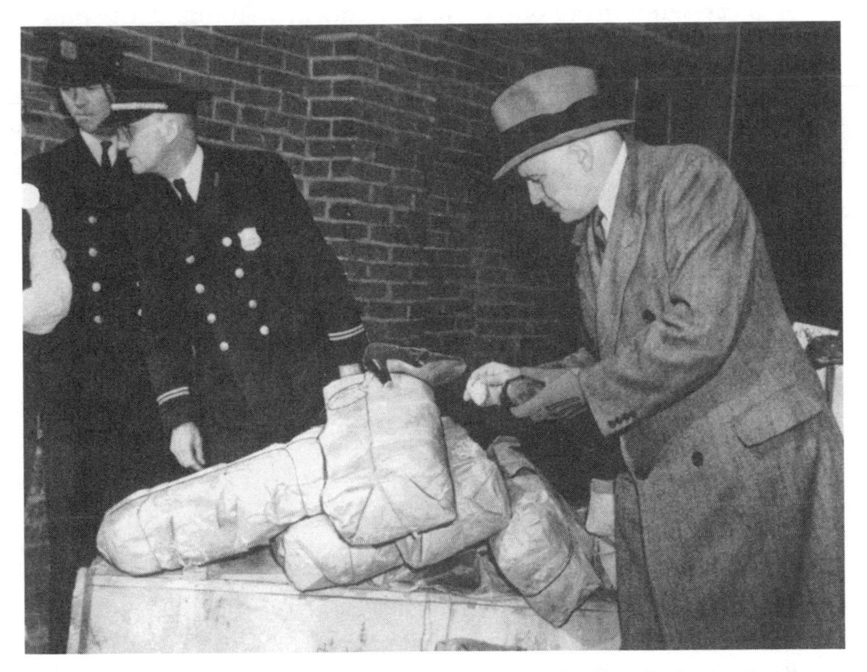

Figure 14.3 Federal Bureau of Narcotics Commissioner Harry J. Anslinger, America's first "drug czar," examines seized drugs in the 1950s (DEA Museum).

Anslinger became the J. Edgar Hoover of drugs, America's first "drug czar." During his more than three decades on the job, Anslinger never wavered from his commitment to a tough law-and-order approach to drugs. Anslinger told judges to "jail offenders, and then throw away the key."[43] In his view, the main lesson to be learned from the failures of Prohibition was that it had not been tough enough. He believed that the key challenge was curtailing the drug supply, especially from abroad. As the top U.S. diplomat on drug issues, Anslinger played a lead role in international meetings and conferences concerned with narcotics, continuously lobbying for the increasingly restrictive measures that came to define the emerging global drug prohibition regime. He also spearheaded international efforts to coordinate drug-related intelligence gathering and sharing.

Because of their compact size and low weight relative to value, smuggled drugs were much harder to detect than smuggled alcohol. This made random searches of people, luggage, and cargo even more inefficient than during the Prohibition years. Anslinger therefore increasingly turned to informants and undercover operations to develop cases and make busts. He consequently "plunged the bureau into the murky business of employing smugglers to catch smugglers," note historians Kathryn Meyer and Terry Parsinnen, with the downside that "using informants brought the agents into the same dark shadowlands as the traffickers they sought to control. At times their identities blurred."[44]

Yet for decades Anslinger turned a blind eye to the spreading rot of corruption within his own agency—which would eventually contribute to its dismantling and reorganization. An investigation initiated decades later found that nearly sixty out of the three hundred FBN agents were corrupt, which included collaborating with traffickers and selling heroin. Ramsey Clark, the U.S. attorney general at the time of the corruption investigation, concluded: "The least you can make of it is that Anslinger was derelict in being so unaware of what was happening in his own agency. Apparently he had decided as a matter of self preservation not to address it."[45]

Meanwhile, to generate the needed support to protect and expand his agency and its mission, Anslinger undertook a sweeping and aggressive campaign in the 1930s and 1940s to mold public antidrug attitudes.

He regularly testified before Congress and became a prolific writer, spreading his antidrug message through all types of media outlets. He persistently blamed particular minority groups, foreigners, and foreign ideological influences for America's drug problem.[46] He aggressively cultivated a rising chorus of demands from sources from within and outside of government that argued for punitive sanctions against the sale and use of opiates and cocaine. Out of this increasingly moralistic and drug-intolerant social context emerged the criminalization of another drug: marijuana.

Killer Weed

Early drafters of the Harrison Act tried to outlaw marijuana but found little organized support for their efforts—and much opposition from the pharmaceutical industry.[47] By the mid-1920s, however, fear of marijuana was growing in the South and West, spurred by rapidly increasing Mexican migration. Although employers welcomed Mexicans as a source of cheap labor, the new immigrants—like the Chinese and others before them—triggered fears of crime and social corruption.

Racist and nativist suspicions about Mexican immigrants came to focus on marijuana use. Before long, local residents had attributed crime-producing powers to the drug. As the Great Depression made the Mexicans an unwelcome surplus labor force in the 1930s, the identification of Mexicans with both crime and marijuana deepened. Pressure on Washington to "do something" mounted from several quarters, including local police forces, citizens' groups, state governors, and the Hearst newspaper chain (whose stories and cartoons detailed the ways the drug enslaved its users).

With his agents already plenty busy, Anslinger was at first reluctant to add marijuana to his list of targets. But by 1936 he had joined the push for federal legislation prohibiting it. He and his agency helped forge a more punitive public consensus against marijuana, and they assisted in crafting and securing passage of legislation and lent vocal support in the debate in Congress. In December 1936, Anslinger told Congress that marijuana was "about as hellish as heroin."[48] Everyone seemed to have forgotten that just a year earlier he had claimed marijuana wasn't even addictive.

The Marijuana Tax Act passed in the summer of 1937 and took effect in October of that year. By that time forty-six states had placed anti-marijuana laws on the books. The Marijuana Tax Act was modeled on some features of the 1914 Harrison Act. Only the nonmedical, untaxed possession or sale of marijuana was outlawed. "Illegitimate transfers" were taxed at $100 a pound—a steep tax considering that marijuana purchased legally cost $2 a pound. Violations brought a fine of $2,000, five years in prison, or both.[49] The antimarijuana campaign had succeeded in adding the substance to the public's list of serious law-enforcement threats: by the time marijuana was outlawed, "common sense" linked its use to deadly crimes. A person under the influence of marijuana could, as Anslinger put it, be provoked by "the slightest opposition, arousing him to a state of menacing fury or homicidal attack. During this frenzied period, addicts have perpetuated some of the most bizarre and fantastic offenses and sex crimes known to police annals."[50] Little

Figure 14.4 Advertisement for the 1936 American film *Reefer Madness*. Decades later it was used by the National Organization for the Reform of Marijuana Laws to illustrate the excesses of the antimarijuana campaign (Granger Collection).

opposition surfaced to Anslinger's efforts to define marijuana as a crime-causing "killer weed" and to ban its use; and in the fearful and moralistic mood of the day, few spoke out against the general trend toward a punitive policy of drug prohibition. The government discouraged opposition by blocking critical testimony, disparaging those who publicly questioned policy assumptions, studiously ignoring contrary evidence, and straining to defend the many questionable claims about drugs propounded by prohibitionists and the media.

If few questioned the criminalization of marijuana, almost no one challenged the basic assumptions of Anslinger's overall drug-suppression strategy. The only outspoken opposition in Congress in the 1930s and 1940s came from Washington representative John M. Coffee. Coffee pointedly condemned the Harrison Act and the federal government for creating a vast smuggling industry: "If we, the representatives of the people, are to continue to let our narcotics authorities conduct themselves in a manner tantamount to upholding and in effect supporting the billion-dollar drug racket, we should at least be able to explain to our constituents why we do so." He argued for going back to the original intent of the Harrison Act, bringing addicts under medical supervision to secure the supply they needed legitimately at low cost: "Morphine which the peddler sells for a dollar a grain would be supplied, of pure quality, for 2 or 3 cents a grain. The peddler, unable to meet such a price, would go out of business—the illicit narcotic drug industry, the billion-dollar drug racket, would automatically cease to exist."[51] Such appeals fell on deaf ears—much to the delight of both drug smugglers and drug law enforcers.

Drugs and Geopolitics

The emerging illicit drug trade was shaped not only by prohibitions but also by geopolitics. As the United States became a dominant player on the world stage, drugs and national security increasingly bumped into each other—at times awkwardly, but also in politically useful ways. Geopolitics trumped drug enforcement during and after World War II, often to the advantage of politically protected traffickers. At the same time, anticommunist anxieties provided added ideological ammunition for America's antidrug campaign. In other words, the United States overlooked drug trafficking when geopolitically convenient, while also disparaging geopolitical rivals as complicit in the drug trade.

Anslinger cultivated close relations with the intelligence community, and he was pleased to have the FBN's surveillance capacities put to good use during the war years when the illicit drug trade had largely dried up with the disruptions in global transportation. For instance, Garland Williams, the head of the FBN's New York office, became director of special training at the Office of Strategic Services (OSS, predecessor of the CIA). Similarly, FBN agent George Hunter White was appointed as director of counterespionage training at the OSS. After the war, the FBN jointly operated safe houses with the CIA in New York and San Francisco, provided CIA operatives with FBN jobs as cover overseas, and even collaborated on mind-control drug research experiments.[52]

Not just drug-control agents but also drug traffickers were recruited in the pursuit of American war objectives. Most notable was the case of Charles "Lucky" Luciano, who had made a name for himself as a bootlegger and also engaged in heroin trafficking and organized prostitution. Arnold Rothstein's illicit drug import business passed on to Luciano and other underlings in the New York underworld, such as Meyer Lansky, Louis Buchalter, and Frank Costello.[53] In 1936 Luciano began a long prison sentence for running a New York prostitution ring. World War II proved to be the break that gave him his get-out-of-jail-free card; he was pardoned and deported to freedom in Italy in 1946 as a reward for his wartime collaboration with U.S. Naval Intelligence.[54]

Luciano made a deal: using his business partner Lansky as a go-between, he agreed to gather intelligence from his contacts in New York's waterfront underworld to protect the city's harbor against German espionage and sabotage, and also use his mafia contacts in Italy to help prepare the way for the 1943 American invasion of Sicily. It remains unclear how useful Luciano's information actually proved to be. In any case, FBI director J. Edgar Hoover was stunned when he heard about it: "This is an amazing and fantastic case," he wrote in a memo. "We should get all the facts, for it looks rotten to me from several angles." When informed that the Office of Chief of Naval Operations "acknowledges that Luciano was employed as an informant," Hoover called it "A shocking example of misuse of Navy authority in interest of a hoodlum. It surprises me they didn't give Luciano the Navy Cross."[55]

After the war, Luciano, along with many other American crime figures of Italian descent, were shipped off to Italy. Bringing with them their illicit business knowledge and connections, many of these deported mobsters proceeded to help revive the postwar international heroin trade and supply the U.S. market. As a *Rome Daily American* article reported in 1951, "An estimated fifty men deported from the U.S. to Italy on narcotics charges since the war are believed to have formed the nucleus of a far-flung dope smuggling network."[56] Luciano was singled out by the FBN as the heroin smuggling ringleader, giving Anslinger a familiar face to blame for the country's drug problem. But the FBN certainly knew that Luciano was just one of many traffickers feeding America's drug habit.[57] And some of these suppliers, including CIA-backed Chinese nationalists using dope money to help fund their anticommunist campaign along the southern Chinese border, were simply overlooked by Anslinger because it was too geopolitically awkward to do otherwise.[58]

Cold War geopolitics also inadvertently helped transform Marseille into the main source of U.S.-bound heroin in the 1950s and 1960s. Marseille, France's second largest city and biggest port, was a key entry point for Marshall Plan aid shipments to Europe. It was also a French communist party stronghold and the epicenter of the country's labor movement, which launched strikes that threatened to disrupt shipping and the postwar economic recovery. Viewing French labor struggles through the prism of the East-West conflict, the CIA secretly recruited and funded Corsican gangs to harass local communist leaders, intimidate trade unionists, and break the picket lines. The CIA's covert operation worked as planned—communist influence and labor activism in Marseille were greatly reduced—but left a lasting unintended legacy: newly empowered and politically protected, these very same gangs and their leaders came to dominate the Corsican underworld and control the Marseille waterfront.

Corsican-run heroin laboratories soon sprang up around Marseille, turning morphine base shipped in from Turkey and elsewhere into high-grade U.S.-bound heroin. The product was of such high quality and purity and the business was run so efficiently that Luciano and his Sicilian partners also turned to the Marseille labs to process their heroin. From there, Luciano's old business partner Lansky, and mafiosi such as Santo Traficante, helped move the product into the U.S. market. This infamous "French Connection"—the inspiration for the 1971 Hollywood film by the same name—was America's main heroin supplier until the early 1970s.[59] Some of this heroin supply arrived in the United States via South America—brought in on the same private planes that smuggled large quantities of tax-evading American contraband goods (ranging from cigarettes and whiskey to Levi's jeans) to Paraguay for regional black market distribution.[60]

Meanwhile, the FBN shrewdly tied the drug threat to the foreign threat of communism. "Red China" was publicly accused of trying to destroy Western society and of generating hard cash through heroin sales to U.S. drug pushers.[61] Anslinger charged that Mao's China was the "greatest purveyor in history of habit-forming drugs" and was "reaping tremendous amounts from its network of narcotics smugglers operating on a world-wide basis."[62] In reality, China had launched a draconian crackdown on drugs, jailing or executing thousands of drug traffickers and dealers and largely removing the country from the narcotics trade. Along with remnants of Chinese nationalist forces, opium production had been pushed to remote areas of Burma, Laos, and Thailand. These rebels not only received covert military supplies from the CIA-owned Civil Air Transport (later renamed Air America) but also used their politically protected transportation link as a cover for drug shipments.[63]

While denouncing China, Anslinger was silent in public about the influx of drugs from allied France even as his own field agents were increasingly preoccupied by it.[64] The political atmosphere of the 1950s created a Congress receptive to Anslinger's designs: Americans were absorbed by hearings on the Mafia and organized crime and were consumed by fears of communist aggression and subversion, heightened by McCarthyism. In the Senate, the subcommittee chaired by Texas Democrat Price Daniel embraced Anslinger's assertions about the Chinese communist threat, concluding that "subversion through drug addiction is an established aim of Communist China."[65] Daniel's subcommittee recommended tougher penalties, arguing that the offenses of "heroin smugglers and peddlers" amounted to "murder on the installment plan."[66] The resulting Narcotic Control Act of 1956 raised mandatory minimum penalties (five to twenty years for the second offense; ten to forty years for the third offense) and permitted juries to impose the death penalty on any adult who sold heroin to a minor.[67]

Nixon's Drug War

Anslinger's decades-long antidrug campaign was just a warm-up to the "war on drugs" declared by President Richard Nixon. Starting in the late 1960s and early 1970s, the country experienced dramatic growth in both drug use and drug enforcement. In 1967 *Life* magazine described the suddenly transformed American drug scene: "Almost overnight the U.S. was embarked on the greatest mass flouting of the law since Prohibition."[68] The new drug culture was part of the new youth culture of the Sixties, one in which defying drug laws mirrored the larger rebellion against traditional authority. Consequently, even as the counterculture revolution rejected mainstream consumerism, illicit drug use became an increasingly important part of American consumer society.

Marijuana was the drug of choice, with "Acapulco Gold" imported from Mexico the most popular. Customs agents seized only seven thousand pounds of marijuana in 1964, most of it coming in from Mexico, but by 1968 seizures had skyrocketed to sixty-five thousand pounds.[69] Even factoring in such seizures, the smuggling incentives in a booming consumer market were overwhelming. Consider, for instance, that a ton of marijuana at the time was worth about $12,000 in the Mexican state of Sinaloa, increased to about $25,000 by the time it reached Tijuana, then increased to $65,000 across the border in San Diego, and sold for as much as $100,000 a ton in Los Angeles and $200,000 a ton in San Francisco. This meant that even if a smuggler were to lose half a shipment it was still hugely profitable.[70]

The biggest transportation challenge to the marijuana smuggler was that the product was both bulky and smelly—and therefore vulnerable to nosy border inspectors and the noses of drug-sniffing dogs. Many smugglers simply played the odds, betting that their pot-filled vehicle would not be searched at the border by blending in with the high volume of regular cross-border traffic. Other smugglers increasingly bypassed border inspections entirely by using small aircraft to deliver their loads.

Heroin was even more profitable than marijuana, pound for pound, and far less cumbersome and detectable. And like marijuana, consumer demand was growing. Whereas the profile of the average American heroin user for much of the 1960s was young, lower-class, and black or Hispanic, by the end of the decade the profile broadened to include returning Vietnam war veterans and suburban whites. By the early 1970s more than half a million people in the United States were estimated to be heroin addicts. In 1971, public opinion polls indicated that Americans considered heroin addiction to be the country's third most serious problem, after Vietnam and the economy.[71]

It was in this changing societal context that President Nixon made drugs a central policy concern and the drug war as we know it today began in earnest. Until then, executive officials above the rank of Federal Bureau of Narcotics Chief Harry Anslinger had rarely occupied themselves with drug-control issues. In 1969 Nixon catapulted drugs to the center of the political stage, declaring it a "national threat." The president helped spearhead new laws, pushed for dramatic funding increases, and reorganized and expanded the federal antidrug bureaucracy. In June 1971 Nixon informed Congress, "The [drug] problem has assumed the dimensions of a national emergency."[72] Media executives received a similar call to arms: "Drug traffic is public enemy number one domestically in the United States today and we must wage a total offensive, worldwide, nationwide, government-wide, and, if I might say so, media-wide."[73]

The president backed his rhetoric with legislative initiatives. The Comprehensive Drug Abuse Prevention and Control Act of 1970 merged previous federal antidrug regulations under one statute. Whereas the 1914 Harrison Act based jurisdiction of drug control on the constitutional power to tax, the 1970 act based jurisdiction on the much more expansive interstate-commerce powers of the Constitution. Antidrug spending ballooned. The federal budget for drug enforcement climbed from $43 million in fiscal 1970 to $321 million in fiscal 1975.[74] A vast new antidrug bureaucracy emerged with the rise in federal spending. The previous thirty years had seen only a slow reorganization and growth in the drug-control apparatus. By the late 1960s the FBN still had a relatively modest budget of $6 million (about twice its 1932 budget) and a staff of some three hundred agents (roughly the same number as in 1932). A second agency, the Bureau of Drug Abuse Control, had been created in the Department of Health, Education, and Welfare in 1965 to regulate hypnotics and stimulants. And in 1968, the last year of the Johnson administration, the two agencies were merged to form the Bureau of Narcotics and Dangerous Drugs (BNDD) and placed in the Justice Department.[75] Nixon moved forcefully to expand the bureaucratic base for his war on drugs. In 1973 he consolidated all agencies involved in drug control, including the Customs Service Drug Investigation Unit, into a new drug superagency—the Drug Enforcement Administration (DEA)—with operational reach around the globe.[76]

Nixon's initiatives expanded the nation's drug war to include an ambitious campaign abroad. The foreign drug war was designed, in Nixon's words, to "strike at the 'supply' side of the drug equation—to halt the drug traffic by striking at the illegal producers of drugs, the growing of those plants from which drugs are derived, and trafficking in these drugs beyond our borders."[77] The concern over foreign supply had long been a focus for nativist and other antivice crusaders. But before Nixon the government's approach was largely rhetorical, diplomatic, and low-profile. Nixon turned foreign supply into a far more prominent issue.

Nixon first went after the Mexican marijuana supply. "Operation Intercept" deployed two thousand agents to the Mexican border in September 1969 to search automobiles and trucks crossing the border in what was officially described as "the country's largest peacetime search and seizure operation by civil authorities." Predictably, the main results were massive border traffic jams, jolts to the economies of border cities, and strongly worded protests from Mexican officials. Few drugs were seized during the two-week operation—smugglers simply took a break, rightly calculating that the crackdown would be short-lived—but the Mexican government got the message that it would have to show more antidrug cooperation and resolve.

Nixon's next foreign target was Turkish opium production, the main morphine base supply source for the Marseille heroin labs.

The United States applied intense diplomatic pressure, threatening to cut off aid if the Turkish government did not stop production and offering reimbursement for losses resulting from reduced poppy cultivation. The Turks complied, and Nixon declared victory. The temporary scarcity of heroin in 1972 and 1973, however, was soon reversed as the slack was taken up by supply from Mexico, Afghanistan, Pakistan, and the Golden Triangle in Southeast Asia.[78] And once again, Cold War geopolitics—especially in Southeast Asia and later in South Asia after the Soviet invasion of Afghanistan—only made things more awkward and complicated, since key U.S. anticommunist allies were also entangled in drug trafficking. As historian Alfred McCoy documents, the CIA was complicit not through corruption or direct involvement in the drug trade but rather through what he describes as a radical pragmatism that tolerated and even facilitated drug trafficking by local allies if it served larger Cold War goals.[79] Politically protected traffickers included suppliers of heroin to tens of thousands of American troops in Vietnam—who in turn helped to smuggle the drug into the United States through a variety of conveyances ranging from GI care packages to body bags.[80]

Meanwhile, the marijuana trade continued to boom in the 1970s, with Colombia rising as a competitor to Mexico as a supplier to the U.S. market. "Santa Marta Gold" from the northern coast of Colombia attracted a higher-end American consumer willing to pay a premium over the price of the competing Mexican product. Colombian suppliers received a huge boost thanks to the fallout from a U.S.-sponsored Mexican marijuana crop eradication campaign in the mid-1970s. Since uprooting marijuana plants by hand was slow and labor-intensive, the Mexican government turned to spraying marijuana fields with the herbicide Paraquat. But farmers simply went ahead and harvested their sprayed crops, and American consumers ended up smoking it—with many getting ill from poisoned pot.[81] The resulting public panic and outcry prompted a federal government investigation, which found that one-fifth of seized marijuana along the border was tainted with the chemical. Marijuana dealers and consumers scrambled to find an alternate supply source, and the Colombians were more than willing to step in. By 1978 they had reportedly taken over an estimated three-quarters of the U.S. market.[82] And it was an enormous market: by 1979, an estimated fifty-five million Americans had used some type of cannabis, including about two-thirds of eighteen-to-twenty-five-year-olds.[83]

Much of the Colombian marijuana supply was smuggled in through the Caribbean to South Florida by boat. Speedboats would zip out and back from the Florida coast, bringing in marijuana loads from mother ships anchored offshore. Government interdiction was minimal, smuggling operations were loosely organized with plenty of freelancers and small local operators (including fishermen who found a much more profitable use for their boats), and the whole business involved only modest risk and relatively little recourse to violence. This was the heyday of marijuana smuggling in South Florida. But it proved to be short-lived. Everything changed by the early 1980s with the avalanche of Colombian cocaine and the ratcheting up of America's war on drugs.

In Darwinian fashion, more sophisticated, organized, and violent traffickers increasingly came to dominate the trade—building on and adapting the old transportation and distribution infrastructure set up for smuggling Colombian marijuana in earlier years. So in a sense, by helping to stimulate Colombian marijuana exports to the United States, the Paraquat-spraying disaster in Mexico inadvertently helped to pave the way for the rise of the Colombian cocaine industry.[84]

Cocaine Wars

Cocaine use in America, which had been largely dormant since the 1930s, began to rise in the late 1960s and early 1970s, in part as a result of stricter federal controls over other stimulants such as speed and other amphetamines.[85] By 1979 the National Institute on Drug Abuse estimated that cocaine use had nearly tripled in two years.[86] By 1980, "the number of cocaine powder sellers [in New York City] outnumbered that of heroin sellers by two to one."[87] Initially, many cocaine users were middle-class and affluent—powder cocaine was a relatively expensive "status drug"—although large numbers of lower-income drug users were inhaling cocaine when they could afford it.[88]

Cocaine was considered by users, and even by many medical authorities, as nonaddictive, for habitual users did not experience the physiological symptoms of heroin withdrawal.[89] As *Time* magazine reported in July 1981, "Superficially, coke is a supremely beguiling and relatively risk-free drug—at least so its devotees innocently claim. A snort in each nostril and you're up and away for 30 minutes or so. Alert, witty and with it. No hangover. No physical addiction. No lung cancer. No holes in the arms or burned-out cells in the brain. Instead, drive, sparkle, energy."[90] The magazine's cover illustration—a martini glass filled with cocaine—captured cocaine's new status as America's most fashionable drug. Similarly, the *Time* cover story also captured the upbeat attitude toward the drug: "Whatever the price, by whatever name, cocaine is becoming the all-American drug. No longer is it a sinful secret of the moneyed elite, nor merely an elusive glitter of decadence in raffish society circles, as it seemed in decades past." It continued: "Today, in part precisely because it is such an emblem of wealth and status, coke is the drug of choice of perhaps millions of solid, conventional and often upwardly mobile citizens. . . ."[91]

Colombian smuggling entrepreneurs were perfectly positioned to feed America's growing appetite for cocaine. Colombia first entered the cocaine business in the early 1970s, building on earlier illicit trades in marijuana and tax-evading contraband goods (especially cigarettes and whiskey). Medellín, the country's most industrialized and export-oriented city, soon became the leading center for the cocaine-export industry. Even as textiles, traditionally the city's vital export sector, fell on hard times, the illicit cocaine-export sector took off. This also had an enormous economic ripple effect throughout the Andean region, fueling a coca cultivation boom in remote areas of neighboring Peru and Bolivia. Hundreds of thousands of Andean peasant farmers turned to growing the raw material used to process Colombian cocaine for the U.S. market.[92]

Medellín's drug trade entrepreneurs, specializing in refining and wholesale trafficking, led the way in turning cocaine into a mass production industry capable of handling large-scale cocaine shipments to the United States. What started out as a business dealing in hundreds of kilos turned into tons of kilos by the late 1970s. Medellín traffickers were also advantaged by the fact that many Colombians from the same region of the country as Medellín had migrated to the east coast of the United States in the late 1960s and early 1970s, providing a ready-made distribution network.[93] Medellín's old elites soon found themselves pushed aside by brash new narco-elites such as Pablo Escobar. Escobar, who began his criminal career stealing gravestones and cars, became the most recognizable face of the international drug trade, even making the *Forbes* list of the top billionaires in the world. Escobar's fame, fortune, and bravado in directly challenging the Colombian government (including assassinating the country's justice minister in 1984) made him the world's most famous outlaw at the time—which in the end would prove to be his undoing.

One of Escobar's business partners, Carlos Lehder Rivas, is credited with pioneering the transportation of cocaine through the Caribbean to the United States by small aircraft. Lehder started out smuggling marijuana but then upgraded to cocaine. At the height of his trafficking career in the late 1970s and early 1980s, Lehder took over Norman's Cay, a tiny island in the Bahamas, and turned it into his own private

Figure 14.5 Colombian cocaine trafficker Pablo Escobar, the most famous smuggler of the modern era. In 1989 *Forbes* magazine listed Escobar as the seventh-richest person in the world (DEA Museum).

airstrip. Government authorities in Nassau were suspected of taking hefty bribes to look the other way, tolerating Lehder's transport business until U.S. pressure and media coverage finally prompted them to shut it down.

But while Lehder was an air transport pioneer of sorts, he was also simply the latest smuggler to exploit the Bahamas as the most convenient transshipment hub in the Caribbean (recall the role of Nassau in blockade running during the American Civil War, and in supplying Rum Row during the Prohibition era). What was new in the case of moving cocaine is that much of it was now coming into the United States not only by sea but also by air. Moreover, the Bahamas also facilitated the laundering of cocaine money, serving as a world-class financial haven useful to dictators, corporate executives, and drug traffickers alike.

With the snowstorm of Colombian cocaine also emerged the myth that the whole business was tightly controlled by a few hierarchically organized trafficking "cartels." The cartel myth was created and perpetuated by politicians, journalists, and law enforcement agents looking for a simple and easily identifiable target.[94] Over time, use of the term *cartel* was so common that it became a permanent part of the drug war vocabulary. But the reality was considerably more complex. By definition, a cartel exerts sufficient control over a market that it can set prices. But the cocaine trade was in fact hypercompetitive—indeed, ruthlessly so, as is evident from violent competition for turf and market share. Cocaine prices plummeted and purity levels increased during the course of the decade. A kilo of cocaine in Miami was worth between $47,000 and $60,000 in 1982, but it plummeted to between $9,000 and $14,000 by late 1987.[95] Overall, wholesale cocaine prices in the United States dropped by 75 percent between 1980 and 1988. Moreover, as law enforcement went after the most visible and well-known trafficking organizations—first targeting Escobar and other leaders of the "Medellín cartel" and then the competing "Cali cartel"—the cocaine business became more fragmented and dispersed, based more on loose, flattened networks than centralized and hierarchical organizations.

As the main gateway to the U.S. drug market in the late 1970s and early 1980s, South Florida became ground zero for both drug profits and drug violence, with competition over cocaine distribution turning the Miami area into the murder capital of the country. No surprise, then, that South Florida also became the main target of President Ronald Reagan's escalating drug interdiction campaign. The South Florida Task Force, under the direction of Vice President George H. W. Bush, was launched with much fanfare in January 1982 to block air and sea drug-smuggling routes in the Southeast. Federal funding for interdiction doubled between 1982 and 1987, mostly concentrated in South Florida and the Caribbean.

Traffickers adjusted. As air interdiction improved, traffickers shifted away from direct flights into Florida and returned to sea routes, ferrying in cocaine loads by speedboat from mother ships waiting offshore. As sea interdiction then improved, traffickers turned to using airdrops rather than mother ships—with speedboat crews picking up floating cocaine packages and ferrying them back to shore. Over time, traffickers shifted not only their methods but also their routes, turning westward to move more of their drug shipments through Central America and Mexico.

A tighter interdiction net also accelerated the switch from smuggling pot to coke: as risks and penalties increased, drug traffickers calculated that it simply made more financial sense to transport the much more compact and profitable white powder. After all, a plane flying in $3 million worth of marijuana could fly in $26 million worth of cocaine.[96] American interdiction efforts consequently turned into a peculiar form of protectionism, with marijuana growers in California, Oregon, and other states the leading beneficiaries.

Escalation

America's transformed drug landscape provided a ready-made target for the Reagan-era conservative backlash. President Reagan's drug-policy agenda was shaped by a large and vocal national constituency that had grown impatient with the permissive attitudes toward drug use and other counterculture activities of the previous decade. At the center of his domestic policy agenda was a set of social policies, articulated most powerfully by the so-called moral majority, which embodied a defense of traditional family values, conservative Christian morality, and patriotism.

President Reagan launched his drug war by using his executive power first to revise executive-branch regulations, organizations, and lines of authority. By the end of his first year in office, Reagan had issued an executive order drafting the entire federal intelligence apparatus into the war on drugs and ordering them to provide guidance to civilian drug enforcement agencies. The president also opened the door, for the first time, to the military's involvement in the war on drugs by securing an amendment to the Posse Comitatus Act, which had outlawed military involvement in civilian law enforcement for more than a century. The Reagan administration argued successfully that the U.S. Navy be allowed to join civilian agencies, such as the Coast Guard, in interdicting smuggling vessels at sea, and all branches of the military were empowered to assist Customs, the Coast Guard, and the DEA with training, equipment, and information. Funding for the military's counterdrug role was $4.9 million in 1982, but it would skyrocket to more than $1 billion by the early 1990s.[97]

In June 1982 Reagan put the federal bureaucracy on notice that the drug war was now a priority mission. The heads of eighteen federal agencies, the vice president, several military leaders, and the commissioner of the IRS were ordered to the White House for a special address: "We're taking down the surrender flag that has flown over so many drug efforts. We're running up the battle flag. We can fight the drug problem, and we can win."[98] In his 1983 State of the Union address, Reagan confirmed, "The administration hereby declares an all-out war on big-time organized crime and the drug racketeers who are poisoning our young people."[99] The media helped fuel the Reagan effort, providing extensive coverage that built up the drug threat beginning in 1982. The administration intended to use "a scorched-earth policy" in drug enforcement, according to former Associate Attorney General Stephen S. Trott. It would not only send traffickers to jail but also lay claim under the new forfeiture laws to "everything they own—their land, their cars, their boats, everything."[100]

The introduction of a new cocaine derivative—"crack," the "poor man's coke"—added fuel to the drug war fire. Smokable cocaine had been around since the late 1970s as cocaine "free base," but not until the mid-1980s was it packaged and mass marketed as crack, with a relatively affordable price that made it popular in poor urban neighborhoods. There was an important racial and class dimension to the reaction to crack: as dealing and use became more visible in urban black and Latino neighborhoods, the crack trade and related violence came to be powerfully tied to negative images of poor minority Americans.[101]

The national panic over the spread of crack cocaine made the drug war an even more potent issue in electoral politics. As *Congressional Quarterly* commented: "In the closing weeks of the congressional election season, taking the pledge becomes a familiar feature of campaign life. Thirty years ago, candidates pledged to battle domestic communism. . . . In 1986, the pledge issue is drugs. Republicans and Democrats all across the country are trying to outdo each other in their support for efforts to crush the trade in illegal drugs."[102] Senator John McCain spoke for many in Congress: "This is such an emotional issue—I mean, we're at war here—that voting no would be too difficult to explain," McCain said of Senate efforts to increase the military role in the drug war in 1988.[103]

Meanwhile, as America's war on cocaine was ramping up, cocaine was quietly becoming entangled in a very different sort of war in Central America: the campaign by U.S.-backed Contra rebels against Nicaragua's Sandinista government. A three-year congressional investigation revealed that some of the same CIA-contracted air transport companies covertly hired to fly supplies to the Contras were also involved in transporting drugs. Although the nature and extent of CIA knowledge and involvement remains murky and steeped in controversy, the available evidence indicates that individual Contras, Contra supporters, and Contra suppliers exploited their political protections as a convenient cover for drug-trafficking operations.[104]

A variation on this dynamic was simultaneously playing out in Afghanistan, where CIA-backed insurgents battling the Soviets were also involved in cultivating and smuggling opium poppies to help fund their political cause. Washington was apparently well aware of the situation but turned a blind eye in pursuit of larger geopolitical goals. "We're not going to let a little thing like drugs get in the way of the political situation," explained a Reagan administration official at the time. "And when the Soviets leave and there's no money in the country, it's not going to be a priority to disrupt the drug trade."[105]

Militarization

The war on drugs was ramped up even further by Reagan's successor, George H. W. Bush, including drafting the military to take on a more frontline antidrug role. In his first prime time televised address to the nation, on September 5, 1989, President Bush held up a bag of crack cocaine. For added shock value, he announced that it had been bought across the street from the White House, in Lafayette Park—though he failed to mention that a bewildered drug dealer had to be lured there by undercover agents to make the buy. The president set the tone: "This is the first time since taking the oath of office that I felt an issue was so important, so threatening, that it warranted talking directly with you, the American people," the president began. He quickly declared a national consensus on the primacy of the issue—"All of us agree that the gravest domestic threat facing our nation today is drugs"—and then declared war, calling for "an assault on every front." Urging Americans to "face this evil as a nation united," Bush proclaimed that "victory over drugs is our cause, a just cause." Bush proposed that "we enlarge our criminal justice system across the board. . . . When requested, we will for the first time make available the appropriate resources of America's armed forces." The president called for a $1.5 billion increase in domestic law-enforcement spending in the drug war and $3.5 billion for interdiction and foreign supply reduction.[106] A *Washington Post*/ABC News poll taken after Bush's speech indicated that 62 percent of those polled were willing to give up "a few of the freedoms we have in this country" for the war on drugs. Eighty-two percent said they were willing to permit the military to join the war on drugs.[107]

Bush took unprecedented steps to widen the drug-fighting authority of federal agencies. To a degree unmatched by previous presidents, he used his power as commander in chief to draft the U.S. military into the drug war, elevating what had been a sporadic and relatively minor role in assisting in civilian enforcement into a major national security mission for the armed forces. In the fall of 1989 Secretary of Defense Dick Cheney declared drugs to be a high-priority mission of the Department of Defense. The fiscal 1989 National Defense Authorization Act charged the Defense Department with three new responsibilities. It was made the lead agency for detecting drug traffic into the country;

Figure 14.6 President George H. W. Bush displays a bag of crack cocaine evidence during his first televised address to the nation, September 5, 1989 (Bettmann/Corbis).

given responsibility for integrating all command, control, and communications for drug interdiction into an effective network; and told to approve and fund state governors' plans for using the National Guard in interdiction and enforcement. Funding for the military's drug-enforcement activities increased from $357 in 1989 to more than $1 billion in 1992.[108]

The Pentagon became noticeably more enthusiastic about taking on drug war duties as the Cold War came to an end. A former Reagan official in the Pentagon commented: "Getting help from the military on drugs used to be like pulling teeth. Now everybody's looking around to say, 'Hey, how can we justify these forces.' And the answer they're coming up with is drugs."[109] One two-star general observed in an interview, "With peace breaking out all over it might give us something to do."[110] The Pentagon inspector general found that a large number of officers consider drug control "as an opportunity to subsidize some non-counternarcotics efforts struggling for funding approval."[111] In 1990, for example, "the Air Force wanted $242 million to start the central sector of the $2.3 billion Over-the-Horizon Backscatter radar network. Once a means of detecting nuclear cruise missiles fired from Soviet submarines in the Gulf of Mexico, Backscatter was now being sold as a way to spot drug couriers winging their way up from South America."[112]

Military equipment and technologies initially designed to deter military invaders were increasingly made available and adapted to deter drug law evaders. For example, Airborne Warning and Control System surveillance planes began to monitor international drug flights; the North American Aerospace Defense Command, which was built to track incoming Soviet bombers and missiles, refocused some of its energies to tracking drug smugglers; X-ray technology designed to detect Soviet missile warheads in trucks was adapted for use by U.S. Customs to find smuggled drugs in cargo trucks; researchers at Los Alamos Laboratory, the birthplace of the atomic bomb, started developing sophisticated new technologies for drug control; and the Pentagon's Defense Advanced Research Projects Agency began using its research on antisubmarine warfare to develop listening devices to detect drug smugglers.[113]

Drug enforcement came to define post–Cold War U.S. security relations with many of its southern neighbors. Reflecting the new priorities, the U.S. Southern Command in Panama was transformed into a de facto forward base for drug interdiction. In 1989 the U.S. military was authorized to make arrests of drug traffickers and fugitives on foreign territory—without the approval of the host country.[114] Drug control even provided the official rationale for the military invasion of Panama and the indictment of Panamanian General Manuel Noriega on drug-trafficking charges, no doubt the most expensive drug bust in history. Although U.S. intelligence reports connecting Noriega to drug trafficking went back as far as 1972, Washington tolerated and overlooked Noriega's shady dealings until he was no longer politically useful.[115]

The intelligence community was also drafted to take on a more frontline drug war role. In 1990 the CIA announced that "narcotics is a new priority."[116] Some observers no doubt found this rather ironic, given that the agency had since its creation shown a chronic willingness to subvert the fight against drugs in the name of fighting communists. The most high-profile example of the CIA's new hands-on antidrug role was the 1992–93 manhunt to help the Colombian government track down and eliminate the drug trafficker Pablo Escobar.[117]

Back home, meanwhile, the drug war was both transforming and overloading the criminal justice system. Fighting drugs was the main driver in the adoption of military models, technologies, and methods (including the proliferation of SWAT teams) in domestic law enforcement.[118] At the same time, the criminal justice system was increasingly overwhelmed with drug cases. By 1990 drug cases accounted for an astonishing 44 percent of all criminal trials and 50 percent of criminal appeals. A dramatic increase in the number of Americans imprisoned made the United States the world's number one jailer, and much of the overload was a consequence of the war on drugs. Drug offenders as a proportion of inmates in federal prisons increased from 25 percent in 1980 to 61 percent in 1993.[119] Bush's "drug czar," William Bennett, was an especially forceful advocate of the administration's hard-line rhetoric and punitive approach, telling a national radio audience that he saw nothing morally wrong with beheading drug traffickers.[120]

The Clinton administration toned down the drug war rhetoric of his predecessors but did little to actually change drug laws or redirect federal drug-control agencies. A proposal to move the DEA, a product of Nixon's drug war, into the FBI was scrapped after generating intense pushback from both the DEA and members of Congress. A modest proposed cut to the interdiction budget was not only withdrawn, but a new position, interdiction coordinator, was created by administration officials who were anxious to reassure conservative critics in Congress that they took drug interdiction seriously. The new coordinator (who was also the head of the Coast Guard) immediately began to press for more funding.[121] President Bill Clinton moved drug policy off the political agenda and out of the public spotlight, but the drug war machinery created and built up by his predecessors continued to grind on. As the governor of Arkansas, Clinton had at one point argued for decriminalizing marijuana. But as a president eager to not appear "soft on drugs"—especially after having acknowledged smoking, though not inhaling, marijuana while in college—Clinton never challenged the marijuana laws that had been significantly toughened in the 1980s. Marijuana arrests more than doubled during Clinton's years in office, reaching record levels.[122]

Overall, the drug war looked little different from that of the Bush era: in 1990, under Bush, some 1,089,500 people were arrested for drug law violations. In 1993, under Clinton, 1,126,300 were arrested. One hundred and seven metric tons of cocaine and 815 kilograms of heroin were seized in 1990, compared to 110.7 tons of cocaine and 1,600.9 kilos of heroin netted in 1993.[123] Washington's relations with much of Latin America continued to be driven by drugs, with virtually all U.S. military and police aid to the region provided under the rubric of drug control by the end of the decade. Colombia became the third-largest recipient of U.S. military assistance (behind Israel and Egypt), with the Colombian government using it to blur the distinction between counterinsurgency and counterdrug operations.

The drug war bureaucracy continued to expand. The DEA's budget went from over $219 million by 1981 to about $800 million under Clinton.[124] And this accounted for only a fraction of the total budget for federal drug-law enforcement, which was more than $8 billion in 1995. Roughly forty federal agencies or programs, in seven of the fourteen cabinet departments, had drug law enforcement responsibilities. Within the Department of Justice alone, the DEA was by the early 1990s just one of fifteen agencies or programs involved in drug control. For instance, the FBI, the Bureau of Prisons, and the Immigration and Naturalization Service all played various drug war roles, from criminal investigations to border checks to prison management. At Treasury, seven agencies had some role in drug enforcement. Customs, for example, was charged with interdicting and disrupting the illegal flow of drugs by air, sea, and land, and the IRS was involved in tracking drug-generated funds and disrupting money laundering. Within the Department of Transportation, the Coast Guard was mandated to eliminate "maritime routes as a significant mode for the supply of drugs to the U.S. through seizures, disruption and displacement."[125] And the Federal Aviation Administration helped identify "airborne drug smugglers by using radar, posting aircraft lookouts, and tracking the movement of suspected aircraft."[126] At the Department of Defense, whose mission was to provide "support to the law enforcement agencies that have counter-drug responsibilities," three new joint antidrug task forces were created.[127] And National Guard units searched cargo, patrolled borders, flew aerial surveillance, eradicated marijuana crops, and lent expertise and equipment to law enforcement agencies.

Resilience and Adaptation

In the face of this extended and expansive U.S. drug war buildup, the illicit drug trade not only survived, it thrived. By the turn of the century, more drugs were more widely available and at higher levels of purity than ever before. In the case of marijuana (by far the nation's favorite illicit drug), 88.5 percent of high school seniors surveyed in 1982 said the drug was "fairly easy" or "very easy" to obtain. In 2000, the percentage of seniors who indicated they could easily obtain the drug was 88.5 percent—even though marijuana penalties, arrests, seizures, and so on had risen sharply. And to the extent that eradicating marijuana crops abroad and interdicting shipments at the border had succeeded, the main effect was to unintentionally give a boost to American pot growers. Partly thanks to suppression efforts against foreign supplies, domestic marijuana production mushroomed into a multibillion-dollar industry, possibly becoming the country's largest cash crop.[128]

Meanwhile, even though Colombia's most notorious trafficking organizations—the so-called Medellín and Cali cartels—were dismantled in the 1990s, cocaine exports were barely dented. Adjusting to a more hostile enforcement environment, trafficking organizations became flatter, more dispersed, and decentralized—making them harder to penetrate and eliminate. Determined drug enforcers had demonstrated that they could successfully eliminate individual traffickers who had become too embarrassing and high-profile, such as Escobar, but this did not translate into elimination, or even a noticeable reduction, of trafficking. Colombian drug entrepreneurs also diversified both in product and in clientele, producing and exporting heroin and shipping more of the cocaine supply to Europe, where prices were much higher and the market was growing.[129]

The drug war inescapably suffered from some of the same fatal flaws and contradictions that had doomed Prohibition earlier in the century. As was the case with alcohol in the 1920s, government policies aimed to make drugs such as cocaine and heroin scarce and expensive by outlawing them. Enforcement indeed raised prices by increasing the risks and costs faced by smugglers. For decades the policy of drug prohibition kept consumer prices far higher than the legal price would be—and as happened with the prohibition of alcohol, this undoubtedly deterred some use. But it was unable to raise prices high enough to keep drugs out of reach. The drug war was unable to raise the cost of doing business high enough to put drug prices out of range for consumers because its success in artificially raising prices also inflated profits. And these profits provided a steady incentive for drug suppliers to remain in the trade and for new suppliers to enter. Because the drug war raised profits as it raised prices, the stick of drug enforcement that was intended to discourage suppliers simultaneously created a carrot of enormous profits, which encouraged suppliers. Such inflated profits repeatedly frustrated supply suppression efforts at home and abroad. In practical terms, this meant that "the average drug organization can afford to lose 70 percent to 80 percent of its product and still be profitable," explained one DEA official. "How do you intend to put that group out of business with a basic policy of trying to suppress its product?"[130]

The drug war was doubly doomed by the mobility and flexibility of the illicit trade. Cocaine, heroin, and marijuana were relatively easy to produce, transport, and sell. The amount of money and skill needed to enter the business was not high. These conditions repeatedly made even successful drug enforcement short-lived. Smugglers could simply put more drugs into the pipeline in order to offset what they projected losing in seizures. And there were always new recruits to take the place of those arrested. Often, attempts to suppress the trade in one locale simply encouraged new recruits or veteran smugglers to set up operations elsewhere. So, while the drug war generated ever more impressive eradication, seizure, and arrest numbers that made politicians and bureaucrats look tough on drugs, this did not translate into an overall reduction in the drug flow.

In short, far from deterring the drug trade, American-led supply-suppression campaigns ended up mostly dispersing and rerouting it. Rather than pushing the trade out of business, drug enforcement had mostly pushed it around—providing a rationale to further expand drug enforcement. And as we'll see in the next chapter, nowhere were the consequences more devastating than along the U.S.-Mexico border.

15

Border Wars and the Underside of Economic Integration

TWO OF MEXICO'S LEADING exports were noticeably left out of the North American Free Trade Agreement (NAFTA): illegal drugs and migrant workers. Instead, higher "tariffs" were imposed through more policing and fence building. But this did not change the fact that the U.S.-Mexico border was the main entry point for smuggling drugs and cheap labor into the country. This was the less celebrated clandestine underside of economic integration between the United States and Mexico at the dawn of the twenty-first century. The U.S.-Mexico borderline became not only the busiest land crossing in the world, for both legal and illegal flows, but also one of the most heavily fortified. This chapter traces this remaking of the border, the longest and most contested geographic divide between rich and poor on the planet. It was here that both the extent and the limits of government policing power were most starkly evident—setting the border-crossing rules and shaping the crossing methods and locations even if unable to fully control who and what crossed the line.

The southwest border had long been a smuggling gateway, yet it was not until the 1990s that the policing of smuggling became a high-profile and high-intensity militarized border campaign commanding enormous public and media attention. This was partly an unintended feedback effect of past policy choices, including a shift in cocaine trafficking to the southwest border in response to the South Florida interdiction buildup in the 1980s examined in the last chapter. Mexican drug smugglers, it turned out, were the leading beneficiaries of the U.S.-led offensive against Colombian trafficking organizations and their Caribbean cocaine-shipping routes. Business also boomed for Mexican *coyotes*—people smugglers—thanks to a tightening of U.S. immigration controls that made it much harder for migrants to cross the border without hiring a professional smuggler. Yet as we will see, this was part of a much older and larger pattern of government interventions inadvertently creating a thriving cross-border smuggling economy.

An Economic Relationship Founded on Smuggling

The popular assertion that we must "regain control" of the border falsely implies that there was once a time when the U.S.-Mexico line was truly under control. Although most of the attention today is on the illicit flow of drugs and migrants, smuggling was a defining feature of the border long before these particular flows were even a concern. Indeed, much of the U.S.-Mexico economic relationship was founded on illicit trade, with a great deal of it flowing from north to south. High tariffs and minimal enforcement meant that much of the goods entering Mexico following independence in 1821 was contraband.[1] Guns and ammunition also flowed south, with Mexican authorities bitterly complaining about the American "traders of blood" who profited from supplying Plains Indians engaged in cross-border raiding and plundering.[2] After the Mexican-American War ended in 1848, trade with Texas increased sharply, much of it in the form of smuggling. Moreover, as we saw earlier, thousands of fugitive slaves smuggled themselves across the border until the end of the American Civil War, and during the war the easternmost point of the Mexican border functioned as an outlet for the smuggling of Confederate cotton to Europe.

Setting up official ports of entry along the border and deploying customs agents to run them reflected the ambitions of government authorities to filter and impose order on all cross-border trade and travel. All crossings in the areas between the ports of entry were by definition classified as illegal. But the locations of the handful of officially sanctioned crossing points along the vast and sparsely populated borderline—sometimes with hundreds of miles between them—were often inconvenient for large numbers of borderland residents, many of whom simply continued to go about their daily border business as before, though this was now treated as unlawful. At the same time, the arrival of the railroad in the late nineteenth century connected border towns to national markets and greatly facilitated and accelerated the cross-border movement of goods and people—licit and illicit—including, as we saw earlier, the smuggling of Chinese laborers barred from legal entry.

The tremendous challenge of imposing controls on border crossings extended not only to goods and people but also to livestock—especially unauthorized cattle crossings. As ranching spread along the border, cattle rustling (stealing and smuggling cattle) became a huge law enforcement headache on both sides of the border. Also troublesome were stray cattle wandering across the line, with retrieval often complicated by inflexible customs agents treating the "self-smuggled" animals as contraband cattle for which duty payment was owed.[3] The first government-erected border fence, along the Baja-California border in 1909, was designed to inhibit the movement of diseased cattle rather than people or goods—though the latter would become the focus of the

Figure 15.1 Smugglers crossing the Rio Grande, as U.S. customs agents watch from the bushes. *Harper's Weekly*, September 4, 1886 (Library of Congress).

urban fencing projects that sprang up during the 1910–1920 Mexican Revolution and then remained afterward.[4]

Of greatest concern during the Revolution was the smuggling of arms and ammunition into Mexico, continuing an old pattern of the United States serving as the favored weapons supplier during periods of social and political unrest south of the border. In South Texas, customs collector Robert Dowe complained that merchants along the border supplied "all comers with arms and cartridges even when aware they were used for revolutionary purposes."[5] In one smuggling scheme, the rebel leader Pancho Villa bartered confiscated cattle for American weapons. One particularly creative gunrunner, Victor Ochoa, used rubber bladders to float large quantities of ammunition across the Rio Grande at night from El Paso to Juarez.[6] Washington deployed tens of thousands of troops to the border in an effort to stem the flow of arms, impose order, and enforce neutrality laws.[7]

Even as much of the demand for smuggled arms dried up with the ending of the Mexican Revolution, the demand for smuggled alcohol shot up with the introduction of Prohibition in the United States in January 1920. Smugglers therefore adapted to the new market environment and simply switched from one commodity to another. Various types of booze—ranging from tequila to mescal to rum—had long been smuggled into the United States from Mexico, but to evade taxes rather than prohibitions. The introduction of Prohibition turned alcohol smuggling into a much bigger, more profitable, and more violent border business. And as smuggling boomed, so too did the policing of smuggling: the size of the U.S. Customs force was fairly small until the Prohibition era, when the number of inspectors along the border rose from 111 in 1925 to 723 in 1930.[8]

More intensive enforcement of Prohibition transformed the illicit trade in alcohol across the border. In south Texas, for example, the trade was initially dominated by Mexican *tequileros,* smugglers on horseback who used mules and donkeys to carry their alcohol supplies across the line in remote areas. Yet even as border authorities were increasingly effective in their operations against the *tequileros,* by the late 1920s they were simply replaced by more sophisticated and violent bootleggers transporting larger volumes of alcohol by car and truck along road networks. Effective enforcement against the *tequileros,* in other words, unintentionally helped pave the way for the rise of a new and more dangerous breed of smuggler.[9]

Many Mexican border towns, such as Tijuana and Juarez, became busy vice districts—offering booze, brothels, and gambling to swarms of American tourists—and also illicit liquor trade centers, helping to build up the border smuggling infrastructure.[10] After repeal, this infrastructure simply adapted to other smuggling opportunities. At the same time, Prohibition helped establish a much greater, even if still limited, federal policing presence along the border.

Meanwhile, the large-scale smuggling of untaxed goods into Mexico, which had been the backbone of border smuggling in the nineteenth century, continued to grow in the twentieth. Although much of the flow went south, smuggling was not entirely one way. The smuggling of candelilla, a strong natural wax from native shrubs, was a thriving export business in some northern Mexican border states by midcentury, thanks to strict government controls on price and production. Also, the smuggling of animals (especially of parrots, sometimes intoxicated with tequila to keep them quiet) from Mexico into the United States became such a profitable business that feuds between rival smugglers could result in their hijacking one another's parrot shipments.[11]

Decades of protectionist Mexican economic policies designed to insulate the country's industries and generate revenue for the government meant that U.S. border towns functioned as unofficial warehouses and shopping centers for consumer durables, ranging from household appliances to automobiles, waiting to be smuggled into Mexico. The Laredo airport became a busy hub for small planes loaded up with televisions, microwave ovens, radios, and other U.S. consumer goods bound for Mexico. Flying was the fastest and cheapest way to get around high Mexican tariffs; going by land required passing through more Mexican customs checkpoints, and therefore spending more on bribes. By the late 1970s, Mexicans were purchasing so many consumer goods in Laredo, Texas, that even though the local residents earned among the lowest wages in the country, Laredo ranked among the highest cities in retail sales per capita.[12]

The situation got so out of hand that the Lopez Portillo administration appealed to the Carter administration to help stem the contraband trade in luxury items, electronics and other appliances, powdered milk, and more, which was estimated to have cost Mexican business $1 billion in losses.[13] Only membership in the General Agreement on Tariffs and Trade in 1986 and the subsequent liberalization of trade (formalized by NAFTA in 1994) enabled Mexico to substantially end this kind of tax-evading smuggling.[14]

But just as smugglers who made their living from contraband saw their business drastically shrink because of market liberalization and the economic opening of the border, the lack of liberalization in other key sectors of the clandestine economic relationship—most notably Mexico's export of drugs and migrant labor and America's high demand for these exports—ensured that border smuggling would continue to flourish.

The Mexican Migration Connection

As we saw earlier, Mexicans were relatively late arrivals to the story of illegal migration to the United States. It was not until 1929 that U.S. border inspectors even made any real effort to regulate the entry of Mexican nationals. Hundreds of thousands of Mexicans fled to the United States during the Mexican Revolution, and an estimated half a million more entered in the 1920s. Mexican workers became the favored source of cheap labor as European and Asian migration dried up. They were considered submissive and disposable: when they were no longer needed during the Great Depression hundreds of thousands of Mexican migrants were simply rounded up and deported.

When America's thirst for cheap labor was renewed in the 1940s as a result of the labor shortages during World War II, Mexican workers were welcomed back. The U.S. Bracero Program, a guest-worker scheme created in 1942, was designed both to ensure a cheap source of labor for southwestern agribusiness interests and to inhibit illegal migration. While in effect, it provided more than 4.5 million individual contracts for temporary employment. The legacy of the program was to institutionalize large-scale labor migration from Mexico to the United States. During the two decades in which the program existed, an interdependent relationship between employers and migrants became entrenched.[15] Moreover, many "temporary" workers ended up settling in the United States, helping to create the permanent migratory networks that formed a bridge and a base for new arrivals.

One consequence of the Bracero Program was that the promise of guaranteed employment unintentionally encouraged illegal border crossings. Large numbers of workers made their way across without going through the cumbersome formal channels of the recruitment process. As migrants streamed north, apprehensions by the Border Patrol jumped from 182,000 in 1947 to more than 850,000 by the end of 1953. In a dramatic effort to impose control, in June 1954 the Eisenhower administration launched Operation Wetback, leading to the deportation of hundreds of thousands of Mexicans. Retired General Joseph Swing, who oversaw the operation, confidently announced in January 1955 that "The day of the wetback is over."[16]

After the Bracero Program was terminated in 1964, the only thing that changed was the legal status of the Mexican workers; they continued to be welcomed by employers who had come to rely on this cheap and flexible labor supply. Employers had little to fear from the law. In 1952 Congress had passed an act that made it illegal to "harbor, transport, or conceal illegal entrants." Employment, however, was conveniently excluded from the category of "harboring," thanks to an amendment (called the Texas proviso) that was a concession to agribusiness interests.[17]

Even as unauthorized immigration increased rapidly in the 1960s and 1970s, it was not matched by a similar increase in immigration law enforcement. Interior enforcement by the Immigration and Naturalization Service (INS), the parent agency of the Border Patrol, was almost nonexistent, and border controls remained at token levels. Anemic enforcement meant that illegal entry across the U.S.-Mexico border remained a relatively simple and inexpensive activity: migrants either smuggled themselves across the border or hired a local *coyote*. The sheer magnitude of the clandestine labor flow, however, heightened competition between smugglers to service it, and with the dispersion of the flow from agricultural to urban areas smuggling gradually became better organized. Still, the use of a professional smuggler remained more a convenience than a necessity. Penalties for smuggling remained low. For example, fewer than 50 percent of smugglers caught between 1973 and 1975 were prosecuted, most on a misdemeanor charge.[18]

Hiring the services of a smuggler generally meant a faster and safer trip across the line and could even include door-to-door service, from the point of departure in the sending community to the point of destination in places such as Los Angeles. This was particularly useful for first-time border crossers. Using a smuggler did involve personal risks (there was potential for theft and physical abuse), but attempting the clandestine border crossing without such help increased the likelihood of assault by border bandits and abuse by authorities.

U.S. Border Patrol agents could cover only about 10 percent of the nearly two thousand miles of border, and the arrests they did make were more apparent than real.[19] Even though the INS insisted that "prompt apprehension and return to country of origin is a positive deterrent to illegal reentry and related violations," migrants simply kept trying to cross until they eventually succeeded.[20] In reality, both the Border Patrol and the illegal border crossers benefited from an arrest system based on "prompt apprehension and return to country of origin." For the Border Patrol, lack of detention space necessitated a speedy removal process predicated on "voluntary departure." And for migrants, a speedy return to the Mexican side was welcomed because it shortened the delay before another crossing attempt.[21] Repeated arrests merely postponed entry but helped Border Patrol agents inflate arrest statistics and improve their internal performance evaluations. External reviewers, however, were less impressed. As one government study bluntly concluded: "Presently the border is a revolving door. . . . We repatriate undocumented workers on a massive scale. . . . The illegals cooperate by agreeing to voluntary departure and significant numbers promptly re-enter. It is not unusual for an illegal to undergo multiple apprehensions and re-entries for there are no serious deterrents."[22]

A clandestine form of cross-border interdependence developed through decades of large-scale Mexican migration. On the U.S. side, employers (particularly in agriculture but in other sectors of the economy as well) became accustomed to a ready supply of cheap labor. At the same time, the Mexican government came to rely on unauthorized migration as a safety valve for the nation's unemployment problem. Remittances from migrant workers provided much-needed foreign exchange—amounting to several billion dollars per year—which was especially important because it went directly to lower-income households. Entire sending communities became economically dependent on such remittances, which also helped fund the northward trip of other community members.

The work opportunities for unauthorized migrants were not only in U.S. agriculture—traditionally the main source of unauthorized employment—but increasingly in urban-based sectors of the economy such as services and construction. As employment options expanded spatially and occupationally, migration became more permanent, less seasonal, and more city-focused, and therefore more visible to the general public. The problem, of course, was that although their illegal status—which made them cheaper and more compliant—was part of what made Mexican workers so attractive to employers, this status reinforced public hostility. And as their numbers grew, expanding beyond the traditional confines of rural agricultural regions in the West, public tolerance eroded.

These changes helped to politicize the issue of illegal immigration in the late 1970s and early 1980s. Years of U.S. congressional debate over what to do about illegal immigration culminated in the passage of the 1986 Immigration Reform and Control Act (IRCA). IRCA introduced employer sanctions for the first time, authorized an expansion of the Border Patrol, and offered a general legalization program (as well as a special legalization program for agricultural workers). Some two million Mexicans were eventually given legal status—far more than initially projected. IRCA proponents argued that this supply of newly legalized workers would saturate the domestic demand for immigrant labor, while sanctions against employers would deter the hiring of illegal workers. This combination, it was hoped, would inhibit further unauthorized migration.

In practice, the new immigration law contributed to the very problem for which it was sold as a remedy. Many onetime immigrants who had gone back to Mexico returned to claim legalization papers. Proof of eligibility was easy to forge with cheap and easy-to-obtain fraudulent papers. And those who were legalized helped facilitate the arrival of new illegal immigrants. Meanwhile, the employer sanctions provisions proved to be mostly symbolic; their main impact was to spark an enormous underground business in fake documents. Since the new law did not require employers to verify the authenticity of the documents, they risked little by hiring illegal workers. And fraudulent papers, though a necessity for migrants, were relatively inexpensive and not difficult to find.

The immediate political effect of IRCA was to defuse domestic pressure by projecting the appearance of "doing something" about illegal immigration. But the law's failings and counterproductive consequences also helped set the stage for an intense anti-immigrant backlash in the early 1990s, with the border becoming the focal point of media coverage, political debate, and public outrage. In just a few years, immigration control along the border went from being a low-profile and politically marginalized activity into a high-intensity campaign commanding unprecedented attention.

The anti-immigration backlash was most acute in California, home to almost half of the unauthorized immigrants estimated to be in the country. California Governor Pete Wilson revived his sagging 1994 electoral campaign by blaming the state's woes on the federal government's failure to control the border. His most effective tool for communicating this message was a television advertisement based on video footage of illegal immigrants dashing across the border from Mexico through the San Ysidro port of entry south of San Diego. Against the background of this chaotic scene, the narrator's voice said: "They keep coming. Two million illegal immigrants in California. The federal government won't stop them at the border, yet requires us to pay billions to take care of them. Governor Wilson sent the National Guard to help the Border Patrol. But that's not all." Governor Wilson then appeared, pledging to do more: "For Californians who work hard, pay taxes and obey the laws, I am suing to force the federal government to control the border and I'm working to deny state services to illegal immigrants. Enough is enough."[23]

The dramatic footage of men, women, and children dashing across the border and weaving through busy traffic was broadcast across the nation, providing a powerful focusing event that galvanized public attention. The images were exploited for political gain by Wilson and projected the message that lax border controls were the root of the illegal immigration problem. Left out of the message was the anemic condition of workplace controls and the economic reliance of key sectors of the California economy on illegal labor, including the nation's largest agriculture industry. A narrow focus on the borderline itself as both the source of the illegal immigration problem and the site of the policing solution drew attention away from the more politically awkward and divisive task of dealing with employer demand, and acknowledging and regulating a well-entrenched clandestine cross-border labor market.

In this heated political climate, in which politicians spanning the political spectrum were scrambling to outdo each other in proposing tough new immigration-control measures, President Bill Clinton launched a high-profile border-enforcement crackdown. Signaling the administration's new commitment, the attorney general and the INS commissioner became frequent visitors to the border, and the attorney general even appointed a special representative to the southwest border—immediately dubbed the "border czar" by the press.

Long viewed as the neglected stepchild of the Department of Justice, the INS suddenly became one of the fastest-growing federal agencies. Indeed, even as most agencies were struggling in the face of budget cuts, the INS was struggling to manage its rapid growth. The INS budget grew from $1.5 billion in fiscal year 1993 to $4 billion in fiscal year 1999, with border enforcement by far the largest budget line item. The size of the Border Patrol along the southwest border more than doubled between fiscal year 1993 and fiscal year 1998, from 3,389 agents to 7,231. By the end of the decade, there were as many Border Patrol agents in the San Diego sector alone as there were along the entire southwest border in the 1970s. As a result of its hiring spree, by the late 1990s the INS had more officers authorized to carry a gun and make arrests than any other federal law enforcement agency.[24]

The new border enforcement campaign also included an influx of new equipment, ranging from infrared night-vision scopes and low-light TV cameras to ground sensors, helicopters, and all-terrain vehicles. The increasingly high-tech nature of border enforcement included a new electronic identification system called IDENT, which stored the fingerprints and photographs of those apprehended. The military also played a supporting role by assisting with the operation of night scopes, motion sensors, and communications equipment, as well as building and maintaining roads and fences. Along the border south of San Diego, for example, army reservists built a ten-foot-high steel wall that extended for fourteen miles. Similarly, in Nogales, Arizona army engineers constructed a fifteen-foot-tall fence that was nearly five miles long. Praising the growing collaboration between the military and law enforcement, INS commissioner Doris Meissner declared, "Think of this as one team, different roles, different uniforms, but with the same game plan—and that is to restore the rule of law to the border."[25]

Congress ensured that the border buildup would continue by passing the Illegal Immigration Reform and Immigration Responsibility Act of 1996. The sweeping immigration law authorized the hiring of a thousand Border Patrol agents a year, reaching a total force of more than ten thousand by 2001. The 1996 law promoted other measures to secure the border, among them a sharp increase in the penalties against migrant smugglers.

The border control offensive was based on a strategy, designed by the INS in 1993–94, called "prevention through deterrence." By using more physical barriers, surveillance equipment, legal sanctions, and law enforcement agents, the objective was to inhibit illegal entry rather than try to catch entrants once they entered the country. The infusion of law enforcement resources at the most popular entry points was designed to disrupt traditional border-crossing methods and routes, forcing migrants to give up or else attempt entry in more difficult and remote areas and at official ports of entry.

The deterrence strategy had its origins in Operation Blockade (later given the more diplomatic name Hold-the-Line), launched in El Paso on September 19, 1993. Some 450 agents were paid overtime to cover a twenty-mile stretch of the borderline. The sudden show of force led to a sharp drop in attempted illegal entries in the area. The high-profile operation drew the applause of Washington, the media, and local residents. It also attracted the attention of political leaders in California, who pushed to replicate the El Paso "success story" along their part of the border.[26]

Impressed by the El Paso show of force and the domestic support it generated, in 1994 the INS announced a comprehensive plan to apply the "prevention through deterrence" strategy across the entire southwestern border. The strategy would first target the busiest entry points: the El Paso and San Diego sectors, which at that time accounted for more than two-thirds of all southwestern border apprehensions. Operation Hold-the-Line in El Paso was thus matched by Operation Gatekeeper south of San Diego in October 1994, targeting the fourteen westernmost miles of the border.[27] The strategy would then be expanded to the Tucson sector and south Texas, where migrants were expected to shift after the El Paso and San Diego sectors had been secured. As envisioned by the Border Patrol, the strategy would eventually be applied along the entire border.[28]

Noticeably left out of this immigration-control offensive was any meaningful focus on the workplace; about 2 percent of the INS budget was devoted to enforcing employer sanctions. There were only seventeen hundred or so INS investigators assigned to cover the entire interior of the country, and less than a fifth of their time was devoted to worksite enforcement.[29] The number of investigations of employers for immigration violations had plummeted since the early 1990s, as had the number and total amount of fines.[30] Equally downplayed in the rush to secure the border was the fact that around 40 to 50 percent of all illegal immigrants in the United States had entered the country legally (for example, as tourists or students) and then simply overstayed their visas.

As expected, tighter border controls in El Paso and San Diego pushed migrants to attempt entry elsewhere along the border. Consequently, apprehensions in the El Paso sector plummeted, but they shot up to the west in New Mexico and Arizona. Similarly, apprehensions in the Imperial Beach sector south of San Diego, traditionally the single most important gateway for illegal entry, declined sharply once Gatekeeper began, but arrests jumped in the more remote areas of east San Diego County.

These shifts in human traffic generated further political pressures and a bureaucratic rationale to geographically expand the border-policing campaign. Operation Safeguard was subsequently launched in Nogales, Arizona, and Operation Gatekeeper, which first concentrated on the fourteen westernmost miles of the border, was extended in October 1996 to cover sixty-six miles. Similarly, in January 1997 Operation Hold-the-Line was extended ten miles west into New Mexico. And in late August 1997 the INS announced Operation Rio Grande in southeast Texas, which included setting up portable floodlights, twenty-foot watchtowers, low-light video cameras, and high-powered infrared vision scopes along the Rio Grande. As part of Operation Rio Grande, the

Border Patrol and the military's Joint Task Force Six started building 240 miles of roadway, a dozen helicopter pads, and fifty high-intensity lights in the Laredo area.[31]

Meanwhile, the heightened Border Patrol presence between the official ports of entry created more pressure at the ports of entry. Operations such as Gatekeeper prompted attempts at illegal entry through the ports of entry, and the INS in turn responded by deploying new port inspectors. Between fiscal year 1994 and fiscal year 1997, the number of INS port inspectors increased from 1,117 to 1,865—a 67 percent rise. The influx of personnel was reinforced by tougher penalties for those attempting entry through fraudulent use of documents.[32]

Breaking up the traditional routes and methods of clandestine entry turned the once relatively simple illegal act of entry without inspection into a more complex underground web of illegality. Past entry methods mostly involved either self-smuggling or limited use of a local smuggler. But with the buildup of border policing, the use of a professional smuggler became more of a necessity. Greater reliance on smugglers, a 1997 report of the Binational Study on Migration concluded, "helps to explain why most migrants attempting unauthorized entry succeed despite significantly more U.S. Border Patrol agents and technology on the border."[33] Indeed, hundreds of thousands of migrants entered the United States illegally every year during the 1990s, with the southwest border the most important entry point. According to the Pew Hispanic Center, the total number of unauthorized foreigners in the country more than doubled in the 1990s, from 3.5 million in 1990 to 8.4 million in 2000, with a majority from Mexico.[34]

As the demand for smuggling services and the risks of crossing the border grew, so too did the price of being smuggled. Prices along parts of the border doubled and in some cases more than tripled. The smuggling fee could exceed a thousand dollars, with the exact price depending on location, the quality of service, and the set of services being purchased. As one Border Patrol agent explained, "It's much like a full-service travel agency, all depending on how much you're willing to spend."[35] The INS argued that the increase in prices was an indicator that the deterrence effort was effective. Yet higher prices were not necessarily a major deterrent, given that smuggling fees tended to be paid for by relatives and friends already in the United States rather than by the migrants themselves. Alternatively, some migrants may have been given the option of paying off the fee by working in a job arranged or provided by the smuggler. Although the cost of being smuggled across the border was not insignificant, it could be earned back in a relatively short period of time spent working in the United States.

Higher prices did not significantly deter migrants, but they did greatly increase the wealth and power of smuggling groups. As Miguel Vallina, the assistant chief of the Border Patrol in San Diego, noted, "the more difficult the crossing, the better the business for the smugglers."[36] INS Commissioner Doris Meissner explained in January 1996 that "as we improve our enforcement, we increase the smuggling of aliens that occurs, because it is harder to cross and so therefore people turn more and more to smugglers." But at the same time that Meissner recognized the Border Patrol had created more business for smugglers, she also emphasized that we are "moving as aggressively as we can . . . so that we can put them [the smugglers] out of business."[37]

Beefed-up policing certainly removed some smugglers, but at the same time it increased the market position of others. Moreover, many of those arrested were the lowest-level and most-expendable members of migrant smuggling organizations: the border guides and drivers who were the "foot soldiers" of the business. Smugglers were first and foremost travel service providers. And as long as there continued to be a strong demand for their services—which the tightening of border controls and the strong domestic employer demand for migrant labor guaranteed—smuggling would persist. The high profits from smuggling—inflated by law enforcement pressure—ensured that there would be smugglers willing to accept the occupational hazards. As one smuggler explained, "Figure it this way. If I work in a factory five days, I make $125 a week. If I take one person across the border, I get $300."[38]

U.S. officials went to great lengths to portray migrants as the victims of smugglers, and they used this both to deflect criticism and to provide a further rationale to crack down on smuggling. Assistant U.S. Attorney Michael Wheat, for example, suggested that "basically, alien smuggling is modern-day slavery. The whole idea behind slavery was moving humans to perform labor. The way the aliens are moved, the way they are treated, this is just a sophisticated form of slavery."[39]

Migrants, however, generally viewed smugglers as simply a "necessary evil," a clandestine business transaction that they willingly engaged in to evade the expanding border enforcement net. Within Mexico, many considered migrant smuggling a shady business, but one that was providing a high-demand service. Smugglers had a clear economic motivation to deliver their "clients" unharmed across the border, since a substantial portion of the payment was typically made only upon delivery. Of course, as was well documented in media accounts, smugglers could be abusive and reckless, and their efforts to bypass law enforcement could place migrants at great risk; hundreds were dying every year trying to cross the border in the harsh and remote terrain where border enforcement was thinnest. Yet smugglers were hired precisely because they generally provided a safer, faster, and more reliable border-crossing experience. Indeed, many smugglers depended on customer satisfaction for future business, since migrants who had a successful experience were likely to recommend their smuggler to other friends and relatives.[40]

Smugglers also became more skilled as border enforcement became more intensive. Although some of the local freelance entrepreneurs who once dominated migrant smuggling along the border were being squeezed out by the border-enforcement offensive, they were replaced by better-organized and more-skilled smuggling organizations. Those smuggling operations that had the greatest transportation and communication capabilities were the ones most capable of evading arrest. Pressured by law enforcement, some smugglers turned to using commercial trucks to move migrants across the border, blending in with the boom in cross-border trucking brought on by the liberalization of trade and transportation. Northbound truck crossings doubled between 1993 and the end of the decade. U.S. port inspectors could realistically search only a small percentage of the trucks crossing the border.

Further complicating the challenge of organized migrant smuggling along the border was an unintended side effect of U.S. efforts to stop the maritime smuggling of Asian migrants. As officials began to target the use of boats to smuggle Asian migrants into the country in 1993, much of the smuggling was diverted to other routes, including land routes through Mexico—a strikingly similar replay of the dynamics of diverted Chinese migrant smuggling a century earlier. The arrival of Chinese smuggling boats, most notably the *Golden Venture* in 1993, attracted tremendous media attention, provoking a law enforcement crackdown. Smugglers reacted by using less visible transportation methods and routes. As Meissner noted, "We've stopped that illegal boat traffic, but there are still a lot of people coming from Asia, mainly through Central America and Mexico."[41] Chinese migrants paid up to $30,000 for the trip, often going into indentured servitude in the United States to pay off the debt. A typical boat from China landing in the northern Mexican state of Baja in 1993 carried human cargo worth $6 million.[42]

As migrant smuggling became a more organized and sophisticated enterprise in reaction to tighter controls, this served to justify tougher laws and tougher enforcement. The number of smugglers being prosecuted mushroomed. In San Diego (the busiest federal court in the country for migrant smuggling cases), prosecutions increased from 33 in 1993 to 233 in 1996.[43] More punitive sentencing guidelines significantly increased the length of prison terms for smugglers. The INS was also given new enforcement powers to target organized smuggling, such as federal racketeering statutes and the authority to use wiretaps and undercover sting operations.

But the U.S. border crackdown did not create a shortage of smugglers. More risks translated into higher smuggling fees. And as the risks for smuggling rose, so too did the incentive for smugglers to use more dangerous methods to avoid law enforcement. This partly explained the increase in high-speed chases and accidents that resulted when smugglers tried to circumvent INS checkpoints along the highways leading north from the border. It also helped to explain a particularly creative but cruel smuggling trend: because the law did not allow jailing illegal migrants with children, children were sometimes bought, rented, or stolen to facilitate the crossing. The children were then often left to fend for themselves on the U.S. side.[44]

Greater enforcement also increased the efforts by smugglers to bribe or buy entry documents from those doing the enforcing. And as smuggling groups became more sophisticated and profitable—as a consequence of the higher demand and cost for their services and the heightened risks involved in providing these services—the capacity and means to corrupt also grew. So even though the border was more heavily policed, it was also more corrupt, with some of those responsible for policing also engaged in informal toll collecting. But the profits and payoffs from migrant smuggling paled in comparison to those of the border's biggest smuggling business: drug trafficking.

The Mexican Drug Connection

The entry of drugs into the mix of smuggling activities in the early twentieth century profoundly changed the dynamics of law enforcement and evasion across the southwest border. U.S. drug prohibition gave a major boost to Mexico's nascent drug-export sector. Marijuana had been grown in Mexico since the nineteenth century, and in the first decades of the twentieth century Chinese immigrants brought opium growing to the states of Sinaloa and Sonora. Restrictive U.S. drug laws were eventually matched by similar laws on the Mexican side of the border, including a ban on the export of heroin and marijuana in 1927. In practice, however, there was little real enforcement. Moreover, during World War II the United States encouraged Mexican opium production (for morphine) and marijuana production (hemp for rope) as part of the war effort.

In the 1950s and 1960s, Mexico was the main marijuana supplier for the U.S. market, but it remained a marginal player in the heroin trade. In the early 1970s, however, Mexico's share of the U.S. heroin market rose sharply, not simply as a result of high consumer demand but because of U.S. antidrug initiatives on the other side of the globe. When the Turkish government, under pressure from the Nixon administration, prohibited opium production and implemented a strict control program in 1972, more production moved to a logical and much closer alternative: Mexico. In other words, the unintended feedback effect of targeting Turkey and severing the Marseille "French Connection" was to partly transplant the opium-production problem to America's backyard. Mexican brown heroin was of lower quality, but it was also cheaper and more accessible, especially on the West Coast.

Partly because of prodding from Washington, in 1975 Mexico launched the most ambitious eradication effort ever undertaken by any country. The results were impressive, drastically reducing Mexican supplies of marijuana and heroin to the U.S. market by the late 1970s. Yet it did not take long for the Mexican drug trade to adjust to the new enforcement environment. Production of marijuana and opium again rapidly expanded (this time in more dispersed and less visible plots), and by the mid-1980s Mexico was an increasingly important transshipment point for South American cocaine bound for the U.S. market. The full significance of this change and its impact on the border region would not be recognized until years later.

Washington's escalating drug war in the 1980s focused on the influx of cocaine through South Florida, treating Mexico as a sideshow. The Maginot Line–style strategy in the southeast did not significantly deter drug imports, but it did influence the location, methods, and organization of drug smuggling. Its most important impact was to push much of the traffic to the Southwest, making Colombian traffickers increasingly reliant on their Mexican counterparts. In other words, the U.S. drug war offensive unintentionally empowered Mexican traffickers. The end result was a redistribution of power within the international drug trade, with the world's most powerful traffickers now next door just across the border.[45]

Testifying at a House Foreign Affairs Committee task force hearing in October 1987, Assistant DEA Administrator David Westrate noted that the enforcement crackdown in the Caribbean had redirected more cocaine shipments through Mexico: "Now that's got a serious downside, other than it opens a major theater for us to address, which is the southwest border. . . . It also has produced a strong linkage between the Colombian major drug organizations and Mexican drug organizations—a connection we did not have before. And I think that clearly is something that's going to cause us fits in the next couple of years."[46] Put differently, the main result of the U.S. interdiction strategy was to create more business for Mexican smuggling organizations and more work for law enforcement.

Apparently the lesson learned from the experience in the southeast was the need to replicate the strategy in the southwest. Coast Guard Admiral Paul Yost testified: "The more money that you spend on it, the more success you are going to have in the interdiction area. . . . We did that in the Caribbean for the last two years, and I'm sure that what we're about to do on the southwest border will also be extremely successful. It is also going to be extremely expensive, and the success-expense ratio is going to be a very direct one."[47]

But measuring such success was politically tricky. At a 1987 Senate hearing held in Nogales, Arizona, Senator Pete Domenici (R-NM) summarized the situation: "Now, I understand that we're shooting at floating targets. I mean, you do well in the Southeast and they [traffickers] move to the Southwest. We'll load up the Southwest and what happens next? Nonetheless, we have to continue the war on drugs. And for us to sustain the resources, you have to have a few field victories of significant size that are measurable."[48] The reply by Customs Commissioner William Von Raab was predictable: "The seizures, which are your typical measure of success, are impressive." Pleased to hear that some progress was being made in controlling the border, none of the committee members questioned what these measures of success actually measured.[49] At the same hearing, Von Raab acknowledged that "there is good news and bad news" in increased drug seizures: "The good news is that we are catching more drugs because we are getting better at doing our jobs. We have more resources. The bad news is that we are catching more because more is coming across."[50]

Meanwhile, the business community along the southwest border was increasingly nervous that heightened drug checks, which caused congestion and traffic jams, were impeding legal commerce. The president of one brokerage firm told a congressional committee, "The significant increases in commercial and civilian traffic coupled with the need to address the drug problem are creating a disastrous situation for manufacturers, importers, and border city retailers." He warned, "If U.S. Customs is going to service the needs of the commercial sector and civilian sectors and at the same time increase their surveillance and interdiction programs for drugs, international trade and relations are going to suffer irreparable harm unless the appropriations for improved facilities and manpower are provided."[51] Such worries reflected the dilemma that U.S. officials had partly created for themselves: they had transplanted much of the cocaine flow from South Florida to the U.S.-Mexico border, but efforts to harden the border against illegal trade collided with the policy goal of facilitating the expansion of legal trade with Mexico.

A dramatic sign that the Mexican drug trade had not only recovered from the crackdown of the 1970s but transformed into a more violent and corrupting enterprise was the 1985 murder of DEA agent

Kiki Camarena in Guadalajara. The affair sent U.S.-Mexican relations into a tailspin. The most visible and immediate U.S. response to Camarena's disappearance was Operation Intercept II in February 1985, involving intensive checks on traffic entering from Mexico and even a partial closing of the border. Its primary purpose, however, was not interdiction but rather to signal disapproval with Mexico's antidrug performance. The diplomatic crisis worsened in 1986. In January, Mexicans were shocked by the DEA-orchestrated kidnapping of Rene Verdugo Urquidez to the United States to stand trial for his alleged role in Camarena's murder. And on March 8 most of the customs houses on the border were temporarily shut down; the official reason given was the need to search for drugs and weapons being smuggled into the United States by Libyan terrorists.

Heated congressional hearings on the Camarena affair turned into a public platform for a much broader interrogation of official corruption in Mexico. For the first time, the U.S.-Mexico war on drugs also became a full-blown cross-border war of words. Although the entrenchment of drug-related corruption in Mexico had long been well known, it was not until the killing of Camarena that U.S. officials publicly pointed fingers at specific individuals within the Mexican political system and security apparatus. Growing alarm over drug-related corruption in Mexico fueled more general anxiety over the security of the border. The House Select Committee on Narcotics Abuse and Control sponsored a series of hearings in the Southwest and concluded in its final report that the border was "totally out of control and threatening not only to the region itself, but to the entire country."[52]

The fallout from the Camarena affair sparked changes on both sides of the border that would have long-lasting consequences. In Washington, Camarena's murder was an important impetus for the U.S. Congress to mandate, as part of the sweeping Anti-Drug Abuse Act of 1986, that the United States make foreign economic and military assistance, votes in multilateral lending institutions, and trade preferences contingent on "full cooperation" with U.S. antidrug objectives. In Mexico, meanwhile, investigations into Camarena's death embarrassed the Mexican government by exposing close links between traffickers and the security apparatus. Largely because of pressures from Washington, the notoriously corrupt Federal Security Directorate was quickly disbanded; and Rafael Caro Quintero, the trafficker accused of being responsible for Camarena's murder, was arrested.

Partly to appease and impress Washington, the Mexican government boosted its antidrug spending. The percentage of the attorney general's budget devoted to drug control rose from around 32 percent in 1985 to more than 60 percent in 1988. At the same time, Mexico continued to expand the role of the military in crop eradication. In 1987, this involved some twenty-five thousand soldiers—up from only five thousand in the late 1970s.[53] Following the U.S. lead, President Miguel De La Madrid Hurtado officially announced that drug trafficking was a national security threat.

These changes were merely a prelude to President Carlos Salinas de Gortari's antidrug initiatives. Salinas's main agenda—sweeping market reforms and building a closer economic relationship with the United States—depended at least in part on projecting a new image of Mexico's drug-control effort and taming American anxiety over the flow of drugs across the border. Fortunately for Salinas, he had key allies in Washington, reflected in the celebrated "spirit of Houston" that emerged from the November 1988 meeting between the recently elected presidents Bush and Salinas.

Yet even as Salinas and Bush began to craft a new and closer economic relationship, the clandestine underside of the relationship was rapidly changing as well. Mexican marijuana and heroin exports were already generating billions of dollars by the late 1980s, making drugs a sizable export industry. But the heightened role of cocaine in Mexican drug smuggling dramatically elevated the financial stakes of the trade. So long as the heroin and marijuana that traditionally dominated the business of drug smuggling across the southwest border were produced within Mexico, Mexican drug smuggling remained primarily a local and regional business. The percentage of cocaine entering the United States through Mexico had been negligible in the early 1980s. But according to the State Department, by 1989 nearly a third of cocaine exports were rerouted through Mexican territory; by 1992, more than half; in later years, as high as 75–80 percent.[54] Whatever the actual amount, the trend was unmistakable.

The U.S. interdiction offensive in the 1980s disrupted not only the traditional routes for cocaine smuggling through the Caribbean and South Florida but also the favored method of such smuggling: light aircraft. Extending the U.S. radar net from the Southeast to the Southwest forced much of the trade out of the air. The United States had built what one senior customs official described as a "Maginot Line of radar" across the border that drastically curtailed air smuggling.[55] Washington drug warriors boasted that the sharp drop in air smuggling demonstrated the effectiveness of interdiction. But the actual effect was to redirect rather than reduce the drug flow. With much of the traffic pushed out of the air, road transportation networks through Mexico to the U.S. market became a much more integral part of the cocaine trade. And the Mexican organizations that controlled smuggling along these routes were more than willing to sell their services—off-loading, storing, and smuggling—to Colombia's cocaine exporters.

As Salinas assumed the Mexican presidency in December 1988, he faced the daunting twin tasks of coping with a more powerful and internationally connected Mexican drug-smuggling business (thanks largely to the "success" of U.S. interdiction in the Caribbean and south Florida) and dealing with rising U.S. political expectations that Mexico demonstrate much greater commitment to doing something about it. Salinas therefore launched an aggressive campaign to revitalize the Mexican antidrug program, declaring that drug trafficking was the number one security threat facing the nation. He reorganized and greatly expanded the country's drug-control apparatus, which was particularly impressive given that it occurred during a time of deep cuts in overall government spending. The resources devoted to drug control by the Mexican attorney general's office tripled from the late 1980s to the early 1990s. Drug control came to dominate the Mexican criminal justice system. Salinas also extended the antidrug role of the military, with about one-third of the military's budget devoted to the effort by the end of the 1980s. Militarization fit well with the new emphasis on defining drugs as a national security threat.

As the Salinas government beefed up its efforts on the Mexican side of the border, U.S. drug-control strategists built up interdiction efforts on their side. The enforcement-induced shift in drug smuggling from the Southeast to the Southwest provided the main rationale. As the Bush administration reported in 1991, "the success of interdiction in the southeastern United States and the Caribbean islands and Sea has caused drug smugglers to shift their focus towards Mexico as a primary transfer point into the United States." As a result, "resources have been enhanced along the Southwest Border." Concretely, that meant 175 new Customs Service inspectors, 200 more Border Patrol agents, twenty-three more canine drug-detection teams, and increased funds for "capital assets such as fencing, ground sensors, traffic checkpoints, aerostats, and other equipment to detect smugglers."[56] Between 1988 and 1993, Customs increased the number of southwest border inspectors by 41 percent and investigators by 21 percent. While Customs focused on the ports of entry, the Border Patrol was designated the lead law enforcement agency for drug interdiction between ports of entry. New fencing projects were initiated to deter drug-laden vehicles from entering the U.S. at unauthorized crossing points.

The border also became much more militarized. As part of the Pentagon's expanded interdiction role, Joint Task Force Six was established, based at Fort Bliss, Texas. The task force involved units of some seventy infantrymen armed with M16 rifles; they were divided into camouflaged four-man teams to cover designated thirty-mile segments of the border. In fiscal year 1990, the task force conducted twenty operations in support of border drug interdiction. By fiscal year 1992 the number of missions had increased to 408.[57] Teams of National Guardsmen were also drafted into counterdrug work, deployed to remote border posts to monitor smuggling in rural areas and to ports of entry for cargo inspection.

The impressive quantitative results of the drug enforcement offensive—more crops eradicated, more traffickers arrested, and more drugs seized—were officially touted as evidence of unprecedented U.S. and Mexican resolve and cooperation in fighting drugs. Mexico boasted that it was confiscating more drugs than any other country in the region—and indeed more drugs were seized during Salinas's first year in office than in the previous six years combined.[58] Year after year, the State Department offered glowing reviews of Mexico's antidrug record. The antidrug performance touted by both U.S. and Mexican officials helped preserve the upbeat mood in U.S.-Mexico relations on the eve of passing NAFTA.

At the same time as the Salinas government was renegotiating its economic partnership with Washington, Mexican smugglers were renegotiating the terms of their partnership with Colombia's cocaine exporters. In the beginning of this business alliance, the Mexicans were simply paid in cash for moving Colombian cocaine across the southwestern border, $1,000–$2,000 for every kilogram. But as the relationship matured, and the Colombians faced growing law enforcement pressure at home and abroad, the leverage of the Mexican smugglers grew. As a result, they increasingly demanded payment in the form of product: 40 to 50 percent of every cocaine shipment, which in turn expanded their own distribution networks, especially in the western parts of the United States. This increased the Mexican share of cocaine profits five to ten times, dramatically changing the financial stakes of smuggling across the border.[59]

At the same time, Mexican drug traffickers diversified by taking over much of the U.S. market for methamphetamines—thanks in part to U.S. crackdowns on domestic producers. Just as had been the case with the U.S. offensive against Colombian traffickers, the offensive against domestic methamphetamine producers played right into the hands of Mexican smugglers.

Mexico's growing stake in the drug trade produced more sophisticated and organized smuggling organizations along the border's main transportation hubs, the most prominent of which were the Gulf, Tijuana, and Juarez drug-trafficking groups. Their meteoric rise would later prompt the head of the DEA to describe them as "the premier law enforcement threat facing the United States."[60] The Mexican government calculated that the gross revenue of Mexican drug-smuggling organizations reached $30 billion in 1994; U.S. officials estimated the profits at $10 billion, putting it ahead of Mexico's leading legal export, oil.[61] Such figures, of course, necessarily represented "guesstimates," at best, but even the most conservative numbers indicated the drug trade had become a leading economic force in Mexico.

Ironically, the most visible operational achievements of the U.S. and Mexican antidrug campaigns were actually aided by an expanding drug trade: well-publicized increases in seizures and arrests on both sides of the border were partly made possible by the fact that there were more drugs to seize and smugglers to arrest. Similarly, record eradication levels were facilitated by bumper crops of marijuana and opium poppy. Impressive drug-enforcement statistics masked the fact that the Mexican crackdown was selective: old-guard smugglers were targeted, while the business of other smugglers expanded. Record arrest and seizure statistics did not lead to less smuggling but simply created openings for more aggressive smugglers on the rise.

As more government resources were devoted to drug control, smugglers also devoted more resources to paying off those doing the controlling. Law enforcement had to be bribed because it could not be entirely bypassed or bullied. The problem was exacerbated by the fact that rather than reforming the criminal justice system, Salinas had simply expanded the size of an already corruption-plagued policing apparatus. The perverse result was to boost opportunities for collecting bribes. The financial rewards of drug enforcement created enormous competition within law enforcement agencies for assignment to key posts along the smuggling corridors. Eduardo Valle, who left the Mexican attorney general's office toward the end of the Salinas administration, claimed that while he was in office the top Mexican drug-enforcement posts were auctioned off to the highest bidder. The price of a particular law enforcement position, he said, depended on changes in drug-smuggling routes along the border: "In Coahuila, for example, there are four or five entrances to the United States. If one crossing point is closed, the price of a federal police chief's position in that area goes down because the post is irrelevant, but the price of the police chief positions in other places goes up. This is openly discussed inside the federal police."[62] The higher the law enforcement position, the higher the payoff. For example, a notebook recovered from the smuggling organization run by Juan Garcia Abrego of the Gulf trafficking organization included a list of payoffs: $1 million to the national commander of Mexico's Federal Judicial Police, $500,000 to the force's operations chief, and $100,000 to the federal police commanders in the city of Matamoros.[63]

Mexico's response to the growing corruption problem within the police was to turn even more to the military for help. The antidrug role of the Mexican military, though enhanced during the Salinas years, expanded much further under President Ernesto Zedillo. By early 1998, military personnel occupied top law enforcement posts in two-thirds of Mexico's states.[64] For example, more than one hundred military personnel were brought into the Federal Attorney General's Office in the border state of Chihuahua. In some states, such as Nuevo Leon, the Federal Judicial Police forces were entirely replaced by soldiers.[65] By the end of the decade, the Mexican secretaries of defense and navy acknowledged that drug control had become the primary mission of their services.[66]

Yet sending in the military in response to corruption within the police also brought with it greater risk of corruption within the military. Indeed, in early 1997 the head of the federal antidrug agency, General Jesus Gutierrez Rebollo, was arrested on charges of working for the Juarez trafficking organization. The agency, which had been patterned after the DEA when it first opened in 1993, was quickly dismantled. Just a few weeks before the scandal, the White House drug policy director, Barry McCaffrey, had described the general as "an honest man who is a no-nonsense field commander of the Mexican army who's now been sent to bring to the police force the same kind of aggressiveness and reputation he had in uniform."[67] No other army commander had displayed more antidrug initiative. The problem was its selective focus, largely leaving the Juarez traffickers untouched while targeting other trafficking groups. This scandal, although an unusually high-profile one, was not an isolated incident. The next month, General Alfredo Navarro Lara was arrested for offering $1 million a month to the top federal justice official in Baja California on behalf of the Tijuana drug-trafficking organization.[68] A White House report indicated that thirty-four senior Mexican military officers had been targeted for disciplinary action as a result of drug-related corruption.[69]

Meanwhile, smugglers were increasingly hiding their drug shipments within the rising tide of commercial trucks, railcars, and passenger vehicles crossing the border. The NAFTA-encouraged boom in cross-border traffic had the side effect of creating a much more challenging job for those border agents charged with the task of weeding out the illegitimate flows from the legitimate ones—a challenge that in turn provided the rationale for a further infusion of law enforcement resources at the official ports of entry. As the 1999 *National Drug Control Strategy Report* explained, "Rapidly growing commerce between the United States and

Mexico will complicate our efforts to keep drugs out of cross-border traffic. Since the southwest border is presently the most porous of the nation's borders, it is there that we must mount a determined coordinated effort to stop the flow of drugs."[70]

Concern that drug smugglers might benefit from NAFTA was deliberately not discussed during the negotiations over the free-trade accord. "This was in the 'too hot to handle' category," noted Gary Hufbauer of the Institute for International Economics, but "it's a painfully obvious problem."[71] An internal report written by an intelligence officer at the U.S. embassy in Mexico City claimed that cocaine traffickers were establishing factories, warehouses, and trucking companies in anticipation of the expected boom in cross-border commerce. Some traffickers reportedly even hired trade consultants to determine what products move most swiftly through border inspection under NAFTA guidelines.[72] NAFTA, it turned out, was good for both licit and illicit commerce, though this was conveniently glossed over by NAFTA boosters eager not to let the drug issue derail the trade agreement.

The sheer volume of border crossings fostered an ideal environment for drug smuggling. By 1997, more than two hundred thousand vehicles were coming into the United States from Mexico every day. That year, U.S. border officials searched more than a million commercial trucks and railway cars crossing from Mexico, and found cocaine in only six.[73] The enforcement challenge, in other words, was the equivalent of finding a needle in a haystack—except the haystack kept getting bigger and the needle was actively trying to avoid detection. Trade between the United States and Mexico tripled between 1993 and 2000, most of which was transported via commercial cargo conveyances across the border. Such conveyances, of course, could carry illegal goods as easily as legal goods. One truck that was stopped near San Diego was smuggling eight tons of cocaine stuffed into cans of jalapño peppers. U.S. officials believed that the shipment belonged to the owner of one of Mexico's largest shipping companies.[74]

For political reasons, customs officials continued to proclaim that efforts to keep drugs out would not be sacrificed in order to keep legitimate trade moving, but commercial realities dictated that the border remain highly porous. The more intensive and intrusive the inspection process, the longer the wait at the border. As one customs official warned, "If we examined every truck for narcotics arriving into the United States along the Southwest border . . . Customs would back up the truck traffic bumper-to-bumper into Mexico City in just two weeks—15.8 days. In 15.8 days, there would be 95,608 trucks backed up into Mexico. That's 1,177 miles of trucks, end to end."[75] By the end of the decade, ninety million cars and four million trucks and railcars were entering the United States from Mexico every year.

But even as increased cross-border traffic placed practical limitations on border controls, domestic political imperatives meant devoting ever more resources to enhancing such controls. In February 1995 Customs announced Operation Hard Line, an intensified effort to target drug smuggling in commercial cargo. Customs received more than six hundred new positions through Hard Line in fiscal year 1997, roughly a 25 percent increase in personnel on the border. A year after the initiation of Hard Line, Customs issued a press release praising the program's "record-breaking success": 24 percent more seizures of cocaine, heroin, and marijuana than in the previous year. Another press release a few days later boasted that the number of drug seizures along the California-Mexico border had increased by 79 percent over the same period the year before. The fine print, though, revealed that although the overall number of drug seizures was up, the actual amount of drugs seized had fallen, indicating that smugglers had adapted to increased enforcement by breaking their loads into smaller packages to reduce their risks.[76] The trend, in fact, was toward more-but-smaller drug shipments—creating more and harder work for drug enforcement. Border inspectors and their drug-sniffing dogs were mostly kept busy making busts of relatively small marijuana shipments.

To keep generating drug seizures without stopping the rising flow of commercial traffic, U.S. border-control strategists increasingly turned to state-of-the-art technologies. Giant Backscatter x-ray machines, large enough to drive a truck through, were installed at more and more ports of entry along the border. In 1995 a Border Research Technology Center was opened in San Diego, with the purpose of adapting various gadgets and gizmos previously restricted to military use to border-control tasks. As Clinton's drug policy director, Barry McCaffrey, put it, "Technology can help us stop drugs while facilitating legal commerce."[77] And this military-aided search for a high-tech fix for the border was just getting started. Indeed, it turned out that the sharp escalation of border enforcement in the 1990s was just a warm-up.

The Border Aftershocks of September 11

Even though the terrorist attacks on September 11, 2001, took place thousands of miles away, the shock waves were intensely felt along the U.S.-Mexico borderline. Ports of entry were virtually shut down, squeezing the arteries that provided the lifeblood to the border economies and the larger U.S.-Mexico economic integration process. In Laredo, Texas, for example, during peak crossing times before the attacks it took about five minutes for a pedestrian to cross a bridge checkpoint and a half-hour for a motorist. Immediately after the attacks, the wait increased up to five hours. Retail sales in U.S. border cities immediately plummeted as Mexican shoppers stayed south of the border. Mexican border towns were similarly shaken by the sharp decline in U.S. visitors. Although the crisis mode of border enforcement eased within a few weeks, the shocks of September 11 left a permanent mark on the border.

In the aftermath of the attacks, politicians from across the political spectrum rushed to pledge allegiance to "securing the border"—and attacked their opponents for not doing enough. In this heated political climate, U.S. border strategists scrambled to take the old drug and immigration enforcement infrastructure and adapt it to the suddenly prioritized counterterrorism mission. It was an awkward fit and a cumbersome retooling job. The INS enforcement apparatus was designed to handle millions of migrant workers entering the country in search of employment, not to detect and deter those few determined individuals arriving to commit terrorist acts. Similarly, Customs agents along the border had until September 2001 been mostly preoccupied with drugs and other contraband.

These already overstretched agencies were now ordered to suddenly reinvent themselves and play a frontline role against terrorism. The new security fear was that the same groups, methods, and routes long used to smuggle migrants and drugs into the country could be used to smuggle in terrorists and weapons of mass destruction. Also worrisome to U.S. authorities was that the same fraudulent document industry that had long provided identification cards for unauthorized migrants could also potentially provide these services to terrorists.

The bureaucratic reinvention process led to a flood of new funding for border enforcement and the consolidation of twenty-two agencies, including Customs and INS, under a new cabinet-level Department of Homeland Security (DHS)—the largest reorganization of the federal government in more than half a century. It would become the third largest cabinet agency (after the Department of Defense and Department of Veterans Affairs), with some 230,000 employees by the end of the decade. A once-obscure term, "homeland security," suddenly became part of everyday security lingo. Similarly, "border security" replaced "border control" as the favored policy term, though it remained vague exactly what this actually meant or entailed. Traditional concerns about drugs and unauthorized migrants were now lumped together with counterterrorism as "transnational security threats." One sign of this change was that the roving border inspectors screening vehicles for smuggled goods and people were renamed "Anti-Terrorism Contraband Enforcement Team." Terrorism was now put at the top of the list of border priorities in official mission statements, even though the day-to-day work of patrolling the border remained overwhelmingly focused on smuggled drugs and migrants.

The changed political climate after September 11 also hardened the U.S. immigration policy debate as the entry of foreigners inescapably came to be viewed through the prism of national security. In the months prior to the terrorist attacks, Mexican President Vicente Fox had high hopes of reaching a migration deal with the United States and creating a more open border, but such hopes were quickly dashed on September 11 as Washington's mood and attention suddenly shifted.[78]

Immigration policy reform stalled and was placed on the back burner, and the prior escalation of U.S. immigration enforcement along the border escalated even further. This included a continuation of the Border Patrol hiring boom that started in the 1990s. By the end of the decade, the size of the Border Patrol exceeded twenty thousand agents—more than doubling since 2000 and a fivefold increase since the early 1990s, turning it into the nation's largest police force. And this did not count the deployment of National Guard troops to the border, including six thousand sent in as a stopgap measure by President George W. Bush in 2006.

The rush to hire and deploy more agents to the border, however, also brought with it greater risks of corruption. Corruption cases proliferated along the border, involving both federal and local law enforcement and extending to military and National Guard troops. Between 2003 and 2010, 129 customs officials and border agents were arrested on corruption-related charges.[79] In one 2005 case, a San Ysidro port inspector was caught waving carloads of illegal immigrants through his lane. Between the ports of entry, several Border Patrol agents in California were caught shuttling illegal migrants across the line and showing smugglers how to evade Border Patrol sensors and cameras. At one point they even removed a group of migrants from custody and, instead of sending them back across the line, dropped them off at a local Walmart parking lot for their smugglers to pick them up. Other Border Patrol agents were caught using interior road checkpoints as de facto tollbooths to collect payoffs from drug traffickers. In one particularly troubling case in 2005, the corruption investigation implicated the assistant area port director, whose job included overseeing anti-smuggling and anticorruption efforts at San Ysidro. Equally troubling was the discovery that the top FBI official in El Paso, who oversaw 220 special agents and employees, was closely associated with a Juarez businessman allegedly tied to drug traffickers.[80]

Paralleling Washington's deployment of thousands of additional border-enforcement personnel, a militia-style border-monitoring campaign called the "Minuteman Project" was launched in early 2005, involving armed civilians in fatigues taking up patrol positions along the Arizona-Mexico border. The initiative—essentially a border publicity stunt designed to draw public attention to the porosity of the border and embarrass the federal government to do more about it—generated hundreds of thousands of dollars in donations and drew recruits from across the country, aided by the use of the Internet and national media coverage.

Continuing the fence fetish that began in the 1990s, in 2006 the U.S. Congress passed the Secure Fence Act, which included approval to build some seven hundred miles of new border fencing, at a cost between $1 million and $3 million for every mile.[81] As governor of Arizona, Janet Napolitano had expressed skepticism about the expansive fencing plan when it was first proposed in 2005, saying "You show me a fifty-foot wall and I'll show you a fifty-one-foot ladder at the border." She also could have mentioned the dozens of tunnels that had been discovered under the border. But once Napolitano was appointed as head of the Department of Homeland Security in the Obama administration, she was noticeably less dismissive about the utility of border fences. Meanwhile, some Arizona officials, frustrated by the slow pace of fence construction, began to seek private donations to build their own border wall.[82]

The post–September 11 security environment also created an opportunity to further militarize immigration control via the broader mandate of "homeland security." In the past, military units operating on the border were formally limited to assisting counterdrug work: "It had to have a counterdrug nexus," noted a spokesperson for Joint Task Force North (which replaced Joint Task Force Six in September 2004). "Now our mission is a major supporter of homeland security." The new expanded mission was to support federal law enforcement agencies in the "interdiction of suspected transnational threats within and along the approaches to the United States," which could include targeting unauthorized immigration.[83] Although further militarization of border

Figure 15.2 U.S. border fence along the Arizona-Mexico border, 2011 (U.S. Customs and Border Patrol).

Figure 15.3 Drug tunnel discovered under the California-Mexico border, 2011 (U.S. Customs and Border Patrol).

control was partly inhibited by the deployment of military forces to Iraq and Afghanistan, some aspects of border policing provided training in desert warfare. For example, an Alaska-based Stryker unit (designed to roll out quickly on eight-wheeled armored vehicles using surveillance and reconnaissance to generate information) on its way to Iraq spent sixty days in the New Mexico desert working alongside the Border Patrol, and it was reportedly responsible for the Border Patrol's apprehension of twenty-five hundred illegal immigrants.[84]

Major military contractors, such as Boeing, Lockheed Martin, Raytheon, and Northrop Grumman, were also recruited to play a larger role in border control—as one press report put it, "Using some of the same high-priced, high-tech tools these companies have already put to work in Iraq and Afghanistan."[85] Reflecting the growing faith in high-tech solutions, in 2004 the Border Patrol began to use unmanned aerial vehicles, the first civilian law enforcement agency in the world to

Figure 15.4 President George W. Bush and Homeland Security Secretary Michael Chertoff view a Predator drone in Yuma, Arizona, used to patrol the U.S.-Mexico border, April 9, 2007 (Jason Reed/Reuters/Corbis).

do so.[86] In September 2005 border officials in Arizona unveiled a new unmanned aerial surveillance system based on the satellite-controlled Predator-B drone used for military operations in the Middle East and elsewhere. By the end of the decade the Department of Homeland Security, which already operated hundreds of manned aircraft—the largest nonmilitary air force in the world—also had a small fleet of Predator drones along the border.[87]

President Obama boasted about the border buildup at a 2010 press conference: "We have more of everything: ICE [Immigration and Customs Enforcement], Border Patrol, surveillance, you name it. So we take border security seriously."[88] But it was not at all clear what the actual deterrent effect of all this border activity was. Many determined migrants and their smuggler guides continued to be redirected rather than deterred by the new border barriers. This included more "express service" of migrants through ports of entry (hidden in vehicles or through fraudulent use of documents, or simply paying compromised inspectors to look the other way) rather than braving the harsh desert and mountain terrain. There was also a surge in the landing of migrants on California beaches by speedboat and other low-profile, radar-evading marine craft. Smugglers charged a premium for these faster and more convenient modes of clandestine entry.[89]

The continued escalation of enforcement certainly made the border more challenging and dangerous to cross, with hundreds of migrants dying each year. Indeed, the border was harder to cross than ever before in the nation's history. It was also increasingly difficult to even reach the border, with more and more U.S.-bound migrants (especially the tens of thousands of non-Mexicans traveling through Mexican territory) facing a gauntlet of extortionist criminals and corrupt cops along their northward journey.

Immigration laws were also more stringently enforced than at any other time; federal prosecutions for immigration law violations more than doubled from 2001 to 2005, replacing drug law violations as the most frequently enforced federal crime.[90] By the end of the decade, violations of immigration law represented more than half of all federal prosecutions (and in the Southwest it was more than 80 percent).[91] One consequence was to fuel a booming business in federally funded private detention centers in the Southwest and elsewhere.[92]

No doubt the hardening of the border was having some deterrent effect on would-be unauthorized border crossers, given that the crossing was made much more difficult and expensive and the odds of being apprehended and detained increased. Still, most of those migrants caught could simply keep trying until they succeeded. Surveys of migrants indicated that almost all the Mexicans who attempted illegal entry eventually made it in—thanks largely to hiring the services of professional smugglers.[93]

Ultimately, the biggest inhibitors to migrant smuggling were not just tougher border enforcement but broader push and pull factors. Demographic, social, and economic shifts within Mexico began to reduce the push to migrate, while at the same time the sharp contraction of the U.S. economy starting in 2007 greatly reduced the pull of employer demand.[94] Just as the economic boom of the 1990s had fueled an enormous influx of illegal workers despite intensified policing efforts to keep them out, the Great Recession discouraged many new migrants from leaving home and even encouraged some to return. Low-wage immigrants were hit particularly hard by the economic downturn, especially in the construction sector.[95] Following an old historical pattern, as the jobs began to dry up so did the migration flow. There were an estimated 11.2 million unauthorized migrants in the country in 2010—more than half of them Mexican—down from a high of 12 million in 2007 but still higher than the 8.4 million in 2000, and triple the 1990 level of 3.5 million.[96]

Meanwhile, the Mexican side of the border had turned increasingly violent and dangerous, much of it fueled by mounting drug-related murders in Mexican border cities. The sharply rising death toll in Juarez, the city most heavily hit, made it one of the most dangerous places in the world. With much fanfare, Mexican President Felipe Calderón declared an all-out war on the country's major drug-trafficking organizations when he took office in 2006. But even though his military-led antidrug offensive weakened the Tijuana, Juarez, and Gulf trafficking organizations, these "successes" unintentionally created an opportunity for rival traffickers, and the ensuing disorganization, disruption, and competitive scramble to control turf, routes, and market share fueled an unprecedented wave of drug violence in Mexico—with most of the weapons that were used to carry out the killings having been smuggled in from the United States.[97]

Applauding Calderón's drug war offensive, Washington pledged $400 million in counterdrug military and police assistance for Mexico in 2008, and it took on an increasingly active behind-the-scenes role within Mexico. This included setting up a "fusion intelligence center" at a northern Mexican military base (modeled on similar centers in Iraq and Afghanistan for counterinsurgency purposes), providing military and police training for thousands of Mexican agents, and deploying CIA operatives and military contractors to Mexico to gather intelligence, assist in wiretaps and interrogations, and help plan raids and other operations.[98] In early 2011 the Pentagon also began to deploy high-altitude Global Hawk drones deep into Mexican territory on drug surveillance missions.[99] More than ever before, Mexico and the border became the front line of America's war on drugs.

Yet much to Mexico's frustration, Washington made only token efforts to curb the clandestine export of U.S. firearms that was arming Mexican drug gangs. Despite Mexico's complaints, there was little domestic political pressure within the United States—and there were

Figure 15.5 Drugs seized from a tunnel discovered under the California-Mexico border, 2011 (Immigration and Customs Enforcement).

plenty of political obstacles—to more intensively police and restrict bulk weapons sales (ranging from handguns to AK-47s) by thousands of loosely regulated gun dealers in Texas and elsewhere near the border. In late 2011, J. Dewey Webb, the special agent responsible for curbing gun smuggling in Texas for the Bureau of Alcohol Tobacco and Firearms, noted that "The United States is the easiest and cheapest place for drug traffickers to get their firearms."[100] Despite the proximity of the drug violence in Mexico and public anxiety about spillover (remarkably, U.S. border cities continued to have some of the lowest violent crime rates in the country), stopping the southbound flow of arms generated far less attention and concern than the northbound flow of drugs.[101]

Washington provided sophisticated surveillance technology and expertise to help Calderón target and remove a growing number of high-profile traffickers. But as had been the case in eliminating high-level Colombian traffickers in the 1990s, this did not translate into an overall reduction of drug trafficking; in fact, Mexican exports of heroin, marijuana, and methamphetamines to the United States were reportedly increasing at the end of the decade.[102] Rather than greatly reducing the drug flow, it seemed that the crackdown was doing more to fuel brutal competition within and between a growing number of rival smuggling organizations and creating a much more fluid and volatile—and therefore violent—market environment. Four criminal organizations dominated the trafficking of drugs into the United States when Calderón took office in 2006, but by 2011 there were seven—with the new traffickers even more willing and able to use violence than the old ones. The most trigger-happy and ruthless of the new groups, Los Zetas, was composed of former members of an elite U.S.-trained Mexican military unit.[103]

Every year, the drug killings in Mexico continued to mount. By mid-2012, drug-related deaths reached roughly fifty thousand since Calderon launched his antidrug offensive in 2006.[104] And there was no end in sight. Many Mexicans, suffering from drug war fatigue and fed up with the escalating violence, no doubt viewed the bloody battle to feed America's seemingly insatiable appetite for illicit drugs as yet another affirmation of the old Mexican saying "Poor Mexico, so far from God, so close to the United States."

EVEN AS THE U.S.-MEXICO border continued to be ground zero in America's campaign against the smuggling of people and drugs in the early twenty-first century, Washington also increasingly viewed these clandestine border crossings as part of a much larger, more ominous, and unprecedented globalized crime threat requiring a U.S.-led global response. In other words, the new challenge was not just a porous border but the shadowy underside of globalization more generally. Yet on closer inspection, one cannot help but get a strong sense of historical déjà vu. As detailed in the next chapter, there is at least as much continuity as transformation in this illicit globalization story—and certainly more than is conventionally recognized amid all the uproar over an allegedly new and rapidly growing danger. Indeed, it seems that no policy debate in Washington has been more devoid of historical memory, learning, and reflection.

16

America and Illicit Globalization in the Twenty-First Century

AMERICA IS UNDER SIEGE, or so we are told. Transnational organized crime "poses a significant and growing threat to national and international security, with dire implications for public safety, public health, democratic institutions, and economic stability," the White House declared in its 2011 *Strategy to Combat Transnational Crime: Addressing Converging Threats to National Security*.[1] Such dire pronouncements had been repeated in Washington policy circles since the 1990s, with U.S. Senator John Kerry exclaiming that America "must lead an international crusade" against a growing global crime threat.[2] Pundits similarly sounded the alarm bells. Jessica Mathews pointed to organized crime and trafficking as the dark side of a fundamental "power shift" away from governments; and Moises Naim boldly labeled the conflict between governments and global crime as "the new wars of globalization," with governments increasingly on the losing side.[3] Crime has gone global, Naim warned, "transforming the international system, upending the rules, creating new players, and reconfiguring power in international politics and economics."[4] International relations scholars echoed these sweeping claims of change, even calling transnational organized crime "perhaps *the* major threat to the world system."[5] One security scholar described transnational organized crime as "the HIV virus of the modern state, circumventing and breaking down the natural defenses of the body politic." Most states in the past "seemed to have the capacity" to keep this threat "under control," but this is "no longer so obviously the case."[6]

There are some common themes in these scary accounts of the illicit side of globalization. Globetrotting criminals, ranging from drug traffickers to migrant smugglers to money-launderers, are increasingly agile, sophisticated, organized, and technologically savvy. Governments, on the other hand, are increasingly overwhelmed, outsmarted, and outmaneuvered. And though the problem is portrayed as a global one, the United States is often depicted as the favorite target market of this new, unprecedented, and rapidly growing threat.

At first glance, this picture of the shadowy underside of globalization seems terrifyingly accurate. Traffickers *are* routinely defying borders, mocking laws, and corrupting and sometimes violently challenging government authorities. These concerns are confirmed in daily media stories and policy statements and reports, and resonate with the popular imagination. It is commonsensical, after all, that the same global transformations in communication, transportation, and finance that aid licit business also aid illicit business. Globalization reduces transaction costs for both licit and illicit market actors. As President Barack Obama put it in July 2011, "During the past fifteen years, technological innovation and globalization have proven to be an overwhelming force for good. However, transnational criminal organizations have taken advantage of our increasingly interconnected world to expand their illicit enterprises."[7]

True enough. But even though this gloomy portrait of illicit globalization contains many truths, it ultimately obscures more than it reveals. Most importantly, its neglect of the past grossly distorts our view of the present. Contrary to conventional wisdom, illicit globalization is not entirely new. Indeed, rather than a new threat to America, it is the continuation of an old American tradition. As we have seen, its starting point goes back not just years or decades but centuries, beginning with the growth of transoceanic commerce and the violation of rigid mercantilist trade restrictions.

So despite the anxious voices inside the beltway who warn us that "smugglers, traffickers, and copycats are hijacking the global economy,"[8] the reality is that these illicit actors have long been integral to the global economy and indeed helped to create it. Smugglers have frustrated government controls from the very start: the modern state emerged with the expansion of long-distance trade, and it is therefore little surprise that efforts to impose controls on such commerce would prove to be imperfect, at best. Evasion, diversion, and subversion were inevitable by-products of restrictive laws and their enforcement. The policing reach of the state has always been greater than the strength of its grip.

This final chapter in our long story evaluates today's conventional wisdom about illicit globalization through the prism of the American experience, past and present, highlighting patterns of continuity and change in America's centuries-old relationship with the world of clandestine commerce and speculating what this may mean for the future. Now, as in the past, this relationship is far more complex and double-edged than standard accounts would lead us to believe.

Continuity and Change

"Transnational organized crime" is the favored term to describe the illicit dimensions of globalization.[9] But it is also a frustratingly broad, vague, and fuzzy term. Many of those who use it tend to focus on large criminal organizations (often misleadingly labeled as "cartels") and mafialike leaders (often given colorful medieval-sounding names such as "crime lords" and "drug barons") rather than particular market sectors or activities. At base, much of what makes the business of organized crime transnational involves some form of profit-driven economic exchange across borders. How transnational, organized, and criminal the exchange is tends to depend on the legal and financial risks. For the most part, transnational organized crime is therefore merely a fancy new term for an old and familiar practice: smuggling. The speed, content, methods, and organization of smuggling have varied greatly across time and place; the basic activity itself has not fundamentally changed. Neither has the necessity for smugglers to go either through law enforcement via camouflage or corruption or around it via circuitous routes.

As in the past, smugglers today sneak in or take out whatever they can, in whatever way they can. This includes prohibited commodities, legal commodities that circumvent sanctions and embargoes or evade taxes and tariffs, stolen or counterfeit commodities, unauthorized migrants, and endangered species. Some of these smuggling activities are little more than a law enforcement nuisance (cross-border vehicle theft); some are obscure (the black market trade in bear bile), and others receive intense policy attention and media scrutiny (illicit drugs and human trafficking); but still others have serious environmental consequences (the outlawed trade in toxic waste) and security implications (sanctions busting and arms trafficking).

The extraordinary diversity of smuggling is illustrated by simply considering the thousands of seized items at New York's JFK Airport during the span of just a few days. They range from the predictable (Cuban cigars, fruits, meats, and vegetables) and fraudulent (counterfeit Tiffany jewelry, fake Viagra, pirated CDs, knock-off Louis Vuitton handbags) to the exotic (undeclared antique pistols, handbags made from endangered species skin) and bizarre (cow dung toothpaste, cow urine, deer blood, animal corpses for witchcraft rituals).[10] And this does not include the human trade, ranging from illicitly importing low-wage nannies, grape pickers, and sex workers to high-priced Cuban baseball players.[11]

At the same time, America is a favorite place for illicit traders from around the world to stash their ill-gotten gains. For all the U.S. finger-pointing at offshore tax havens and money-laundering centers such as the Cayman Islands, the state of Delaware is one of the easiest places in the world to hide money via shell companies, with the diverse clientele ranging from Serbian cigarette smugglers to Russian arms dealers to Fortune 500 corporations.[12]

Today's smugglers are as diverse as what is being smuggled, from disorganized to highly organized. In the case of drug smugglers, for instance, they include not only the everyday "mules" smuggling dope in their vehicle, luggage, or body (swallowing condoms filled with heroin or cocaine and tied shut with dental floss) but also grandmas smuggling in their meds as well as jocks smuggling in their steroids from Mexico and Canada. Smugglers range from self-smugglers (migrants sneaking across borders) to individuals smuggling goods for their own personal consumption, to independent and small-scale entrepreneurs, loose networks of transnational gangs, and highly developed and sophisticated criminal organizations.

Even though the global reach of some smuggling groups has accelerated with the integration of the global economy, the image of an octopuslike network of crime syndicates that runs the underworld through its expansive tentacles is a fiction invented by sensationalistic journalists, opportunistic politicians, and Hollywood scriptwriters. If this picture matched reality, the challenge to law enforcement would actually be far less difficult: one would need only to cut off the head of the octopus and the tentacles would die with it. Even the most developed and sophisticated smuggling schemes tend to be defined more by fragmentation and loose informal networks than by concentration and hierarchical organization.

The conventional account of illicit globalization repeatedly tells us that there has been a dramatic upsurge in the volume of illicit trade in the last few decades. This may well be true; after all, such trade would simply have to keep pace with the licit economy to grow at an impressive rate. But that does not mean this trade has necessarily increased as an overall percentage of global commerce. And indeed, the liberalization of trade in recent decades has sharply reduced incentives to engage in smuggling practices designed to evade taxes and tariffs, which were historically a driving force of illicit commerce. With the lowering of trade barriers as part of the process of globalization, smuggling is increasingly about evading prohibitions and bans rather than import duties. Behind this bifurcated trend, the United States has been the world's leading advocate of both market liberalization and selective market criminalization. So rather than an extreme example of "globalization out of control," the prevalence of illicit global commerce today partly reflects how limited and incomplete globalization actually is. In other words, smuggling would be defined away in a truly "borderless world" in which free trade and labor mobility reigned in all sectors of the economy.

Standard accounts of illicit globalization also tell us that borders and border defenses are increasingly overrun and overwhelmed—with the U.S.-Mexico line, the most important crossing point for illicit drugs and labor in the world, pointed to as a particularly glaring illustration. Calling for tougher border enforcement is therefore an easy political sell in Washington, and every administration is vulnerable to the charge that it is not doing enough to "secure the border." But we too often forget that America has always had leaky borders. As we saw in the previous chapter, smuggling across the southwestern border was a defining feature of the U.S.-Mexico relationship from the very start. The same is true of the U.S.-Canada border—though today this history is often forgotten, given all the attention to the southern border. And as was the case with smuggled Chinese in the late nineteenth century and smuggled booze in the 1920s, the northern border continues to be an important clandestine crossing point for people and drugs, including Chinese migrants, "Ecstasy" (MDMA) tablets, prescription pills, and high-potency British Columbian marijuana ("BC Bud").[13]

Moreover, we should remind ourselves that much of today's U.S.-Mexico border smuggling problem is self-created, an unintended consequence of past government actions. The "successful" U.S. crackdown on Colombian cocaine trafficking through the Caribbean and South Florida in the 1980s pushed the cocaine trade to the southwest and vastly increased the power and wealth of Mexican traffickers—with devastating consequences for Mexican society. Similarly, the increased sophistication, organization, and profitability of migrant smuggling across the border is largely a self-made problem: migrants used to have the option of smuggling themselves into the country, but with the dramatic tightening of border controls they now have little choice but to place their lives in the hands of professional smugglers. The border remains porous, but it is far more difficult and dangerous to cross than ever before. The fact that migrants keep crossing is made possible by the hiring of smugglers but ultimately reflects Washington's unwillingness to seriously target domestic employers. Not surprisingly, unauthorized entries have slowed substantially in recent years with the slowdown in the economy and reduced employer demand.

The ability to weed out illicit from licit border crossings has long depended on the nature of the smuggled commodity; the ease of production, concealment, and transport; the availability of legal substitutes; and the nature and level of consumer demand. It is little surprise, therefore, that law enforcement has been least effective in suppressing the illicit drug trade. Drugs have all the traits of the ideal smuggled commodity: high-value and low-weight; compact; easy to produce, transport, and hide; and having intense consumer demand requiring constant replenishment. These characteristics also apply to the most lethal and addictive legal drug—tobacco—which is smuggled in large quantities to evade high taxes rather than bans. It is striking to note that global cigarette exports are about one-third higher than imports, with the mysteriously missing third explained by diversion via smuggling channels. America's favorite brand, Marlboro, is also one of the world's most smuggled brands—with Philip Morris at one point paying the European Union $1.25 billion to settle charges of complicity.[14]

Policing campaigns often fail to eliminate the targeted illicit trade but nevertheless function as an alternative form of regulation: as we have seen again and again throughout the nation's history, the method, intensity, and focus of law enforcement significantly shape the location and form of smuggling, the size and structure of the smuggling operation, and its cost and profitability. For instance, U.S. efforts to restrict Chinese immigration in the late nineteenth century prompted both a sharp increase in Chinese smuggling and a geographic shift in clandestine entry to land borders, and this dynamic was repeated again a century later. A similar pattern has long been evident in the geographic displacement effects of U.S.-promoted drug eradication and interdiction campaigns—for example, pushing the heroin trade from Turkey to Mexico in the 1970s, and pushing cocaine trafficking from the Caribbean to Mexico in later years (much to the delight of Mexican smugglers).

We should therefore not lose sight of the fact that, even if not always terribly effective, it is the very existence of government controls and efforts to tighten them that makes it necessary for illicit traders to adapt and devise such creative and elaborate evasive maneuvers. Some smuggling activities are so profitable—and sometimes violent—precisely because governments impose and enforce prohibitions. Prohibitions can therefore function as price supports, which can attract new market entrants willing to accept the occupational hazards so long as consumer demand remains high. Even corruption can be considered a peculiar form of regulation, the equivalent of an informal tax on illicit trade that smugglers pay for non-enforcement of the law. But instead of filling government coffers, the corruption tax lines private pockets.

As has always been the case, the sheer volume of border crossings means that governments prioritize some smuggling concerns more than others. In this regard, the United States has shaped the global anti-smuggling agenda more than any other nation. No country has been more aggressive and more successful in exporting its favored prohibitions and policing practices.[15] When one digs beneath the surface of many United Nations and other multilateral anti-smuggling initiatives, one inevitably finds U.S. funds, personnel, model legislation, and diplomatic endeavors. But U.S. attention and concern is highly selective and uneven. Washington has persistently blocked UN attempts to impose more stringent controls on small-arms trafficking—and the political muscle of the NRA has made sure there is no tampering with notoriously loose domestic gun laws. The United States spends billions of dollars trying to stop the smuggling of drugs into the country while doing relatively little to impede the smuggling of guns out.[16]

Similarly, compare Washington's crackdown on the unauthorized entry of migrants to its muted response to the entry of black-market babies. Guatemalan infants, even if obtained through shady channels, have been far more welcomed than Guatemalan workers. From 1997 to 2006, the number of Guatemalan children adopted by Americans increased by some 400 percent, to more than 4,500 per year. Guatemala, long known to have the world's worst corruption and fraud record in foreign adoptions, finally put a stop to U.S. adoptions in 2008 in an effort to curb child trafficking.

The baby smuggling problem extends well beyond Guatemala. In Cambodia, an American baby broker collected $9 million in adoption fees by arranging eight hundred adoptions of Cambodian children between 1997 and 2001. American investigators later charged that the broker was complicit in purchasing, defrauding, coercing, or stealing Cambodian children and was also complicit in fabricating child identity documents. Although buying, stealing, and trafficking children across borders—what one legal scholar has dubbed "child laundering"—is a global problem, the United States imports more infants than all other countries combined.[17]

The United States is also one of the world's largest importers of smuggled antiquities, which is a relatively low priority on Washington's anti-smuggling agenda. The United States has only implemented part of the 1970 UNESCO Convention on the Means of Prohibiting and Preventing the Illicit Import, Export and Transfer of Cultural Property. And it was not until 2008 that the U.S. finally signed on to the 1954 Hague Convention for the Protection of Cultural Property in the Event of Armed Conflict. Not only was the looting of the National Museum in Baghdad part of the collateral damage from the 2003 U.S. military invasion of Iraq, but hundreds of stolen Iraqi artifacts turned up in the United States.[18]

Though old European imperial powers, such as England and France, acquired their vast antiquities collections through conquest and colonialism—proudly on display at the British Museum and the Louvre—American collectors in the postcolonial era have had to rely more on smuggling channels. And it is not just private collectors who have been implicated, but also leading museums such as the J. Paul Getty Museum and the Metropolitan Museum of Art. For instance, Greek and Italian authorities charged Marion True, the curator of the Getty, with antiquities theft. In the aftermath of a smuggling scandal that implicated the Getty and other major U.S. museums, forty looted masterpieces were returned to Italy between 2007 and 2011.[19]

The United States profoundly influences not only which illicit trades are—and are not—at the top of the international anti-smuggling agenda, but also how they are policed. Washington's approach to suppressing the trafficking of women, for example, has focused far more on criminalizing the traffic than protecting the human rights of those being trafficked. And as was the case with the "white slavery" moral panic of a century ago, the subplot of much of today's American-led international antitrafficking campaign is an attempt to suppress prostitution more generally. The United States also continues to be the leading promoter of the supply-side-focused global drug prohibition regime, though there are signs that the international consensus is weakening.[20] The State Department even hands out annual report cards grading countries on how well they're doing in fighting human trafficking and the international drug trade.[21]

It is important to remind ourselves that the cross-border economic flows that the United States and other governments define as illicit in the first place has changed with shifting political winds and social norms. Through their law-making and law-enforcing authority, governments set the rules of the game even if they cannot entirely control the play and outcome. Changes in laws and the intensity with which those laws are enforced have profound effects on the incidence and profitability of smuggling. New laws turn once-legal trades into illegal trades, resulting in a sudden and sometimes significant rise in smuggling. Indeed, a century ago much of what today preoccupies U.S. border inspectors—most notably drug trafficking, by far the largest and most profitable illicit global trade—was not even criminalized. And some of today's illicit trades were criminalized only relatively recently. Illicit globalization is therefore not only about more expansive transnational crime but also more ambitious prohibitions.

Take, for instance, the multibillion-dollar illicit wildlife trade that has flourished in recent decades in the wake of national and international efforts to protect endangered species.[22] Animal smuggling across America's borders in earlier eras primarily meant cattle rustling and evading quarantines and tariffs; today it mostly means violating bans on the trade in endangered wildlife. This includes the poaching of tens of thousands of endangered Mexican parrots for the U.S. market (the majority of which die during capture or in transit), yet this remains a largely overlooked border smuggling problem, given all the attention on the smuggling of drugs and migrants.[23] And as in the case of drugs and migrants, Mexico is both a major source country and also a key transit point for U.S.-bound illicit wildlife trafficking from all over the world.[24] Wildlife trade bans are imperfect, unevenly enforced, and widely violated, yet some rare species would no doubt be extinct in their absence. At the same time, all the focus on stopping smuggling distracts from the larger threat to wildlife: habitat destruction and human encroachment.

The methods of animal smuggling today are both comical and tragic. In one incident not long ago, inspectors at Miami International Airport discovered, crammed into a single large suitcase arriving from Buenos Aires, five boa constrictors, seven rainbow boas, seven parrot snakes, two rattlesnakes, 107 Chaco tortoises, 103 red-footed tortoises, seventy-six tartaruga turtles, ninety tree frogs, twenty tarantulas, ten scorpions, twenty red tegu lizards, and a handful of other lizards.[25] And this was just one suitcase belonging to a low-level smuggler from Argentina. Other animal smugglers have tried more creative schemes. At Los Angeles International Airport, a man tried to sneak in two pygmy monkeys stuffed down his pants. Somehow he had escaped notice by the flight attendants on the long trip from Asia. In another case, a man attempted to smuggle in reptiles from South Asia in his prosthetic leg.[26] Other smugglers have opted to illicitly ship via the mail service—postal workers in Los Angeles found three hundred live tarantulas in one package arriving from Germany. Investigators later claimed that the smuggler had made about $300,000 in the illicit tarantula trade.[27]

The flourishing illicit international wildlife trade is a particularly striking illustration of the relatively recent criminalization of a previously legal trade. But the opposite is also evident. We should recall that some of today's licit trades were previously criminalized and considered a serious transnational crime threat. Most notably, alcohol-smuggling networks that linked the United States to international suppliers created an enormous policing challenge during the Prohibition era, and it was then eliminated with the stroke of a pen with the repeal of the Volstead Act in 1933. Corruption related to illicit trade has never been as serious a problem in America as it was during the Prohibition years, when it seemed as if entire police forces were bought off. At the height of Prohibition, the U.S.-Canada border was a bootlegging superhighway rivaling the smuggling role of the U.S.-Mexico border today. Similarly, much of what the United States classified as "obscene" material and considered a major smuggling problem during the purity crusades of the late nineteenth and early twentieth centuries—ranging from sexual images to racy novels to condoms—is now legal, thanks to court rulings rolling back the Comstock-era laws.

If these historical episodes are any guide, it is worth contemplating that illicit trade today may be licit trade tomorrow. Take the case of marijuana, by far the most popular illicit drug in America. Enforcing marijuana prohibition takes up much of the time and energy of U.S. border agents; the vast majority of border drug busts involve relatively small marijuana seizures. Marijuana law violations are also responsible for hundreds of thousands of U.S. arrests every year, more than for all other illicit drugs combined. According to an October 2011 Gallup poll, a record 50 percent of Americans favor legalizing pot, which is up from 12 percent in 1969, when the first Gallup poll on the subject was conducted. A 2010 Gallup survey found that 70 percent of Americans favored making it possible for doctors to prescribe marijuana for pain and suffering. The proliferation of "medical marijuana" in some states reflects this softening public attitude; there are reportedly more marijuana dispensaries in California than Starbucks coffee shops.[28] Even the television evangelist Pat Robertson has called for legalizing marijuana.[29] If hard economic times and shrinking budgets persist, state leaders may become increasingly tempted by the prospect of new revenue generated by taxing marijuana. It is worth recalling that the Great Depression dealt the final deathblow to alcohol prohibition, when politicians suddenly became more eager to tax booze than to police it.

And just as illicit trade today may be licit trade tomorrow, the American historical experience reminds us that the opposite is also conceivable: licit trade may become illicit. Just as few people during the eighteenth century could have imagined a global prohibition on the slave trade, so too is it difficult to imagine an entirely legitimate trade today being banned. Consider the case of tobacco. Full prohibition seems like a remote possibility in the immediate future. Yet tobacco use in America is increasingly stigmatized and causes far more deaths every year than all illegal drugs combined. Tobacco use is the leading cause of preventable deaths in dozens of countries. Regardless of the legal fate of tobacco, it is important to recall that many of the illicit trades that preoccupy U.S. law enforcers today were legal a century ago—and therefore looking ahead, it is not difficult to imagine that some trades that will be prohibited a century from now are legal today.

The Technology Factor

A dominant theme in standard narratives of illicit globalization is the crime-enabling role of new technologies, such as the Internet.[30] This is certainly important. But it is also simply the latest—and not necessarily the most significant—chapter in an old story. Law enforcement officials in the United States and elsewhere have long bemoaned the crime-facilitating effects of new technologies, and they have repeatedly used this as a justification to expand their policing powers and reach.[31] It is far from evident that recent technological innovations have had a more transformative impact upon illicit commerce than in earlier eras, and indeed the impact may be considerably less. Consider the profound effect of the steamship, the railway, the telegraph, the telephone, the automobile, and the airplane in enhancing cross-border mobility and communication, both licit and illicit.[32] These technologies proliferated long before globalization even became a buzzword.

And it is important to realize that rarely do new technologies actually create new crimes. Rather, they simply provide a new means to commit old crimes—such as theft and vandalism, in the case of the Internet.

Technology is also double-edged, not just challenging but also aiding governments. It is certainly not a one-way street in which law evaders always have the edge and an ever-increasing technological advantage. Consider how the development of photography and fingerprinting revolutionized criminal investigations and long-distance police cooperation.[33] Photography and other technological innovations have long played a key role in the development of government-issued travel documents, including the introduction of the modern passport (which was not required to enter the United States until World War I).[34] The invention of the telephone enabled faster and more efficient communication between smugglers, but as we saw during the Prohibition years, this also created the opening to justify a controversial new law enforcement weapon: wiretapping. And the growing use of the automobile for bootlegging provided the legal rationale to give American police the power to stop and search vehicles without a warrant. In more recent years, computers have certainly aided licit and illicit business alike, but this has created an opportunity and rationale for more invasive law enforcement: American border inspectors are now allowed to search not only luggage but also laptops and other electronic storage devices, raising yet another concern about the erosion of Fourth Amendment protections (protections created by the country's founders with fresh memories of the hated searches carried out by British customs agents).[35] Similarly, the proliferation of GPS tracking devices facilitates both legal and illegal trade, but they also provide a new method of surveillance; their use to monitor and track suspect vehicles without a warrant is the latest test for the courts of the prohibition against unreasonable searches.[36]

The role of new technologies in enabling law enforcement is, if anything, growing, with the United States at the forefront of this trend. Even as new technologies facilitate illicit border crossings, these advances also greatly increase government tracking and surveillance capabilities. New communication and transportation technologies have also dramatically lowered the costs and increased the intensity of transgovernmental law enforcement networks, allowing American authorities to interact with their foreign counterparts more rapidly and frequently. In short, we greatly understate the degree to which the same technological transformations that have facilitated the globalization of crime also facilitate the globalization of crime control.

New technologies will continue to increase government capacity to track and police the cross-border flow of people, cargo, money, and information. The digitization of U.S. border controls and the creation of "virtual borders," for instance, has ranged from the use of more expansive and sophisticated databases for "data mining" and computer tracking systems for prescreening cargo and passenger manifests to the creation of more tamper-resistant travel documents and "smart" IDs with biometric identifiers (such as digital fingerprints and facial and retinal scans). Cargo inspections traditionally done at ports of entry have also increasingly been pushed outward through prescreening and preclearance, facilitated by the development of "smart containers" and the use of new cargo-tagging and tracking devices.

Many commercial activities facilitated by new technologies, such as electronic banking, also leave digital fingerprints that government authorities can detect and trace.[37] Illicit online financial transactions are often constrained by the need for electronic payment, which can leave a record. This is partly the reason so many illicit activities in cyberspace—ranging from circulation of pirated music to child porn—involve a barter exchange economy based on file sharing rather than profit-driven commercial transactions (no wonder, then, that the widely reported claim that Internet child porn is a $20 billion a year business turned out to be bogus[38]). Cybercops have failed to eliminate these electronic smuggling activities, but they have succeeded in taking some of the profit out of them. At the same time, the persistence of these illicit online transactions furnishes the rationale for more police investigations and sting operations in cyberspace. This has included setting up a government "Cyber-smuggling Center," an outgrowth of U.S customs initiatives against child pornography in the 1990s.

The very anonymity of the Web that facilitates illicit exchange and makes prosecution difficult also makes it hard for cybersmugglers and other cybercriminals to differentiate between an accomplice and an informant or undercover cop. This vulnerability, for example, has made the online "carding" business (trading stolen credit card numbers) a high-risk business, as "carding forums" are increasingly infiltrated by cybercops—with one major carding forum even turning out to be a law enforcement sting operation. And this, in turn, has pushed cybersmuggling deeper into the digital underworld.[39]

Policing cyberspace will continue to develop as a new frontier of anti-smuggling initiatives that coexists and intermingles with traditional policing.[40] Recent U.S. cyberpolicing initiatives include targeting major search engines for facilitating illegal online transactions, such as unauthorized downloading of music and movies, and allowing advertising for illegally acquired prescription drugs. In August 2011 Google agreed to a $500 million settlement for its failure to turn away advertising from illicit businesses, notably online Canadian pharmacies that use Google to place targeted ads pushing illicitly imported prescription drugs.[41] In January 2012, the Justice Department and the FBI announced a grand jury indictment against seven individuals connected to the popular website Megaupload, an Internet service that allows users to anonymously share large files. They were charged with operating an international criminal conspiracy responsible for hundreds of millions of dollars in online copyright violations. The founder of the site, Kim Dotcom (previously Kim Schmitz), along with three others, were arrested in New Zealand. The international hacker collective Anonymous quickly retaliated by "taking down" the website of the Justice Department, along with the websites of the Motion Picture Association of America and the Recording Music Industry Association of America.[42] According to Cisco Systems' Visual Networking Index, more than a fourth of all online activity involves using peer-to-peer and locker sites—mostly for illegal sharing and downloading.[43]

The difficulty of carrying out a full-blown crackdown against online piracy was dramatically demonstrated by the backlash against two proposed bills in Congress that initially had considerable bipartisan support: the Stop Online Piracy Act (in the House of Representatives) and the Protect Intellectual Property Act (in the Senate). In a startling display of the new ability to harness the power of the Internet to both protest and lobby, free-speech advocates teamed up with tech companies, websites, and broadband service providers to derail legislative initiatives supported by Hollywood, the entertainment industry, and the U.S. Chamber of Commerce. The outpouring of criticism, ranging from Internet activists to web powerhouses, charged that the proposed new laws were too broad and heavy-handed, would stifle creativity and innovation, and would lead to censorship. The protests included Google placing a black banner across its home page and the English-language version of Wikipedia going dark on January 18, 2012. Key political supporters of the legislation quickly pulled out, and the White House also signaled concerns. It was a stunning turn of events and a setback for traditional media companies, but the political battle over online piracy was just getting started.[44]

In some cases, scientific and technological breakthroughs not only facilitate illicit trade but can also enable entirely new types of illicit trade. For instance, the black market for human organs, especially kidneys, has been made possible by advances in organ-transplant procedures. Yet we should keep in mind that future scientific advances in the development of artificial organs could greatly reduce black market demand. New scientific procedures may also enable DNA theft and illicit cloning as a form of smuggling in the not-too-distant future—but this can also be expected to open up new forms of policing through more advanced genetic testing and tracing. One can also imagine the development of synthetic cocaine or heroin—as part of the growing trend toward use of synthetic drugs—that could radically shake up (and potentially domesticate) the international drug trade. At the same time, scientists are reportedly working on an "addiction vaccine," which could greatly curtail licit and illicit drug markets alike.[45] And even if this proves illusive, scientists will likely continue to unlock the mysteries of addiction in ways that should improve treatment. Advances in science and technology can also create legal substitutes that inhibit illicit trade, as evident in the invention of Viagra and its potential as a substitute for illicitly trafficked animal parts traditionally used as aphrodisiacs. At the same time, the predictable downside has been to also create a thriving new black market in Viagra, including counterfeits.[46]

Complicity

Too often gone unnoticed in conventional accounts of illicit globalization is that governments at times create and exploit illicit trade networks to pursue their own interests. So rather than illicit globalization simply threatening governments, it is also sometimes harnessed by governments for their own ends. Although attracting the most attention, state-sponsored illicit trade is not restricted to a handful of "rogue states" such as Myanmar (formerly Burma) and North Korea. In the U.S. case, illicit finance and gunrunning have long been closely tied to covert operations. The Cold War, not globalization, provided the most important impetus. The CIA exploited illicit networks for a variety of geopolitical purposes in the Cold War years, including to fund and supply insurgents around the globe, from Southeast Asia to Afghanistan to Central America. At times this involved turning a blind eye to the drug-trafficking activities of anticommunist allies. Though the details are murky and enmeshed in controversy, it is clear that security imperatives sometimes collided with and trumped concerns about drug trafficking.[47]

Washington's strategic use of illicit trade networks extended into the post–Cold War era, ranging from encouraging and facilitating arms embargo busting in the Balkans in the 1990s to tolerating and even supporting drug-connected Afghans allied in the fight against the Taliban and al-Qaeda in more recent years. For instance, Ahmed Wali Karzai, the brother of the Afghan president, was widely suspected of ties to the drug trade before he was assassinated, but he was also allegedly on the CIA payroll.[48]

These contemporary cases receive the most attention, but this is in some ways an old story—a modern-day variant of a practice that dates back in American history at least as far as the War of 1812, when U.S. military forces led by Andrew Jackson made a short-term alliance of convenience with the band of pirate-smugglers led by Pierre and Jean Laffite in repelling the British in the Battle of New Orleans. The Laffites were treated as heroes and granted presidential pardons as a reward for their patriotic assistance—and they then promptly returned to their illicit business activities.

U.S. intelligence connections to illicit traders have repeatedly generated damaging blowback effects. Again, this is an old story. Let out of jail as a reward for his cooperation and collaboration with U.S. Naval Intelligence during World War II, the New York mobster Charles "Lucky" Luciano was deported to Italy, but he then became a leading heroin supplier to the U.S. market. Similarly, the CIA covertly aided

Corsican gangs in Marseille against France's leftist labor movement, but these same gangs then set up the famed "French Connection," which became the main heroin supplier to the United States in the 1950s and 1960s.

Or take the case of the Haqqani network in Afghanistan and Pakistan, whose criminal activities include the smuggling of drugs, precious gems, and stolen lumber. This network enjoyed covert CIA backing in the 1980s in fighting Soviet forces, but in 2011 it was responsible for orchestrating a bold daylong attack on the American embassy in Kabul and was described as the most dangerous security threat to U.S. forces in Afghanistan. As the *New York Times* put it, in the 1980s they were supplied with U.S. missiles; now they are the targets of CIA missiles. Texas Representative Charlie Wilson, whose support for the Mujahedeen was the subject of the Hollywood film *Charlie Wilson's War*, had even described the elder Haqqani leader, Jalaluddin Haqqani, as "goodness personified."[49]

A very different sort of government complicity in illicit trade involves intellectual property theft. The United States and other industrial powers are understandably frustrated that China has been so resistant to external pressure to more aggressively crack down on counterfeiting and pirating intellectual property, including knockoffs ranging from Luis Vuitton handbags to fake Rolex watches, which one can find just as easily on Canal Street in New York or Santee Alley in Los Angeles as in Silk Alley in Beijing.[50] For many reasons beyond corruption, it seems that it is simply not in China's immediate interests to curb such illicit business practices. But some historical perspective is useful here. As we saw earlier, the U.S. government tolerated and even encouraged intellectual piracy and technology smuggling during the country's initial industrialization process. Theft and smuggling were integral to America's early economic development strategy. China today in some ways is merely following in America's footsteps, albeit in an age when industrial espionage and other forms of intellectual property theft can take place via the Internet.[51] If the past is any guide to the future, it is possible that China will become a serious advocate of intellectual property protection only when it has more of its own intellectual property to protect—just as was the case of the United States once it became an industrial powerhouse.

Intellectual piracy in nineteenth-century America extended well beyond illicit technology transfers. American authors and filmmakers today are of course upset that bootleg copies of their books and films almost immediately make it to the black market in China and elsewhere. For instance, forged editions of Bill Clinton's autobiography *My Life* quickly appeared in Chinese, filled with glaring editorial alterations, including Clinton confessing his admiration for Mao.[52] The United States has been at the forefront of international efforts to push other countries to crack down on intellectual property theft. Yet in the nineteenth century it was British authors such as Charles Dickens who were outraged by the widespread copying of their works in America without their authorization—and the unwillingness of the U.S. government to do anything about it. The American copyright law of 1831 was silent on the issue of international literary piracy, and this did not change until 1891. It was not until America's own authors (notably among them Mark Twain) became victims of such theft that the country began to promote emerging international copyright standards.

The Conflict Connection

The illicit side of globalization is also increasingly blamed for fueling contemporary armed conflicts, and vice versa. Indeed, the link between illicit commerce and conflict is considered a defining attribute of "new wars," from the Balkans to West Africa.[53] But despite the label, the connection between illicit trade and conflict is not a post–Cold War invention. It goes back not just decades but centuries. One need only look to the early American historical experience: much to the dismay of the British imperial authorities, illicit "trading with the enemy" kept French forces clandestinely supplied by American colonial merchants during the Seven Years War, and transatlantic smuggling kept George Washington's Continental Army supplied during the American War of Independence. Much to the delight of the British, American colonial merchants illicitly traded with the enemy and helped keep English forces supplied during the War of 1812, and Confederate cotton smuggling helped keep English mills supplied during the American Civil War. Much is made of the importance of "conflict commodities" in sustaining recent conflicts, from cocaine in Colombia to so-called blood diamonds in Sierra Leone. But few of today's illicit exports from conflict zones rival the importance of Confederate cotton—we could call it "blood cotton"—in fueling a war that cost more American lives than any other conflict in U.S. history.

Then, as now, it was often difficult to clearly differentiate between greed and grievance in motivating rebellion. There is certainly no evidence to suggest that today's insurgents are more profit-driven than some of their American predecessors; one need only examine the large and lucrative privateering business—which the British defined as piracy because they did not recognize the legal authority of the rebels to commission privateering vessels—during the American War of Independence to realize how much the profit motive can contribute to a revolutionary cause. The grievances were real, but so too were the fortunes made from war.

Illicit international trading networks are also frequently blamed for undermining UN sanctions, most powerfully dramatized by large-scale embargo busting by Serbia and Iraq in the 1990s.[54] But no contemporary sanctions episode has been as ambitious—or as widely violated—as Thomas Jefferson's self-imposed embargo on American trade with the rest of the world. Designed to punish European powers by denying them American exports, Jefferson's ill-fated embargo was instead massively (and sometimes violently) evaded from within. The illicit trade was so blatant and defiant of federal authority in some places that Jefferson called it an insurrection.

Illicit trade in recent years is also blamed for impeding and complicating postwar reconstruction in places such as Bosnia and Kosovo. But long forgotten is that this was also true for the United States in the aftermath of the Revolutionary War. The very smuggling practices that aided the War of Independence turned into an obstacle for the newborn American state. The powerful legacy of colonial smuggling contributed to merchant resistance to centralized state authority and regulation of commerce. Smuggling now undermined American rather than British revenue collection and greatly complicated U.S. border management and foreign relations. This was a particularly serious problem for the nascent federal government, given that most of its revenue derived from duties imposed on imports.

Illicit trade was therefore a major challenge to early American state making—just as it is for state-making efforts around the globe today. At the same time, concerns about smuggling stimulated government growth and the creation of a border management infrastructure, notably the establishment of the customs service as one of the first pillars of the federal government. Efforts to combat pirates and embargo busters also contributed to the early development of the navy. In other words, illicit trade and related activities were double-edged, both undermining and building up the new American state. The same is true today, suggesting more continuity with the past than is typically recognized. We should be careful not to overstate or misinterpret the historical parallels, but neither should they be glossed over.

BRINGING IN HISTORY TO reevaluate illicit globalization in the early twenty-first century is crucial for a number of reasons: because it is so conspicuously absent from contemporary debates about transnational crime, because it corrects for the hubris of the present and the common tendency to view recent developments as entirely new and unprecedented, and because it helps us make sense of why we are where we are and even where we might be headed. Today's efforts to secure America's borders are part and parcel of historical processes that date back centuries, when Britain deployed substantial naval resources in an ill-fated effort to suppress illicit colonial trade, and the newborn U.S. federal government tried to impose some semblance of control over its vast land and water borders. The depth and extent of contemporary anti-smuggling efforts would have been unimaginable to U.S. border enforcers a century and more ago, but the basic challenges would not.

As has always been the case, there are inherent limits to how much we can deter, detect, and interdict unauthorized flows of goods and people across our borders, especially while maintaining an open society and keeping borders open for legal trade and travel. An average of nearly a million people; more than sixty thousand truck, rail, and sea containers; and about a quarter-million privately owned vehicles legally entered the United States *every day* in 2010. That same year, more than $2 trillion in legal imports crossed our borders. Facilitating this enormous volume of licit border crossings while attempting to enforce laws against illicit crossings is and will remain an inherently cumbersome and frustrating task. Reconciling the imperatives of globalization with the domestic pressures for tighter border enforcement will no doubt continue to present a hugely challenging policy conundrum, placing great strain on the nation's gatekeepers.

But this predicament need not lead to more collective hyperventilating about seemingly out-of-control borders and illicit globalization gone amok. We need to take a deep breath. The sky is not falling. Accounts of illicit globalization that suggest otherwise are not only overblown but can lead to counterproductive policy prescriptions. Urgent calls to "do something" to "regain control" provide ammunition for politicians and bureaucrats to justify high-profile and expensive crackdowns that may be politically popular but that ultimately fail. It can also contribute to growing calls to further securitize and militarize anti-smuggling efforts at home and abroad, regardless of the effectiveness of using military resources for law enforcement tasks. The temptation to do so has increased considerably in the wake of the September 11 terrorist attacks, as is evident in the growing convergence between counterterrorism and countersmuggling missions. Failure to find the smuggled "nuke in a box" is the ultimate nightmare scenario, however unlikely it may be.[55] But whether that smuggling nightmare—we could call it "catastrophic smuggling"—ever becomes a reality will depend more on intelligence gathering and international cooperation than on random border searches.

Meanwhile, some American anti-smuggling initiatives continue to generate enormous collateral damage, particularly the campaigns to suppress the smuggling of people and drugs. The tightening of immigration controls has prompted migrant smugglers to turn to more daring and dangerous border-crossing strategies, leading to hundreds of migrant deaths per year. Further barricading the border has substituted for repairing a deeply dysfunctional immigration system.[56] The American-led global antidrug campaign has also contributed to extraordinary levels of crime, violence, corruption, and other ills. These supply-focused policing initiatives endlessly chase the symptoms rather than the source of the problem at home. Blaming foreign drug traffickers and migrant smugglers is politically easier than confronting America's twin addictions to mind-altering substances and cheap migrant labor.

It is perhaps no coincidence that the United States, the world's leading promoter of the war on drugs, is also the world's leading jailer. With about 5 percent of the world's population, America has about 25 percent of the world's incarcerated population. Indeed, it incarcerates more people for drug law violations than Western Europe incarcerates for all offenses combined. The number of people in jail for drug law violations in the United States shot up from around forty thousand in 1980 to about half a million by 2010. Like the British in their crusade against the illicit slave trade in the nineteenth century, the United States leads a crusade of sorts against drugs—but whereas the former was about freeing people, the war on drugs is about locking them up, with African Americans a disproportionate number of those behind bars.[57]

Battles over illicit trade will no doubt continue to profoundly shape America and its engagement with its neighbors and the rest of the world in the twenty-first century. The particular smuggling activities and policing priorities will surely shift over time, as they always have, but it is safe to predict that America's centuries-old illicit trading tradition will remain alive and well.

EPILOGUE

LET'S RETURN BRIEFLY to the place where our smuggling story began: my adopted hometown of Providence, Rhode Island, which played such a prominent role in illicit trade during the colonial era and early years of the new republic. Let's start in my undergraduate lecture class at Brown on "The Politics of the Illicit Global Economy." I ask students how many of them have ever bought counterfeit goods; a majority of hands go up. I ask how many are right now wearing a knock-off product; a few hands go up. I then ask how many have illegally downloaded movies or music—and almost all hands go up, which is perhaps to be expected, given that all they have to do is type "download music for free" in Google to find links to illegal copies of all sorts of entertainment.

Of course, illegally buying and consuming alcohol before reaching the legal age of twenty-one—facilitated by the underground trade in fake IDs—is so common and taken for granted that I don't even have to ask my students for a show of hands. I also don't ask them about illegal drugs. I already know the answer. The campus newspaper conducts a regular substance use poll. In one poll more than 40 percent of the students polled indicated they had used marijuana that semester;[1] marijuana is apparently more widely used on campus than tobacco.[2] Students also illegally buy or sell prescription pills; Adderall and Ritalin are particularly popular.[3]

I also don't ask my students from immigrant families about their legal status or how they or their parents got into the United States. Again, as the campus newspaper reports, Brown has its own unauthorized immigrant student population—not to mention an unknown number of immigrant employees who have at some point resorted to using fraudulent papers.[4]

Yet none of this should lead us to frown upon Brown alone for such behavior. Far from it. Pick any university across the country and you will find similar stories. Look hard enough and dig deep enough, and you will inevitably find traces of all sorts of smuggling in all sorts of places. Brown, like other institutions of higher education, is a smuggler university within a smuggler nation embedded in a smuggler world. Indeed, it has always been so; a founder of the university, after all, was perhaps Rhode Island's richest smuggler. John Brown would no doubt be proud that the smuggler tradition remains alive and well. He would also certainly find some of today's smuggling activities bewildering, since there were no drug prohibitions in his day and nothing remotely resembling pirated music recordings and knock-off Gucci bags—though pirated industrial technology would certainly be familiar, given that his brother Moses and others in his family invested quite a bit in it and played a role in America's early industrialization.

John Brown would also notice that Rhode Island is no longer the smuggling hub it was during his heyday. Even if Rhode Island still dabbles in illicit commerce and cannot shake off its old reputation for corruption and shady business dealings (*Newsweek* has labeled it the state with the highest per capita corruption in the country[5]) it is now merely a bit player in the world of smuggling compared to its early history. In the early years, Rhode Island's fiercely independent merchants smuggled in West Indies molasses to manufacture rum and later illicitly imported British technology and machinists to produce textiles, helping to launch the American industrial revolution. They were also leading slave traffickers in flagrant defiance of state and federal laws. But the distilleries and mills are long gone, as is the African slave trade. Like my students, Rhode Islanders now participate in the smuggling economy mostly as consumers rather than producers or traders.

John Brown the illicit slave trader would also surely be startled to see that a black woman had recently served as president of the university he helped found. The slave trade that he so defiantly defended forcibly brought to America the ancestors of Ruth Simmons—the first African American president of an Ivy League institution, whose office was located in a university building partly built by slave labor. Simmons was praised for forming a Steering Committee on Slavery and Justice to examine the university's early links to slavery and slave trafficking, including John Brown's role. Yet Simmons was also the subject of controversy when it was reported that, as a board member of Goldman Sachs—the now infamous firm that paid a $550 million fine in 2010 to settle federal securities fraud charges[6]—she accepted millions of dollars in stock options and approved millions more in controversial bonuses for its widely reviled top executives at a time when the nation was undergoing the worst financial meltdown since the Great Depression. Simmons's role at Goldman Sachs raised eyebrows across campus, provoked outrage in the *Providence Journal*, and drew the scrutiny of the business page of the *New York Times*.[7] She nevertheless survived the episode remarkably unscathed, and is widely celebrated as Brown's most successful president.

Certainly in comparison, my students involved as consumers in the smuggling economy are mere amateurs; yet they are the ones who have violated the law. And that brings me to my final point. Even though America very much remains a smuggler nation (along with its counterpart, the ever-expanding police nation) it seems clear that curbing reckless behavior in the licit side of the economy is the country's most formidable challenge today.[8] The policing face of the state, while increasingly prominent, is noticeably selective in who and what it targets. The Securities and Exchange Commission is a tiny player in the massive federal criminal justice bureaucracy. Despite the intensity of the financial crisis and its aftershocks, policing Wall Street remains a half-hearted sideshow compared to policing border smuggling. It is far easier, after all, to go after drug couriers and smuggled migrants than the financial speculators who made such extraordinary profits in the years leading up to the financial crisis. John Brown, who loathed government interference and made his fortune by blurring the lines between licit and illicit business, would be envious.

NOTES

Introduction

1. This interactive dynamic is an adaptation and variation of Charles Tilly's notion that "states make war and war makes states." See Charles Tilly, *Coercion, Capital, and European States: AD 990–1992* (Oxford: Blackwell, 1992).
2. The relevant historical literature is enormous, but most works tend to focus more narrowly on a particular commodity or smuggling activity, specific historical events and limited time periods, or a geographically confined place or area. Some of the literature focuses on "organized crime" more generally, which includes a much wider assortment of domestic crimes such as extortion, loan sharking, and racketeering. See, for example, Michael Woodiwiss, *Organized Crime and American Power: A History* (Toronto: University of Toronto Press, 2003).
3. As detailed in the chapters that follow, Astor, the wealthiest man in America at the time of his death in 1848, made his initial fortune trading illicit alcohol for Indian furs, engaged in "trading with the enemy" during the War of 1812, and dabbled in opium smuggling to China. Astor was far from unique. Stephen Girard, also one of the richest men in country when he died in 1831, had built up much of his early fortune through smuggling of various sorts, including in the China opium trade. For brief profiles of Astor and Girard in the context of the early U.S. economy, see Michael Lind, *Land of Promise: An Economic History of the United States* (New York: HarperCollins, 2012), 65–75.

4. For an influential recent account, see Moises Naim, *Illicit: How Smugglers, Traffickers, and Copycats Are Hijacking the Global Economy* (New York: Doubleday, 2005).
5. Adam Smith, *An Inquiry into the Nature and Cause of the Wealth of Nations* (Charleston, SC: Forgotten Books, 2008), 686.
6. See, for instance, Stephen Skowronek, *Building a New American State: The Expansion of National Administrative Capacities, 1877–1920* (Cambridge: Cambridge University Press, 1982), Part I. In describing the "exceptional character of the early American state," Skowronek notes that European observers, including Tocqueville, Marx, and Hegel, considered America to be peculiarly stateless in comparison to the European tradition.
7. Students of American political development have been curiously neglectful of the prominence of the customhouse in their accounts of the early American state. But see Gautham Rao, *The Creation of the American State: Customhouses, Law, and Commerce in the Age of Revolution* (Ph.D. dissertation, University of Chicago, 2008), 35. More generally, on the too-often-overlooked role of government regulation in early America, see William J. Novak, *The People's Welfare: Law and Regulation in Nineteenth-Century America* (Chapel Hill: University of North Carolina Press, 1996).
8. Ira Katznelson, Martin Shefter, and other scholars have persuasively argued that we should look more closely at international influences on American political development. Yet their much-needed call to examine how America has been "shaped by war and trade" does not extend to illicit trade or the role of illicit trade in wartime. See Katznelson and Shefter, eds., *Shaped by War and Trade: International Influences on American Political Development* (Princeton, NJ: Princeton University Press, 2002).
9. On the international dimensions of policing, see Peter Andreas and Ethan Nadelmann, *Policing the Globe: Criminalization and Crime Control in International Relations* (New York: Oxford University Press, 2006); Nadelmann, *Cops Across Borders: The Internationalization of U.S. Criminal Law Enforcement* (University Park: Penn State Press, 1993).
10. On the politics of moral crusades more generally, see especially James A. Morone, *Hellfire Nation: The Politics of Sin in American History* (New Haven: Yale University Press, 2003).
11. On the use of counterfactual analysis, see Philip E. Tetlock and Aaron Belkin, eds., *Counterfactual Thought Experiments in World Politics* (Princeton: Princeton University Press, 1996); and Richard New Lebow, *Forbidden Fruit: Counterfactuals and International Relations* (Princeton: Princeton University Press, 2010).
12. For a useful historical introduction, see Alan L. Karras, *Smuggling: Contraband and Corruption in World History* (Lanham, MD: Rowman & Littlefield, 2010). For an overview of the contemporary illicit global economy more broadly, see H. Richard Friman, ed., *Crime and the Global Political Economy* (Boulder, CO: Lynn Rienner, 2009).

13. Michael Connor, *Duty Free: Smuggling Made Easy* (Boulder, CO: Paladin, 1993); Connor, *Sneak It Through: Smuggling Made Easier* (Boulder, CO: Paladin, 1983); Connor, *How to Hide Anything* (Boulder, CO: Paladin, 1984).
14. Luca Bastello, *I Am the Market: How to Smuggle Cocaine by the Ton, in Five Easy Lessons* (New York: Faber and Faber, 2010). Also see Hawkeye Gross, *Drug Smuggling: the Forbidden Book* (Boulder, CO: Paladin, 1992).
15. Ed Rosenthal, *Marijuana Grower's Handbook* (San Francisco: Quick American Archives, 2010); Jorge Cervantes, *Marijuana Horticulture* (Vancouver, WA: Van Patten, 2006).

Chapter 1

1. As Barbara Tuchman puts it, "Subject to infinite variables of winds and currents, of supply and demand, of crops and markets, trade has a way of carving its own paths not always obedient to the mercantilist faith." Tuchman, *The First Salute: A View of the American Revolution* (New York: Knopf, 1988), 21.
2. Bernard Bailyn, *Atlantic History: Concept and Contours* (Cambridge, MA: Harvard University Press, 2005), 88.
3. Bailyn, *Atlantic History*, 89.
4. For a useful overview, see Wim Klooster, "Inter-Imperial Smuggling in the Americas, 1600–1800," in *Soundings in Atlantic History: Latent Structures and Intellectual Currents, 1500–1830*, ed. Bernard Bailyn and Patricia L. Denault (Cambridge, MA: Harvard University Press, 2009).
5. For a discussion of the differences between the North and South in the colonial smuggling economy, see George Louis Beer, *The Commercial Policy of England Toward the American Colonies* (New York: Columbia College, 1893), 132–34. Some accounts suggest there was more illicit trade in the Southern colonies than has been conventionally assumed. See Samuel G. Margolin, *Lawlessness on the Maritime Frontier of the Greater Chesapeake, 1650–1750* (Ph.D. dissertation, College of William and Mary, 1992).
6. See, for example, W. A. Cole, "Trends in Eighteenth Century Smuggling," *Economic History Review* 10, no. 3 (1958): 395–410.
7. See Cathy Matson, *Merchants and Empire: Trading in Colonial New York* (Baltimore: Johns Hopkins University Press, 1998), 207.
8. Bailyn, *Atlantic History*, 90.
9. Bailyn, *Atlantic History*, 90.
10. John Adams to William Tudor, 11 August 1818, in John Adams, *The Works of John Adams, Second President of the United States: With a Life of the Author, Notes and Illustrations, by his Grandson Charles Francis Adams*, ed. Charles Francis Adams, 10 vols. (Boston: Little, Brown, 1856), 10:345.
11. See Thomas Barrow, *Trade and Empire: The British Customs Service in Colonial America, 1660–1775* (Cambridge, MA: Harvard University Press, 1967), 55.

12. George Louis Beer, *The Old Colonial System, 1660–1754* (Gloucester: Peter Smith, 1958), II:282–83.
13. Barrow, *Trade and Empire*, 31.
14. Colonial and English Channel smuggling are briefly compared in Beer, *The Commercial Policy in England Toward the American Colonies*, 132.
15. Carl E. Prince and Mollie Keller, *The U.S. Customs Service: A Bicentennial History* (Washington, DC: U.S. Department of the Treasury, 1989), 2.
16. For a more detailed discussion, see Barrow, *Trade and Empire.*
17. Gautham Rao, *The Creation of the American State: Customhouses, Law, and Commerce in the Age of Revolution* (University of Chicago, PhD dissertation, Department of History, December 2008), 35.
18. R. Auchmuty, quoted in Barrow, *Trade and Empire*, 141.
19. Arthur Meier Schlesinger, *The Colonial Merchants and the American Revolution, 1763–1776* (New York: Facsimile Library, 1939), 43.
20. Klooster, "Inter-Imperial Smuggling in the Americas, 1600–1800," 167.
21. See in general James Blaine Hedges, *Browns of Providence Plantations: Colonial Years* (Providence: Brown University Press, 1968).
22. Quoted in Russell Bourne, *Cradle of Violence: How Boston's Waterfront Mobs Ignited the American Revolution* (Hoboken, NJ: Wiley, 2006), 53.
23. And this in turn left a paper trail for historians. The insurance records also document bribes—"gifts"—to the Boston deputy collector of customs. See John W. Tyler, *Smugglers and Patriots: Boston Merchants and the Advent of the American Revolution* (Boston: Northeastern University Press, 1986), 15–16.
24. Gilman M. Ostrander, "The Colonial Molasses Trade," *Agricultural History* 30, no. 2 (April 1956): 82.
25. For a more detailed discussion, see Ostrander, "The Colonial Molasses Trade"; and Richard Pares, *Yankees and Creoles: The Trade Between North America and the West Indies Before the American Revolution* (Cambridge, MA: Harvard University Press, 1956).
26. Ian Williams, *Rum: A Social and Sociable History* (New York: Nation Books, 2005), 89.
27. Schlesinger, *The Colonial Merchants and the American Revolution, 1763–1776*, 43.
28. Ostrander, "The Colonial Molasses Trade," 84.
29. Williams, *Rum*, 90.
30. Charles William Taussig, quoted in Williams, *Rum*, 85.
31. William Smith McClellan, *Smuggling in the American Colonies at the Outbreak of the Revolution: With Special Reference to the West Indies Trade* (New York: Moffat, Yard, 1912), 36.
32. Ostrander, "The Colonial Molasses Trade," 83.
33. Elaine Forman Crane, *A Dependent People: Newport, Rhode Island in the Revolutionary Era* (New York: Fordham University Press, 1985), 84.

34. Letter reprinted in Rhode Island Historical Society, *Proceedings of the Rhode Island Historical Society, 1877–88* (Providence: printed for the Society, 1888), 81–82.
35. See Sydney V. James, *Colonial Rhode Island: A History* (New York: Scribner, 1975), 272.
36. McClellan, *Smuggling in the American Colonies*, 36.
37. Barrow, *Trade and Empire*, 144.
38. On the rise of American consumer culture, see T. H. Breen, "'Baubbles of Britain': The American and Consumer Revolutions of the Eighteenth Century," *Past and Present*, no. 119 (May 1988): 73–104.
39. Matson, *Merchants and Empire*, 207.
40. Colonial Society of Massachusetts, *Publications of the Colonial Society of Massachusetts*, vol. vi. Transactions, 1899, 1900 (Boston: published by the Society, 1904), 6:299–304. Bollan goes on to inform the Lords "That the persons concerned in this Trade are many, Some of them of the greatest Fortunes in this Country, and who have made great Gains by it, and having all felt the Sweets of it, they begin to Espouse and Justify it, Some openly some Covertly, and having perswaded themselves that their Trade ought not to be bound by the Laws of Great Britain, they labour, and not without Success to poison the Minds of all the Inhabitants of the Province. . . ."
41. Quoted in Barrow, *Trade and Empire*, 148.
42. Quoted in Barrow, *Trade and Empire*, 148.
43. For a more general discussion, see Jack S. Levy and Katherine Barbieri, "Trading with the Enemy During Wartime," *Security Studies* 13, no. 3 (Spring 2004): 1–47.
44. Fauquier to Board of Trade, as quoted in Barrow, *Trade and Empire*, 163.
45. Thomas M. Truxes, *Defying Empire: Trading with the Enemy in Colonial New York* (New Haven: Yale University Press, 2008), 93.
46. *Correspondence of William Pitt when Secretary of State with Colonial Governors and Military and Naval Commissioners in America, Edited under the Auspices of the National Society of the Colonial Dames of America*, ed. Gertrude Selwyn Kimball (New York: Macmillan, 1906), 2:351–55.
47. Francis Bernard, quoted in Charles Rappleye, *Sons of Providence: The Brown Brothers, the Slave Trade, and the American Revolution* (New York: Simon and Schuster, 2006), 32.
48. Francis Fauquier, quoted in Barrow, *Trade and Empire*, 162.
49. Quoted in Rappleye, *Sons of Providence*, 32.
50. Rappleye, *Sons of Providence*, 32.
51. Robert Rogers, *A Concise Account of North America* (1765; reprint New York: Johnson Reprint, 1966), 57.
52. Quoted in Barrow, *Trade and Empire*, 161.
53. Quoted in Barrow, *Trade and Empire*, 167.
54. Barrow, *Trade and Empire*, 167.
55. McClellan, *Smuggling in the American Colonies*, 53.

56. Quoted in Truxes, *Defying Empire*, 4.
57. *Correspondence of William Pitt*, ed. Kimball, 2:320–21.
58. *Correspondence of William Pitt*, 2:373–78.
59. Joseph Sherwood's letter is available in *The Correspondence of the Colonial Governors of Rhode Island, 1723–1775*, ed. Gertrude Selwyn Kimball (Boston: Houghton Mifflin, 1903), 320.
60. Truxes, *Defying Empire*, 1.
61. Truxes, *Defying Empire*, 5.
62. Truxes, *Defying Empire*, 6.
63. Truxes, *Defying Empire*, 84.
64. Truxes, *Defying Empire*, 12–18.
65. Colden's letter to Amherst is available in New-York Historical Society. *Collections of the New York Historical Society for the Year 1876* (New York: printed for the Society, 1877), 195–96.
66. Quoted in Truxes, *Defying Empire*, 39.
67. Truxes, *Defying Empire*, 152–54.

Chapter 2

1. In a survey of the literature, one historian observes that smuggling is an aspect of the economy of British America that "receives nowhere the attention it deserves." See David Hancock, "Rethinking the Economy of British America," in *The Economy of Early America*, ed. Cathy Matson (University Park: Penn State Press, 2006), 81.
2. James M. Volo, *Blue Water Patriots: The American Revolution Afloat* (Lanham, MD: Rowman & Littlefield, 2006), 3.
3. See Thomas Barrow, *Trade and Empire: The British Customs Service in Colonial America, 1660–1775* (Cambridge, MA: Harvard University Press, 1967), 173.
4. As Morgan and Morgan describe the customs collectors, "Too many of them sat placidly in England enjoying their large salaries, while their ill-paid and irresponsible deputies collected bribes instead of customs in America." See Edmund S. Morgan and Helen M. Morgan, *The Stamp Act Crisis: Prologue to Revolution* (Chapel Hill: University of North Carolina Press, 1995), 23.
5. Morgan and Morgan, *Stamp Act Crisis*, 24.
6. Quoted in Barrow, *Trade and Empire*, 179.
7. For Adams's description of the Otis speech, see *Novanghus and Massachussettensis: Political Essays, Published in the Years 1774–1775* (1819; reprint Bedford, MA: Applewood, 2009), 244–47.
8. *Peter Oliver's Origin and Progress of the American Rebellion: A Tory View*, ed. Douglas Adair and John A. Schutz (Stanford: Stanford University Press, 1967), 48–50.

9. Quoted in Russell Bourne, *Cradle of Violence: How Boston's Waterfront Mobs Ignited the American Revolution* (Hoboken, NJ: Wiley, 2006), 83.
10. Barrow, *Trade and Empire*, 191.
11. Robert Middlekauff, *The Glorious Cause: The American Revolution, 1763–1789*, rev. ed. (New York: Oxford University Press, 2005), 69.
12. Barrow, *Trade and Empire*, 202.
13. Historian Oliver M. Dickerson argues that the greatly reduced amount of customs racketeering in Canada, which was due to Governor Guy Carleton's intolerance for such practices, partly explains why Canada remained loyal to Britain. Dickerson also points out that only the merchant class in Virginia, Maryland, and North Carolina remained loyal and suggests that this was because customs racketeering was less prevalent in these places. See Dickerson, *The Navigation Acts and the American Revolution* (Philadelphia: University of Pennsylvania Press, 1951), 222, 255.
14. *The Political Thought of Benjamin Franklin*, ed. Ralph L. Ketcham (1965; reprint Indianapolis, IN: Bobbs-Merrill, 2003), 262. Italics in original.
15. Barrow, *Trade and Empire*, 197.
16. Quoted in Dickenson, *The Navigation Acts*, 230.
17. Quoted in McClellan, *Smuggling in the American Colonies*, 88.
18. Stephen Hopkins, *The Rights of the Colonies Examined* (Providence: William Goddard, 1765), 12.
19. Morgan and Morgan, *Stamp Act Crisis*, 28.
20. Quoted in John W. Tyler, *Smugglers and Patriots: Boston Merchants and the Advent of the American Revolution* (Boston: Northeastern University Press, 1986), 17.
21. Middlekauff, *The Glorious Cause*, 194.
22. Barrow, *Trade and Empire*, 235.
23. Sir Angus Fraser, foreword to Carl E. Prince and Mollie Keller, *The U.S. Customs Service: A Bicentennial History* (Washington, DC: Department of the Treasury, 1989), xi.
24. Barrow, *Trade and Empire*, 227.
25. Quoted in Barrow, *Trade and Empire*, 228.
26. Middlekauff, *The Glorious Cause*, 170–73.
27. Barrow, *Trade and Empire*, 233.
28. Barrow, *Trade and Empire*, 234.
29. Barrow, *Trade and Empire*, 240; 244–45.
30. Prince and Keller, *The U.S. Customs Service*, 23.
31. *Providence Gazette* (10 June 1769), as quoted in Prince and Keller, *The U.S. Customs Service*, 25.
32. This description of the incident is taken from Barrow, *Trade and Empire*, 246.

33. Quoted in Barrow, *Trade and Empire*, 246.
34. Quoted in Barrow, *Trade and Empire*, 247.
35. Charles Rappleye, *Sons of Providence: The Brown Brothers, the Slave Trade, and the American Revolution* (New York: Simon & Schuster, 2006), 113–14.
36. Quoted in Benjamin L. Carp, *Defiance of the Patriots: The Boston Tea Party and the Making of America* (New Haven: Yale University Press, 2010), 72.
37. Quoted in Carp, *Defiance of the Patriots*, 55.
38. Carp, *Defiance of the Patriots*, 77.
39. Niall Ferguson, *Empire: The Rise and Demise of the British World Order and the Lessons for Global Power* (New York: Basic Books, 2004), 72. Other historians also point to the importance of tea-smuggling interests. See especially Tyler, *Smugglers and Patriots*.
40. Barrow, *Trade and Empire*, 250.
41. Middlekauff, *The Glorious Cause*, 272.
42. Quoted in Neil L. York, "Clandestine Aid and the American Revolutionary War Effort: A Re-Examination," *Military Affairs* 43, no. 1 (February 1979): 26; Helen Augur, *The Secret War of Independence* (New York: Duell, Sloane and Pearce, 1955), 194–96.
43. Ian Williams, *Rum: A Social and Sociable History* (New York: Nation Books, 2005), 162.
44. As one of the wealthiest merchants in the colonies, Hancock is widely described in the historical literature as complicit in smuggling, but the extent of such involvement remains unknown. What is known is that Hancock played a lead role in publicly defying and denouncing what was increasingly viewed in the colonies as an unjust and abusive crackdown on smuggling.
45. The essay by "Massachussettensis" is available in John Adams, *Novanghus and Massachussettensis: Political Essays, Published in the Years 1774–1775* (1819; reprint Bedford, MA: Applewood, 2009), 161.
46. Quoted in Rappleye, *Sons of Providence*, 126.

Chapter 3

1. William Moultrie, *Memoirs of the American Revolution, so far as it Related to the States of North and South Carolina, and Georgia* (New York: D. Longworth, 1802), I:63–64.
2. Elizabeth Miles Nuxoll, *Congress and the Munitions Merchants: The Secret Committee of Trade During the American Revolution, 1775–1777* (New York: Garland, 1985), 283–86.
3. Moultrie, *Memoirs of the American Revolution*, I:78.
4. Neil L. York, "Clandestine Aid and the American Revolutionary War Effort: A Re-Examination," *Military Affairs* 43, no. 1 (February 1979): 27.
5. George C. Herring, *From Colony to Superpower: U.S. Foreign Relations Since 1776* (New York: Oxford University Press, 2008), 18; Orlando

W. Stephenson, "The Supply of Gunpowder in 1776," *American Historical Review* 30, no. 2 (January 1925): 277, 279.
6. Stephenson, "The Supply of Gunpowder in 1776," 279.
7. See *The Writings of George Washington: 1775–1776*, ed. Worthington Chauncey Ford (New York: Putnam, 1889), 3:299.
8. Stephenson, "The Supply of Gunpowder in 1776," 274.
9. James. A. Huston, *Logistics of Liberty: American Services of Supply in the Revolutionary War and After* (Newark: University of Delaware Press, 1991), 111.
10. Nuxoll, *Congress and the Munitions Merchants*, 8–9.
11. Robert H. Patton, *Patriot Pirates: The Privateer War for Freedom and Fortune in the American Revolution* (New York: Pantheon, 2008), 16.
12. Charles Rappleye, *Sons of Providence: The Brown Brothers, the Slave Trade, and the American Revolution* (New York: Simon & Schuster, 2006), 210–211.
13. Quoted in *American Archives: Fourth Series, Containing a Documentary History of the English Colonies in North America from the King's Message to Parliament of 7 March 1774 to the Declaration of Independence of the United States*, ed. Peter Force (Washington, DC: Published by M. St. Clair Clarke and Peter Force, 1840), 3:1688.
14. *The Writings of George Washington from the Original Manuscript Sources, 1745–1799*, ed. John C Fitzpatrick (Washington, DC: U.S. Government Printing Office, 1936), 13:335.
15. *The Writings of George Washington*, 3:459.
16. York, "Clandestine Aid," 27.
17. Quoted in William Armstrong Fairburn, *Merchant Sail* (Center Lovell, ME: Fairburn Marine Educational Foundation, 1955), 1:379. Derby wrote this letter to his ship captain, Nathaniel Silsbee, stationed at Hispaniola.
18. Patton, *Patriot Pirates*, 17.
19. York, "Clandestine Aid," 27.
20. York, "Clandestine Aid," 27.
21. Huston, *Logistics of Liberty*, 105.
22. By 1777, the British naval blockade had tightened enough to make the smuggling business riskier and thus discourage private merchants. However, by this time greater French support had been secured, leading to official French aid in 1778 with the Treaty of Amity and Commerce. See York, "Clandestine Aid," 28–29.
23. York, "Clandestine Aid," 28.
24. York, "Clandestine Aid," 28.
25. See Thomas Perkins Abernethy, "The Commercial Activities of Silas Deane in France," *American Historical Review* 39 (April 1934): 477–85.
26. Indeed, neutrality violations provided the pretext for more than 150 British seizures of French vessels in the first half of 1778 prior to France's

entry into the war. James M. Volo, *Blue Water Patriots: The American Revolution Afloat* (Lanham, MD: Rowman & Littlefield, 2006), 232.

27. Patton, *Patriot Pirates*, 77.
28. George L. Clark, *Silas Deane, A Connecticut Leader in the American Revolution* (Charleston, SC: Nabu Press, 2010 reprint, original 1913), 90.
29. Clark, *Silas Deane*, 90.
30. Clark, *Silas Deane*, 90–91.
31. See Elizabeth S. Kite, "French 'Secret Aid' Precursor to the French American Alliance 1776–1777," *French-American Review* I (1948): 151; John J. Meng, "A Footnote to Secret Aid in the American Revolution," *American Historical Review* 43, no. 4 (July 1938): 791.
32. C. H. Van Tyne, "French Aid Before the Alliance of 1778," *American Historical Review* 31, no. 1 (October 1925): 40.
33. *Correspondence of the American Revolution; Being Letters of Eminent Men to George Washington from the Time of his Taking Command of the Army to the End of his Presidency*, ed. Jared Sparks (Boston: Little, Brown, 1853), 1:394.
34. Clark, *Silas Deane*, 89–91.
35. Nuxoll, *Congress and the Ammunitions Merchants*, 444–45.
36. Robert Middlekauff, *The Glorious Cause: The American Revolution, 1763–1789*, rev. ed. (New York: Oxford University Press, 2005), 405. See also Samuel Flagg Bemis, *The Diplomacy of the American Revolution* (1935; reprint Bloomington: Indiana University Press, 1957), 23–28; and Julian P. Boyd, "Silas Deane: Death by a Kindly Teacher of Treason?" *William and Mary Quarterly*, 3rd series, 16 (1959): 165–87, 319–42.
37. Huston, *Logistics of Liberty*, 110.
38. Quoted in Patton, *Patriot Pirates*, 109.
39. Quoted in Nancy Rubin Stuart, *The Muse of the Revolution: The Secret Pen of Mercy Otis Warren and the Founding of a Nation* (Boston: Beacon Press, 2008), 141.
40. Patton, *Patriot Pirates*, 115.
41. Patton, *Patriot Pirates*, 115.
42. Robert A. East, *Business Enterprise in the American Revolutionary Era* (New York: Columbia University Press, 1938), 65.
43. See Volo, *Blue Water Patriots*.
44. As William Whipple wrote to the former Continental Congress delegate Josiah Bartlett from Portsmouth, New Hampshire, on 12 July 1778: "[Y]ou may depend no public ship will ever be manned while there is a privateer fitting out. The reason is plain:—those people who have the most influence with the seamen think it their interest to discourage the public service [the navy], because by that they advance promote their own interest, viz., Privateering." Whipple's letter can be found in *The Papers of Josiah Bartlett*, ed. Frank C. Mevers (Hanover, NH: University Press of New England, 1979), 196.

45. This was a source of great frustration for those attempting to build up a viable navy. While stationed in Providence with the five-vessel Continental fleet in the fall of 1776, Continental Navy officer John Paul Jones denounced those who "wink at, encourage, and employ deserters from the navy." Quoted in Patton, *Patriot Pirates*, 80.
46. Entitled "A Song for the Montgomery," this chantey was written for the privateer *Montgomery*, based out of Providence. This is reprinted in *Naval Documents of the American Revolution*, ed. William James Morgan (Washington, DC: Naval History Division, Department of the Navy, 1972), 6:117.
47. Middlekauff, *The Glorious Cause*, 535.
48. Volo, *Blue Water Patriots*, 47.
49. Nathanael Greene, "Letters of General Nathanael Greene to Colonel Jeremiah Wadsworth," *The Pennsylvania Magazine of History and Biography* 22, no. 2 (1898): 211.
50. Greene, "Letters of General Nathanael Greene to Colonel Jeremiah Wadsworth," 214.
51. E. James Ferguson, "Business, Government, and Congressional Investigation in the Revolution," *William and Mary Quarterly*, 3rd series, 16, no. 3 (July 1959): 313–15.
52. East, *Business Enterprise in the American Revolutionary Era*, 229.
53. Morris's letter is available in *Letters of Delegates to Congress, 1774–1789*, ed. Paul H. Smith, et al. (Washington, DC: Library of Congress, 1976), 5:147.
54. Quoted in Patton, *Patriot Pirates*, 73.
55. For a detailed account, see Nuxoll, *Congress and the Munitions Merchants*. The committee was composed of men with experience in international trade, and much of the committee's dealings went through merchants and others with close connections to committee members. According to Nuxoll, "The Committee's far-flung commercial activities helped build the wealth and political careers of many merchants" (vi).
56. See Charles Rappleye, *Robert Morris: Financier of the American Revolution* (New York: Simon & Schuster, 2010); Clarence L. Ver Steeg, *Robert Morris: Revolutionary Financier: With an Analysis of his Earlier Career* (Philadelphia, University of Pennsylvania Press, 1954); Nuxoll, *Congress and the Munitions Merchants*.
57. Morris's letter is available in New-York Historical Society, *Collections of the New York Historical Society for the Year 1886* (New York: printed for the Society, 1887), 174.
58. Patton, *Patriot Pirates*, xix.
59. Patton, *Patriot Pirates*, 158, 165.
60. Quoted in Patton, *Patriot Pirates*, 172.
61. Huston, *Logistics of Liberty*, 106.
62. Patton, *Patriot Pirates*, 67, 71–72.

63. Quoted in Patton, *Patriot Pirates*, 216.
64. Nuxoll, *Congress and the Munitions Merchants*, 455.
65. Barbara W. Tuchman, *The First Salute: A View of the American Revolution* (New York: Knopf, 1988), 18. See also Franklin Jameson, "St. Eustatius in the American Revolution," *American Historical Review* 8, no. 4 (July 1903): 683–708; Ronald Hurst, *The Golden Rock: An Episode of the American War of Independence* (Annapolis, MD: Naval Institute Press, 1996).
66. Tuchman, *The First Salute*, 19, 21.
67. Huston, *Logistics of Liberty*, 109.
68. Abraham Van Bibber's letter (written with his business partner Richard Harrison) is available in *Archives of Maryland: Journal and Correspondence of the Maryland Council of Safety, July 7–31 December 1776*, ed. William Hand Browne (Baltimore: Maryland Historical Society, 1893), 12:457).
69. Quoted in Tuchman, *The First Salute*, 16.
70. Quoted in Tuchman, *The First Salute*, 13.
71. Huston, *Logistics of Liberty*, 109–10.
72. Hence the title of Tuchman's book *The First Salute* (New York: Random House, 1988).
73. East, *Business Enterprise in the American Revolutionary Era*, 177.
74. Tellingly, during the war Nova Scotia imported British goods valued at ten times higher than what it could domestically consume. Stuart D. Brandes, *Warhogs: A History of War Profits in America* (Lexington: University of Kentucky Press, 1997), 42. According to Brandes, Canada was the biggest leak in the British embargo of the colonies.
75. Thomas Victor Goodrich, *The Opening of the British West Indies Trade to American Vessels* (Madison: University of Wisconsin Press, 1908), 10–11.
76. Middlekauff, *The Glorious Cause*, 420.
77. East, *Business Enterprise in the American Revolutionary Era*, 181.
78. See Arthur D. Pierce, *Smuggler's Woods: Jaunts and Journeys in Colonial and Revolutionary New Jersey* (New Brunswick, NJ: Rutgers University Press, 1984), 39.
79. East, *Business Enterprise in the American Revolutionary Era*, 181.
80. Quoted in East, *Business Enterprise in the American Revolutionary Era*, 182.
81. See Richard Buel, *Dear Liberty: Connecticut's Mobilization for the Revolutionary War* (Middletown, CT: Wesleyan University Press, 1980), 257–67.
82. Buel, *Dear Liberty*, 261.
83. Brandes, *Warhogs*, 42.
84. Buel, *Dear Liberty*, 257.
85. Washington's letter available in Charles S. Hall, *Life and Letters of Samuel Holden Parsons: Major-General in the Continental Army and Chief Judge of the Northwestern Territory, 1737–1789* (Binghamton, NY: Otseningo, 1905), 725.

86. Quoted in East, *Business Enterprise in the American Revolutionary Era*, 31.
87. Washington's letter available in *The Writings of George Washington: 1780–1782*, ed. Worthington Chauncey Ford (New York: Putnam, 1891), 6:135.
88. Quoted in Brandes, *Warhogs*, 44.
89. Letter available in Gertrude E. Meredith, *The Descendants of Hugh Amory, 1605–1805* (London: privately printed at the Chiswick Press, 1901), 231.
90. John Welsh, as quoted in East, *Business Enterprise in the American Revolutionary Era*, 52.
91. The paragraph above is drawn from Brandes, *Warhogs*, 42–43.
92. Tuchman, *The First Salute*, 196, 201.
93. Pembroke Papers (1780–1794); Letters and Diaries of Henry, Tenth Earl of Pembroke and his Circle, ed. Lord Herbert (London: Cape, 1950), 179.

Chapter 4

1. See Alexander Hamilton, "Federalist No. 12," *The Federalist Papers: Alexander Hamilton, James Madison, and John Jay*, ed. Ian Shapiro (New Haven: Yale University Press, 2009).
2. The newly appointed federal customs collector at Penobscot, Maine, wrote to Hamilton at the end of 1789: "Under the State government by far the greatest part of these vessels [i.e., coasting ships] found means to avoid the regulation then prescribed. . . . Coasters have so long trampled upon the Revenue Laws of this State with impunity that they now think they are bound by no Laws." Quoted in Leonard D. White, *The Federalists: A Study in Administrative History* (New York: Macmillan, 1948), 461.
3. George C. Herring, *From Colony to Superpower: U.S. Foreign Relations Since 1776* (New York: Oxford University Press, 2008), 52.
4. On the anemic nature of the early American state, see Sheldon D. Pollack, *War, Revenue, and State Building: Financing the Development of the American State* (Ithaca, NY: Cornell University Press, 2009). Brian Balogh, in contrast, argues that the early American state was less weak and hollow than conventionally assumed but operated in a subtler and more "out of sight" manner. See Balogh, *A Government out of Sight: The Mystery of National Authority in Nineteenth-Century America* (Cambridge: Cambridge University Press, 2009).
5. Carl E. Prince and Mollie Keller, *The U.S. Customs Service: A Bicentennial History* (Washington, DC: U.S. Department of the Treasury, 1989), 37.
6. See Prince and Keller, *The U.S. Customs Service*, 71.
7. Quoted in "Federalist No. 35," *The Federalist Papers*, 168.
8. *The Papers of Alexander Hamilton,* ed. Harold C. Syrett (New York: Columbia University Press, 1965), 8:398.
9. *Gazette of the United States*, as quoted in White, *The Federalists*, 462.

10. *Annals of Congress*, 1st Cong., 1st sess., 311.
11. Joshua Smith, "Patterns of Northern New England Smuggling, 1783–1820," in William S. Dudley and Michael J. Crawford, eds., *The Early Republic and the Sea: Essays on the Naval and Maritime History of the Early United States* (Washington, DC: Brassey's, 2001), 37.
12. Charles R. Ritcheson, *Aftermath of Revolution: British Policy Toward the United States, 1783–1795* (Dallas: Southern Methodist University, 1969), 212.
13. See especially Joshua M. Smith, *Borderland Smuggling: Patriots, Loyalists, and Illicit Trade in the Northeast, 1783–1820* (Gainesville: University Press of Florida), 2006.
14. Werner Levi, "The Earliest Relations Between the United States of America and Australia," *Pacific Historical Review* 12, no. 4 (December 1943): 354–55.
15. *The Trader's Book*, 1809, mss 9001-T, loose manuscripts, Rhode Island Historical Society, 54.
16. Quoted in Charles C. Stelle, "American Trade in Opium to China Prior to 1820," *Pacific Historical Review* 9, no. 4 (December 1940): 427 (note 12).
17. Quoted in Stelle, "American Trade in Opium to China Prior to 1820," 427 (note 12).
18. Jacques M. Downs, "American Merchants and the China Opium Trade, 1800–1840," *Business History Review* 42, no. 4 (Winter 1968): 419.
19. Downs, "American Merchants and the China Opium Trade, 1800–1840," 425.
20. On the economic importance of this export boom, see Claudia D. Goldin and Frank D. Lewis, "The Role of Exports in American Economic Growth During the Napoleonic Wars, 1793–1807," *Explorations in Economic History* 17 (January 1980): 6–25.
21. Quoted in Gautham Rao, *The Creation of the American State: Customhouses, Law, and Commerce in the Age of Revolution* (University of Chicago, PhD dissertation, Department of History, December 2008), 180.
22. Melvin H. Jackson, *Privateers in Charleston: A French Palatinate in South Carolina* (Washington, DC: Smithsonian Institution Press, 1969), 108.
23. Rao, *Creation of the American State*, 182–83.
24. Quoted in Gordon S. Wood, *Empire of Liberty: A History of the Early Republic, 1789–1815* (New York: Oxford University Press, 2009), 202.
25. Douglas C. North, *The Economic Growth of the United States 1790–1860* (Englewood Cliffs, NJ: Prentice-Hall, 1961), 25.
26. Herring, *From Colony to Superpower*, 115.
27. Wood, *Empire of Liberty*, 623.
28. Wood, *Empire of Liberty*, 641.
29. Quoted in Donald R. Hickey, *The War of 1812: A Forgotten Conflict* (Urbana: University of Illinois Press, 1989), 11.
30. Wood, *Empire of Liberty*, 642.

31. Wood, *Empire of Liberty*, 646.
32. John Odiorne to James Locke, as quoted in Rao, *Creation of the American State*, 146.
33. This section draws heavily from Rao, *Creation of the American State*, 187–216; and Donald R. Hickey, "America's Response to the Slave Revolt in Haiti, 1791–1806," *Journal of the Early Republic* 2, no. 4 (Winter 1982): 361–79.
34. Hickey, "America's Response to the Slave Revolt in Haiti," 362–363.
35. Rao, *Creation of the American State*, 188–89; Hickey, "America's Response to the Slave Revolt in Haiti," 365.
36. Hickey, "America's Response to the Slave Revolt in Haiti," 367.
37. Quoted in Rao, *Creation of the American State*, 190.
38. Rao, *Creation of the American State*, 193. See also Rayford W. Logan, *The Diplomatic Relations of the United States with Haiti, 1776–1891* (Chapel Hill: University of North Carolina Press, 1941), 139.
39. Rao, *Creation of the American State*, 194–95.
40. Quoted in Hickey, "America's Response to the Slave Revolt in Haiti," 370.
41. *Thomas Jefferson: Thoughts on War and Revolution*, ed. Brett F. Woods (New York: Algora, 2009), 179.
42. Quoted in Rao, *Creation of the American State*, 201–2.
43. Quoted in Rao, *Creation of the American State*, 205.
44. Quoted in Hickey, "America's Response to the Slave Revolt in Haiti," 374.
45. Quoted in Rao, *Creation of the American State*, 212–13.
46. Hickey, "America's Response to the Slave Revolt in Haiti," 378.
47. Rao, *Creation of the American State*, 222.
48. Quoted in Rao, *Creation of the American State*, 298.
49. Quoted in Prince and Keller, *The U.S. Customs Service*, 73.
50. Quoted in Rao, *Creation of the American State*, 302.
51. MacDonald comments that "almost no shipper felt bound by conscience or patriotism to obey the embargo if he could successfully violate it, for the law deprived him of his property and livelihood in the interest of a policy that he regarded as questionable on grounds of constitutionality, morality, and plain good sense." See Forrest MacDonald, *The Presidency of Thomas Jefferson* (Lawrence: University Press of Kansas, 1976), 149.
52. *Thomas Jefferson: Thoughts on War and Revolution*, 222.
53. *The Works of Thomas Jefferson*, ed. Paul Leicester Ford (New York: Putnam, 1905), 11:41.
54. Burton Spivak, *Jefferson's English Crisis: Commerce, Embargo, and the Republican Revolution* (Charlottesville: University Press of Virginia, 1979), 162. Leonard Dupee White notes that one ship cleared from Boston to Charleston even blamed bad weather for having to veer off course and ending up in Lisbon: "On 14 January 1809, the schooner

Charles cleared Boston for Charleston in ballast, but turned up in Lisbon. The master alleged that stress of weather had forced him 'bear away' for that distant port." See White, *The Jeffersonians: A Study in Administrative History, 1801–1829* (New York: Macmillan, 1951), 445.

55. Rao, *Creation of the American State*, 309–11.
56. H. N. Muller, "Smuggling into Canada: How the Champlain Valley Defied Jefferson's Embargo," *Vermont History* 38, no. 1 (Winter 1970): 5–21.
57. Prince and Keller, *The U.S. Customs Service*, 75.
58. Quoted in Prince and Keller, *The U.S. Customs Service*, 75.
59. Quoted in Prince and Keller, *The U.S. Customs Service*, 75. See also Richard F. Casey, "North Country Nemesis: The Potash Rebellion and the Embargo of 1807–09," *New York Historical Society Quarterly* 64 (1980): 31–49.
60. Flour was in such high demand in British Nova Scotia and New Brunswick during this period that many farmers in Eastern Maine switched to cultivating wheat, producing a sudden spike in wheat production despite the less-than-ideal conditions. See Jamie H. Eves, "'The Poor People Had Suddenly Become Rich': A Boom in Maine Wheat, 1793–1815," *Maine Historical Society Quarterly* 27, no. 3 (Winter 1987): 114–41.
61. Smith, *Borderland Smuggling*, 10–11.
62. Smith, *Borderland Smuggling*, 60.
63. Smith, "Patterns of Northern New England Smuggling," 40–42.
64. Smith, *Borderland Smuggling*, 52.
65. Louis Martin Sears, *Jefferson and the Embargo* (New York: Octagon, 1966), 80.
66. Robin Higham, "The Port of Boston and the Embargo of 1807–1809," *American Neptune* 16 (July 1956): 189–210.
67. *The Writings of Albert Gallatin,* ed. Henry Adams (Philadelphia: Lippincott, 1879), 1:448.
68. Christopher Ward, "The Commerce of East Florida During the Embargo, 1806–1812: The Role of Amelia Island," *Florida Historical Quarterly* 68, no. 2 (October 1989): 160–79.
69. Prince and Keller, *The U.S. Customs Service*, 78.
70. Peter S. Palmer, *History of Lake Champlain: From Its First Exploration by the French in 1609 to the Close of the Year 1814*, 4th ed. (Harrison, NY: Harbor Hill, ed. 1983), 158–59. On embargo resistance turned violent, see also Joshua Smith, "Murder on Isle au Haut: Violence and Jefferson's Embargo in Coastal Maine, 1808–1809" *Maine History* 39, no. 1 (Spring 200): 17–40.
71. In the case of Massachusetts, for example, see Douglas Lamar Jones, "The Caprice of Juries: The Enforcement of the Jeffersonian Embargo in Massachusetts," *American Journal of Legal History* 24, no. 4 (October 1980): 307–30.

72. *The Writings of Albert Gallatin*, 1:397. Gallatin is specifically referring to courts in the Lake Ontario region.
73. Prince and Keller, *The U.S. Customs Service*, 81.
74. Herring, *From Colony to Superpower*, 120.
75. Spencer C. Tucker, *The Jeffersonian Gunboat Navy* (Columbia: University of South Carolina Press, 1993), 86–90.
76. Quoted in Rao, *Creation of the American State*, 318. This statute is reprinted in Frederick T. Wilson, *Federal Aid in Domestic Disturbances, 1787–1903* (Washington, DC: Government Printing Office, 1903), 52.
77. Quoted in Rao, *Creation of the American State*, 347–48. For more on Rhode Island smuggling during this period, see Harvey Strum, "Rhode Island and the Embargo of 1807," *Rhode Island History* 52, no. 2 (May 1994): 59–67.
78. Quoted in Prince and Keller, *The U.S. Customs Service*, 77.
79. Prince and Keller, *The U.S. Customs Service*, 76.
80. Rao, *Creation of the American State*, 371, 403.
81. King notes that "Baltimore, which a few years before had encountered difficulty getting authorization to employ one cutter, was told to hire three." See Irving H. King, *The Coast Guard Under Sail: The U.S. Revenue Cutter Service, 1789–1865* (Annapolis, MD: Naval Institute Press, 1989), 49.
82. Smith, *Borderland Smuggling*, 68–69.
83. According to Smith, "In 1807, the federal presence in Eastport [Maine] consisted of an unarmed customs collector, and perhaps a half a dozen part-time assistants. By 1812, the federal government bolstered that presence with a new and more effective collector, a permanent U.S. deputy marshal, a fortification garrisoned by a half company of artillerists, and a revenue cutter." See Smith, *Borderland Smuggling*, 11.
84. In his third annual message on 5 November 1811, President Madison not only complained about smuggling but declared that it was worse "when it blends with a pursuit of ignominious gain a treacherous subserviency, in the transgressors, to a foreign policy adverse to that of their own country." *A Compilation of the Messages and Papers of the Presidents, 1789–1902*, ed. James D. Richardson (Washington, DC: Bureau of National Literature and Art, 1907), 1:495.

Chapter 5

1. Quoted in Gordon S. Wood, *Empire of Liberty: A History of the Early Republic, 1789–1815* (New York: Oxford University Press, 2009), 670.
2. Thomas Jefferson, for example, boldly proclaimed in August 1812 that "the acquisition of Canada this year, as far as the neighborhood of Quebec, will be a mere matter of marching." See *The Writings of Thomas Jefferson*, ed. Albert Ellery Bergh (Washington, DC: issued under the auspices of the Thomas Jefferson Memorial Association of the United States, 1907), 13:180.

3. In Baltimore, for example, "a class of merchants—for instance, the McKim, Hollingworth and Hollins families, George Stiles, and Senator Samuel Smith—who had been central to the illegal, armed St. Domingue trade, and systematic undermining of the Non-Intercourse Act of 1809, and the Non-Importation Act of 1811, operated a fleet of privateers." Gautham Rao, *The Creation of the American State: Customhouses, Law, and Commerce in the Age of Revolution* (Ph.D. dissertation, University of Chicago, 2008), 428. See also Jerome R. Garitree, *The Republic's Private Navy: The American Privateering Business as Practiced by Baltimore in the War of 1812* (Middletown, CT: Wesleyan University Press, and Mystic Seaport, 1977).
4. This is emphasized by Donald Hickey, "American Trade Restrictions During the War of 1812," *Journal of American History* 68, no. 3 (December 1981): 517–38.
5. Donald R. Hickey, *The War of 1812: A Forgotten Conflict* (Urbana: University of Illinois Press, 1989), 225. Until 1814 the war with the United States was largely a sideshow for Britain as it continued to focus on continental Europe. But with Napoleon's defeat the British moved more of their forces to the American war.
6. Quoted in Hickey, *The War of 1812*, 168.
7. Quoted in Hickey, *The War of 1812*, 216.
8. Alan Taylor, *The Civil War of 1812: American Citizens, British Subjects, Irish Rebels, and Indian Allies* (New York: Vintage, 2011), 290–92.
9. George C. Herring, *From Colony to Superpower: U.S. Foreign Relations Since 1776* (New York: Oxford University Press, 2008), 128.
10. Quoted in Hickey, *The War of 1812*, 226.
11. H. N. Muller III, "A 'Traitorous and Diabolical Traffic': The Commerce of the Champlain-Richelieu Corridor During the War of 1812," *Vermont History* 44, no. 2 (Spring 1976): 90–91.
12. This is the main argument of Donald G. Alcock, "The Best Defense Is . . . Smuggling? Vermonters During the War of 1812," *Canadian Review of American Studies*, 25, no. 1 (Winter 1995): 73–91.
13. Quoted in Muller, "A 'Traitorous and Diabolical Traffic,'" 91.
14. J. I. Little, *Loyalties in Conflict: A Canadian Borderland in War and Rebellion, 1812–1840* (Toronto: University of Toronto Press, 2008), 43.
15. Quoted in Hickey, *The War of 1812*, 227.
16. Hickey, "American Trade Restrictions During the War of 1812," 535.
17. Hickey, *The War of 1812*, 226.
18. Muller, "A 'Traitorous and Diabolical Traffic,'" 83.
19. Quoted in Little, *Loyalties in Conflict*, 46.
20. Stuart D. Brandes, *Warhogs: A History of War Profits in America* (Lexington: University of Kentucky Press, 1997), 56.
21. Muller, "A 'Traitorous and Diabolical Traffic,'" 90.
22. See *Official Correspondence with the Department of War: Relative to the Military Operations of the American Army under the Command of Major*

General Izard, on the Northern Frontier of the United States in the Years 1814 and 1815 (Philadelphia: Thomas Dobson, 1816), 57.

23. Quoted in Don Whitehead, *Border Guard: The Story of the United States Customs Service* (New York: McGraw-Hill, 1963), 44.
24. Hickey, *War of 1812*, 227. This illicit trade sometimes also included use of counterfeit American bank notes forged in Lower Canada. The problem of counterfeit American bank notes coming in from Canada predated the war, but the Canadian government cracked down on the forgers only in December 1813, when a substantial amount of bogus Lower Canadian army bills manufactured in Boston were about to be introduced via northern Vermont. See Little, *Loyalties in Conflict*, 48–49. For a more detailed discussion of counterfeiting in early America, see Stephen Mihm, *A Nation of Counterfeiters: Capitalists, Con Men, and the Making of the United States* (Cambridge, MA: Harvard University Press), 2007.
25. Harvey Strum, "Smuggling in Maine During the Embargo and the War of 1812," *Colby Library Quarterly* 19, no. 2 (June 1983): 90–97.
26. Joshua Smith, "Patterns of Northern New England Smuggling, 1782–1820," in William S. Dudley and Michael J. Crawford, eds., *The Early Republic and the Sea: Essays on the Naval and Maritime History of the Early United States* (Washington, DC: Brassey's, 2001).
27. Joshua Smith, quoted in Margaret Nagle, "The Golden Era of Smuggling," *Today Magazine* (University of Maine), December 2001/January 2002.
28. For a more detailed account, see Alan S. Taylor, "The Smuggling Career of William King," *Maine Historical Society Quarterly* 17 (Summer 1977): 19–38.
29. Quoted in Michael J. Crawford, "The Navy's Campaign Against the Licensed Trade in the War of 1812," *American Neptune* 46, no. 3 (1986): 167.
30. When Madison was informed of this British favoritism toward New England in the license trade, he told Congress in February 1813 that this was an "insulting attempt on the virtue, the honor, the patriotism, and the fidelity of our brethren of the Eastern States." Quoted in Hickey, "American Trade Restrictions During the War of 1812," 528.
31. Hickey, "American Trade Restrictions During the War of 1812," 533.
32. Brandes, *Warhogs*, 56.
33. Quoted in Hickey, "American Trade Restrictions During the War of 1812," 537.
34. Quoted in Hickey, *The War of 1812*, 171.
35. *The Documentary History of the Campaign upon the Niagara Frontier in the Year 1813*, ed. E. Cruikshank (Welland, Ontario: Tribune Office, 1905), 3:194.
36. Quoted in the *Vermont Republican* 18 April 1814, available in *Records of the Governor and Council of the State of Vermont*, ed. E. P. Walton (Montpelier: J. & J. M. Poland, 1878), 6:497–98.

37. Wood, *Empire of Liberty*, 689.
38. Brandes, *Warhogs*, 57.
39. Brandes, *Warhogs*, 58.
40. Harvey Strum, "Smuggling in the War of 1812," *History Today* 29, no. 8 (August 1979): 537.
41. Strum, "Smuggling in the War of 1812," 537.
42. William C. Davis, *Pirates Laffite: The Treacherous World of the Corsairs of the Gulf* (Orlando: Harcourt, 2005), 48.
43. Davis, *Pirates Laffite*, 48–49.
44. Quoted in Whitehead, *Border Guard*, 46.
45. Davis, *Pirates Laffite*, 80.
46. Arsène Lacarrière Latour, *Historical Memoir of the War in West Florida and Louisiana in 1814–15* (1816, reprint Bedford, MA: Applewood, 2009), 15.
47. Whitehead, *Border Guard*, 50.
48. Davis, *Pirates Laffite*, 89.
49. Davis, *Pirates Laffite*, 97, 107.
50. Quoted in Davis, *Pirates Laffite*, 111.
51. Davis, *Pirates Laffite*, 111.
52. Quoted in Charles Gayarré, *History of Louisiana: The American Domination* (1882, reprinted Gretna, LA: Pelican, 1965), 4:370. Italics in original.
53. Quoted in Jack C. Ramsay Jr., *Jean Laffite: Prince of Pirates* (Austin: Eakin Press, 1996), 40.
54. Davis, *Pirates Laffite*, 132.
55. Davis, *Pirates Laffite*, 164.
56. For more details, see John Sugden, "Jean Laffite and the British Offer of 1814," *Louisiana History* 20, no. 2 (Spring 1979): 159–67.
57. Davis, *Pirates Laffite*, 174–75.
58. Quoted in Whitehead, *Border Guard*, 52.
59. Davis, *Pirates Laffite*, 188.
60. Quoted in Ramsay, *Jean Laffite*, 60.
61. Quoted in Ramsay, *Jean Laffite*, 60.
62. Hickey, *War of 1812*, 207.
63. Robert C. Vogel, "Jean Laffite, the Baratarians, and the Battle of New Orleans: A Reappraisal," *Louisiana History* 41, no. 3 (Summer 2000): 265.
64. Quoted in Whitehead, *Border Guard*, 54.
65. See Robert V. Remini, *The Battle of New Orleans: Andrew Jackson and America's First Military Victory* (New York: Penguin, 1999).
66. Quoted in *Official Letters of the Military and Naval Officers of the United States, During the War with Great Britain in the Years 1812, 13, 14, and 15,* ed. John Brannan (Washington City: Way & Gideon, 1823), 478.
67. Quoted in Ramsay, *Jean Laffite*, 82.
68. See especially Jane Lucas DeGrummond, *The Baratarians and the Battle of New Orleans* (Baton Rouge: Louisiana State University Press, 1961).

69. Wilburt S. Brown, *The Amphibious Campaign for West Florida and Louisiana: A Critical Review of Strategy and Tactics at New Orleans* (Tuscaloosa: University of Alabama Press, 1969), 31.
70. Hickey, *War of 1812*, 305.
71. Vogel, "Jean Laffite, the Baratarians, and the Battle of New Orleans," 276.

Chapter 6

1. See especially Doron S. Ben-Atar, *Trade Secrets: Intellectual Piracy and the Origins of American Industrial Power* (New Haven: Yale University Press, 2004); David J. Jeremy, *Transatlantic Industrial Revolution: The Diffusion of Textile Technologies Between Britain and America, 1790–1830s* (Cambridge, MA: MIT Press, 1981).
2. Thomas C. Cochran, *Frontiers of Change: Early Industrialism in America* (New York: Oxford University Press, 1981), 64.
3. Quoted in Ben-Atar, *Trade Secrets*, 86.
4. See Doron Ben-Atar, "Alexander Hamilton's Alternative: Technology Piracy and the Report on Manufactures," *William and Mary Quarterly* 52, no. 3 (January 1995): 389–414.
5. *The Papers of Alexander Hamilton,* ed. Harold C. Syrett (New York: Columbia University Press, 1966), 10:272.
6. This is emphasized in Carroll W. Pursell, Jr. *The Machine in America: A Social History of Technology* (Baltimore: Johns Hopkins University Press, 1995), 39.
7. *The Papers of Alexander Hamilton*, 10:308.
8. One plan in 1787 involved dispatching an agent, Andrew Mitchell, to England to obtain models and patterns of machinery, but Mitchell was busted by British customs on his way out of the country. See Anthony F. C. Wallace and David J. Jeremy, "William Pollard and the Arkwright Patents," *William and Mary Quarterly* 34, no. 3 (July 1977): 410.
9. Ben-Atar, *Trade Secrets*, 97.
10. Robert Glen, "Industrial Wayfarers: Benjamin Franklin and a Case of Machine Smuggling in the 1780s," *Business History* 23, no. 3 (November 1981): 309–26.
11. *The Writings of George Washington,* ed. Worthington Chauncey Ford (New York: Putnam, 1891), 12:6–7.
12. *A Compilation of the Messages and Papers of the Presidents, 1789–1902*, ed. James D. Richardson (Washington, DC: Bureau of National Literature and Art, 1907), 1:66.
13. Ben-Atar, *Trade Secrets*, xv.
14. Ben-Atar, *Trade Secrets*, 169.
15. In 1836 foreigners were finally given the right to hold a U.S. patent without restriction. But whereas U.S. citizens or those declaring an intent to become a U.S. citizen paid only $30 for a patent, foreigners paid

$300—and British subjects paid $500. Pat Choate, *Hot Property: The Stealing of Ideas in an Age of Globalization* (New York: Knopf, 2005), 29.

16. Ben-Atar, *Trade Secrets*, 204.
17. Choate, *Hot Property*, 30.
18. Quoted in Carroll W. Pursell Jr., "Thomas Digges and William Pearce: An Example of the Transit of Technology," *William and Mary Quarterly* 21, no. 4 (October 1964): 551.
19. Pursell, *The Machine in America*, 37–39. Moreover, as Pursell points out, not only did the Americans successfully appropriate the British technologies, they then appropriated British improvements on these earlier technologies: "Meanwhile, improvements continued to be made in England, and each, in turn, was imported. The mule was made self-acting about 1830 by Richard Roberts of Manchester, but because the export of textile machinery was still forbidden by British law, it, too, had to be brought over discreetly." Pursell, *The Machine in America*, 50.
20. Wallace and Jeremy, "William Pollard and the Arkwright Patents," 413.
21. Quoted in Herbert Heaton, "The Industrial Immigrant in the United States, 1783–1812," *Proceedings of the American Philosophical Society* 95, no. 5 (October 1951): 523.
22. Quoted in American Historical Association, *Annual Report of the American Historical Association for the Year 1896* (Washington, DC: U.S. Government Printing Office, 1897), 1:613.
23. Ben-Atar, *Trade Secrets*, 116.
24. For a detailed discussion of the evolution of British restrictions, from which this paragraph draws, see David J. Jeremy, "Damming the Flood: British Government Efforts to Check the Outflow of Technicians and Machinery, 1780–1843," *Business History Review* 51, no. 1 (Spring 1977): 1–34; and Jeremy, "British Textile Technology Transmission to the United States: The Philadelphia Region Experience, 1770–1820," *Business History Review* 47, no. 1 (Spring 1973): 24–52.
25. Heaton, "The Industrial Immigrant in the United States, 1783–1812," 519.
26. Ben-Atar, *Trade Secrets*, 114.
27. Jeremy, "Damming the Flood," 3.
28. Jeremy, "Damming the Flood," 14.
29. Quoted in Ben-Atar, *Trade Secrets*, 80.
30. Ben-Atar, *Trade Secrets*, 141.
31. Jeremy, "Damming the Flood," 30.
32. *The Papers of George Washington: Presidential Series*, ed. Mark A. Mastromarino (Charlottesville: University Press of Virginia, 2000), 9:182–83.
33. Jeremy, *Transatlantic Industrial Revolution*, 76.
34. Quoted in Ben-Atar, *Trade Secrets*, 79.

35. Heaton, "The Industrial Immigrant in the United States, 1783–1812," 520.
36. See Michael Kraus, "Across the Western Sea (1783–1845)," *Journal of British Studies* 1, no. 2 (May 1962): 94.
37. Quoted in Heaton, "The Industrial Immigrant in the United States, 1783–1812," 526.
38. *The Papers of Alexander Hamilton,* ed. Harold C. Syrett (New York: Columbia University Press, 1965), 8:18.
39. Quoted in Ben-Atar, *Trade Secrets,* 156.
40. Jeremy, *Transatlantic Industrial Revolution,* 78.
41. Ben-Atar, *Trade Secrets,* 142.
42. Quoted in Pursell, "Thomas Digges and William Pearce," 552.
43. Ben-Atar, *Trade Secrets,* 145.
44. Quoted in Ben-Atar, *Trade Secrets,* 146.
45. *The Papers of Alexander Hamilton,* ed. Harold C. Syrett (New York: Columbia University Press, 1966), 11:242.
46. *The Papers of Alexander Hamilton,* 11:243–44.
47. Quoted in Ben-Atar, *Trade Secrets,* 116–17.
48. Quoted in Ben-Atar, *Trade Secrets,* 174.
49. Quoted in Pursell, *The Machine in America,* 40.
50. Quoted in Ben-Atar, *Trade Secrets,* 143.
51. Quoted in Pursell, *The Machine in America,* 41.
52. Quoted in Pursell, *The Machine in America,* 42.
53. Jeremy, *Transatlantic Industrial Revolution,* 86.
54. Quoted in Jeremy, *Transatlantic Industrial Revolution,* 86.
55. Jeremy, *Transatlantic Industrial Revolution,* 87.
56. Jeremy, *Transatlantic Industrial Revolution,* 84.
57. Jeremy, *Transatlantic Industrial Revolution,* 87.
58. Jeremy, *Transatlantic Industrial Revolution,* 88.
59. For more details on the diffusion of the Slater system, see David R. Meyer, *The Roots of American Industrialization* (Baltimore: Johns Hopkins University Press, 2003), 96–107. On the Slater story more generally, see E. H. Cameron, *Samuel Slater: Father of American Manufactures* (Freeport, ME: Bond Wheelwright, 1960); and Barbara M. Tucker, *Samuel Slater and the Origins of the American Textile Industry, 1790–1860* (Ithaca, NY: Cornell University Press, 1984).
60. Pursell, *The Machine in America,* 44.
61. Jeremy, *Transatlantic Industrial Revolution,* 92.
62. Nathan Appleton, *Introduction of the Power Loom, and Origin of Lowell* (Lowell, MA: B. H. Penhallow, 1858), 8–9.
63. Choate, *Hot Property,* 31.
64. Jeremy, *Transatlantic Industrial Revolution,* 95.
65. Ben-Atar, *Trade Secrets,* 203.
66. Jeremy, "Damming the Flood," 31.

Chapter 7

1. William E. Unrau, *White Man's Wicked Water: The Alcohol Trade and Prohibition in Indian Country, 1802–1892* (Lawrence: University Press of Kansas, 1996).
2. See Eric Jay Dolin, *Fur, Fortune, and Empire: The Epic History of the Fur Trade in America* (New York: Norton, 2010).
3. Other common trade items included blankets, cloth, guns, powder, knives, and additional utensils. The cumulative effect over time was to undermine Indian self-sufficiency and create a dependence on white traders.
4. Ian Williams, *Rum: A Social and Sociable History* (New York: Nation Books, 2005), 114.
5. See especially Peter C. Mancall, *Deadly Medicine: Indians and Alcohol in Early America* (Ithaca, NY: Cornell University Press, 1995).
6. Mancall, *Deadly Medicine*, 14.
7. Mancall, *Deadly Medicine*, 16.
8. Mancall, *Deadly Medicine*, 68.
9. See John W. Frank, Roland S. Moore, and Genevieve M. Ames, "Public Health Then and Now: Historical and Cultural Roots of Drinking Problems Among American Indians," *American Journal of Public Health* 90, no. 3 (March 2000), 346. For a more general discussion, see also National Institute on Alcohol Abuse and Alcoholism, *Alcohol Use Among American Indians and Alaska Natives: Research Monograph 37* (Washington, DC: U.S. Department of Health and Human Services, 2002).
10. Mancall, *Deadly Medicine*, 26.
11. Quoted in Williams, *Rum*, 110.
12. Williams, *Rum*, 111.
13. Quoted in Clarence Walworth Alvord and Clarence Edwin Cartera, eds., *The Critical Period, 1763–1765.* Illinois State Historical Collections (Springfield: Illinois State Historical Library, 1915), 10:334–35.
14. Quoted in Mancall, *Deadly Medicine*, 162.
15. Quoted in Mancall, *Deadly Medicine*, 162.
16. Quoted in Mancall, *Deadly Medicine*, 101.
17. Quoted in Pennsylvania Provincial Council, *Minutes of the Provincial Council of Pennsylvania: From the Organization to the Termination of the Proprietary Government* (Philadelphia: J. Severns, 1852), 3:275.
18. Quoted in Pennsylvania Provincial Council, *Minutes of the Provincial Council of Pennsylvania: From the Organization to the Termination of the Proprietary Government* (Harrisburg: Theo. Fenn, 1851), 4:91.
19. Williams, *Rum*, 102.
20. Quoted in William L. McDowell Jr., ed., *The Colonial Records of South Carolina: Documents Relating to Indian Affairs, 21 May 1750–7 August 1754* (Columbia: South Carolina Archives Department, 1958), 12.
21. Williams, *Rum*, 99–100.

22. Larzer Ziff, ed., *The Portable Benjamin Franklin* (New York: Penguin, 2005), 117.
23. Mark Edward Lender and James Kirby Martin, *Drinking in America: A History* (New York: Free Press, 1987), 31.
24. Barton H. Barbour, *Fort Union and the Upper Missouri Fur Trade* (Norman: University of Oklahoma Press, 2001), 150–51.
25. The 1832 law stated that no "ardent spirits" should be introduced into Indian country "under any pretence." The 1834 revision specified various penalties, including forfeiture and a $500 fine for providing alcohol to an Indian, and forfeiture and a $300 fine for transporting alcohol into Indian country. Illegal stills could be dismantled and owners fined $1,000. Trading licenses could also be revoked. The 1847 revision established a two-year prison sentence for selling alcohol to Indians and a one-year sentence for transporting alcohol into Indian country. Indian witnesses were also given equal status as whites in legal proceedings.
26. Anthony F. C. Wallace, *Jefferson and the Indians: The Tragic Fate of the First Americans* (Cambridge, MA: Harvard University Press, 1999), 211–12.
27. Unrau, *White Man's Wicked Water*, x.
28. Unrau, *White Man's Wicked Water*, x.
29. Unrau, *White Man's Wicked Water*, 18.
30. Unrau, *White Man's Wicked Water*, 10.
31. Hiram Martin Chittenden, *The American Fur Trade of the Far West*, vol. 1 (Stanford: Academic Reprints, 1954), 23.
32. Quoted in Gustavus Myers, *History of the Great American Fortunes*, vol. 1 (Chicago: Charles H. Kerr, 1911), 115.
33. Charles Larpenteur, *Forty Years a Fur Trader on the Upper Missouri: The Personal Narrative of Charles Larpenteur, 1833–1872*, ed. Elliott Coues (New York: Harper, 1898), 57.
34. Quoted in Francis Paul Prucha, *Documents of United States Indian Policy* (Lincoln: University of Nebraska Press, 2000), 44.
35. Quoted in Unrau, *White Man's Wicked Water*, 10.
36. Quoted in Francis Paul Prucha, *Broadax and Bayonet: The Role of the United States Army in the Development of the Northwest, 1815–1860* (Lincoln: University of Nebraska Press, 1995), 74–75.
37. Quoted in Unrau, *White Man's Wicked Water*, 14.
38. Quoted in William E. Unrau, "Indian Prohibition and Tribal Disorganization in the Trans-Missouri West, 1802–1862," *Contemporary Drug Problems* 21, no. 4 (Winter 1994): 528.
39. W. J. Rorabaugh, *Alcoholic Republic: An American Tradition* (New York: Oxford University Press, 1979), 160.
40. Rorabaugh, *Alcoholic Republic*, 159.
41. Detroit was created as a fur trade outpost by the Frenchman Antoine de la Mothe de Cadillac, who argued that selling alcohol to Indians was justified on sanitary grounds. With the main Indian diet based on

fish and smoked meat, Cadillac suggested that "a little brandy after the meal . . . seems necessary to cook the bilious meats and the crudities they leave in their stomach." Quoted in Frank E. Ross, "The Fur Trade of the Western Great Lakes Region," *Minnesota History* 19, no. 3 (September 1938): 279. Cadillac not only profited greatly from the alcohol-for-fur trade but was also apparently a con artist and imposter, pretending to be of noble descent by creating a fake aristocratic name and family coat of arms, the same one used centuries later by the American automobile of that name. See Edward Butts, *Outlaws of the Lakes* (Toronto: Lynx Images, 2004), 16–17.

42. In the case of early Chicago as a fur trade village dominated by Astor's company, see John D. Haeger, "The American Fur Company and the Chicago of 1812–1835," *Journal of the Illinois State Historical Society* 61, no. 2 (Summer 1968): 117–39. Haeger also notes that the American Fur Company was the key in organizing the Indian treaty of 1833 that proved to be a milestone in the history of Chicago, laying the foundation for rapid population growth in subsequent decades.
43. Chittenden, *The American Fur Trade of the Far West,* 1:21.
44. Quoted in Chittenden, *The American Fur Trade of the Far West,* 1:21.
45. More generally, Gustavus Myers writes: "Astor's company was a law unto itself. That it employed both force and fraud and entirely ignored all laws enacted by Congress, is as clear as daylight from the Government reports of that period." Myers adds that "if there was one serious crime at that time it was the supplying of the Indians with whisky. . . . To say that Astor knew nothing of what his agents were doing is a palliation not worthy of consideration; he was a man who knew and attended to even the pettiest of details of his varied business." See Myers, *History of the Great American Fortunes,* 1:114–15.
46. Quoted in Myers, *History of the Great American Fortunes,* 1:118.
47. Quoted in Barbour, *Fort Union and the Upper Missouri Fur Trade,* 167–68.
48. For a detailed account of this episode, see Barbour, *Fort Union and the Upper Missouri Fur Trade,* 166–71.
49. Larpenteur, *Forty Years a Fur Trader on the Upper Missouri,* 74.
50. Jeanne P. Leader, "The Pottawatomies and Alcohol: An Illustration of the Illegal Trade," *Kansas State History* 2, no. 3 (Autumn 1979): 162.
51. This paragraph is based on Unrau, *White Man's Wicked Water,* 67–68.
52. Unrau calculates that by 1845 "total monetary obligations sanctioned by treaties with the removal of Indians . . . amounted to $26,983,068." For a breakdown of these funds by tribe, see Unrau, *White Man's Wicked Water,* 45.
53. Clyde N. Wilson, ed., *The Papers of John C. Calhoun* (Columbia: University of South Carolina Press, 1980), 13:191.
54. Quoted in Unrau, "Indian Prohibition and Tribal Disorganization," 527.
55. Quoted in Unrau, "Indian Prohibition and Tribal Disorganization," 527.

56. Quoted in Unrau, *White Man's Wicked Water*, 9.
57. Unrau, *White Man's Wicked Water*, 9.
58. U.S. Congress, *American State Papers: Indian Affairs Volume Four Part Two 1832* (Whitefish, MT: Kessinger, 2005), 655.
59. Quoted in Unrau, *White Man's Wicked Water*, 24.
60. Quoted in Unrau, *White Man's Wicked Water*, 26.
61. Unrau, *White Man's Wicked Water*, 41.
62. Quoted in Unrau, *White Man's Wicked Water*, 52.
63. This paragraph draws from Unrau, *White Man's Wicked Water*, 34, 42.
64. Quoted in Gary C. Stein, "A Fearful Drunkenness: The Liquor Trade to the Western Indians as Seen by European Travelers in America, 1800–1860," *Red River Valley Historical Review* 2, no. 2 (1974): 15.
65. Quoted in George Frederick Ruxton, *In the Old West*, ed. Horace Kephart (New York: Outing, 1916), 166.
66. Rufus B. Sage, *Scenes in the Rocky Mountains and in Oregon, California, New Mexico, Texas, and the Grand Prairies; or, Notes by the Way, During an Excursion of Three Years, with a Description of the Countries Passed through, Including their Geography, Geology, Resources, Present Condition, and the Different Nations Inhabiting Them* (Philadelphia: Carey & Hart, 1846), 28.
67. Charles Latrobe, *The Rambler in North America* (original 1836; reprint Carlisle, MA: Applewood, 2007), 2:212.

Chapter 8

1. The first U.S. Census, in 1790, recorded fewer than seven hundred thousand slaves, but by the outbreak of the Civil War there were almost four million, with more than half of them connected in some form to cotton cultivation. See Anne Farrow, Joel Lang, and Jennifer Frank, *Complicity: How the North Promoted, Prolonged, and Profited from Slavery* (New York: Ballantine, 2006), 26.
2. For a comprehensive review of these state and federal laws, see W.E.B. Dubois, *The Suppression of the African Slave-Trade to the United States of America 1638–1870* (New York: Russell & Russell, 1965, first published 1898).
3. Quoted in Don E. Fehrenbacher, *The Slaveholding Republic* (New York: Oxford University Press, 2001), 141–42.
4. On the importance of cotton, see Gene Dattel, *Cotton and Race in the Making of America* (Chicago: Ivan R. Dee, 2009).
5. Ernest Obadele-Starks, *Freebooters and Smugglers: The Foreign Slave Trade in the United States After 1808* (Fayetteville: University of Arkansas Press, 2007), 61.
6. Farrow et al., *Complicity*, xxvii, 4. On New York's commercial rise and its connection to cotton, see Sven Beckert, *The Monied Metropolis: New York City and the Consolidation of the American Bourgeoisie, 1850–1896* (New York: Cambridge University Press, 2001).

7. Warren S. Howard, *American Slavers and the Federal Law, 1837–1862* (Berkeley: University of California Press, 1963), 13; Donald L. Canney, *Africa Squadron: The U.S. Navy and the Slave Trade, 1842–1861* (Washington, DC: Potomac, 2006), 56–57.
8. In a twenty-year period the squadron captured only thirty-six ships. Canney, *Africa Squadron*, xiii.
9. Fehrenbacher, *The Slaveholding Republic*, 174.
10. It should be noted that at this point the United States wanted to be able to search British vessels, not so much to enforce antislave-trade laws but rather to enforce the Union blockade of Confederate ports. Thus, as U.S. concerns suddenly shifted, Washington's long-standing stance against mutual search and seizure dramatically softened. American involvement in the slave trade quickly plummeted. In his annual address to Congress in December 1863, President Lincoln stated, "It is believed that, so far as American ports and American citizens are concerned, that inhuman and odious traffic has been brought to an end." Quoted in Don E. Fehrenbacher, ed., *Lincoln: Speeches and Writings: 1859–1865* (New York: Literary Classics of the United States, 1989), 538.
11. Quoted in Daniel P. Mannix, *Black Cargoes: A History of the Atlantic Slave Trade, 1518–1865* (New York: Viking, 1962), 205.
12. Hugh Thomas notes, for example, that from 1837 to 1860 there were seventy-four court cases in the United States on slave-trading-related charges, but few captains were convicted and the others received minimal sentences. Thomas, *The Slave Trade* (New York: Simon and Schuster, 1997), 774.
13. Howard, *American Slavers and the Federal Law*, 196–99.
14. Ron Soodalter, *Hanging Captain Gordon: The Life and Trial of an American Slave Trader* (New York: Atria, 2006), 26.
15. Soodalter, *Hanging Captain Gordon*, 54.
16. Soodalter, *Hanging Captain Gordon*, 42–43; Howard, *American Slavers and the Federal Law*, 102–10.
17. For more details, see Soodalter, *Hanging Captain Gordon*.
18. Obadele-Starks, *Freebooters and Smugglers*, 187.
19. Farrow et al., *Complicity*, 123.
20. Quoted in Charles Rappleye, *Sons of Providence: The Brown Brothers, the Slave Trade, and the American Revolution* (New York: Simon and Schuster, 2006), 248.
21. Quoted in Edward A. Park, ed., *The Works of Samuel Hopkins* (Boston: Doctrinal Tract and Book Society, 1852), 1:123.
22. Quoted in Rappleye, *Sons of Providence*, 299.
23. Rappleye, *Sons of Providence*, 304.
24. Quoted in Rappleye, *Sons of Providence*, 260.
25. Farrow et al., *Complicity*, 110.
26. According to Fehrenbacher, a cargo of slaves could be worth up to fifteen times the value of the ship. See *The Slaveholding Republic*, 197.

27. Jay Coughtry, *The Notorious Triangle: Rhode Island and the African Slave Trade, 1700–1807* (Philadelphia: Temple University Press, 1981), 217.
28. Quoted in Coughtry, *The Notorious Triangle*, 218.
29. For more details on this episode, see Rappleye, *Sons of Providence*, 317–18; and Coughtry, *The Notorious Triangle*, 27–28.
30. Rappleye, *Sons of Providence*, 312.
31. Rappleye, *Sons of Providence*, 338.
32. Farrow et al., *Complicity*, 111.
33. Fehrenbacher, *The Slaveholding Republic*, 141.
34. Rappleye, *Sons of Providence*, 337.
35. Coughtry, *The Notorious Triangle*, 229.
36. Quoted in Farrow et al., *Complicity*, 112.
37. Farrow et al., *Complicity*, 112.
38. Quoted in Dattel, *Cotton and Race in the Making of America*, 91.
39. Quoted in Dattel, *Cotton and Race in the Making of America*, 90.
40. Quoted in Soodalter, *Hanging Captain Gordon*, 71.
41. Obadele-Starks, *Freebooters and Smugglers*, 176.
42. Thomas, *The Slave Trade*, 773.
43. Quoted in Thomas, *The Slave Trade*, 773.
44. Howard, *American Slavers and the Federal Law*, 167; Soodalter, *Hanging Captain Gordon*, 83–87.
45. Farrow et al., *Complicity*, 125.
46. Only one-sixth of indictments in New York City produced convictions. Between 1837 and 1861, there were about 125 prosecutions, and of these just 20 led to prison sentences (averaging two years per sentence). Of these, ten received presidential pardons. See Soodalter, *Hanging Captain Gordon*, 9.
47. Quoted in Farrow et al., *Complicity*, 124.
48. Thomas, *The Slave Trade*, 568.
49. David Eltis, "The U.S. Transatlantic Slave Trade, 1644–1867: An Assessment," *Civil War History* 54, no. 4 (2008): 372.
50. Howard, *American Slavers and the Federal Law*, 30.
51. Howard, *American Slavers and the Federal Law*, 32.
52. Quoted in Thomas, *The Slave Trade*, 729.
53. David Eltis, "The U.S. Transatlantic Slave Trade, 1644–1867," 376.
54. Howard, *American Slavers and the Federal Law*, 32.
55. David Eltis, *Economic Growth and the Ending of the Transatlantic Slave Trade* (New York: Oxford University Press, 1987), 271–72. Eltis notes, "In the last twenty years of the trade, a count of 136 ships for which information on place of construction can be found indicates that 64 percent were built in the United States."
56. Howard, *American Slavers and the Federal Law*, 37–39.
57. Thomas, *The Slave Trade*, 729.
58. Quoted in Fehrenbacher, *The Slaveholding Republic*, 164.

59. Quoted in Fehrenbacher, *The Slaveholding Republic*, 164.
60. Fehrenbacher, *The Slaveholding Republic*, 177–78.
61. Fehrenbacher, *The Slaveholding Republic*, 179.
62. For a discussion, see Fehrenbacher, *The Slaveholding Republic*, 137.
63. Howard, *American Slavers and the Federal Law*, 29.
64. Government slave auctions were typically set up by the U.S. marshal's office. "The sale of slaves by the United States marshals," the *New Orleans Bee* observed in 1830, "was not uncommon in everyday life of Louisiana." Quoted in Obadele-Starks, *Freebooters and Smugglers*, 81.
65. Joe G. Taylor, "The Foreign Slave Trade in Louisiana after 1808," *Louisiana History: The Journal of the Louisiana Historical Association* 1, no. 1 (Winter 1960): 37, 43.
66. Quoted in Fehrenbacher, *The Slaveholding Republic*, 148.
67. Taylor, "The Foreign Slave Trade in Louisiana After 1808," 38.
68. Quoted in Adam Rothman, *Slave Country: American Expansion and the Origins of the Deep South* (Cambridge, MA: Harvard University Press, 2005), 193.
69. Quoted in Rothman, *Slave Country*, 193.
70. Quoted in Rothman, *Slave Country*, 193.
71. William C. Davis, *Three Roads to the Alamo* (New York: HarperCollins, 1998), 60.
72. Quoted in "Early Life of the Southwest—the Bowies," *DeBow's Review* 13, no. 4 (October 1852): 381.
73. Richard Drake, "Revelations of a Slave Smuggler (1808–1853)," excerpted in Robert Edgar Conrad, ed., *In the Hands of Strangers: Readings on Foreign and Domestic Slave Trading and the Crisis of the Union* (University Park: Penn State Press, 2001), 73. Historians question the authenticity of Drake's account yet still cite it because it reveals credible knowledge of slave trafficking, especially the parts related to the United States.
74. Frances J. Stafford, "Illegal Importations: Enforcement of the Slave Trade Laws Along the Florida Coast, 1810–1828," *Florida Historical Quarterly* 46, no. 2 (October 1967): 124–33.
75. Jennifer Heckard, *The Crossroads of Empire: The 1817 Liberation and Occupancy of Amelia Island, East Florida* (Ph.D. Dissertation, University of Connecticut, 2006), 8–9.
76. For more details, see T. Frederick Davis, "MacGregor's Invasion of Florida, 1817," *Quarterly of the Florida Historical Society* 7, no. 1 (July 1928): 1–71.
77. Stafford, "Illegal Importations," 126.
78. Rothman, *Slave Country*, 193.
79. Quoted in Charles H. Bowman Jr., "Vicente Pazos and the Amelia Island Affair, 1817," *Florida Historical Quarterly* 53, no. 3 (January 1975), 293.
80. U.S. Congress, Senate Committee on Foreign Relations, *Compilation of Reports on Foreign Relations* (Washington, DC: U.S. Government Printing Office, 1901), 6:25.

81. This is emphasized by Richard G. Lowe, "American Seizure of Amelia Island," *Florida Historical Quarterly* 45, no. 1 (July 1966): 18–30.
82. Obadele-Starks, *Freebooters and Smugglers*, 79.
83. For a more detailed account, see especially Paul D. Lack, "Slavery and the Texas Revolution," *Southwestern Historical Quarterly* 89, no. 2 (October 1985): 181–202. Also see Obadele-Starks, *Freebooters and Smugglers*, 85–87.
84. Lack, "Slavery and the Texas Revolution," 186.
85. Sean Kelley, "Blackbirders and Bozales: African-Born Slaves on the Lower Brazos River of Texas in the Nineteenth Century," *Civil War History* 54, no. 4 (December 2008): 413; Lack, "Slavery and the Texas Revolution," 186.
86. Obadele-Starks, *Freebooters and Smugglers*, 86–87.
87. Larry Gara, *The Liberty Line: The Legend of the Underground Railroad* (Lexington: University Press of Kentucky, 1996 ed.).
88. Lathan A. Windley, "Runaway Slave Advertisements of George Washington and Thomas Jefferson," *Journal of Negro History* 63, no. 4 (October 1978): 373–74.
89. Ethan A. Nadelmann, *Cops Across Borders: The Internationalization of U.S. Criminal Law Enforcement* (University Park: Penn State Press, 1993).
90. Sean Kelley, "'Mexico in His Head': Slavery and the Texas-Mexico Border, 1810–1860," *Journal of Social History* 37, no. 3 (Spring 2004): 709–23; Ronnie C. Tyler, "Fugitive Slaves in Mexico," *Journal of Negro History* 57, no. 1 (January 1972): 1–12.
91. Obadele-Starks, *Freebooters and Smugglers*, 127.
92. Nadelmann, *Cops Across Borders*, 36.
93. James McPherson, *Battle Cry of Freedom: The Civil War Era* (New York: Oxford University Press, 2003), 81.
94. In the 1850s, Indiana, Iowa, and Illinois went so far as to pass exclusion laws prohibiting the immigration of any blacks regardless of whether they were free or not.
95. Carol Wilson, *Freedom at Risk: The Kidnapping of Free Blacks in America, 1780–1865* (Lexington: University Press of Kentucky, 1994).
96. Wilson, *Freedom at Risk*, 18.
97. Fehrenbacher, *The Slaveholding Republic*, 215.
98. Quoted in Gara, *The Liberty Line*, 117.
99. For a more detailed analysis, see Stanley W. Campbell, *The Slave Catchers: Enforcement of the Fugitive Slave Law, 1850–1860* (New York: Norton, 1972).
100. John Reuben Thompson, "The Editor's Table: The Fugitive Slave Bill," *Southern Literary Messenger* (November 1850), 697.
101. Gara, *The Liberty Line*, 114.
102. Frederick Douglass, *My Bondage and My Freedom* (New York: Washington Square Press, 2003, originally published 1855), 365.

103. Fehrenbacher, *The Slaveholding Republic*, 234.
104. Fehrenbacher, *The Slaveholding Republic*, 238.
105. Gara, *The Liberty Line*, 128; Fehrenbacher, *The Slaveholding Republic*, 251.
106. Campbell, *The Slave Catchers*, 110.
107. On the origin and popularization of the word *contraband* to describe escaped slaves, see Kate Masur, "A Rare Phenomenon of Philological Vegetation: The Word 'Contraband' and the Meanings of Emancipation in the United States," *Journal of American History* 93, no. 4 (March 2007): 1050–84.
108. Testimony of the Superintendent of Contrabands at Fortress Monroe, Virginia, before the American Freedmen's Inquiry Commission, 9 May 1863, reprinted in Conrad, ed., *In the Hands of Strangers*, 492–94.

Chapter 9

1. James McPherson, *Battle Cry of Freedom: The Civil War Era* (New York: Oxford University Press, 1988), 318–19.
2. Two clandestinely acquired vessels, named the *Florida* and *Alabama*, wreaked havoc on the U.S. merchant marine, greatly damaging America's prominence in commercial shipping. Stephen R. Wise, *Lifeline of the Confederacy: Blockade Running During the Civil War* (Columbia: University of South Carolina Press, 1988), 49; McPherson, *Battle Cry of Freedom*, 547.
3. Dean B. Mahin, *One War at a Time: The International Dimensions of the American Civil War* (Washington, DC: Brassey's, 2000), 84.
4. George C. Herring, *From Colony to Superpower: U.S. Foreign Relations Since 1776* (New York: Oxford University Press, 2008), 226–27.
5. Quoted in McPherson, *Battle Cry of Freedom*, 383.
6. Quoted in Mahin, *One War at a Time*, 84.
7. Quoted in McPherson, *Battle Cry of Freedom*, 383.
8. For the most detailed account of the British role, see Amanda Foreman, *A World on Fire: Britain's Crucial Role in the American Civil War* (New York: Random House, 2011).
9. Mahin, *One War at a Time*, 86.
10. McPherson notes that Britain in turn would cite this precedent "a half-century later to justify seizure of American ships carrying contraband to neutral Holland intended for overland trans-shipment to Germany." McPherson, *Battle Cry of Freedom*, 387.
11. Quoted in Mahin, *One War at a Time*, 162.
12. Wise, *Lifeline of the Confederacy*, 221.
13. Wise, *Lifeline of the Confederacy*, 221.
14. McPherson, *Battle Cry of Freedom*, 380.
15. Wise, *Lifeline of the Confederacy*, 7.
16. Quoted in Gene Dattel, *Cotton and Race in the Making of America* (Chicago: Ivan R. Dee, 2009), 198.
17. Wise, *Lifeline of the Confederacy*, 107.

18. Quoted in Mahin, *One War at a Time*, 167.
19. Quoted in Mahin, *One War at a Time*, 166.
20. Quoted in Rodman L. Underwood, *Waters of Discord: The Union Blockade of Texas During the Civil War* (Jefferson, NC: McFarland, 2008), 55.
21. Wise, *Lifeline of the Confederacy*, 132.
22. Quoted in Mahin, *One War at a Time*, 170.
23. See especially James A. Irby, *Backdoor at Bagdad: The Civil War on the Rio Grande* (El Paso: Texas Western Press, 1977).
24. Quoted in Underwood, *Waters of Discord*, 72.
25. Fredericka Meiners, "The Texas Border Cotton Trade, 1862–1863," *Civil War History* 13, no. 9 (December 1977): 293–94.
26. Robert W. Delaney, "Matamoros, Port of Texas During the Civil War," *Southwestern Historical Quarterly* 58, no. 4 (April 1955): 473–74.
27. Quoted in Underwood, *Waters of Discord*, 71.
28. Wise, *Lifeline of the Confederacy*, 88.
29. Wise, *Lifeline of the Confederacy*, 110–11.
30. McPherson, *Battle Cry of Freedom*, 380.
31. Quoted in Dattel, *Cotton and Race in the Making of America*, 195.
32. David G. Surdam, *Northern Naval Superiority and the Economics of the American Civil War* (Columbia: University of South Carolina Press, 2001), 6.
33. Some scholars argue that the importation of luxury items actually helped the South, since it made blockade running profitable. See Robert B. Ekelund Jr. et al., "The Unintended Consequences of Confederate Trade Legislation," *Eastern Economic Journal* 30, no. 2 (Spring 2004): 187–205.
34. Thomas Boaz, *Guns for Cotton: England Arms the Confederacy* (Shippensburg, PA: Burg Street Press, 1996), 62.
35. The list of banned items included brandy and other spirits, carpets and rugs, carriages and carriage parts, furniture, marble, wallpaper, bricks, coconuts, gems, antiques, and coin collections. See Wise, *Lifeline of the Confederacy*, 145.
36. Mahin, *One War at a Time*, 91. The most important exception to this was the handful of ships operated by the Ordinance Bureau, the only Confederate agency that directly carried out its own blockade running.
37. Mahin, *One War at a Time*, 173.
38. Wise, *Lifeline of the Confederacy*, 217.
39. McPherson, *Battle Cry of Freedom*, 381–82.
40. Surdam, *Northern Naval Superiority and the Economics of the American Civil War*, 6.
41. Quoted in E. Merton Coulter, "Commercial Intercourse with the Confederacy in the Mississippi Valley, 1861–1865," *Mississippi Valley Historical Review* 5, no. 4 (March 1919): 384.
42. Stanley Lebergott, "Why the South Lost: Commercial Purpose in the Confederacy, 1861–1865," *Journal of American History* 70, no. 1 (June 1983): 72–73.

43. Stuart D. Brandes, *Warhogs: A History of War Profits in America* (Lexington: University of Kentucky Press), 95.
44. Ludwell H. Johnson, "Trading with the Union: The Evolution of Confederate Policy," *Virginia Magazine of History and Biography* 78, no. 3 (July 1970): 308.
45. These border states were exempted from Chase's May 1861 order severing trade with "all persons or parties in armed insurrection against the Union." Yet he also noted that "it is obviously improper to permit contraband whose ultimate destination may reach the rebel forces to be forwarded to those states." Quoted in Robert F. Futrell, *Federal Trade with the Confederate States, 1861–1865: A Study of Governmental Policy* (Ph.D. dissertation, Vanderbilt University, 1950), 11.
46. Quoted in Carl E. Prince and Mollie Keller, *The U.S. Customs Service: A Bicentennial History* (Washington, DC: U.S. Department of the Treasury, 1989), 130.
47. Quoted in Prince and Keller, *The U.S. Customs Service*, 130.
48. Quoted in Prince and Keller, *The U.S. Customs Service*, 131.
49. Sellew A. Roberts, "The Federal Government and Confederate Cotton," *American Historical Review* 32, no. 2 (January 1927): 271.
50. Joseph H. Parks, "A Confederate Trade Center Under Federal Occupation: Memphis, 1862–1865," *Journal of Southern History* 7, no. 3 (August 1941): 294.
51. Parks, "A Confederate Trade Center Under Federal Occupation," 298.
52. Futrell, *Federal Trade with the Confederate States, 1861–1865*, 298.
53. Parks, "A Confederate Trade Center Under Federal Occupation," 299.
54. Quoted in Surdam, *Northern Naval Superiority and the Economics of the American Civil War*, 197.
55. Futrell, *Federal Trade with the Confederate States*, 227.
56. Futrell, *Federal Trade with the Confederate States*, 228.
57. Quoted in Futrell, *Federal Trade with the Confederate States*, 228.
58. Futrell, *Federal Trade with the Confederate States*, 102.
59. Quoted in Futrell, *Federal Trade with the Confederate States*, 291–92.
60. Parks, "A Confederate Trade Center Under Federal Occupation," 296.
61. Quoted in Surdam, *Northern Naval Superiority and the Economics of the American Civil War*, 173–74.
62. Quoted in McPherson, *Battle Cry of Freedom*, 621.
63. Quoted in McPherson, *Battle Cry of Freedom*, 622.
64. Brandes, *Warhogs*, 95.
65. Quoted in Brandes, *Warhogs*, 95.
66. Quoted in Futrell, *Federal Trade with the Confederate States*, 391.
67. Quoted in McPherson, *Battle Cry of Freedom*, 623.
68. Quoted in Futrell, *Federal Trade with the Confederate States*, 77.
69. Jonathan D. Sarna, *When General Grant Expelled the Jews* (New York: Schocken Books, 2012), ix.

70. Quoted in Roberts, "The Federal Government and Confederate Cotton," 268–69.
71. Futrell, *Federal Trade with the Confederate States*, 370.
72. Futrell, *Federal Trade with the Confederate States*, 462.
73. Ludwell H. Johnson, "Contraband Trade During the Last Year of the Civil War," *Mississippi Valley Historical Review* 49, no. 4 (March 1963): 641.
74. Quoted in Futrell, *Federal Trade with the Confederate States*, 415.
75. Surdam notes that Lincoln did not turn down a single permit request by friends and family. See David G. Surdam, "Traders or Traitors: Northern Cotton Trading During the Civil War," *Business and Economic History* 28, no. 2 (Winter 1999), 305.
76. Quoted in Futrell, *Federal Trade with the Confederate States*, 225.
77. See especially Ludwell H. Johnson, "Northern Profit and Profiteers: The Cotton Rings of 1864–1865," *Civil War History* 12, no. 2 (June 1966): 101–15.
78. Surdam, "Traders or Traitors," 310.
79. Brandes, *Warhogs*, 94.
80. Quoted in Coulter, "Commercial Intercourse with the Confederacy in the Mississippi Valley, 1861–1865," 393–94.
81. Quoted in Surdam, *Northern Naval Superiority and the Economics of the American Civil War*, 203.
82. Dattel, *Cotton and Race in the Making of America*, 198.
83. Quoted in Prince and Keller, *The U.S. Customs Service*, 135.
84. Robert W. Delaney, "Matamoros, Port for Texas During the Civil War," *Southwestern Historical Quarterly* 58, no. 4 (April 1955): 479.
85. Underwood, *Waters of Discord*, 73–74.
86. Quoted in Prince and Keller, *The U.S. Customs Service*, 136.
87. Quoted in Prince and Keller, *The U.S. Customs Service*, 137.
88. This paragraph is drawn from Ludwell H. Johnson, "Commerce Between Northeastern Ports and the Confederacy, 1861–1865," *Journal of American History* 54, no. 1 (June 1967): 33–34.
89. Prince and Keller, *The U.S. Customs Service*, 139. They note that Chase and Barney collaborated in many other financial schemes. For more details, also see Thomas Graham Belden and Marva Robins Belden, *So Fell the Angels* (Boston: Little, Brown, 1956).
90. Prince and Keller, *The U.S. Customs Service*, 140.
91. See Mary Kaldor, *New and Old Wars: Organized Violence in a Global Era* (Stanford: Stanford University Press, 1999).

Chapter 10

1. For a more detailed account of smuggling during this period, see especially Andrew Wender Cohen, *Contraband: The War on Smuggling and the Birth of the American Century* (New York: Norton, forthcoming).

2. Alfred E. Eckes, *Opening America's Market: U.S. Foreign Trade Policy Since 1776* (Chapel Hill: University of North Carolina Press, 1995), 28.
3. Eckes, *Opening America's Market*, 28.
4. Eckes, *Opening America's Market*, 29.
5. Quoted in Jack Beatty, *Age of Betrayal: The Triumph of Money in America: 1865–1900* (New York: Vintage, 2008), 70.
6. Schmeckelbier provides a detailed list of forbidden imports, ranging from the well-known to the highly obscure. See Laurence Frederick Schmeckelbier, *The Customs Service: Its History, Activities and Organization* (Baltimore: Johns Hopkins University Press, 1924), 73–74.
7. George F. Howe, "The New York Custom-House Controversy, 1877–1879," *Mississippi Valley Historical Review* 18, no. 3 (December 1931): 350.
8. The information on seizures, indictments, fines, and penalties is drawn from Andrew Wender Cohen, "Smuggling, Globalization, and America's Outward State, 1870–1909," *Journal of American History* 97, no. 2 (September 2010): 372, 382.
9. This had been true since the early years of the republic. See especially Gautham Rao, *The Creation of the American State: Customhouses, Law, and Commerce in the Age of Revolution* (Ph.D. dissertation, University of Chicago, 2008).
10. For a more detailed discussion, see Ari Hoogenboom, *Outlawing the Spoils: A History of the Civil Service Reform Movement, 1865–1883* (Urbana: University of Illinois Press, 1968). Also see Howe, "The New York Custom-House Controversy," 350–63.
11. "The Moiety System," *New York Times*, 8 March 1874; Hoogenboom, *Outlawing the Spoils*, 104.
12. Cohen, "Smuggling, Globalization, and America's Outward State, 1870–1909," 382.
13. Don Whitehead, *Border Guard* (New York: McGraw-Hill, 1963), 66.
14. "Smuggling in the United States," *Frank Leslie's Popular Monthly* 6, no. 1 (July 1878): 3.
15. John Dean Goss, *The History of Tariff Administration in the United States from Colonial Times to the McKinley Administrative Bill* (New York: Columbia University, 1897), 69–70.
16. Whitehead, *Border Guard*, 65.
17. *Commissions to Examine Certain Custom-Houses of the United States,* 24 May 1877, 16.
18. Carl E. Prince and Mollie Keller, *The U.S. Customs Service: A Bicentennial History* (Washington, DC: U.S. Department of Treasury, 1989), 150, 152.
19. Quoted in Prince and Keller, *The U.S. Customs Service*, 152.
20. Prince and Keller, *The U.S. Customs Service*, 159. For a more general discussion of the reform movement, see Hoogenboom, *Outlawing the Spoils.*
21. *Commissions to Examine Certain Custom-Houses of the United States,* 21 May 1877, 111.

22. Quoted in Prince and Keller, *The U.S. Customs Service*, 155–56.
23. Goss, *The History of Tariff Administration*, 75.
24. Thomas Gangs Thorpe, "New York Custom-House," *Harper's New Monthly Magazine* (June 1871): 26.
25. Richard Wheatley, "The New York Custom-House," *Harper's New Monthly Magazine* (June 1884): 38.
26. Quoted in Sven Beckert, *The Monied Metropolis: New York City and the Consolidation of the American Bourgeoisie, 1850–1896* (Cambridge: Cambridge University Press, 2001), 69.
27. Cohen, "Smuggling, Globalization, and America's Outward State, 1870–1909," 374.
28. See Kristin L. Hoganson, *Consumers' Emporium: The Global Production of American Domesticity, 1865–1920* (Chapel Hill: University of North Carolina Press, 2007).
29. Beckert, *The Monied Metropolis*, 154.
30. "Seize Fine Dresses on American Line," *New York Times*, 30 March 1909.
31. "Smuggling a Bridal Outfit," *New York Times*, 20 May 1870.
32. Cohen, "Smuggling, Globalization, and America's Outward State, 1870–1909," 374.
33. Of course, there were exceptions to the "high value, low bulk" petty smuggling pattern, including a case in which a sailor was caught trying to sneak in fifteen monkeys in violation of the 20 percent monkey tariff. "The Monkey Duty," *New York Times*, 7 October 1883.
34. See, for example, "Heavy Importers' Frauds," *New York Times*, 24 March 1870 (reporting on two cases of importers caught in a false invoicing scam in which large amounts of laces, velvets, and silks were classified as cotton and other cheap fabric); and "Wholesale Smuggling," *New York Times*, 16 February 1872 (reporting on cases of fraudulent entry and invoicing).
35. "More Smuggling Frauds," *New York Times*, 26 February 1870; "The Sugar Tariff Ring," *New York Times*, 14 April 1880. On the types of sugar fraud, see Goss, *The History of Tariff Administration*, 73–74.
36. Cohen, "Smuggling, Globalization, and America's Outward State, 1870–1901," 374.
37. The *New York Times* reported this claim but suggested it was exaggerated. See "The Custom-House and the Tariff," *New York Times*, 22 October 1881.
38. "Book Smuggling—A New Phase of Fraud," *New York Times*, 18 January 1869.
39. Peter Faszi and Martha Woodmansee, "Copyright in Transition," in *A History of the Book in America*, ed. Carl F. Kaestle and Janice A. Radway, vol. 4 (Chapel Hill: University of North Carolina Press, 2009), 94. Also see James J. Barnes, *Authors, Publishers, and Politicians: The Quest for an Anglo-American Copyright Agreement, 1815–1854* (London: Routledge,

1974); Zorina Khan, "Does Copyright Piracy Pay? The Effects of U.S. International Copyright Laws on the Market for Books, 1790–1920," *NBER Working Paper Series* (January 2004).

40. The American copyright law of 1790 covered only authors who lived in the United States. See Adrian Johns, *Piracy: The Intellectual Property Wars from Gutenberg to Gates* (Chicago: University of Chicago Press, 2009), 196. According to Johns, "America's first major domestic publishing venture was a Bible with a false imprint attributing it to the king's printer in London." See Johns, *Piracy*, 183.
41. Sidney P. Moss, *Charles Dickens' Quarrel with America* (Troy, NY: Whitson, 1984); Lawrence H. Houtchens, "Charles Dickens and International Copyright," *American Literature* 13, no. 1 (March 1941): 18–28.
42. Quoted in Johns, *Piracy*, 203.
43. Thorpe, "The New York Custom-House," 23.
44. William H. Theobald, *Defrauding the Government: True Tales of Smuggling, from the Note-Book of a Confidential Agent of the United States Treasury* (New York: Myrtle, 1908), 442–43.
45. Quoted in Theobald, *Defrauding the Government*, 439.
46. Thorpe, "The New York Custom-House," 23. The article warns that women are so disrespectful of tariffs that when they "achieve suffrage, free-traders will ever be in the halls of Congress."
47. "Smuggling Tricksters," *New York Times*, 3 April 1870. Approximately seventy thousand smuggled cigars were reportedly seized every year. See "Smuggling in the United States," 3.
48. Theobald, *Defrauding the Government*, 444–45.
49. "Smuggling in the United States," 7.
50. "Miles of Women Smugglers," *Washington Post*, 8 March 1908.
51. Headline dated 13 September 1902. For more details on her remarkable career, see Cohen, "Smuggling, Globalization, and America's Outward State," 374–75.
52. H. W. Brands, *American Colossus: The Triumph of Capitalism, 1865–1900* (New York: Doubleday, 2010), 544.
53. Hoganson, *Consumers' Emporium*, 22, 168, 171.
54. Ethan Nadelmann, *Cops Across Borders: The Internationalization of U.S. Criminal Law Enforcement* (University Park: Penn State Press, 1994), 28.
55. Quoted in "The Smuggling Mania," *Literary Digest*, 1 October 1910, 528.
56. *New York Times*, 4 September 1910.
57. For a more general discussion of the laws related to border inspections and the limits of Fourth Amendment protections, see Gregory L. Waples, "From Bags to Body Cavities: The Law of Border Search," *Columbia Law Review* 74, no. 1 (January 1974): 53–87.
58. Quoted in "The Smuggling Mania," *Literary Digest*, 1 October 1910, 528.

59. Cohen, "Smuggling, Globalization, and America's Outward State, 1870–1909," 393.
60. "Getting Home: Latter-Day Experiences in the New York Custom House," *New York Times*, 19 September 1909.
61. The turn-of-the-century field notes of a Treasury Department special agent, William Theobald, provide detailed accounts of following wealthy Americans abroad and then catching them trying to smuggle in diamonds and jewelry—including pearl necklaces from Tiffany's—on their return trip. See Theobald, *Defrauding the Government*, 231.
62. Theobald, *Defrauding the Government*, 483.
63. "Ex-Gov. Rollins Caught Smuggling," *New York Times*, 14 May 1910.
64. "Nab a Pious, Rich Man," *Chicago Daily Tribune*, 23 May 1897.
65. Cohen, "Smuggling, Globalization, and America's Outward State, 1870–1909," 386–88.
66. Quoted in Cohen, "Smuggling, Globalization, and America's Outward State, 1870–1909," 393.
67. See Cohen, "Smuggling, Globalization, and America's Outward State, 1870–1909."
68. William Franklin Shanks, "Policemen of the Sea," *Harper's New Monthly Magazine* (March 1869): 445.
69. "Books Show 75% of U.S. Tourists are Smugglers," *Chicago Daily Tribune*, 15 May 1929.

Chapter 11

1. Donna Dennis, *Licentious Gotham: Erotic Publishing and Its Prosecution in Nineteenth Century New York* (Cambridge, MA: Harvard University Press, 2009), 128.
2. Carl E. Prince and Mollie Keller, *The U.S. Customs Service: A Bicentennial History* (Washington, DC: U.S. Department of Treasury, 1989), 255.
3. David Loth, *The Erotic in Literature* (New York: Julian Messner, 1961), 143.
4. Wayne E. Fuller, *Morality and the Mail in Nineteenth-Century America* (Urbana: University of Illinois Press, 2003), 227.
5. See especially Dennis, *Licentious Gotham*, 203–5.
6. For a more detailed account, see Fuller, *Morality and the Mail*, chapter 5.
7. Carmine Sarracino and Kevin M. Scott, *The Porning of America: The Rise of Porn Culture, What It Means, and Where We Go from Here* (Boston: Beacon Press, 2008), 7.
8. Gaines M. Foster, *Moral Reconstruction: Christian Lobbyists and the Federal Legislation of Morality, 1865–1920* (Chapel Hill: University of North Carolina Press, 2002), 48.
9. Prince and Keller, *The U.S. Customs Service*, 256.
10. Paul S. Boyer, *Purity in Print: Book Censorship in America from the Gilded Age to the Computer Age*, 2nd ed. (Madison: University of Wisconsin

Press, 2002), 29. The playwright George Bernard Shaw is credited for coining "Comstockery," describing it as "the world's standing joke at the expense of the United States. . . . It confirms the deep-seated conviction of the world that America is a provincial place." Quoted in Andrea Tone, *Devices and Desires: A History of Contraceptives in America* (New York: Hill and Wang, 2001), 23.

11. See Helen Lefkowitz Horowitz, *Rereading Sex: Battles over Sexual Knowledge and Suppression in Nineteenth-Century America* (New York: Vintage, 2002), 390–93.
12. Aine Collier, *The Humble Little Condom: A History* (Amherst, NY: Prometheus, 2007), 144.
13. Quoted in Nicola Beisel, *Imperiled Innocents: Anthony Comstock and Family Reproduction in Victorian America* (Princeton, NJ: Princeton University Press, 1997), 105.
14. Quoted in Dennis, *Licentious Gotham*, 275–76.
15. James Morone, *Hellfire Nation: The Politics of Sin in American History* (New Haven: Yale University Press, 2003), 230.
16. Dennis, *Licentious Gotham*, 143.
17. Quoted in Sarracino and Scott, *The Porning of America*, 8.
18. This point is stressed by Dennis, *Licentious Gotham*, 301. Much to the dismay of Comstock's successor, John Saxton Sumner, New York's erotic book publishing industry made a dramatic comeback in the 1920s and 1930s. See Jay A. Gertzman, *Bookleggers and Smuthounds: The Trade in Erotica 1920–1940* (Philadelphia: University of Pennsylvania Press, 2002).
19. Dennis, *Licentious Gotham*, 250.
20. Dennis, *Licentious Gotham*, 280.
21. Dennis, *Licentious Gotham*, 294.
22. Dennis, *Licentious Gotham*, 277. She notes that expected profits in legitimate publishing, by comparison, were only 10–20 percent.
23. Dennis, *Licentious Gotham*, 286–87.
24. The wording of the 1873 law was so broad that any purity crusader must have been pleased: "That no obscene, lewd, or lascivious book, pamphlet, picture, paper, print, or other publication of an indecent character, or any article or thing designed or intended for the prevention of contraception or the procuring of abortion, or any article or thing intended or adapted for any indecent or immoral use or nature, nor any . . . book, pamphlet, advertisement or notice of any kind giving information, directly or indirectly, where, or how, or of whom, or by what means either of the things before mentioned may be obtained or made . . . shall be carried in the mail." Quoted in Beisel, *Imperiled Innocents*, 39–40.
25. Quoted in Collier, *The Humble Little Condom*, 146.
26. Janet Farrell Brodie, *Contraception and Abortion in Nineteenth Century America* (Ithaca, NY: Cornell University Press, 1994), 210.

27. T.J.B. Buckingham, "The Trade in Questionable Rubber Goods," *India Rubber World*, 15 March 1964, 164.
28. Collier, *The Humble Little Condom*, 138.
29. Quoted in Tone, *Devices and Desires*, 69.
30. Robert Jutte, *Contraception: A History* (Malden, MA: Polity Press, 2008), 152.
31. Brodie, *Contraception and Abortion in Nineteenth Century America*, 208.
32. Jutte, *Contraception*, 131.
33. Quoted in Jutte, *Contraception*, 131.
34. Tone, *Devices and Desires*, 38. Also see Linda Gordon, *The Moral Property of Women: A History of Birth Control Politics in America*, 3rd ed. (Urbana: University of Illinois Press, 2002), 33–34.
35. Quoted in Collier, *The Humble Little Condom*, 146.
36. For a more detailed account, see Collier, *The Humble Little Condom*, 146–49.
37. The advertising campaign included a doctor's endorsement: "Vaseline, charged with four to five grains of salicylic acid, will destroy spermatozoa, without injury to the uterus or vagina." Quoted in Tone, *Devices and Desires*, 28–29.
38. As Tone writes, "No reputable company was reckless enough to make contraceptives its primary articles of commerce." See Tone, *Devices and Desires*, 48.
39. Collier, *The Humble Little Condom*, 146.
40. Tone, *Devices and Desires*, 30; 193–95.
41. Tone, *Devices and Desires*, 47–48.
42. Collier, *The Humble Little Condom*, 155.
43. Tone, *Devices and Desires*, 50–51; 103; 184–88; Collier, *The Humble Little Condom*, 154–57.
44. Collier, *The Humble Little Condom*, 151.
45. Tone, *Devices and Desires*, xvi, 64–66.
46. Dorothy Wardell, "Margaret Sanger: Birth Control's Successful Revolutionary," *American Journal of Public Health* 70, no. 7 (July 1980): 739; Collier, *The Humble Little Condom*, 153.
47. Tone, *Devices and Desires*, 126–27; Wardell, "Margaret Sanger," 741.
48. See especially Tone, *Devices and Desires*, 32–36.
49. Tone, *Devices and Desires*, 27–28.
50. Collier, for example, cites two turn-of-the-century surveys, one in New York and the other in Boston, in which a large percentage of the women respondents reported regular use of birth control. Collier, *The Humble Little Condom*, 174.
51. On birthrates and their relationship to the availability of birth control, see James Reed, *From Private Vice to Public Virtue: The Birth Control Movement and American Society Since 1830* (New York: Basic Books, 1978); Brodie, *Contraception and Abortion in Nineteenth Century America*, 2; Gordon, *The Moral Property of Women*, 22; Tone, *Devices and Desires*, 68.

52. Quoted in Tone, *Devices and Desires*, 103.
53. Tone, *Devices and Desires*, 105.
54. Tone, *Devices and Desires*, 106–8.
55. Tone, *Devices and Desires*, 127.
56. Tone, *Devices and Desires*, 126, 293 (note 4).
57. Quoted in Lawrence M. Friedman, *Crime and Punishment in American History* (New York: Basic Books, 1993), 326.
58. David J. Langum, *Crossing over the Line: Legislating Morality and the Mann Act* (Chicago: University of Chicago Press, 1994), 18.
59. George Kibbe Turner, "The City of Chicago: A Study of the Great Immoralities," *McClure's Magazine* 28 (April 1907): 581–82.
60. George Kibbe Turner, "The Daughters of the Poor: A Plain Story of the Development of New York City as a Leading Centre of the White Slave Trade of the World, under Tammany Hall," *McClure's Magazine* 34 (November 1909): 45–61.
61. For more detailed accounts, see Brian Donovan, *White Slave Crusades: Race, Gender, and Anti-Vice Activism, 1887–1917* (Urbana: University of Illinois Press, 2006); Langum, *Crossing over the Line*, 33–34; Amy R. Lagler, *"For God's Sake, Do Something": White Slavery Narratives and Moral Panic in Turn-of-the-Century American Cities* (Ph.D. dissertation, Michigan State University, 2000).
62. Edwin W. Sims, "White Slave Trade," in Ernest A. Bell, ed., *Fighting the Traffic in Young Girls, or War on the White Slave Trade* (s.n. 1910), 57.
63. Quoted in "To Curb White Slavery; Taft Consulted on Plan to Reach Traffic Through Inter-State Commerce Law," *New York Times*, 25 November 1909.
64. State of the Union Address of William H. Taft, 7 December 1909.
65. Quoted in Langum, *Crossing over the Line*, 28.
66. Langum notes that "The transportation of adult, willing prostitutes would always constitute the great bulk of Mann Act prosecutions." See Langum, *Crossing over the Line*, 48.
67. Langum, *Crossing over the Line*, 4, and chapter 3.
68. Quoted in Langum, *Crossing over the Line*, 33.
69. Morone, *Hellfire Nation*, 257.

Chapter 12

1. See Aristide Zolberg, *A Nation by Design: Immigration Policy in the Fashioning of America* (Cambridge, MA: Harvard University Press, 2006). Zolberg emphasizes that America's early efforts to regulate immigration have often been overlooked because this was handled at the state level rather than by the federal government until the 1880s.
2. This is celebrated by Hernando De Soto as an overlooked success story in the development of capitalism in the United States. See De Soto,

The Mystery of Capital: Why Capitalism Triumphs in the West and Fails Everywhere Else (New York: Basic Books, 2000), chapter 5.

3. Quoted in De Soto, *The Mystery of Capital*, 122.
4. Quoted in De Soto, *The Mystery of Capital*, 124.
5. See Joel Achebach, "George Washington's Western Adventure," *Washington Post*, 6 June 2004.
6. See Andrew R. L. Cayton, *The Frontier Republic: Ideology and Politics in the Ohio Country, 1780–1825* (Kent, OH: Kent State University Press, 1986), especially chapter 1.
7. Cited in Mark T. Kanazawa, "Possession Is Nine Points of the Law: The Political Economy of Early Public Land Disposal," *Explorations in Economic History* 33, no. 2 (April 1996): 230.
8. See, for example, Roy M. Robbins, "Preemption: A Frontier Triumph," *Mississippi Valley Historical Review* 18, no. 3 (December 1931): 331–49.
9. Gregory H. Nobles, *American Frontiers: Cultural Encounters and Continental Conquest* (New York: Hill & Wang, 1997), 141.
10. Zolberg, *A Nation by Design*, 176, 181. The March 1868 treaty between the United States and China stipulated the right of Chinese to emigrate and to work in the United States.
11. The nation's Chinese population increased from fewer than ten thousand in 1850 to more than a hundred thousand in 1880.
12. On the importance of the Page law in the initiation of federal immigration control, see Kerry Abrams, "Polygamy, Prostitution, and the Federalization of Immigration Law," *Columbia Law Review* 105, no. 3 (April 2005): 641–716.
13. According to some accounts, this turned into a sophisticated transnational business. See Robert Chao Romero, "Transnational Immigrant Smuggling to the United States via Mexico and Cuba, 1882–1916," *Amerasia Journal* 30, no. 3 (2004/2005): 11–12.
14. See, for instance, Tung Chin, *Paper Son: One Man's Story* (Philadelphia: Temple University Press, 2000). See also Erika Lee, *At America's Gates: Chinese Immigration During the Exclusion Era, 1882–1943* (Chapel Hill: University of North Carolina Press, 2003), 203–4.
15. Quoted in Lee, *At America's Gate*, 202.
16. Clifford Alan Perkins, *Border Patrol: With the Immigration Service on the Mexican Boundary, 1910–54* (El Paso: Texas Western Press, 1978), 13.
17. Carl E. Prince and Mollie Keller, *The U.S. Customs Service: A Bicentennial History* (Washington, DC: U.S. Department of Treasury, 1989), 176–77.
18. Lee, *At America's Gate*, 214–16.
19. Quoted in Lee, *At America's Gates*, 43.
20. Adam M. McKeown notes that at the turn of the century China was the only country in the world where it was required to obtain an immigration visa from a U.S. consulate. See McKeown, *Melancholy Order: Asian*

Migration and the Globalization of Borders (New York: Columbia University Press, 2008), 224.

21. For a more detailed discussion, see John Torpey, *The Invention of the Passport: Surveillance, Citizenship, and the State* (Cambridge: Cambridge University Press, 2000), 96–100.
22. Daniel J. Tichenor makes the more general point that efforts to control immigration, regardless of effectiveness, have "produced significant national state-building in U.S. political history." See Tichenor, *Dividing Lines: The Politics of Immigration Control in America* (Princeton, NJ: Princeton University Press, 2002), 7.
23. On the importance of the Chinese exclusion laws in building up the nation's initial immigration control machinery, see especially Lee, *At America's Gates*, 22.
24. Kitty Calavita, "The Paradox of Race, Class, Identity, and 'Passing': Enforcing the Chinese Exclusion Acts, 1882–1910," *Law and Social Inquiry* 25, no. 1 (2000): 15, note 10.
25. We obviously do not know the precise number of Chinese who entered the country illegally across the U.S.-Canada and U.S.-Mexico borders, but according to Lee an estimated seventeen thousand Chinese clandestinely entered this way between 1882 and 1920. See Lee, *At America's Gates*, 151.
26. "Smuggling Chinese from Canada," *New York Times*, 28 September 1884 (on fees for smuggling Chinese into the U.S. from Ontario); "The Chinese Question," *New York Times*, 27 November 1885 (on the continued dependence on Chinese labor in the Northwest); "How the Chinese Are Smuggled," *New York Times*, 8 September 1896 (on the use of Montreal as a transit point for smuggling Chinese immigrants).
27. Quoted in Julian Ralph, "The Chinese Leak," *Harper's New Monthly Magazine* (March 1891): 516.
28. Quoted in McKeown, *Melancholy Order*, 144.
29. Lee, *At America's Gates*, 176.
30. Lee, *At America's Gates*, 153.
31. Quoted in Lee, *At America's Gates*, 153.
32. Quoted in Lee, *At America's Gates*, 170.
33. Quoted in McKeown, *Melancholy Order*, 142.
34. Lee, *At America's Gates*, 154.
35. Ralph, "The Chinese Leak," 521.
36. The case is detailed in Sarah M. Griffith, "Border Crossings: Race, Class, and Smuggling in Pacific Coast Chinese Immigrant Society," *Western Historical Quarterly* 35, no. 4 (Winter 2004): 473–92.
37. Prince and Keller, *The U.S. Customs Service*, 191.
38. See, for example, William H. Siener, "Through the Back Door: Evading the Chinese Exclusion Act Along the Niagara Frontier, 1900–1924," *Journal of American Ethnic History* 27, no. 4 (Summer 2008): 34–70.

39. Ralph, "The Chinese Leak," 516.
40. According to a U.S. Immigration Bureau spokesman, "Since Canada places a head-tax of $500 on Chinese entering that country [in January 1904], the duty of guarding the Canadian border had been simplified, as the supply of Chinese to be smuggled has been practically limited to recruits gathered from among the Chinamen admitted to Canada prior to the assessment of the head-tax mentioned." Quoted in Kenneth Bruce McCullough, *America's Back Door: Indirect International Immigration Via Mexico to the United States from 1875 to 1940* (Ph.D. dissertation, Texas A&M University, 1992), 110–11.
41. The 1894 Canadian Agreement between the U.S. government and Canadian transportation companies essentially made possible the extension of U.S. immigration law beyond the U.S. border. See Marian L. Smith, "The Immigration and Naturalization Service (INS) at the U.S.-Canadian Border, 1893–1993: An Overview of Issues and Topics," *Michigan Historical Review* 26, no. 2 (Fall 2000): 129.
42. Lee, *At America's Gates*, 176–79.
43. See Kennett Cott, "Mexican Diplomacy and the Chinese Issue, 1876–1910," *Hispanic American Historical Review* 67, no. 1 (1987): 63–85.
44. Quoted in Lee, *At America's Gate*, 181.
45. Quoted in Patrick Ettinger, *Imaginary Lines: Border Enforcement and the Origins of Undocumented Immigration, 1882–1930* (Austin: University of Texas Press, 2009), 13.
46. Ettinger, *Imaginary Lines*, 14.
47. Lee, *At America's Gates*, 157.
48. Ettinger, *Imaginary Lines*, 99.
49. Ettinger, *Imaginary Lines*, 100.
50. Quoted in Ettinger, *Imaginary Lines*, 100.
51. Quoted in Lee, *At America's Gates*, 159.
52. Quoted in Ettinger, *Imaginary Lines*, 93.
53. Quoted in James Bronson Reynolds, "Enforcement of the Chinese Exclusion Law," *Annals of the American Academy of Political Science* 34, no. 2 (1909): 368.
54. Quoted in Lee, *At America's Gates*, 159.
55. See especially Lee, *At America's Gates*, 162–64.
56. Quoted in Ettinger, *Imaginary Lines*, 60.
57. Lee, *At America's Gates*, 184.
58. Lee, *At America's Gates*, 185.
59. "Bribes from Chinese: Customs Officers Accused of Accepting Them," *Washington Post*, 25 August 1901.
60. In addition to trachoma, the list included "tuberculosis, favus, syphilis, gonorrhea, leprosy, delirium tremens, idiocy, hernia, valvular heart disease, pregnancy, poor physique, chronic rheumatism, nervous afflictions, malignant disease, deformities, senility, debility, varicose veins, bad eyesight,

and any disease or deformity which might interfere with an immigrant's ability to earn a living." See McCullough, *America's Back Door*, 200.

61. See Ettinger, *Imaginary Lines*, 71.
62. Ettinger, *Imaginary Lines*, 105. On the smuggling of Jews across the border, see Libby Garland, "Not-quite-closed Gates: Jewish Alien Smuggling in the Post-Quota Years," *American Jewish History* 94, no. 3 (September 2008): 197–224.
63. Quoted in Ettinger, *Imaginary Lines*, 106–7.
64. Ettinger, *Imaginary Lines*, 107.
65. See, for example, "Smuggle Chinese by the Thousand: Eight Arrests Made in Huge Conspiracy of Trainmen, Mexicans, and Chicago Orientals," *Chicago Daily Tribune*, 29 May 1909.
66. For a more detailed account, see Ettinger, *Imaginary Lines*, 109.
67. See Perkins, *Border Patrol*, 2.
68. Perkins, *Border Patrol*, 52–53. As Perkins tells the story, Charlie Sam invited him for a drink to announce that he was retiring and moving back to China. During their friendly conversation over drinks, Sam allegedly confessed that he was responsible for organizing the smuggling of Chinese through El Paso and recounted how on one occasion he had barely eluded an undercover sting operation set up by Perkins and his men. According to Perkins, "we parted with many good wishes for our unknown futures." Perkins also recounts (p. 40) a meeting with Pancho Villa during the Mexican Revolution in which Villa unsuccessfully tried to recruit him to smuggle arms, in violation of the U.S. embargo.
69. Ettinger, *Imaginary Lines*, 115.
70. As retired Border Patrol agent Clifford Perkins notes in his memoir, "The Service recognized the decreasing importance of the problem [Chinese smuggling] by changing my designation from Chinese Inspector to Immigrant Inspector on 1 July 1917, although my duties remained the same." See Perkins, *Border Patrol*, 49.
71. For more details and context, see especially John Higham, *Strangers in the Land: Patterns of American Nativism* (New Brunswick, NJ: Rutgers University Press, 2002).
72. Zolberg describes this as the emergence of "remote control," by which is meant "the elaboration of an extensive immigration bureaucracy abroad." See Zolberg, *A Nation by Design*, 264.
73. Quoted in McCullough, *America's Back Door*, 48.
74. Quoted in Siener, "Through the Back Door," 60.
75. Quoted in McCullough, *America's Back Door*, 49.
76. Quoted in McCullough, *America's Back Door*, 230.
77. Quoted in McCullough, *America's Back Door*, 51–52.
78. Quoted in McCullough, *America's Back Door*, 52–53.
79. Quoted in McCullough, *America's Back Door*, 6.
80. McCullough, *America's Back Door*, 6, 230–31.

81. Quoted in Tichenor, *Dividing Lines*, 172.
82. These are detailed in Perkins, *Border Patrol*, 89–90.
83. Quoted in Ettinger, *Imaginary Lines*, 155.
84. Quoted in Ettinger, *Imaginary Lines*, 156.
85. See A. H. Uln, "New U.S. Border Police Force Now Combats Smugglers," *New York Times*, 10 May 1925. The most detailed history is provided by Kelly Lytle Hernandez, *Migra! A History of the U.S. Border Patrol* (Berkeley: University of California Press, 2010).
86. See, for example, "Bootlegged Immigrants," *New York Times*, 5 May 1924. While painting an alarming picture of the problem, the editorial notes: "The exact number of bootlegged immigrants is not known. They have been estimated at from 17,000 to 200,000 a year."
87. See "Smuggling Aliens into the USA," *Washington Post*, 14 September 1924. The subheading in bold warns of "Dealers Who Bootleg Whole Boatloads of Human Souls!"
88. Quoted in Ettinger, *Imaginary Lines*, 162.
89. Perkins, *Border Patrol*, 55.
90. Quoted in Zolberg, *A Nation by Design*, 257.
91. Quoted in Aristide Zolberg and Robert Smith, *Migration Systems in Comparative Perspective: An Analysis of the Inter-American Migration System with Comparative Reference to the Mediterranean-European System* (Washington, DC: U.S. Department of State, Bureau of Population, Refugees, and Migration, 1996), 9.
92. Zolberg, *A Nation by Design*, 257.
93. For a more detailed discussion, see S. Deborah Kang, "Crossing the Line: The INS and the Federal Regulation of the Mexican Border," in *Bridging National Borders in North America: Transnational and Comparative Histories*, ed. Benjamin H. Johnson and Andrew R. Graybill (Durham, NC: Duke University Press, 2010).

Chapter 13

1. W. J. Rorabaugh, *The Alcoholic Republic: An American Tradition* (New York: Oxford University Press, 1979), 21.
2. John Kobler, *Ardent Spirits: The Rise and Fall of Prohibition* (1973 reprint, New York: Da Capo Press, 1993), 31–33; Daniel Okrent, *Last Call: The Rise and Fall of Prohibition* (New York: Scribner, 2010), 7–8.
3. Quoted in Rorabaugh, *The Alcoholic Republic*, 97.
4. Rorabaugh, *The Alcoholic Republic*, 8, 99.
5. Quoted in Okrent, *Last Call*, 7.
6. James Morone, *Hellfire Nation: The Politics of Sin in American History* (New Haven: Yale University Press, 2003), 292.
7. More generally, see Holly Berkley Fletcher, *Gender and the American Temperance Movement of the Nineteenth Century* (New York: Routledge, 2007).

8. Quoted in Sean Dennis Cashman, *Prohibition: The Lie of the Land* (New York: Free Press, 1981), 22.
9. Okrent, *Last Call*, 101.
10. Quoted in Kobler, *Ardent Spirits*, 11.
11. Thomas M. Coffey, *The Long Thirst: Prohibition in America, 1920–1933* (New York: Norton, 1975), 69.
12. Mark Edward Lender and James Kirby Martin, *Drinking in America: A History* (New York: Free Press, 1987), 154.
13. Quoted in Michael Woodiwiss, *Organized Crime and American Power* (Toronto: University of Toronto Press, 2001), 183.
14. Quoted in Woodiwiss, *Organized Crime and American Power*, 183.
15. Quoted in Michael Woodiwiss, *Crime, Crusades and Corruption: Prohibitions in the United States, 1900–1987* (London: Pinter, 1988), 9.
16. Okrent, *Last Call*, 132.
17. Thomas R. Pegram, *Battling Demon Rum* (Chicago: Ivan R. Dee, 1998), 159.
18. For these and additional details, see Michael A. Lerner, *Dry Manhattan: Prohibition in New York City* (Cambridge, MA: Harvard University Press, 2007), 68.
19. Quoted in Edward Behr, *Prohibition: Thirteen Years That Changed America* (New York: Arcade, 1996), 241.
20. Quoted in Okrent, *Last Call*, 232.
21. See especially Garrett Peck, *Prohibition in Washington DC: How Dry We Weren't* (Charleston, SC: History Press, 2011), 125–31.
22. For these and other details, see Kobler, *Ardent Spirits*, 244.
23. Quoted in Peck, *Prohibition in Washington DC*, 133.
24. Quoted in Cashman, *Prohibition*, 132.
25. Quoted in Behr, *Prohibition*, 164.
26. For more details, see Okrent, *Last Call*, 324–25.
27. Behr, *Prohibition*, 164.
28. Carl E. Prince and Mollie Keller, *The U.S. Customs Service: A Bicentennial History* (Washington, DC: U.S. Department of Treasury, 1989), 217.
29. The Jones law amended Volstead by turning liquor law violations into felonies. The penalty for first-time offenders, initially six months in jail or a fine of $1,000, was increased to up to five years in jail and/or $10,000.
30. Quoted in Woodiwiss, *Organized Crime and American Power*, 198.
31. Lender and Martin, *Drinking in America*, 145.
32. Quoted in Okrent, *Last Call*, 172.
33. Malcolm F. Willoughby, *Rum War at Sea* (Washington, DC: U.S. Department of Treasury, 1964), 29.
34. Lawrence Spinelli, *Dry Diplomacy: The United States, Great Britain, and Prohibition* (Lanham, MD: Rowman & Littlefield, 2008), 3.
35. Quoted in Okrent, *Last Call*, 160.
36. Okrent, *Last Call*, 160.

37. Okrent, *Last Call*, 161.
38. Spinelli, *Dry Diplomacy*, 3.
39. William P. Helm, Jr., "20 to 50 Ships Supply New York Liquor Trade," *New York Times*, 3 September 1924.
40. See, for example, Robert Carse, *Rum Row: The Liquor Fleet That Fueled the Roaring Twenties* (Mystic, CT: Flat Hammock Press, 2007, reprint of 1928 book).
41. "332 Foreign Ships Found in Rum Trade," *New York Times*, 3 February 1925.
42. See Jean Pierre Andrieux, *Rumrunners: The Smugglers from St. Pierre and Miquelon and the Burin Peninsula from Prohibition to Present Day* (St. John's, Newfoundland, Can.: Flanker Press, 2009), 22.
43. Andrieux, *Rumrunners*, 30, 67.
44. Coffey, *The Long Thirst*, 178.
45. Frederick F. Van de Water, *The Real McCoy* (Mystic, CT: Flat Hammock Press, 2007, originally published 1931), 5–6.
46. Willoughby, *Rum War at Sea*, 43.
47. Willoughby, *Rum War at Sea*, 163.
48. David Kahn, *The Codebreakers: The Comprehensive History of Secret Communication from Ancient Times to the Internet* (New York: Scribner, 1996), 802–54.
49. Harold Waters, *Smugglers of Spirits: Prohibition and the Coast Guard Patrol* (New York: Hastings House, 1971), 17.
50. Waters, *Smugglers of Spirits*, 17.
51. Everett S. Allen, *The Black Ships: Rumrunners of Prohibition* (Boston: Little, Brown, 1979), 53, 110.
52. Former Coast Guardsman Harold Waters notes that smugglers often repurchased their seized boats at bargain prices: "No starry-eyed outsider ever made a bid at these auctions, not with the cold-eyed gunmen standing around to discourage 'outside' bidding. Very often we would catch the very same boat and its very same crew, who were meanwhile out on bail, all over again." Waters, *Smugglers of Spirits*, 56.
53. Quoted in Allen, *The Black Ships*, 53.
54. Waters, *Smugglers of Spirits*, 62.
55. Willoughby, *Rum War at Sea*, 58.
56. Okrent, *Last Call*, 280.
57. See Kobler, *Ardent Spirits*, 262–65.
58. Quoted in Okrent, *Last Call*, 170.
59. Waters, *Smugglers of Spirits*, 114.
60. Quoted in Waters, *Smugglers of Spirits*, 152.
61. Waters, *Smugglers of Spirits*, 167.
62. Waters, *Smugglers of Spirits*, 199.
63. See especially Philip P. Mason, *Rumrunning and the Roaring Twenties: Prohibition on the Michigan-Ontario Waterway* (Detroit: Wayne State University Press, 1995).

64. Amounting to more than two hundred bottles per person in the area, this was far in excess of local consumption capacity. See Okrent, *Last Call*, 124.
65. Mason, *Rumrunning and the Roaring* Twenties, 42.
66. Charles A. Selden, "Our 'Rum Capital': An Amazing Picture," *New York Times*, 27 May 1928.
67. Okrent, *Last Call*, 256–57.
68. Mason, *Rumrunning and the Roaring Twenties*, 109; Coffey, *The Long Thirst*, 317.
69. Michael Woodiwiss, *Crime, Crusades, and Corruption*, 28.
70. Mason, *Rumrunning and the Roaring Twenties*, 42–43.
71. Quoted in Mason, *Rumrunning and the Roaring Twenties*, 111.
72. Woodiwiss, *Organized Crime and American Power*, 191.
73. Mason, *Rumrunning and the Roaring Twenties*, 37.
74. Okrent, *Last Call*, 342.
75. "Official Report Admits Failure of Prohibition," *Chicago Daily Tribune*, 4 December 1928, 4.
76. See Cashman, *Prohibition*, 30; and Spinelli, *Dry Diplomacy*, 129.
77. Behr, *Prohibition*, 130.
78. Charles O. Smith, "Rum Treaty Proposals as Seen by Canadians," *New York Times*, 13 January 1929.
79. Quoted in Morrow Mayo, "Rum Running on the Detroit River," *Nation*, 4 September 1929, 244.
80. "Canada's Colossal Smuggling 'Industry,'" *Literary Digest*, 29 May 1926.
81. One smuggler defiantly boasted to the *Detroit Free Press*: "The government can block the river. Let them. Airplanes cost less than a good speedboat. Fly loads right to Chicago. They'll have a tough time stopping us. We'll fly right over their heads and laugh at them." Quoted in Kobler, *Ardent Spirits*, 268.
82. Mason, *Rumrunning and the Roaring Twenties*, 146.
83. Quoted in Okrent, *Last Call*, 259.
84. For more details, see Allan S. Everest, *Rum Across the Border: The Prohibition Era in Northern New York* (Syracuse, NY: Syracuse University Press, 1978), 24, 37, 46–47.
85. This sometimes included former border agents. For example, Ralph Hackmeister, nicknamed the "terror of rumrunners" until 1922, resigned from the customs patrol and a year later was arrested on charges of rumrunning (the charges were later dropped for insufficient evidence). Edward Cronk, a former border agent at Malone, was convicted and jailed for rumrunning and hijacking a shipment of alcohol. When he left the border force, he publicly announced his intention to become a smuggler and confidently predicted that he would never be caught. See Everest, *Rum Across the Border*, 77.
86. This account of Fay's career is taken from Coffey, *The Long Thirst*, 22–23, 53–55, 122, 161–62, 173. Fay's business ventures had many ups and

downs. Trying to go legit, Fay became the head of the New York Chain Milk Association, but his career in the milk business was cut short when he was indicted for conspiracy in restraining the milk trade. Fay was later shot to death by a drunk and disgruntled nightclub employee. See Coffey, *The Long Thirst*, 250, 313–14.

87. Olmstead's story is recounted in more detail in Emmett Watson, *Once upon a Time in Seattle* (Seattle: Lesser Seattle, 1992). Also see Behr, *Prohibition*, 138–39; and Okrent, *Last Call*, 284–85.
88. Kobler, *Ardent Spirits*, 254.
89. Quoted in John C. Burnham, *Bad Habits* (New York: NYU Press, 1003), 66.
90. For these and other details on the Bronfman story, see Okrent, *Last Call*, 149–58.
91. Morone, *Hellfire Nation*, 283.
92. Claire Bond Potter, *War on Crime: Bandits, G-Men, and the Politics of Mass Culture* (New Brunswick, NJ: Rutgers University Press, 1998), 12–13.
93. Cashman, *Prohibition*, 124–25; Okrent, *Last Call*, 164.
94. Quoted in Morone, *Hellfire Nation*, 329.
95. Okrent, *Last Call*, 283.

Chapter 14

1. See "Why People Take Drugs," in Andrew Weil, *The Natural Mind* (New York: Houghton Mifflin, 1986), 17–38.
2. The literature here is vast. For an especially useful historical introduction, see David T. Courtwright, *Forces of Habit: Drugs and the Making of the Modern World* (Cambridge, MA: Harvard University Press, 2001).
3. On the pivotal U.S. role in globalizing drug prohibition, see Peter Andreas and Ethan Nadelmann, *Policing the Globe: Criminalization and Crime Control in International Relations* (New York: Oxford University Press, 2006).
4. Quoted in Courtwright, *Forces of Habit*, 34.
5. David F. Musto, *The American Disease: Origins of Narcotics Control* (New York: Oxford University Press, 1987), 7.
6. James A. Inciardi, *The War on Drugs: Heroin, Cocaine, Crime, and Public Policy* (Palo Alto, CA: Mayfield, 1986), 6–7.
7. James A. Inciardi, *The War on Drugs III* (Boston: Allyn & Bacon, 2002), 24.
8. Troy Duster, *The Legislation of Morality: Law, Drugs, and Moral Judgment* (New York: Free Press, 1970), 7.
9. Edward M. Brecher and the editors of *Consumer Reports*, eds., *Licit and Illicit Drugs* (Boston: Little, Brown, 1972), 7.
10. Douglas Clark Kinder, "Shutting Out the Evil: Nativism and Narcotics Control in the United States," *Journal of Policy History* 3, no. 4 (1991): 472–73.

11. Musto, *American Disease*, 6.
12. Kinder, "Shutting Out the Evil," 473.
13. John Helmer, *Drugs and Minority Oppression* (New York: Seabury Press, 1975), 13.
14. Brecher et al., *Licit and Illicit Drugs*, 44.
15. Arnold H. Taylor, *American Diplomacy and the Narcotics Traffic, 1900–1939: A Study in International Humanitarian Reform* (Durham, NC: Duke University Press, 1969), 27.
16. Taylor, *American Diplomacy and the Narcotics Traffic*, 37.
17. Musto, *American Disease*, 39.
18. Quoted in Musto, *American Disease*, 34.
19. Charles Reasons, "The Politics of Drugs: An Inquiry in the Sociology of Social Problems," *Sociological Quarterly* 15, no. 3 (Summer 1974): 393.
20. Brecher et al., *Licit and Illicit Drugs*, 49.
21. The actual level of opium use was highly contested. See William Butler Eldridge, *Narcotics and the Law: A Critique of the American Experiment in Narcotic Drug Control* (New York: NYU Press, 1962), 7.
22. Eldridge, *Narcotics and the Law*, 9.
23. Brecher et al., *Licit and Illicit Drugs*, 49.
24. Musto, *American Disease*, 123.
25. *New York Times*, 18 December 1918, quoted in Rufus King, *The Drug Hang-Up* (New York: Norton, 1972), 26.
26. Musto, *American Disease*, 190; Inciardi, *War on Drugs*, 98.
27. U.S. Department of Justice, Drug Enforcement Administration, *A Chronicle of Federal Drug Law Enforcement* (Washington, DC: Department of Justice, 1977), 22, 24.
28. Physician and pharmacist lobbies were still strong enough to block sweeping new legislation in Congress. Reasons, "The Politics of Drugs," 398.
29. See Jerald Cloyd, *Drugs and Information Control* (Westport, CT: Greenwood Press, 1982), 62.
30. "Breakers of Narcotics Laws Outnumber Wet Convicts," *New York Times*, 24 January 1927; John C. McWilliams, "Through the Past Darkly: The Politics and Policies of America's Drug War," *Journal of Policy History* 3, no. 4 (1991): 364.
31. Eric C. Schneider, *Smack: Heroin and the American City* (Philadelphia: University of Pennsylvania Press, 2008), chapter 1.
32. Alan A. Block and William J. Chambliss, *Organized Crime* (New York: Elsevier, 1981), 53.
33. Kathryn Meyer and Terry Parssinen, *Webs of Smoke: Smugglers, Warlords, Spies, and the History of the International Drug Trade* (Lanham, MD: Rowman & Littlefield, 1998), 243; David T. Courtwright, "The Road to H: The Emergence of the American Heroin Complex, 1898–1956," in *One-Hundred Years of Heroin*, ed. David Musto (Westport, CT: Auburn House, 2002).

34. Jill Jonnes, *Hep-Cats, Narcs, and Pipe Dreams* (Baltimore: Johns Hopkins University Press, 1999), 77.
35. Quoted in Jonnes, *Hep-Cats, Narcs, and Pipe Dreams*, 77.
36. Quoted in Musto, *The American Disease*, 197.
37. Jonnes, *Hep-Cats, Narcs, and Pipe Dreams*, 96.
38. Meyer and Parssinen, *Webs of Smoke*, 253, 260; Jonnes, *Hep-Cats, Narcs, and Pipe Dreams*, 109.
39. See Courtwright, "The Road to H," 11; Schneider, *Smack*, 7–8.
40. See Joseph F. Spillane, "Making a Modern Drug War: The Manufacture, Sale, and Control of Cocaine in the United States, 1880–1920," in *Cocaine: Global Histories*, ed. Paul Gootenberg (London: Routledge, 1999), 39–41.
41. Jonnes, *Hep-Cats, Narcs, and Pipe Dreams*, 84.
42. For a detailed account, see John C. McWilliams, *The Protectors: Harry J. Anslinger and the Federal Bureau of Narcotics, 1930–1962* (Newark: University of Delaware Press, 1990).
43. Quoted in Eric Schlosser, *Reefer Madness* (New York: Houghton Mifflin, 2004), 20.
44. Meyer and Parssinen, *Webs of Smoke*, 247.
45. Quoted in Jonnes, *Hep-Cats, Narcs, and Pipe Dreams*, 197.
46. Kinder, "Shutting Out the Evil," 479.
47. "At that time, and for at least a decade longer, the drugs [pharmaceutical] trades saw no reason why a substance used chiefly in corn plasters, veterinary medicine, and nonintoxicating medicaments should be so severely restricted." Musto, *American Disease*, 216.
48. Quoted in McWilliams, "Through the Past Darkly," 366. Also see Harry J. Anslinger and Courtney Ryley Cooper, "Marijuana: Assassin of Youth," *American Magazine*, July 1937.
49. Brecher et al., *Licit and Illicit Drugs*, 69, 77.
50. Quoted in McWilliams, "Through the Past Darkly," 368.
51. Quoted in King, *Drug Hang-Up*, 65.
52. The information in this paragraph comes from Jonnes, *Hep-Cats, Narcs, and Pipe Dreams*, 165.
53. Douglas Valentine, *The Strength of the Wolf: The Secret History of America's War on Drugs* (London: Verso, 2006), 10.
54. For more details, see Rodney Campbell, *The Luciano Project: The Secret Wartime Collaboration of the Mafia and the U.S. Navy* (New York: McGraw-Hill, 1977); Tim Newark, *Mafia Allies: The True Story of America's Secret Alliance with the Mob in World War II* (St. Paul, MN: Zenith, 2007), chapter 7.
55. Quoted in Jonnes, *Hep-Cats, Narcs, and Pipe Dreams*, 146.
56. Quoted in Jonnes, *Hep-Cats, Narcs, and Pipe Dreams*, 167.
57. The FBN apparently maintained a secret black list that included the names of hundreds of traffickers. See Jonnes, *Hep-Cats, Narcs, and Pipe Dreams*, 160–61.

58. William B. McCallister, "Habitual Problems: The United States and International Drug Control," in *Federal Drug Control: The Evolution of Policy and Practice*, ed. Jonathon Erlen and Joseph Spillane (Binghamton, NY: Pharmaceutical Products Press, 2004), 193. See also Richard M. Gibson and Wenhua Chen, *The Secret Army: Chiang Kai-Shek and the Drug Warlords of the Golden Triangle* (New York: Wiley, 2011).
59. For an in-depth account, see Alfred W. McCoy, *The Politics of Heroin: CIA Complicity in the Global Drug Trade*, rev. ed. (Chicago: Lawrence Hill, 2003), chapter 2; Jonnes, *Hep-Cats, Narcs, and Pipe Dreams*, chapter 9; and Cornelius Friesendorf, *U.S. Foreign Policy and the War on Drugs: Displacing the Cocaine and Heroin Industry* (London: Routledge, 2007), 42–44.
60. Evert Clark and Nicholas Horrock, *Contrabandista!* (New York: Praeger, 1973), 111, 192–94.
61. Musto, *American Disease*, 231.
62. Quoted in Jonnes, *Hep-Cats, Narcs, and Pipe Dreams*, 177.
63. Pierre-Arnoud Chouvy, *Opium: Uncovering the Politics of the Poppy* (Cambridge, MA: Harvard University Press, 2010), 96.
64. See Jonnes, *Hep-Cats, Narcs, and Pipe Dreams*, 177, 186. More generally, see McCoy, *Politics of Heroin*, chapter 2.
65. Kinder, "Shutting Out the Evil," 484.
66. Arnold S. Trebach, *The Heroin Solution* (New Haven: Yale University Press, 1982), 164.
67. Cited in McWilliams, "Through the Past Darkly," 371; and Musto, *American Disease*, 231.
68. Quoted in Timothy Green, *The Smugglers* (New York: Walker, 1969), 86.
69. Elaine Shannon, *Desperados: Latin Drug Lords, U.S. Lawmen, and the War America Can't Win* (New York: Viking, 1988).
70. This pricing information comes from Green, *The Smugglers*, 109.
71. The information on heroin in this paragraph comes from Letizia Paoli, Victoria A. Greenfield, and Peter Reuter, *World Heroin Market* (New York: Oxford University Press, 2009).
72. "President's Message on Drug Control Programs," *Congressional Quarterly Almanac* 26 (1971): 94A.
73. Quoted in Edward Jay Epstein, *Agency of Fear: Opiates and Political Power in America*, rev. ed. (New York: Verso, 1990), 178.
74. Peter Goldberg, "Federal Government's Response to Illicit Drugs, 1969–1978," in *The Facts About "Drug Abuse,"* Drug Abuse Council (New York: Free Press, 1980), 57.
75. Musto, *American Disease*, 234, 239–41.
76. Steven Wisotsky, *Beyond the War on Drugs* (Amherst, NY: Prometheus, 1990), 250. On the global reach of U.S. drug enforcement, see especially Ethan Nadelmann, *Cops Across Borders: The Internationalization of U.S. Criminal Law Enforcement* (University Park: Penn State Press, 1993).

77. "President's Message on Drug Control Programs," 95A.
78. Epstein, *Agency of Fear*, 83–92; Musto, *American Disease*, 256–57.
79. McCoy, *Politics of Heroin*.
80. Thomas Darmondy, *Opium: Reality's Dark Dream* (New Haven: Yale University Press, 2012), 239.
81. "Nation: Panic over Paraquat," *Time*, 1 May 1978.
82. Shannon, *Desperados*, 72–73.
83. Courtwright, *Forces of Habit*, 44.
84. Shannon, *Desperados*, 76.
85. Brecher et al., *Licit and Illicit Drugs*, 302–5. On pp. 304–5 Brecher and his co-editors write: "The decade [of the 1960s] began with almost all stimulants being supplied by reputable manufacturers; their low-cost amphetamines had almost driven cocaine off the market. The withdrawal of intravenous amphetamines from the legal market opened the door for the illicit speed labs. The Drug Abuse Control Amendments of 1965 curbed the direct diversion of legal amphetamines to the black market; this opened the door for the smuggling of exported amphetamines back into the United States. By 1969, law-enforcement efforts had raised black market amphetamine prices and curbed amphetamine supplies sufficiently to open the door for renewed cocaine smuggling."
86. According to the National Institute on Drug Abuse (NIDA), 4.4 million people had used cocaine within the past thirty days, at least 9.7 million within the past year, and at least 15 million at least once at some time in the past. These figures, which represent a 250–300 percent increase over the NIDA survey in 1977, were considered low by other official estimates. Wisotsky, *Beyond the War on Drugs*, 12–14.
87. Bruce D. Johnson and John Muffler, "Sociocultural Aspects of Drug Use and Abuse in the 1990s," in *Substance Abuse: A Comprehensive Text*, ed. Joyce H. Lowinson et al. (Baltimore: Williams and Wilkins, 1992), 124.
88. Johnson and Muffler, "Sociocultural Aspects of Drug Use and Abuse in the 1990s."
89. See Musto, *American Disease*, 274; and Wisotsky, *Beyond the War on Drugs*, 7.
90. Quoted in Ryan Grim, *This Is Your Country on Drugs: The Secret History of Getting High in America* (New York: Wiley, 2010), 73–74.
91. Quoted in Grim, *This Is Your Country on Drugs*, 73.
92. On the history and development of the Andean cocaine industry, see especially Paul Gootenberg, *Andean Cocaine: The Making of a Global Drug* (Chapel Hill: University of North Carolina Press, 2009).
93. On the rise of Medellín as a cocaine-export center, see Mary Roldan, "Colombia: Cocaine and the 'Miracle' of Modernity in Medellin," in *Cocaine: Global Histories* ed. Paul Gootenberg (New York: Routledge, 1999), 166–67.
94. On the mythical nature of Colombia's "drug cartels," see Michael Kenney, *From Pablo to Osama: Trafficking and Terrorist Networks, Government*

Bureaucracies, and Competitive Adaptation (University Park: Penn State Press, 2008), 88–90.

95. Paul Eddy with Hugo Sabogal and Sarah Walden, *The Cocaine Wars* (New York: Norton, 1988), 98.
96. Eddy et al., *The Cocaine Wars*, 151.
97. Wisotsky, *Beyond the War on Drugs*, 250; Office of National Drug Control Policy, *National Drug Control Strategy: Budget Summary* (Washington, DC: U.S. Government Printing Office, 1994), 23, 184–85.
98. Arnold S. Trebach, *Great Drug War* (New York: Macmillan, 1987), 152.
99. "Major Crime Package Cleared by Congress," *Congressional Quarterly Almanac* 40 (1984): 213–24.
100. Trebach, *Great Drug War*, 184.
101. See, for example, the discussion in Craig Reinarman and Harry Levine, "Crack in Context: Politics and Media in the Making of a Drug Scare," *Contemporary Drug Problems* 16, no. 4 (Winter 1989): 537–39, 555–59.
102. "Four Key Issues Playing Role in Congressional Contests," *Congressional Quarterly*, 18 October 1986, 2599.
103. Chris Adams, "Second Thoughts on the Military as Narcs," *Washington Post*, 15 June 1988.
104. See the report from the Senate Committee on Foreign Relations, Subcommittee on Terrorism, Narcotics and International Operations *Drugs, Law Enforcement and Foreign Policy* (Washington, DC: U.S. Government Printing Office, 1989). See also Peter Dale Scott and Jonathan Marshall, *Cocaine Politics: Drugs, Armies, and the CIA in Central America* (Berkeley: University of California Press, 1998).
105. Quoted in Elaine Sciolino with Stephen Engelberg, "Fighting Narcotics: U.S. Is Urged to Shift Tactics," *New York Times*, 10 April 1988.
106. "Text of Address by President Bush," *Washington Post*, 6 September 1989.
107. Poll cited in Tom Wicker, "The Wartime Spirit," *New York Times*, 3 October 1989.
108. "National Drug Control Strategy: Budget Summary" (Washington, DC: White House, 1992), 23; Office of National Drug Control Policy, *National Drug Control Strategy Budget Summary* (Washington, DC: U.S. Government Printing Office, 1994), 184–85.
109. Lawrence Korb, assistant secretary of defense, quoted in "Faced with Peace, Pentagon Wants to Enlist in Drug War," *The State* (Columbia, SC), 17 December 1989.
110. Quoted in "Faced with Peace, Pentagon Wants to Enlist in Drug War," *The State* (Columbia, SC), 17 December 1989. Military officials have made similar arguments. For example, Lt. Charles L. Diaz explained: "DoD should consider expanding its funding justification to include increased federal funds for its 'new' drug detection and monitoring mission. . . . Shifting the emphasis of a portion of DoD's budget toward

its new peace-time mission will help DoD retain certain resources and manpower while satisfying domestic pressure to increase the drug interdiction effort." Diaz, "DoD Plays in the Drug War," *Proceedings/Naval Review* 116, no. 5 (1990): 84, 86.

111. David C. Morrison, "Police Action," *National Journal* 24, no. 5 (1992): 267–70.
112. Morrison, "Police Action," 268.
113. Eric Schmitt, "Colorado Bunker Built for Cold War Shifts Focus to Drug Battle," *New York Times*, 18 July 1993; William Matthews, "Toys Dusted Off for War on Drugs," *Federal Times*, 16 April 1990; "DOD Studies X-Ray Techniques for Examining Cargo Containers," *Drug Enforcement Report*, 23 May 1994; Frank Greve, "Ailing Defense Contractors Urged to Arm the Drug War," *Miami Herald*, 15 July 1990.
114. Michael Isikoff and Patrick E. Tyler, "U.S. Military Given Foreign Arrest Powers," *Washington Post*, 16 December 1989.
115. Sciolino with Engelberg, "Fighting Narcotics." More generally, see John Dinges, *Our Man in Panama* (New York: Random House, 1991).
116. Jeff Gerth, "CIA Shedding Its Reluctance to Aid in Fight Against Drugs," *New York Times*, 25 March 1990.
117. For a detailed account, see Mark Bowden, *Killing Pablo: The Hunt for the World's Greatest Outlaw* (New York: Penguin, 2002).
118. See especially Peter B. Kraska, ed., *Militarizing the American Criminal Justice System: The Changing Roles of the Armed Forces and the Police* (Boston: Northeastern University Press, 2001).
119. Curtis Stiner, "U.S. Legal Group Debates Reform as Drug Cases Inundate System," *Christian Science Monitor*, 12 February 1990; Ronald Ostrow, "In Ranking Jailers, U.S. Easily No. 1," *Los Angeles Times*, 11 February 1992; and Mark Pazniokas, "Tough Stands on Crime May Ignore Reality," *Hartford Current*, 20 October 1994.
120. "Off with Their Heads? Thoughts from the Drug Czar," *Washington Post*, 20 June 1989.
121. Office of National Drug Control Policy, *National Drug Control Strategy: Budget Summary* (1995), 235.
122. Schlosser, *Reefer Madness*, 48.
123. All figures are from Office of National Drug Control Policy, *National Drug Control Strategy* (1995), 144–45.
124. See U.S. Department of Justice, Drug Enforcement Administration, "A Chronicle of Federal Drug Law Enforcement," *Drug Enforcement* 7, no. 2 (1980): 52–64; Office of National Drug Control Policy, *National Drug Control Strategy Budget Summary* (1994), 12.
125. Office of National Drug Control Policy, *National Drug Control Strategy Budget Summary* (1994), 140–41.
126. Office of National Drug Control Policy, *National Drug Control Strategy Budget Summary* (1994), 144.

127. Sid Balman Jr. "An Electronic Picket Faces Smugglers," *Air Force Times*, 18 June 1990.
128. This paragraph draws from Schlosser, *Reefer Madness*, 14, 71.
129. Paul Gootenberg, "Cocaine's Long March North, 1900–2010," *Latin American Politics and Society* 54, no. 1 (Spring 2012): 168.
130. Michael Matza, "'Narc' No More," *Philadelphia Inquirer*, 2 April 1990.

Chapter 15

1. Jorge A. Hernandez, "Trading Across the Border: National Customs Guards in Nuevo Leon," *Southwestern Historical Quarterly* 100, no. 4 (1997): 433–51.
2. Brian Delay, "19th Century Lessons for Today's Drug-War Policies," *Chronicle of Higher Education*, 27 July 2009.
3. Rachel St. John, *Line in the Sand: A History of the Western U.S.-Mexico Border* (Princeton, NJ: Princeton University Press, 2011), 99–100.
4. St. John, *Line in the Sand*, 203, and chapter 5,
5. Quoted in George T. Diaz, *Contrabandista Communities: States and Smugglers in the Lower Rio Grande Borderlands, 1848–1945* (Ph.D. dissertation, Southern Methodist University, 2010), 111.
6. Louis R. Sadler, "The Historical Dynamics of Smuggling in the U.S.-Mexican Border Region, 1550–1998," in *Organized Crime and Democratic Governability: Mexico and the U.S.-Mexican Borderlands*, ed. John Bailey and Roy Godson (Pittsburgh: University of Pittsburgh Press, 2000), 164.
7. St. John, *Line in the Sand*, 122–23. Also see Charles H. Harris III and Louis R. Sadler, *The Border and the Revolution: Clandestine Activities of the Mexican Revolution, 1910–1920* (Silver City, NM: High Lonesome, 1988). On the particular importance of El Paso, see Harris and Sadler's *The Secret War in El Paso: Mexican Revolutionary Intrigue, 1906–1920* (Albuquerque: University of New Mexico Press, 2009), chapters 6 and 16.
8. Ethan A. Nadelmann, *Cops Across Borders: The Internationalization of U.S. Criminal Law Enforcement* (University Park: Penn State Press, 1993), 30.
9. See especially George T. Diaz, "Twilight of the Tequileros: Prohibition Era Smuggling in the South Texas Borderlands, 1919–1933," in *Smugglers, Brothels, and Twine: Historical Perspectives on Contraband and Vice in North America's Borderlands*, ed. Elaine Carey and Andrae M. Marak (Tucson: University of Arizona Press, 2011).
10. See St. John, *Line in the Sand,* chapter 6. On Tijuana's development as the premier vice district, see especially Paul J. Vanderwood, *Satan's Playground: Mobsters and Movie Stars at America's Greatest Gaming Resort* (Durham, NC: Duke University Press, 2010).
11. See Timothy Green, *The Smugglers: An Investigation into the World of the Contemporary Smuggler* (New York: Walker, 1969), 292.
12. Tom Miller, *On the Border: Portraits of America's Southwestern Frontier* (New York: Harper & Row, 1981): 52.

13. Marshall Carter, "Law, Order, and the Border: El Paso Del Norte" (revision of a paper prepared for the annual meeting of the National Council on Geographic Education, Mexico City, November 1979), 6.
14. Sadler, "The Historical Dynamics of Smuggling in the U.S.-Mexican Border Region, 1550–1998," 175.
15. Kitty Calavita, *Inside the State: The Bracero Program, Immigration, and the INS* (New York: Routledge, 1992).
16. Quoted in Kelly Lytle Hernandez, *Migra! A History of the U.S. Border Patrol* (Berkeley: University of California Press, 2010), 196.
17. See Kitty Calavita, "U.S. Immigration and Policy Responses: The Limits of Legislation," in *Controlling Immigration: A Global Perspective*, ed. Wayne Cornelius et al. (Stanford: Stanford University Press, 1994), 60.
18. See Comptroller General of the United States, *Smugglers, Illicit Documents, and Schemes Are Undermining U.S. Controls over Immigration: Report to Congress by the Comptroller General of the United States* (Washington, DC: Government Printing Office, 30 August 1976), 5–6, 18.
19. Comptroller General of the United States, *Illegal Entry at United States–Mexico Border: Multiagency Enforcement Efforts Have Not Been Effective in Stemming the Flow of Drugs and People, Report to the Congress by Comptroller General of the United States* (Washington, DC: Government Printing Office, 2 December 1977), 7.
20. INS annual report, 1978, cited in Sherrie A. Kossoudji, "Playing Cat and Mouse at the U.S.-Mexican Border," *Demography* 29, no. 2 (1992): 161.
21. Josiah Heyman calls this dynamic the "voluntary departure complex." See his "Putting Power into the Anthropology of Bureaucracy: The Immigration and Naturalization Service at the Mexico-United States Border," *Current Anthropology* 36, no. 2 (1995): 261–87.
22. Domestic Council's Committee on Illegal Aliens, Preliminary Report, December 1976, quoted in Comptroller General of the United States, *Illegal Entry at United States-Mexico Border*, 17.
23. Quoted in Katrina Burgess and Carlos Gonzalez Gutierrez, "Reluctant Partner: California in U.S.-Mexico Relations" (unpublished manuscript, n.d.), 29–30.
24. *Migration News*, February 1998.
25. News conference with Doris Meissner and Janet Reno, Washington, DC, 12 January 1996.
26. For a more detailed account, see Timothy J. Dunn, *Blockading the Border and Human Rights: The El Paso Operation That Remade Immigration Enforcement* (Austin: University of Texas Press, 2009).
27. See especially Joseph Nevins, *Operation Gatekeeper and Beyond: The War on "Illegals" and the Remaking of the U.S.-Mexico Boundary*, 2nd ed. (New York: Routledge, 2010).
28. U.S. Border Patrol, "Border Patrol Strategic Plan 1994 and Beyond: National Strategy" (Washington, DC: U.S. Border Patrol, July 1994).

29. William Branigin, “Reaping Abuse for What They Sew,” *Washington Post*, 16 February 1997.
30. *Migration News*, April 1996; *Migration News*, November 1998.
31. For a more detailed account, see David Spener, “Smuggling Migrants Through South Texas: Challenges Posed by Operation Rio Grande,” in *Global Human Smuggling*, ed. David Kyle and Rey Koslowski (Baltimore: Johns Hopkins University Press, 2001).
32. *Migration News*, February 1997.
33. *Migration Between Mexico and the United States: Binational Study* (Mexico City and Washington, DC: Mexican Foreign Ministry and U.S. Commission on Immigration Reform, 1997), 28.
34. *Migration News*, April 2011. According to another estimate, 3.3 million unauthorized Mexicans immigrants settled in the United States between 1990 and 1999. See David Spener, *Clandestine Crossings: Migrants and Coyotes on the Texas-Mexico Border* (Ithaca, NY: Cornell University Press, 2009), 9.
35. Jesse Katz and Tony Perry, “Smugglers of Immigrants Fill Growing Demand,” *Los Angeles Times*, 7 April 1996.
36. Sebastian Rotella, “Tough Border Policies a Boon for Smugglers,” *Los Angeles Times*, 5 February 1995.
37. News conference with Doris Meissner and Janet Reno, *Federal News Service*, 12 January 1996.
38. Quoted in Sebastian Rotella, “Station of Dreams: Tijuana Bus Terminal Haven for Immigrant Smuggling Rings,” *Los Angeles Times,* 11 May 1992.
39. Rotella, “Tough Border Policies a Boon for Smugglers.”
40. For a detailed account of the relationship between migrants and smugglers, see Spener, *Clandestine Crossings*.
41. Quoted in Sam Dillon, “Smuggling Ring Smashed,” *New York Times,* 30 May 1996.
42. Sebastian Rotella, *Twilight on the Line: Underworlds and Politics at the Mexican Border* (New York: Norton, 1998), 75–78.
43. *Annual Report of the Office of the United States Attorney, Southern District of California* (Washington, DC: U.S. Department of Justice, 1996).
44. International Organization for Migration, “Organized Crime Moves into Migrant Trafficking,” *Trafficking in Migrants Quarterly Bulletin* No. 11, June 1996.
45. More generally, Gootenberg argues that the unintended cumulative impact of U.S. drug enforcement over many decades was to push the cocaine trade ever closer to the United States. See Paul Gootenberg, “Cocaine’s Long March North, 1900–2010,” *Latin American Politics and Society* 54, no. 1 (Spring 2012): 159–80.
46. Quoted in John Moore, “No Quick Fix,” *National Journal* 19 (November 1987): 2957.

47. Testimony of Admiral Paul Yost, U.S. Coast Guard, before the House Select Committee on Narcotics Abuse and Control, *U.S. Narcotics Control Efforts in Mexico and on the Southwest Border*, 99th Cong., 2d sess., July 1986, 34.
48. See Senate Subcommittee, *Southwest Border Law Enforcement and Trade*, 19 August 1987, 25.
49. Senate Subcommittee, *Southwest Border Law Enforcement and Trade*, 25, 191, 200.
50. Senate Subcommittee, *Southwest Border Law Enforcement and Trade*, 191, 202.
51. Statement of Russell L. Jones, president of Richard L. Jones Customhouse Brokers, before Senate Subcommittee of the Committee on Appropriations, *Southwest Border Law Enforcement and Trade*, 100th Cong., 1st sess., 19 August 1987, 143–44.
52. House Select Committee on Narcotics Abuse and Control, *Southwest Border Hearings (El Paso, Texas, Tucson, Arizona, San Diego, California) and Mexico Trip Report (Nogales, Mexico City, Culiacan)*, 99th Cong., 2d sess., 12–19 January 1986, 3.
53. Maria Celia Toro, "Drug Trafficking from a National Security Perspective," in *Mexico: In Search of Security*, ed. Bruce M. Bagley and Sergio Aguayo Quezada (Coral Gables, FL: North South Center, University of Miami, 1993), 326.
54. State Department estimates cited in Peter H. Smith, "Semiorganized International Crime: Drug Trafficking in Mexico," in *Transnational Crime in the Americas*, ed. Tom Farer (New York: Routledge, 1999), 195.
55. Congressional Research Service, *Drug Interdiction: U.S. Programs, Policy, and Options for Congress*, report prepared by the Senate Caucus on International Narcotics Control, September 1996, proceeds of a seminar held by the Congressional Research Service, 12 December 1995, 19–20.
56. Office of National Drug Control Policy, *National Drug Control Strategy* (1991), 102–3.
57. Oversight Hearing on Border Drug Interdiction, Senate Subcommittee on Treasury, Postal Service, and General Government, Committee on Appropriations, *Border Drug Interdiction*, 103d Cong., 1st sess., 25 February 1993, 133.
58. U.S. Department of State, *Department of State Dispatch*, 26 November 1990, 294.
59. Tim Golden, "Mexico and Drugs: Was U.S. Napping?" *New York Times*, 11 July 1997.
60. Quoted in Douglas Farah and Molly Moore, "Mexican Drug Traffickers Eclipse Colombian Cartels," *Washington Post*, 30 March 1997.
61. General Accounting Office, *Drug Control: Counternarcotics Efforts in Mexico (Appendix II: Comments from the Drug Enforcement*

Administration) (Washington, DC: General Accounting Office, June 1996), 26.

62. Tom Gjelten, "Mexican Military Will Help Fight Drug Wars," National Public Radio, *Morning Edition*, 23 May 1995.
63. Sam Dillon, "Victory or Deceit?" *New York Times*, 12 May 1996.
64. "Time for Retreat?" *Economist*, 8 March 1997, 44–47.
65. Donald Schulz, *Between a Rock and a Hard Place: The United States, Mexico, and the Agony of National Security*, Strategic Studies Institute Special Report (Carlisle Barracks, PA: Strategic Studies Institute, U.S. Army War College, 24 June 1997), 4.
66. Department of State, *International Narcotics Control Strategy Report* (Washington, DC: Department of State, March 1999).
67. Press conference with Barry McCaffrey, director, Office of National Drug Control Policy, and Jorge Madrazo, Mexican attorney general, Washington, DC, 29 January 1997.
68. Andrew Reding, "Facing Political Reality in Mexico," *Washington Quarterly* 20, no. 4 (1997): 103–17.
69. Office of National Drug Control Policy, *Report to Congress*, 1:35.
70. Office of National Drug Control Policy, *National Drug Control Strategy Report* (Washington, DC: Office of National Drug Control Policy, 1999), 69–70.
71. Quoted in Tim Weiner with Tim Golden, "Free Trade Treaty May Widen Traffic in Drugs, U.S. Says," *New York Times*, 24 May 1993.
72. Weiner with Golden, "Free Trade Treaty May Widen Traffic in Drugs, U.S. Says"; Tim Golden, "Mexican Drug Connection Grows as Cocaine Supplier to U.S.," *New York Times*, 30 July 1995.
73. Christopher S. Wren, "U.S. Drug Chief Seeks Overhaul of Strategy to Stop Illegal Flow from Mexico," *New York Times*, 20 September 1998.
74. See Peter Andreas, "When Policies Collide: Market Reform, Market Prohibition, and the Narcotization of the Mexican Economy," in *The Illicit Global Economy and State Power*, ed. H. Richard Friman and Peter Andreas (Lanham, MD: Rowman & Littlefield, 1999), 134.
75. Remarks of Harvey G. Pothier, deputy assistant commissioner, Office of Air Interdiction, U.S. Customs Service, in Congressional Research Service, *Drug Interdiction*, 22.
76. Customs Service press releases, 26 and 28 February 1996.
77. Testimony of Barry R. McCaffrey, House Subcommittee on Criminal Justice, Drug Policy, and Human Resources, Government Reform and Oversight Committee, 106th Cong., 1st sess., 25 February 1999.
78. For a more detailed discussion, see Marc R. Rosenblum, *U.S. Immigration Policy Since 9/11: Understanding the Stalemate over Comprehensive Immigration Reform* (Washington, DC: Woodrow Wilson International Center for Scholars and Migration Policy Institute, August 2011).
79. "U.S. Official Held 'Drug Smuggling,'" *BBC News*, 19 October 2011.

80. These and other corruption cases are profiled in Tim Gaynor, *Midnight on the Line: The Secret Life of the U.S.-Mexico Border* (New York: St. Martin's Press, 2009), chapter 9.
81. For background on border fencing projects, see Blas Nunez-Neto and Yule Kim, *Border Security: Barriers Along the U.S. International Border* (Washington, DC: CRS Report to Congress, updated 13 May 2008).
82. Marc Lacey, "Arizona Officials, Fed up with U.S. Border Efforts, Seek Donations to Build Border Fence," *New York Times*, 19 July 2011.
83. Quoted in Bill Hess, "Military's Use on the Border Expands," *Sierra Vista Herald*, 21 April 2005.
84. Hess, "Military's Use on the Border Expands."
85. Eric Lipton, "Bush Turns to Big Military Contractors for Border Control," *New York Times*, 18 May 2006. The rush to fund private military contractors to come up with a technological fix for the border proved expensive, and the plan was canceled in early 2011 after already spending an estimated $1 billion. See Rey Koslowski, *The Evolution of Border Controls as a Mechanism to Prevent Illegal Immigration* (Washington, DC: Migration Policy Institute, February 2011), 11.
86. "Message from the Commissioner," in *National Border Patrol Strategy: Office of Border Patrol* (Washington, DC: U.S. Customs and Border Protection, Department of Homeland Security, 2004).
87. For a critical evaluation of the cost-effectiveness of such initiatives, see Tom Barry, *International Policy Report: Fallacies of High-Tech Fixes for Border Security* (Washington, DC: Center for International Policy, April 2010), 6.
88. Quoted in Edward Alden and Bryan Roberts, "Are U.S. Borders Secure?" *Foreign Affairs* 90, no. 4 (July/August 2011): 20.
89. Ken Dermota, "Human Smugglers Launch 'Coyote Express' into US," *Agence France Presse*, 18 May 2007; Richard Marosi, "Border Battle over Illegal Immigration Shifts to Beaches," *Los Angeles Times*, 24 March 2011.
90. Eric Lichtblau, "Prosecutions in Immigration Doubled in Last Four Years," *New York Times*, 29 September 2005.
91. Tom Barry, *Border Wars* (Cambridge, MA: MIT Press, 2011), 104.
92. Nina Bernstein, "Companies Use Immigration Crackdown to Turn a Profit," *New York Times*, 28 September 2011.
93. Alden and Roberts, "Are U.S. Borders Secure?" 24.
94. Damien Cave, "For Mexicans Looking North, a New Calculus Favors Home," *New York Times*, 5 July 2011.
95. Douglas S. Massey, "Isolated, Vulnerable, and Broke," *New York Times*, 4 August 2011.
96. For these and other estimates, including data sources and methodology used, see Jeffrey S. Passel and D'Vera Cohn, *Unauthorized Immigrant Population: National and State Trends 2010* (Washington, DC: Pew Hispanic Center, 1 February 2011).

97. Randal C. Archibold, "2-Nation Border Conference Discusses Gun Trafficking," *New York Times*, 16 August 2008.
98. The use of private U.S. military contractors made it possible to get around Mexican laws prohibiting foreign military personnel from carrying out operations on Mexican territory. Ginger Thompson, "U.S. Widens Role in Battle Against Mexican Drug Cartels," *New York Times*, 6 August 2011.
99. Ginger Thompson and Mark Mazzetti, "U.S. Drones Fight Mexican Drug Trade," *New York Times*, 15 March 2011.
100. Quoted in Chris McGreal, "How Mexico's Drug Cartels Profit from the Flow of Guns Across the Border," *Guardian* (UK), 8 December 2011.
101. On the domestic political and bureaucratic obstacles to curbing gunrunning to Mexico, see especially James Verini, "Mexican Roulette," *Foreign Policy* 30 (August 2011).
102. National Drug Intelligence Center, *National Drug Threat Assessment 2010* (Washington, DC: U.S. Department of Justice, February 2010).
103. For an overview, see June S. Beittel, *Mexico's Drug Trafficking Organizations: Source and Scope of the Rising Violence* (Washington, DC: Congressional Research Service, 7 January 2011).
104. The Justice in Mexico Project at the Trans-border Institute (University of San Diego) has carried out the most careful and detailed tracking of Mexican drug violence.

Chapter 16

1. *Strategy to Combat Transnational Organized Crime: Addressing Converging Threats to National Security* (Washington, DC: White House, 19 July 2011).
2. John Kerry, *The New War: The Web of Crime That Threatens America's Security* (New York: Touchstone, 1998), 32.
3. Jessica Mathews, "Power Shift," *Foreign Affairs* (January/February 1997): 50; Moises Naim, "The Five Wars of Globalization," *Foreign Policy* 76 (January/February 2003): 50–66.
4. Moises Naim, *Illicit: How Smugglers, Traffickers, and Copycats Are Hijacking the Global Economy* (New York: Doubleday, 2005), 5.
5. Susan Strange, *The Retreat of the State: The Diffusion of Power in the World Economy* (New York: Cambridge University Press, 1996), 121.
6. Phil Williams, "Transnational Organized Crime and the State," in *The Emergence of Private Authority in Global Governance*, ed. Rodney Bruce Hall and Thomas J. Biersteker (Cambridge: Cambridge University Press, 2003), 161, 165. More recently, see Robert Mandel, *Dark Logic: Transnational Criminal Tactics and Global Security* (Stanford: Stanford University Press, 2010).
7. President's letter, *Strategy to Combat Transnational Organized Crime: Addressing Converging Threats to National Security* (Washington, DC: White House, 19 July 2011).

8. This is the subtitle of Naim's book, *Illicit*.
9. For a recent critical review of the now-expansive criminological literature in this area, see *Routledge Handbook of Transnational Organized Crime*, Felia Allum and Stan Gilmour, eds. (London: Routledge, 2012). For a nuanced account of the challenges criminal organizations face in expanding their reach across borders, see Federico Varese, *Mafias on the Move: How Organized Crime Conquers New Territories* (Princeton: Princeton University Press, 2011).
10. The collection of items seized between 16 and 20 November 2009 was captured in more than a thousand photographs by Taryn Simon, *Contraband* (Gottingen, Germany: Steidl, 2010).
11. The Los Angeles baseball agent Gus Dominguez was indicted in October 2006 for arranging the smuggling of five Cuban baseball players (four pitchers and a shortstop) into the country. He reportedly paid smugglers $225,000 to clandestinely transport the players from Cuba to Florida by boat and then by car to California. The agent auctioned the players off to various Major League Baseball teams. See Michael Lewis, "Commie Ball: A Journey to the End of a Revolution," *Vanity Fair*, 8 July 2008.
12. Leslie Wayne, "How Delaware Thrives as a Corporate Tax Haven," *New York Times*, 30 June 2012. The article quotes Lanny A. Breuer, assistant attorney general for the criminal division of the Justice Department, who claims that "Shells are the No. 1 vehicle for laundering illicit money and criminal proceeds."
13. For a detailed account of British Columbia's booming marijuana export sector, see Misha Glenny, *McMafia: A Journey Through the Global Criminal Underworld* (New York: Knopf, 2008), chapter 10.
14. Mark Tran, "Philip Morris reaches $1.25bn EU agreement," *Guardian* (UK), 9 July 2004. In 1992 Italian authorities also accused Philip Morris of collusion in smuggling and punished the company by banning Marlboro imports. But this only prompted more smuggling, and Italy lifted the ban. Raymond Bonner, "2 Cases Shed Light on Cigarette Smuggling in Italy," *New York Times*, 2 September 1997.
15. For a more detailed account, see Peter Andreas and Ethan Nadelmann, *Policing the Globe: Criminalization and Crime Control in International Relations* (New York: Oxford University Press, 2006).
16. The arms trade in general, whether licit or illicit, tends to be a shady business, with the United States the world's most important player. See Andrew Feinstein, *The Shadow World: Inside the Global Arms Trade* (New York: Farrar, Straus, and Giroux, 2011).
17. David M. Smolin, "Child Laundering: How the Intercountry Adoption System Legitimizes and Incentivizes the Practices of Buying, Trafficking, Kidnapping, and Stealing Children," *Berkeley Electronic Press Legal Series working paper*, no. 749, August 2005; E. J. Graff, "The Lie We Love," *Foreign Policy* (November/December 2008); Karen Dubinksy, *Babies*

Without Borders: Adoption and Migration Across the Americas (New York: NYU Press, 2010), chapter 4; John Feffer, "The Baby Trade," *Huffington Post* (21 December 2010); John Leland, "For Adoptive Parents, Questions Without Answers," *New York Times*, 16 September 2011.

18. Many, but not all, of the looted items were recovered. See Matthew Bogdanos, *Thieves of Baghdad* (New York: Bloomsbury, 2005).
19. Jason Felch and Ralph Frammolino, *Chasing Aphrodite: The Hunt for Looted Antiquities at the World's Richest Museum* (New York: Houghton Mifflin, 2011).
20. See David R. Bewley-Taylor, *International Drug Control: Consensus Fractured* (Cambridge: Cambridge University Press, 2012). More generally, see Sharon Waxman, *Loot: The Battle over the Stolen Treasures of the Ancient World* (New York: Times Books, 2008); and Peter Watson and Cecilia Todeschini, *The Medici Conspiracy: The Illicit Journey of Looted Antiquities, from Italy's Tomb Raiders to the World's Greatest Museums* (New York: Public Affairs, 2006).
21. For human trafficking, see the annual *Trafficking in Persons Report*; for drug trafficking, see the annual *International Narcotics Strategy Report*, both produced by the U.S. State Department.
22. The main international agreement is the 1973 Convention on International Trade in Endangered Flora and Fauna (CITES).
23. See "The Illegal Parrot Trade in Mexico: A Comprehensive Assessment," *Defenders of Wildlife*, 14 February 2007. For a broader analysis of the illicit parrot trade, see R. T. Naylor, *Crass Struggle* (Montreal: McGill-Queens University Press, 2011), chapter 10.
24. Naylor, *Crass Struggle*, 297.
25. Bryan Christy, *The Lizard King: The True Crimes and Passions of the World's Greatest Reptile Smugglers* (New York: Twelve, Hachette Book Group, 2009), 144.
26. Jennifer Steinhauser, "Wildlife Smugglers Test Their Skills, Even at the Airport," *New York Times*, 6 April 2007.
27. Rebecca Cathart, "German Charged with Shipping Tarantulas," *New York Times*, 3 December 2010.
28. Michel Martin, "In California, Marijuana Dispensaries Outnumber Starbucks," National Public Radio, 15 October 2009.
29. Jesse McKinley, "Pat Robertson Says Marijuana Use Should Be Legal," *New York Times*, 7 March 2012.
30. On "cybercrime," see, for example, Misha Glenny, *DarkMarket: Cyberthieves, Cybercops, and You* (New York: Knopf, 2011).
31. See especially Mathieu DeFlem, "Technology and the Internationalization of Policing: A Comparative Historical Perspective," *Justice Quarterly* 19, no. 3 (September 2002): 453–75.
32. R. T. Naylor, *Wages of Crime* (Ithaca, NY: Cornell University Press, 2002), 5.

33. See Simon A. Cole, *Suspect Identities: A History of Fingerprinting and Criminal Investigation* (Cambridge, MA: Harvard University Press, 2001).
34. See Jane Kaplan and John Torpey, eds., *Documenting Individual Identity: State Practices in the Modern World* (Princeton, NJ: Princeton University Press, 2001); and Craig Robertson, *The Passport in America: The History of a Document* (New York: Oxford University Press, 2010).
35. For a general discussion, see David K. Shipler, *The Rights of the People: How Our Search for Security Invades Our Liberties* (New York: Knopf, 2011).
36. "The Court's GPS Test," *New York Times*, 5 November 2011.
37. On electronic finance, see Eric Helleiner, "Electronic Money: A Challenge to the Sovereign State?" *Journal of International Affairs* 51 (1998): 387–409.
38. Carl Bialik, "Measuring the Child-Porn Trade," *Wall Street Journal*, 18 April 2006.
39. Glenny, *DarkMarket*, 266.
40. For a useful introduction, see Jack M. Balkin et al., eds., *Cybercrime: Digital Cops in a Networked Environment* (New York: NYU Press, 2007).
41. Edward Wyatt, "Lines Drawn in Anti-Piracy Bill," *New York Times*, 14 December, 2011.
42. Ben Sisario, "7 Charged as F.B.I. Closes a Top File-Sharing Site," *New York Times*, 19 January 2012.
43. Eduardo Porter, "The Perpetual War: Pirates and Creators," *New York Times*, 4 February 2012.
44. Jenna Wortham, "A Political Coming of Age for the Tech Industry," *New York Times*, 17 January 2012.
45. Douglas Quenchia, "An Addiction Vaccine, Tantalizingly Close," *New York Times*, 4 October 2011.
46. "Viagra Blackmarket Thriving," BBC News, 25 February 2000; Ruben Castaneda, "Md. Man Pleads Guilty to Selling Fake Viagra on Craigslist," *Washington Post*, 30 September 2011; Catherine Humble, "Inside the Fake Viagra Factory," *Telegraph* (UK), 23 August 2005.
47. See especially Alfred W. McCoy, *The Politics of Heroin: CIA Complicity in the Global Drug Trade*, 2nd rev. ed. (Chicago: Lawrence Hill, 2003).
48. Dexter Filkings, Mark Mazzetti, and James Risen, "Brother of Afghan Leader Said to Be Paid by CIA," *New York Times*, 27 October 2009.
49. Mark Mazzetti, Scott Shane, and Alissa J. Rubin, "Brutal Haqqani Crime Clan Bedevils U.S. in Afghanistan," *New York Times*, 24 September 2011.
50. Dana Thomas, *Deluxe: How Luxury Lost Its Luster* (New York: Penguin, 2007), chapter 9.
51. According to a November 2011 U.S. intelligence report, "Chinese actors are the world's most active and persistent perpetrators of economic espionage," with much of it done via "internet espionage." Thom Shanker, "U.S. Report Accuses China and Russia of Internet Spying," *New York Times*, 3 November 2011.

52. Naim, *Illicit*, 1.
53. See Mary Kaldor, *New Wars: Organized Violence in a Global Era* (Stanford: Stanford University Press, 1999).
54. See Peter Andreas, “The Criminalizing Consequences of Sanctions: Embargo Busting and Its Legacy,” *International Studies Quarterly* 49, no. 2 (2005): 335–60. For a more general discussion, see R. T. Naylor, *Patriots and Profiteers: Economic Warfare, Embargo Busting, and State-Sponsored Crime*, 2nd ed. (Montreal: McGill-Queens University Press, 2008).
55. On the threat of nuclear terrorism in general, see, for example, Graham Allison, *Nuclear Terrorism: The Ultimate Preventable Catastrophe* (New York: Holt, 2005). For a more skeptical view, see John Mueller, *Atomic Obsession: Nuclear Alarmism from Hiroshima to Al-Qaeda* (New York: Oxford University Press, 2009).
56. For a nuanced recent evaluation, see Mariano-Florentino Cuellar, “The Political Economies of Immigration Law,” *UC Irvine Law Review*, vol. 2, no. 1 (2012): 1–90.
57. This paragraph and the previous one draw from Peter Andreas and Ethan Nadelmann, *Policing the Globe: Criminalization and Crime Control in International Relations* (New York: Oxford University Press, 2006), 251–252. America’s oversized prison population leads some critics to charge that the United States has become a “penal state.” See Loïc Wacquant, *Prisons of Poverty* (St. Paul-Minneapolis: University of Minnesota Press, 2009). Also see Michelle Alexander, *The New Jim Crow: Mass Incarceration in the Age of Colorblindness* (New York: New Press, 2010).

Epilogue

1. Jonathan Staloff, “Alcohol, Pot Use on Campus Measured,” *Brown Daily Herald*, 3 December 2010.
2. Franklin Kanin, “More Students Use Marijuana than Tobacco, Poll Finds,” *Brown Daily Herald*, 3 December 2007.
3. Natalie Villacorta, “To Get an Edge, Students Turn to Illicit Study Drug Use,” *Brown Daily Herald*, 6 April 2011.
4. Colin Chazen, “Undocumented: Students in ‘Limbo,’ ” *Brown Daily Herald*, 27 January 2009.
5. Nancy Cook, “The Most ‘Per Capita’ Corruption,” *Newsweek*, 10 May 2010.
6. According to the Securities and Exchange Commission, Goldman profited by secretly betting against the same mortgage investments it sold to customers. See Louis Story and Gretchen Morgenson, “U.S. Accuses Goldman Sachs of Fraud in Mortgage Deal,” *New York Times*, 16 April 2010.
7. Graham Bowley, “At Brown, Spotlight on the President’s Role at a Bank,” *New York Times*, 1 March 2010. Also see Charles Pinning, “Brown’s President and Goldman Sachs,” *Providence Journal*, 25 February 2010.

8. The fact that much of such behavior remains legal reflects corporate lobbying power to avoid greater regulation rather than the severity of social consequences. See Nikos Passas and Neva Goodwin, eds., *It's Legal but it Ain't Right: Harmful Social Consequences of Legal Industries* (Ann Arbor: University of Michigan Press, 2005), 2.

INDEX

Page numbers written in italics denote illustrations.